THE WORST PRESIDENT IN HISTORY

THE LEGACY OF BARACK OBAMA

MATT MARGOLIS
& MARK NOONAN

VICTORY
B O O K S

The Worst President in History: The Legacy of Barack Obama
Copyright © 2016 by Matt Margolis & Mark Noonan

For further information, please contact the authors via email at
worstpresident44@gmail.com

Book Design by Logotecture

Edited by Matthew Souders

Cover photo by White House photographer Pete Souza
is a United States Government Work, and is in the public domain.

Victory Books

ISBN 978-0692310915

First Edition

Printed in the United States

For my son, Isaac.
May your life not be burdened by the damage done during the Obama years. Hopefully, your generation will make wiser decisions, informed by history and reason, learning always from our mistakes.

—Matt Margolis

To my late father, George Childs Noonan, Jr. Marine, mathematician, philosopher and patriot. Shortly before he died in 2009, he warned me that bad times were coming for America. He has been proved correct, and I pray that we recover his spirit so that we may restore our nation to greatness.

—Mark Noonan

Contents

Introduction

When Americans are asked "Who is the worst president in history?" and "Who is the best president in history?" one man ranks high on both lists: Barack Hussein Obama. How can he appear on both lists so frequently? The truth is, polls won't tell you much except that Americans have stronger feelings—good and bad—about recent presidents than those of many years past, Obama included. In a December 2011 interview with *60 Minutes*, Obama said he would rank himself as *fourth* best president in terms of legislative accomplishments—an assessment so laughable that the comment was edited out of the initial broadcast.[1] As opinionated as we Americans are about how Obama measures up, history will be the ultimate judge... not recent polls, and certainly not Obama himself.

If told honestly, historical accounts of Obama's presidency will *not* be kind. The goal of this book is to make sure the truth about Obama's record is not forgotten so that history can make an honest, informed assessment of the Obama presidency. Many will want Obama's legacy to be viewed favorably just because of the historic nature of his rise to the nation's highest office, but we are committed to truth, not enslaved at the altar of political correctness. Given everything we've learned throughout Obama's tenure, we decided it was time to compile a historical primer on his disastrous Presidency. So far, we've documented 200 reasons why Barack Obama is the worst president in history. Some examples are more egregious than others, but each reveals inconvenient facts about Obama's real legacy. This isn't about partisanship. This is about the truth.

Obama is keenly aware that he needs to play a role in enshrining the version of his legacy he wants history to remember. Upon leaving the White House, he plans to raise $1 billion for his presidential library and a global foundation—double the amount raised by George W. Bush for his presidential library.[2] One billion dollars is *a lot* of money, but it's not enough to cover up the epic failures of his presidency, which we've compiled in the following pages: his lapses in judgment at home and abroad, failed policies, the radicalism of his appointees, his rejection of constitutional limitations, his demagoguery, and, most importantly, his utter failure to lead on the world stage.

It's true that all presidents, even those who are judged favorably, are flawed people with imperfect records. But, sometimes, history ignores the most valuable lessons of our most transformative political figures. Bill Clinton takes credit for a booming economy that would have never happened had it not been for Newt Gingrich and his *Contract with America*. Franklin Delano Roosevelt is credited with ending the Great Depression despite the fact that he prolonged it. Today, we have a President who claims credit for creating millions of jobs despite no increases in workforce participation and stagnant GDP growth. So, while Obama works hard to tell the story his way, we will provide a fact-based narrative.

Unlike his predecessors, Obama must contend with a vigilant, informed opposition made possible by alternative media outlets. No longer will any President be able to rely on a complicit, elite vanguard of media lackeys more interested in maintaining their status and access than in uncovering the truth. But this information age advantage is lost if we don't each contribute what we can to the proper recording of history. To that end, we will document the truth about Obama's record for future generations, so they will know the true history and won't be doomed to repeat the mistakes of the past. History will be the ultimate judge; we just want to make sure that future historians have a fighting chance to get it right.

Domestic Issues

George W. Bush's presidency came to be defined by an event that forced Americans to look beyond their borders and consider a world overrun by anger, desperation, and want. Far beyond our safe and quiet homes, and our self-involved concerns, the world was becoming increasingly hostile as strains of radical Islam took control of more and more of the populace. Bush answered the devastating terror attack of 9/11 by crafting a foreign policy philosophy that would define him as a leader. Readers of this book can judge for themselves whether Bush was up to the task of handling the signature problems of his time in the White House, but we begin here, in our analysis of President Obama, with a simple question: What were the defining problems of his time?

It turns out that this question has a more complex answer than it did for many former Presidents, but we can say, with clarity, that the first problems he faced were decidedly toward the home front, at least in the minds of most Americans. Their leading concerns, when they went to vote in 2008, were far less likely to be the war on terror or the ambitions of China or Russia, and far more likely to be the recent economic collapse, the state of American politics, the ongoing debt crisis, or the perceived weaknesses of our education or healthcare systems. Obama skillfully campaigned as a man who would be the answer to those problems – a man who would unite Americans, answer populist calls for domestic reforms, revive our flagging economy and "nation-build at home, not in Iraq". Then, his focus seemed on point, even if you disagreed with his prescribed fixes. Then, he seemed to be an optimist – something Americans sorely needed.

Unfortunately, the position demands far more than shining rhetoric, calls for unity and optimism, and lofty ideals. The

Obama we got bore little resemblance to the man who stood on that stage in Denver between soaring Roman columns and promised us that he would look across the aisle, consider any reasonable proposal, comb every line item, and explain it all to every American. The Obama we got was divisive, insular, and resistant to compromise. The man who took possession of the Oval Office was a pessimist and was often accused of being antisocial and detached. And, on matters of domestic policy, this man was far from a unifying populist who sought the council of Americans – he was beholden to special interests and his administration was besotted with ideas that Americans loudly rejected when polled. His flip-flops, evolutions, and pivots were a confusing array of partisan ploys and domineering lectures that left Americans more divided on social issues and domestic policy than they've been at any time since the Civil War.

Was Obama up to the task, when confronted with those first defining problems? We think not.

1. Decline of American Optimism

We begin with that very question of optimism. No President can control the mood of the American people by himself, but when an administration presides over an era where Americans lose confidence in their civic institutions and their future, it must be viewed as a sign of trouble for the man at the top. According to a Gallup Poll taken just a couple of weeks before Obama's second inauguration, only thirty-nine percent of Americans had a positive view of the country. According to Gallup, this is the smallest number since 1979.[3]

> *The challenges President Obama faces as he begins his second term in office are evident from the fact that less than four in 10 Americans rate the nation's current situation on the positive end of a zero to 10 scale and that slightly less than half project that the state of the nation will be positive in five years. Both of these assessments are among the more negative Gallup has measured since the Eisenhower administration.*[4]

4

For all of Obama's hope and change rhetoric, Americans are so distressed and discouraged that the only silver lining Obama's got is that things probably can't get much worse.

To compare, at the start of George W. Bush's first term, seventy-three percent of Americans had a positive view of America, and that number remained above fifty percent until Obama's presidency.[5] As of this writing, only 25.6 percent of Americans think that the nation is headed in the right direction, according to *RealClearPolitics* aggregates of polling data on the question.

2. Domestic Policy Flip-Flops

We're, admittedly, not fans of Obama's work as President, but we were occasionally given hope that his record would be less partisan than we feared. Even this polarizing figure hit on some domestic themes and ideas that we were hoping he'd stick with as his administration got to work. Unfortunately, he has often changed his mind for the worse. Here are a few examples of Obama's domestic policy flip-flops:

- In 2006, then-Senator Obama called a proposal to raise the debt ceiling a "leadership failure" but, as President, Obama has requested multiple increases in the debt ceiling and unilateral power to raise it at his whim.[6]

- In 2008, Obama campaigned on cutting the deficit in half; through his first term, Obama raised the annual deficit to a trillion dollars or more per year.

- Obama said he would not employ lobbyists in the White House, but has, instead, given many waivers to allow lobbyists to work there.[7]

- Obama promised a robust, manned space program, even agreeing to Bush Administration policy of returning to the moon by 2020. But, Obama killed funding for the Constellation space shuttle, which was to bring America back to the moon, and with the termination of the Space Shuttle program, the United States no longer has a manned space program.[8]

- Obama promised that as President he would reduce earmarks "to less than $7.8 billion a year, a level they last achieved in 1993." But earmarks for FY2010, the last year before Republicans took control of the House, totaled $15.9 billion.[9]

- Obama promised that he would eliminate income taxes on American seniors making $50,000 or less; those people are still waiting for the administration to make this a priority.[10]

- Obama promised to adhere to "pay-go" budgeting in which all new expenditures be paid for either by spending reductions elsewhere or tax increases.[11] At no time has Obama obeyed "pay-go" rules and has chastised all GOP attempts to enforce it.

- Obama routinely blamed President Bush for high gas prices, but when gas prices have skyrocketed to record levels on his watch, Obama has suddenly decided that the President didn't have any power to affect gas prices.[12]

- In 2008, Obama touted the use of gas pipelines across Canada as a means of improving America's economy and energy security.[13] As president, he blocked the Keystone pipeline, which would bring oil from Canada into the United States, and of course, create jobs.[14]

- During the 2008 Democratic primary, Obama strongly attacked Hillary Clinton's health care plan requiring an individual mandate.[15] Of course, Obamacare has an individual mandate.[16]

3. No Wall Street or Banker Prosecutions

In 2008, during the financial crisis, candidate Barack Obama promised to bring a "new era of responsibility and accountability to Wall Street and to Washington."[17] When he took office in 2009, he undoubtedly had a mandate to prosecute Wall Street bankers responsible for the systemic fraud that contributed to the crisis. But there have been no arrests or prosecutions of any banker involved in the fiscal collapse.[18] The criminal fraud was undeniable; yet, in 2012, Barack Obama defended the lack of prosecutions because "a lot of that stuff wasn't necessarily illegal, it was just immoral or inappropriate or reckless."[19]

Worse yet, even though Obama publicly promised to hold Wall Street accountable, the so-called "architects of the financial crisis" have actually been protected by the Obama administration.[20] Wall Street donated a lot of money to Obama's campaign in 2008, and has since gained significant influence in his administration. "President Obama has repeatedly turned to nominees with close Wall Street ties for high-level economic positions," wrote Senator Elizabeth Warren (D-MA) in the Huffington Post in November 2014, including Jack Lew, Obama's Treasury Secretary during his second term. One wonders how, precisely, Obama's mind was changed upon entering the Oval Office? Perhaps it had something to do with his many Wall Street financial backers.

And, it seems, the bankers, too, were getting special treatment. Cronyism inside the Department of Justice, and political donations made to the Obama campaign are the likely reasons for Barack Obama and Attorney General Holder's failure to criminally charge any Wall Street bankers, according to a report by the Government Accountability Institute (GAI).[21]

One of Holder's deputy Attorney Generals actually had $20 million worth of work done for the ill-famed AIG Insurance firm at the heart of the 2008 financial crash.[22] Obama was also collecting more donations from Wall Street than any of the Republican candidates for president. From the GAI report:

> *In the weeks before and after the Senate report on Goldman Sachs,*
> *several Goldman executives and their families made contributions*
> *to Obama's Victory Fund and related entities, and some*
> *contributors maxed out at the largest individual donation allowed,*

$35,800. Five senior Goldman Sachs executives wrote more than $130,000 in checks to the Obama Victory Fund. Two of these executives had never donated to Obama before and had previously only given small donations to individual candidates.[23]

For Obama, the line between right and wrong is on a check made out to his campaign. As long as it is signed, and there are a lot of zeros on it, nothing is wrong and everything is negotiable.

4. Betraying the Victims of Hurricane Sandy

Hurricane Sandy ripped into the East Coast of the United States in the final week of the 2012 presidential election campaign, and Obama sensed an opportunity to appear unifying and presidential. He and Republican Governor Chris Christie posed for a photo op and he spoke briefly for the press about the need to pull together as a nation to help the victims of this tragedy. With the photos taken and spread relentlessly around the mainstream media, Obama returned to campaigning and, judging by his subsequent actions, forgot all about the hurricane or its impact on New Jersey and New York.

While the Obama campaign basked in the warm glow of overwhelmingly positive post-Sandy coverage (which may have helped clinch the deal for Obama's reelection), the people of New Jersey and New York suffered through a level of government incompetence not seen since the Katrina disaster. Staten Island victims were left behind after FEMA packed up and left the area— a week after Obama promised to help the affected areas, vowing "No bureaucracy. No red tape."[24]

Hurricane Sandy victims learned, the hard way, that they merely played a supporting role in helping Obama play the part of a decisive leader in a time crisis right before the election. Gas shortages throughout the region stranded tens of thousands in their homes up to three weeks after the storm hit[25]. It took nearly a month to restore power to the hardest hit areas and many were short of food and clothing. Major streets remained impassable for up to three weeks. Hurricane victims felt betrayed by Obama for breaking his promise to get them the help they needed.[26] By April 2014, one federal recovery program had only managed to rebuild six homes, with 20,000 homeowners still on the waiting list.[27] These people lost their homes and livelihoods, but Obama only saw them as campaign props. Once he was safely reelected, did Obama decide to grace the people of New Jersey with another visit or lend a Presidential hand in clearing away the bureaucratic obstruction on relief efforts? No. He went golfing.[28]

5. The Government Response to California's Central Valley Drought

In February 2014, Barack Obama visited California's Central Valley to address an ongoing drought that has been devastating local farmers and families. While there, he promised millions in aid in the form of government handouts and pork for environmental activists. He also took the opportunity to blame the plight of the farmers on global warming.[29] There's just one problem: the water shortages, while exacerbated by an ongoing drought, were primarily caused by government mismanagement. Back in 2009, the Obama administration, using the Endangered Species Act for cover, diverted water needed for irrigation away from California's Central Valley farmers and families to protect the delta smelt (a small, guppy-like fish) and salmon.[30] The government, not global warming, caused the problem.

A significant source of the nation's fruit, nuts, and vegetables, California's Central Valley only became fertile farmland because of irrigation.[31] California is no stranger to droughts, but without the water for irrigation, consumers across the country will see prices at the grocery store go up, as farmers are forced to cut back crops.[32] While the issue of water usage in California has been long and contentious, Obama's environmental activism, not global warming, is destroying this important farmland. And what was Obama's response to a bill that would restore water to California's Central Valley? He threatened to veto it.[33]

6. The Government Response to the BP Oil Spill

On April 20, 2010, an explosion on the Deepwater Horizon drilling rig killed eleven workers and injured another sixteen. The rig burned and sank, resulting in what would become the worst oil spill in American history. The response of the Obama administration was shameful.

Louisiana Governor Bobby Jindal described the Obama administration's response as lackadaisical, with Obama far more concerned with his image and the criticism he was getting than addressing the actual problem.[34] To be sure, many within the administration were all too happy to appear in media interviews and blame Republicans and the oil industry for the problem. The environmental rhetoric was full of sound and fury, but signified nothing.

In fact, the Obama administration's response to the BP Oil spill was arguably much worse than the federal government's response to Hurricane Katrina. According to the 1988 Stafford Act, states are in charge in the event of on-shore natural disasters, not the federal government.[35] The federal government's role in Katrina was to provide any resources requested by the governor. The BP oil spill happened in federal waters, therefore the Obama administration was always in charge. Unfortunately, it wasn't up to the task.

The National Commission on the BP Deepwater Horizon Oil Spill and Offshore Drilling (established by Obama via executive order) found that the Obama administration grossly underestimated the amount of oil flowing into the Gulf of Mexico, slowed response efforts, and withheld its worst-case estimates from the public and overstated the effectiveness of the cleanup efforts.[36]

Given Obama's past criticisms of the government's response to Hurricane Katrina, one might think he'd have done a better job, and not had his administration lie to protect his image.

7. Cutting Medicaid for States Defunding Planned Parenthood

Whatever your views on abortion, if you are fair-minded and interested in pursuing the truth and making ethical choices, when allegations of criminal wrongdoing surface, it is every citizen's duty to take those allegations seriously, and the duty of the states to take notice and investigate. In June of 2015, a group of undercover investigative journalists calling themselves "The Center for Medical Progress" began posting a series of "sting" videos[37] in a style similar to those once posted by activist James O'Keefe. In these new videos, CMP investigators posed as agents for a biotechnology firm and attempted to form a business relationship with Planned Parenthood to facilitate the sale of tissue, organs, and intact cadavers extracted from second-trimester abortions. Should Planned Parenthood have profited in any way from such sales, it would be a Federal crime.

As this series of sting videos continued surfacing, a number of states began considering measures that would strip Medicaid funding from Planned Parenthood clinics in their states. In response, Obama threatened officials in all states that such actions might violate Federal law[38].

We can certainly debate the merits of the research done by CMP, and the legality of responding to the CMP sting through state-level cuts to Medicaid spending on Planned Parenthood. But there's a problem for Obama and his Justice Department. Pro-life Kansas had, long before this controversy erupted, already chosen to eliminate state spending on Planned Parenthood clinics shortly after the election of Tea Party Republican Scott Brownback in 2013. The Obama administration took Kansas to court, claiming that such cuts violated Title X funding laws by denying women equal access to reproductive healthcare. They lost. Realizing that punishing states who responded to the video exposé would be impossible through the courts, Obama issued an executive order cutting Kansas Medicaid payouts by roughly the same amount (around $400,000) that had been redirected from Planned Parenthood to other women's health clinics already. [39]

The leftwing argument against defunding Planned Parenthood is that it violates Title X guarantees of equal access to reproductive care to eliminate Medicaid spending at Planned Parenthood clinics. But this claim would depend on the belief that Planned Parenthood provides services that cannot be obtained elsewhere and that the money being taken out of Planned Parenthood coffers is not being reinvested in women's health options. But this is precisely the argument that played out in court, and it didn't fly there. What authority, then, is given to Obama to punish women seeking reproductive care in Kansas for the State's decision to end its support of Planned Parenthood? Why is the administration picking one private sector entity to provide women with reproductive healthcare access?

8. Skyrocketing College Costs

Under President Obama, the average cost of college tuition has increased by 8 percent across all types of institutions, be they public, private, two-year or four-year schools.[40] Despite campaigning on increasing access to Pell Grants, Obama actually *cut* Pell Grants, which increased average college costs by an average of nearly a thousand dollars per year per student.[41]

These increases in college costs were more than double the rate of inflation,[42] and, combined with the decline of family incomes, significantly increased the burden of obtaining a higher education on Obama's watch. Obama forgot to mention this to all those youngsters who voted for his reelection.

Making matters even worse for college students, Obama's policies have prevented the robust economic growth necessary to absorb each year's graduating class into the workforce. As previously noted, youth employment rates have fallen dramatically in the Obama years. On top of that, full employment rates for recent college graduates dropped below 50% in 2011 – this is a first since the statistic began to be tracked.[43]

9.   Racial Quotas for School Discipline

In the summer of 2012, Obama issued an executive order that effectively called for racial quotas in school discipline policies. The executive order, titled "White House Initiative on Educational Excellence for African Americans," linked the high dropout rate of African American students with "methods that result in disparate use of disciplinary tools." and established a new bureaucracy to enforce proportionate outcomes in school discipline policies based on race.[44] By making such a decree, Obama *assumes* that schools discipline students differently based on race. He thinks he can solve the problem by mandating that schools discipline students based on the color of their skin, not by the content of their character.

According to Roger Clegg, the president of the Center for Equal Opportunity, Obama's executive order has missed the mark completely, and ignores the true source of the problem. Clegg told *The Daily Caller*, "A disproportionate share of crimes are committed by African Americans, and they are disproportionately likely to misbehave in school... [because] more than 7 out of 10 African-Americans (72.5 percent) are born out of wedlock... versus fewer than 3 out of 10 whites."[45]

Michael Meyers, the executive director of the New York Civil Rights Commission, said of Obama, "With the stroke of his presidential pen, Obama has ignored and denies the substantial and irreversible racial progress we as a nation have made; with great alacrity, and without any shame, he has embraced the separatists' mission, credo and agenda that dictate blacks should be regarded as different and educated differently, and treated differentially, from all other American students."[46] Martin Luther King Jr. would be very disappointed.

10. Radical Attorneys General

Obama's Justice Department has, since his cabinet was first filled, taken its cues from the top. The Attorney General of the United States is charged with ensuring that the laws of the United States are strictly and fairly enforced for all Americans. Unfortunately, for President Obama, the primary job of the Attorney General has been to provide cover for his administration's serial violations of law and precedent, and to pursue a radical, racialized interpretation of the Civil Rights Act.

Attorney General Eric Holder's radical past ought to have disqualified him from being the nation's chief law enforcement officer. In 1970, Holder was a Columbia University freshman, and a leader of a black separatist group on campus, the Student Afro-American Society (SAAS). With SAAS, Holder participated in a five-day armed takeover of an abandoned ROTC office on campus.[47]

Holder's radical past certainly explains the actions of his Justice Department, described elsewhere in this book, from his failure to prosecute New Black Panther Party members over voter intimidation during the 2008 election, to his inappropriate involvement in the Trayvon Martin and Michael Brown shooting death cases, and including his stonewalling of high-profile investigations (including Fast and Furious and the IRS Scandal), harassing reporters for doing their job, and allowing millions of illegal voters to remain on the voter rolls.

Despite his tenure being marred by partisan actions, controversy and scandal, Holder was one of the longest-serving members of Obama's original Cabinet.

After the disasters of Holder's tenure, Obama could have made a clean sweep, but instead, he turned to far-left radicals like Al Sharpton for advice on Holder's replacement.[48] Loretta Lynch was selected to be Attorney General for Obama's last two years in office. Lynch's racialist views on justice should have disqualified her as well. She has claimed that reasonable voter ID laws are racist and is pledged to continue lawsuits against them. Lynch has also said that discipline in schools has a racist, disparate impact on minority children.[49] According to Lynch, being "tough on crime" is just code for being tough on blacks.[50] During her confirmation hearings, Lynch declared that she believes illegal aliens have the same rights to work as American citizens, and that she didn't believe Obama's unilateral executive amnesty was, in fact, amnesty.[51]

While Lynch is clearly just like Holder in her radical views on racial issues, she's also well-suited to continue Holder's policy of very selective law enforcement. As U.S. Attorney for the Eastern District of New York, Lynch signed off on mega-bank HSBC's avoiding prosecution for their massive money laundering for drug cartels and State-sponsors of terrorism—a fact she omitted from her Senate questionnaire.[52] HSBC was, according to Lynch's then-boss Eric Holder, too big to prosecute. Lynch's tenure, as of this writing, has included many other bouts of radical partisanship, including a pledge to defend states that criminalize speech against climate change doctrine, a push to prosecute states that attempt to defend religious liberty on issues like gay marriage and gender identification, and an aggressive interventionist policy against states attempting to enact voter ID laws. None of this should be surprising given her past views, and none of it will stop until she is replaced.

11. Giving Up U.S. Control of the Internet

Thus far, we've seen Obama act is a divisive figure, inflaming racial tensions, using tragedies to score political points, and punishing states that don't back his agenda. But surely, on the issue of technology, America's first presidential candidate to announce on Twitter would be a better fit and make better choices, right? Not so much.

In March of 2014, the Obama administration announced that the United States would begin to relinquish oversight of the Internet Corporation for Assigned Names and Numbers (ICANN), which oversees the assignment of domain names—paving the way for an international organization (most likely the UN's International Telecommunication Union) to take over.[53] There are many good reasons why this is a bad idea. The *Wall Street Journal's* L. Gordon Crovitz explained: "Russia, China and other authoritarian governments have already been working to redesign the Internet more to their liking, and now they will no doubt leap to fill the power vacuum caused by America's unilateral retreat."[54]

> *The U.S. role in protecting the open Internet is similar to its role enforcing freedom of the seas. The U.S. has used its power over the Internet exclusively to protect the interconnected networks from being closed off, just as the U.S. Navy protects sea lanes. Imagine the alarm if America suddenly announced that it would no longer patrol the world's oceans.*[55]

What can we expect if the International Telecommunication Union (ITU) takes over the role of overseeing the internet? Nothing good; nothing in favor of freedom, to be sure. During a 2012 conference, countries in the ITU voted in favor of a treaty giving governments the authority to block citizens' access to the global internet. But, that's not all.

> *In the past few years, Russia and China have used [the ITU] to challenge the open Internet. They have lobbied for the ITU to replace Washington as the Icann [sic] overseer. They want the ITU to outlaw anonymity on the Web (to make identifying dissidents easier) and to add a fee charged to providers when people gain access to the Web "internationally"—in effect, a tax on U.S.-based sites such as Google and Facebook. The unspoken aim is to*

discourage global Internet companies from giving everyone equal access.[56]

If this is a gesture to the global community by Obama in light of the NSA scandal, internet freedom seems like a huge price to pay. Ceding oversight of the internet to an international agency will harm freedom, harm America and make tyrannical regimes worldwide far more powerful in the arena of ideas.

12. Net Neutrality

Obama's lack of understanding of the appeal of the internet, and its crucial role in promoting human freedom and flourishing, is even better-highlighted by his administration's support of so-called "Net Neutrality". Ignoring the desires of the American people, and the requirements of the Constitution, in 2014, Obama began pressuring the Federal Communications Commission to regulate the internet as a public utility using authority granted under Title II of the Communications Act of 1934. The innocuously termed "net neutrality" would not only give the government more control over the internet, but would also tax internet usage itself.[57] According to Phil Kerpen, a leading free-market policy analyst and advocate, Obama's plan "includes a new 16.1 percent tax on your Internet bill that would automatically rise every three months – all without the approval of the people's elected representatives in Congress."[58] As the taxes increased, private investment would suffer, causing price increases to accelerate.

Michael Mandel, the chief economic strategist for the Progressive Policy Institute, said that Obama's plan for Title II regulation of the Internet is bad for the economy and "putting the Federal Communications Commission in charge of regulating broadband rates and micromanaging Web services, as the president proposes, would slow innovation and raise costs."[59] According to FCC Commissioner Ajit Pai, the public is being deliberately mislead by the FCC about the scope of net neutrality.

According to Pai, Obama's plans would give the FCC the "power to micromanage virtually every aspect of how the Internet works," including regulating prices.[60]

Obama claimed that these new rules would "keep the Internet open and free," but, given that a whopping 61 percent of Americans oppose his version of "net neutrality", it's clear that the public didn't buy it.[61] Of course, Obama has never been one to let public opinion or the Constitution get in his way. When Republicans in Congress attempted to build up support for legislation countering the excessive Obama-backed rules changes, the Obama administration, true to form, declared legislation wasn't necessary because, they claimed, the FCC already had authority to change the rules under Title II.[62]

Thankfully, in 2015, the FCC chose to implement a far less punitive, far more limited version of Net Neutrality which stuck to the idea that the internet should be open and unfettered by corporate gamesmanship.[63] Their rules were 400 pages long, but contained no significant tax increases and excised the vast majority of the antiquated Title II regulations. The FCC did its job admirably under the circumstances, but pressure from Obama nearly capsized the internet in a sea of red tape and taxes. Battles like this highlight the enormous power that the nation's chief executive holds over Americans that cannot by countered by the other branches and the necessity of selecting a president who believes, as Calvin Coolidge did, that the less he does to wield that power, the better off we'll be.

13. Releasing Criminal Illegal Aliens

The American people have a wide variety of views on the matter of immigration. Obama is certainly not alone in believing amnesty is the right thing to do. But, releasing convicted violent criminals who entered the United States illegally is not in the best interest of American citizens – this should not be a controversial position. Yet, Obama, in his quest for amnesty, has done just that.

Over 36,000 convicted criminal aliens awaiting deportation proceedings were released in 2013 by U.S. Immigration and Customs Enforcement (ICE). According to a report by the Center for Immigration Studies, many of the criminals released had been convicted of serious crimes, including 193 homicides, 426 sexual assaults, 303 kidnappings, 1,075 aggravated assaults, and an astounding 15,635 DUIs. Other convicts released had been found guilty of robbery, arson, assault, sex offenses, larceny, and burglary.[64] In addition to the 36,000 awaiting deportation proceedings, the Obama administration also caught and released 68,000 criminal aliens in 2013 who weren't put into deportation proceedings.[65]

According to Jessica M. Vaughn, the Director of Policy Studies at the Center for Immigration Studies, the policies of the Obama administration "frequently have allowed political considerations to trump public safety factors and, as a result, aliens with serious criminal convictions have been allowed to return to the streets instead of being removed to their home countries."[66]

Obama has argued that changing our immigration policy is "the right thing to do for our economy, our security, and our future."[67] Only in the Obama administration could releasing tens of thousands of convicted criminals back into the U.S. population just because they are illegal aliens be considered "the right thing to do" for our security.

14. The Border Crisis

Obama's lack of understanding regarding the mechanics of immigration didn't stop with freeing criminals for political purposes. In 2012, having been unable to get the DREAM Act through Congress, he did so via executive order instead. Despite this usurpation of the Constitution, he called it "the right thing to do." With the federal government no longer deporting young illegal immigrants, what's the worst that could happen?

What happened was a massive wave of "unaccompanied minors" illegally crossing the border into the United States in 2014 and 2015.[68] These unaccompanied young illegal aliens not only included innocent young children and toddlers, but also criminal gangs.[69] More than 100,000 illegal alien minors have crossed the border from Central America—a full-blown border crisis.[70] These illegal aliens are often found to be ill, sometimes with diseases as serious as tuberculosis and measles.[71] Some may have family or friends in the United States already, others appear to have been sent north in the hope that their families will be able to follow once Obama grants them amnesty. Border Patrol forces are overwhelmed, local communities are feeling the bite of increased spending on law enforcement and health care to deal with the kids, and, in the chaos, we are at grave risk that criminals and terrorists may join the flood and enter the United States.[72]

In response to the crisis, Obama not only refused to visit the border, but he went on vacation.[73] Fingers were pointed at George W. Bush and the Republicans for the ongoing crisis.[74] When not blaming Bush and the GOP, the White House was claiming that "today, border security is stronger than it ever has been."[75] Depending on how you look at the situation at the border, Obama simultaneously wanted all the credit and none of the blame.

As much as Obama doesn't want to accept blame for the border crisis, a joint report from the Department of Homeland Security (DHS) and Immigration and Customs Enforcement (ICE) contradicted publicly made claims about the cause of the crisis. According to the report, the lack of deportations is a significant factor for the influx of Central American minors coming into the United States illegally.[76]

Evidence also suggests that the Obama administration anticipated the crisis well before it exploded. In January 2014, the Department of Homeland Security posted a Request for Information (RFI) for "Escort Services for Unaccompanied Alien Children."[77]

The border crisis is the result of bad policies enacted by Obama via executive action. Nevertheless, Obama refused to accept any responsibility for the crisis and, by all appearances, isn't taking it seriously. Meanwhile, the crisis continues to get worse, America becomes less secure each day along the border, and the long-term costs to the American people and the illegal aliens continues to grow.

15. Executive Amnesty

Obama still wasn't done with immigration, though. We just discussed his decision to grant amnesty to illegal immigrants who arrived here as children—a move he argued was within the limits of his authority, though many people doubted his claim.[78] Possibly to deflect such criticism, Obama continued to make the case that he couldn't unilaterally change immigration laws, insisting that it was a problem for Congress to solve.[79] However, after Congress failed to pass immigration reform, Obama began to threaten to use executive action to grant amnesty to illegals.[80] Worried that such a move would make an already treacherous electoral environment even worse for Democrats, Obama waited until after the 2014 midterms to formally announce *another* executive action on immigration. This time, he granted amnesty to as many as five million illegal immigrants.[81]

With the announcement, President Obama had truly stretched his executive authority beyond the breaking point. But, you don't need to take our word for it, one just needs to ask Barack Obama. As a candidate for president, he said, "I take the Constitution very seriously. The biggest problems that we're facing right now have to do with [the president] trying to bring more and more power into the executive branch and not go through Congress at all. And that's what I intend to reverse when I'm President of the United States of America."[82] For years as president, he repeatedly acknowledged the limitations on his executive powers, including acting alone on amnesty. "I am president, I am not king. [...] I can't just make the laws up by myself."[83] Yet, that is ultimately what he did, once the 2014 midterms were over.

Freed from the need to even pretend to care about what the law says or what the people want, Obama's post-election amnesty was both unconstitutional and unprecedented. According to Mark Krikorian, the executive director of the Center for Immigration Studies, unlike Obama's unilateral executive amnesty, previous executive actions on immigration by Ronald Reagan and George H.W. Bush "were modest attempts at faithfully executing legislation duly enacted by Congress."[84] Leaked documents also indicate that border patrol agents were being trained to hold the vast majority of illegal immigrants as off-limits to deportation.[85] The consequences of Obama's amnesty are quite serious and severe. States stand to lose potentially billions of dollars when illegal immigrants granted amnesty protections use state services and benefits, including unemployment benefits, at the expense of taxpaying citizens and legal immigrants.[86] The IRS also ruled that illegal immigrants granted amnesty would be eligible for tax refunds, even if they didn't pay taxes.[87] Illegal immigrants would also be able to get driver's licenses and social security numbers, making it easier for them the vote in elections.[88] That is certainly no coincidence.

In February of 2015, federal judge Andrew S. Hanen blocked implementation of Obama's amnesty.[89] That didn't stop Obama from threatening Immigration and Customs Enforcement (ICE) officials with unspecified "consequences" if they didn't follow his amnesty rules.[90] In April of 2015, Hanen refused the Obama administration's appeal of his earlier ruling,[91] According to Hanen, Obama's threat of punishment for those who enforce our immigration laws amounts to "total non-enforcement" of the law. He also accused the Obama administration of misleading him when they claimed no part of Obama's amnesty had been implemented yet. We will all get to see just how far into law-breaking President Obama wants to go. After all, Obama needs these new recipients of government benefits voting for the

Democratic Party, and he certainly hasn't let the rule of law get in is way so far.

16. Common Core through Bribery

Since the *No Child Left Behind Act* (NCLB) was passed in 2001, schools have had to meet certain requirements in mathematics, reading and writing, as set by their state in order to maintain federal funding. Obama promised to reform the program to make it more effective. His plan for reforming NCLB was a full embrace of "Common Core" standards – essentially, the establishment of a Federal monopoly on education standards.[92]

States were essentially bribed into accepting Common Core standards with *Race to The Top* grant money and with NCLB waivers.[93] As of this writing, all but nine states have adopted and maintain common core standards, most of them in response to such bribes – the number reached as high as 46 with common core curricula before the backlash began and Oklahoma led the charge to opt out. Obama administration But, according to the Heritage Foundation, the Obama administration didn't actually have the power to bribe the states in this manner:

> *[...]the Secretary of Education has waiver authority under NCLB statute, but that authority does not extend to granting waivers in exchange for adopting Administration-approved policy. Rather than pursuing policy change through the reauthorization of NCLB, the Department circumvented Congress by granting waivers from the law.*[94]

Since Common Core began replacing state education standards in 2010, there has been plenty of criticism from both right and left-leaning states about what is seen as a federal takeover of education. The problems with the Common Core curriculum and standards have become increasingly apparent and too numerous to list here, but they range from the absurd (*Hunger Games* is considered more complex literature than *The Grapes of Wrath*[95]) to the frightening (getting the right answer to a math problem isn't as important as the kids at least thinking about what they got wrong[96]). Even Common Core's earliest proponents have found themselves no longer supporting Obama's favored education standards, and have called for changes, and delays.[97] Sounds a lot like the botched Obamacare rollout... except, in this case, Obama can't share any blame with congressional Democrats.

17. Inaction on Housing Foreclosures

We've already covered a lot of ground, domestically, but what of the problem that caused the 2007/2008 financial collapse – what of home foreclosures? In 2006, there were 717,522 foreclosure filings on American homes. After the housing crash, this jumped up to the 2.8 million range for 2009 and 2010 as the housing market appeared to hit a bottom.[98]

All through 2012, there was a lot of happy talk in the media about a housing recovery, but for 2012, the number of properties subjected to foreclosure was still a staggering 1.8 million.[99] The happy talk was, of course, at the service of Obama's reelection effort but, around the country, foreclosures continue to affect Americans. Fifty-seven percent of the metro areas monitored by RealtyTrac showed an increase in foreclosure activity.[100]

In 2013, the overall picture of the housing market improved slightly, but remained bleak. There were 1.36 million foreclosures, nineteen percent of all homes were rated as "deeply underwater" on their mortgages, and overall foreclosures were still above the norm for a healthy economy.[101] Adding to this bad news, RealtyTrac figures show that the pace of foreclosures started to rise again in early 2014.[102] Too many people tried desperately in the stagnant Obama economy to save their homes, but found few options. Unable to refinance, unable to sell and also unable to afford their homes due to job cuts, pay cuts and tax hikes, people are now throwing in the towel and giving their homes back to the banks.

While Obama was shoveling huge amounts of taxpayer dollars into General Motors and the big banks, when it came to helping out average American homeowners, he suddenly discovered that it was time to be cautious. He never backed legislation to force lenders to come to terms with borrowers whose homes were worth vastly less than the mortgage amount, nor did he pay attention to homeowners who found that lenders were being very uncooperative in working out deals to stave off foreclosure.[103] It seems strange that a populist figure like Obama would miss such easy chances to help struggling Americans deal with the loss of equity that came with the real estate market bust, but, as we've already discussed, Obama isn't much of a populist once the campaign ends.

18. Collapse of Home Values

In September of 2012, the average value of an American home had climbed back to prices last seen in 2003.[104] This is actually considered an improvement because, earlier in the Obama administration, prices had dropped, in some estimates, to levels not seen since the 1990s. This means most people who bought a home from about 2004 until the housing collapse in 2007 now own a home worth less than they paid for it. For most Americans, their home is their largest source of wealth, so this collapse in home values has been devastating, especially to the middle class. Furthermore, the slight rise in home values since 2010 has been built on financial sand. As it turns out, when the US taxpayer was forced to bail out the failed Freddie Mac and Fannie Mae lenders, most of the money wound up being used to merely transfer the bad loans to the Federal Housing Administration (FHA). As a lot of the loans were non-performing when sent to the FHA and the economy has not improved, all that this accomplished was to move the disaster from one government-backed entity to another.

The only way this would have worked is with a bullish economy. If we'd had economic growth of 4 or 5 percent per year since the end of the recession, this would not have been a problem, but we didn't have that. Our anemic growth has not only stunted American wages and reduced American employment; it has also ensured that the FHA will require repeated bailouts. In 2012, FHA was over-leveraged as badly as Lehman Brothers was before its collapse triggered the 2008 financial crisis.[105] As a result, in 2013, the FHA needed a $1.7 billion bailout to cover their losses from troubled loans—it was the first time in its 79-year history that it needed a bailout.[106] And, following this bailout, the stagnation in real estate values has continued, meaning it's only a matter of time before another taxpayer-funded giveaway to the FHA is required.

19. Obama's Supreme Court Nominees

The Supreme Court of the United States experienced two vacancies during Obama's first term, and while there was no question that Obama would see his nominees confirmed by the Democrat-controlled Senate, there are some serious questions as to whether his two nominees should have been chosen in the first place.

After the retirement of Justice David Souter in 2009, Barack Obama nominated Sonia Sotomayor to replace him. Controversy soon arose when her comments on how gender and nationality can and should bias one's judgment in interpreting the law were exposed. Sotomayor said, several times over the years, that she hoped that "a wise Latina woman with the richness of her experiences would more often than not reach a better conclusion than a white male who hasn't lived that life."[107] Her past writings and associations also raised questions about her attitude towards race and equal justice under the law. As a college student, Sotomayor described herself as a Puerto Rican nationalist, and had clearly negative attitudes toward the United States.[108] According to Obama's own Department of Homeland Security, Puerto Rican nationalists are potential domestic terrorists.[109]

Obama's second chance to nominate someone for the Supreme Court came when Justice John Paul Stevens retired. This time, he nominated his Solicitor General, Elena Kagan. Alas, she too has a radical past – this time as an activist opposed to the US Military. While dean of Harvard Law School, Elena Kagan banned military recruiters from campus in protest over the military's now-defunct "don't-ask-don't-tell" policy regarding homosexuals. According to Elaine Donnelly of the Center for Military Readiness, Kagan's "only significant record indicates deliberate hostility and opposition to laws protecting the culture and best interests of the American military."[110] Veterans were not the only group outraged by the nomination. The group '9/11 Families' took issue with the fact that, as Obama's Solicitor General, she helped to shield the Saudi royal family from lawsuits for their alleged role in funding the terrorist attacks.[111]

Sotomayor's radical racialist views, and Kagan's anti-military record cast them far outside the mainstream of American values and jurisprudence. That Obama selected them for lifetime appointments to the highest court in the country says a lot about just how out of the mainstream he really is.

20. War on Coal

We'll talk more about the economy later, but let's also take a moment to consider the impact Obama has had on our energy bills since he took office, since it's a leading concern for many Americans who are struggling to get by. Coal is, by far, the largest source of electricity production in the United States. As of 2011, coal produced forty-two percent of America's electricity, with the next highest source being natural gas at twenty-five percent. "Renewables", Obama's much-touted "green energy", provided only thirteen percent. And while coal, as a source of electricity, has become less prevalent over the years (it was at a peak of fifty-three percent in the 1990s), it is still projected to provide fully thirty-five percent of our electricity in 2040, at a time when "renewables" will still only account for sixteen percent.[112] Given its ubiquity, great care should be taken by the United States government to ensure a steady supply of coal in the short term. But that is not how Obama sees it: he believes that coal is a critical threat to the environment and has taken it upon himself to destroy the coal industry before his tenure is at an end.

In fact, that was one of Obama's 2008 campaign promises: he stated that anyone could build a coal-fired electricity plant, if they wanted, but that his policies would bankrupt them.[113] In this, we have a definite promise kept by Obama: he has gone after the coal industry as if it were the source of all evil in the world. Using the heavy club of the Environmental Protection Agency (EPA), Obama has made it so that more than 200 coal-fired power plants will shut down over the next three to five years.[114]

There is no word from Obama on what will replace these coal-fired power plants, nor what average, working folks will do as they either suffer blackouts or have their power bill shoot up as more expensive sources of electricity are used, nor what his plans are to replace the divot his policies have left in the struggling economies of coal-producing states like Kentucky, West Virginia, and Pennsylvania.

21. War on Oil

While Obama has lavished taxpayer money on "green energy", he has been an enemy of the American oil industry. When Obama took office, the national average gas price was under $2.00 per gallon. Obama set about "correcting" this as soon as he could.

Using the 2010 BP oil spill in the Gulf of Mexico as a pretext, President Obama issued a moratorium on offshore oil drilling, ostensibly so that drilling procedures could be reviewed to ensure safety. But Obama's 2010 budget proposal, submitted to Congress two months before the BP oil spill, indicated that government revenues from offshore oil drilling would drop from $1.5 billion in 2009 to $413 million in 2015. Obama clearly envisioned big restrictions on offshore drilling, he just needed an environmental disaster to use as political cover.[115]

After the moratorium was issued, gas prices, which were already creeping back up, spiked to nearly $4.00 a gallon.[116] The national average gas price would stay above $3.00 per gallon for a record 1,410 days, which stymied the struggling economic recovery.[117]

Obama also opposed the Keystone XL pipeline, which would deliver 700,000 barrels a day of crude oil from Canada to coastal Texas oil refineries and create an estimated 20,000 jobs. Obama delayed making a final decision until after the 2014 midterm elections. Of course, after Republicans won control of the Senate, Obama threatened to veto any bill approving construction of the pipeline.[118] Later, he made good on that threat, stating:

> *Because this act of Congress conflicts with established executive branch procedures and cuts short thorough consideration of issues that could bear on our national interest -- including our security, safety, and environment -- it has earned my veto.[119]*

Never mind the fact that a State Department environmental impact study on the proposed pipeline and concluded that not only would it have minimal impact on greenhouse gas emission, but it would create thousands of jobs[120].

Obama's war on oil didn't stop there. He has done as much as possible to slow down, if not stop, oil production in the United States. His administration cut back the amount of federal land available for shale oil production,[121] and blocked oil exploration in Alaska, a potential source of an estimated 27 billion barrels of oil and thousands of jobs.[122] Federal drilling permits have also been delayed. It's no surprise that, on Obama's watch, oil and natural gas production on federal land went down 6 percent and 28 percent. Oil and natural gas production on private and state land, however, went up 61 percent and 33 percent.[123] Not that Obama hasn't tried to get in the way of private sector efforts. In 2011 he proposed more than $60 billion in tax and fee increases on American energy production,[124] and in 2012, Obama proposed exempting oil and gas companies from eligibility to receive a tax credit that encourages domestic manufacturing.[125]

Thanks to the boom in private oil and natural gas production, Americans finally got the much-needed relief at the gas pump in 2014. According to the AAA, the plunge in gas prices saves American drivers more than $500 million per day.[126] It's a good thing Obama's war on oil failed; otherwise, the slim economic recovery we've managed may never have come at all.

22. Title IX Abuses

In George Orwell's famous dystopian tale *1984*, the Ministry of Truth has, as its primary objective, the job of manipulating the language to suit the needs of the bureaucracy (not to mention the rewriting of history to create a narrative that suits those same needs). Obama has, on more than one occasion, embodied this vision with alarming accuracy by simply altering the interpretation of an existing law, then using the full force of the federal government to impose his new interpretations on the country. Elsewhere in this book, we discuss similar tactics he used when dealing with immigration reform, gun control, and the environment, but perhaps his most blatant foray into the rewriting of decades-old legislation is his treatment of Title IX and the Civil Rights Act regarding gender issues.

The Obama administration expanded Title IX's definition of sexual harassment as "any unwelcome conduct of a sexual nature," making colleges and university responsible for sexual harassment and assaults that occur both on and off-campus, and lowering the standards of evidence to prove the guilt of the accused. According to Jessica Gavora, a former senior policy advisor at the Department of Justice, Obama's new standards effectively killed protections for academic freedom and free expression on college campuses.[127]

When North Carolina's House Bill 2 (H.B.2.) brought the issue of "gender expression" and bathroom usage into the national spotlight in 2016, the Obama administration again overstepped its authority by unilaterally redefining existing laws. On May 4,

2016, Obama's Justice Department, headed by Loretta Lynch, wrote a letter to Governor McCrory informing him that "as a result of compliance with and implementation of North Carolina House Bill 2 ("H.B. 2"), both you and the State of North Carolina are in violation of Title VII of the Civil Rights Act of 1964." While Title VII makes it unlawful to discriminate based on (biological) sex, it does not say or imply that individuals can use whatever bathroom or locker rooms they want based on "gender identity" or "gender expression."[128] This redefinition also conflates sex with gender, which is expressly not mentioned in the CRA.

The Obama administration doubled down just over a week later when it declared that the departments of Justice and Education will both "treat a student's gender identity as the student's sex for purposes of enforcing Title IX," and issued a directive to all public school districts in the country to allow students to use the bathrooms matching their "gender identity." Let's leave aside the implications a decision like this has for states attempting to exercise their right to define their public education systems as they see fit, as should be guaranteed by the 10th Amendment to the Constitution. Title IX only makes reference to *biological* sex, not "gender identity" or "gender expression," ergo, this decree amounts to rewriting Title IX without the assent of Congress.[129] Even though Obama clearly believes sex and gender are entirely different, that didn't stop him from treating them as the same in order to redefine a decades-old law when it suited his needs.

Obama publicly defended his directive by stating, "I think that it is part of our obligation as a society to make sure that everybody is treated fairly, and our kids are all loved, and that they're protected and that their dignity is affirmed."[130] The dignity and privacy of women and young girls who don't want to share bathrooms and changing facilities with men, however, apparently isn't relevant. The *New York Times* noted that the Obama administration directive, "does not have the force of law, but it contains an implicit threat: Schools that do not abide by the Obama administration's interpretation of the law could face lawsuits or a loss of federal aid."[131] Despite the threat of losing federal aid, state and local officials across America pushed back against Obama's transgender bathroom decree. As of this writing, twelve states, including North Carolina, have publicly spoken against Obama's instruction, and have promised to challenge it.[132]

According to Mario Loyola, a senior fellow at the Wisconsin Institute for Law, Obama's reinterpretation of Title IX, is an egregious abuse of power. "In order to 'change the law,' the Obama administration simply pretends that a 1972 act of Congress means whatever the latest progressive fashion trend requires it to mean — even though not a single member of Congress in 1972 would have supported the new "interpretation," much less voted for a law expressly stating what the Obama administration now claims the law says."[133]

23. Climate Change Radicalism

This book is not meant as an indictment of left-wing ideas and policies, per say, but as a condemnation for the particularly unlawful, ineffective, or otherwise bafflingly illogical approaches that Obama and his administration have taken to achieving their goals. This tendency toward extremism and unlawfulness is perhaps most apparent on the issue of climate change. Obama's "colosseum" speech at the Democratic National Convention in Denver in 2008 included a now-infamous promise, "We'll be able to look back and say [...] this was the moment when the rise of the oceans began to slow and our planet began to heal [...]." [134]

He fancied himself the savior of the Earth's climate system in those days, and has gone to extraordinary lengths to leave a legacy of climate change activism despite opposition from Congress, the courts, other nations, and the American people. In service to Obama's belief that climate change is our biggest threat, even as ISIS marches through the Middle East slaughtering by the thousands, he has spent his entire presidency pushing policies which are an outrage against common sense. We've already mentioned a couple of his worst mistakes in the green jobs sphere, but let's recap the whole sorry list:

- He and his representatives and appointees, including Secretary of State John Kerry, have repeatedly made the claim that climate change is a bigger threat than terrorism.[135]

- He and his surrogates have, on many occasions, linked Islamic terrorism to climate change, making the ludicrous claim that Jihadis would be less prone to violence if there weren't a Syrian drought.[136]

- He and his cronies throughout the green energy sphere have wasted billions on renewable energy boondoggles from ABC batteries to Solyndra to solar and wind projects now in the process of shutting down.[137]

- While our men and women fight in our defense, Obama ordered the Defense Department to implement Directives that make climate change preparedness a priority for troops.[138]

- While claiming that the right was anti-science, he has filled the budget of NASA with climate change pork, denying the agency its core mission: space exploration.[139]

- He and his friends at the highest levels of the Department of Energy and the EPA have targeted coal country for extermination—the former head of the EPA even said that people resisting the anti-coal push should be 'crucified'.[140]

- Attorney General Loretta Lynch has indicated that her DOJ would act to support state initiatives to target climate 'deniers' with prosecution and civil lawsuits and intends to defend states pursuing such laws in court.[141]

- The Obama administration has shifted funds intended for military improvements to climate change causes.[142]

- He has made carbon dioxide a pollutant by executive fiat despite its healthful benefits to biomass productivity, subjecting the entire energy sector to massive regulatory burdens and limits on their productivity in the process.[143] The EPA was instructed to pursue that policy—carbon dioxide was officially branded a pollutant in 2009 and subsequent efforts were heavily focused on using this designation to control the energy sector.[144]

- He failed to get cap and trade passed through Congress, so he tried to start the process in the energy-guzzling Northeast Corridor by creating an interstate energy cooperative.[145] The Supreme Court issued a stay on this so-called "clean power plan" - which boils down to a regional cap and trade system - in February of 2016.[146]

- Without the approval of Congress, he entered the US into an international climate change mitigation treaty in 2015. Such an action is illegal by the United States Constitution.[147]

- And in 2016, he diverted funds that were initially earmarked for infectious disease control to climate change research, just as the Zika virus was threatening to break across the US border into Texas and Congress was forced to appropriate further discretionary spending to combat Zika.[148]

Doing even a few of these things would mark Obama a zealot on this issue, and this list is hardly exhaustive. The entire Obama Presidency has been marked by a dogmatic obsession with climate change as the go-to explanation for every wrong, the first argument in favor of every new regulation, and the first deflection for every personal failing. The lengths to which Obama and his surrogates are willing to go - the logic they'll bend - to bring the conversation back to climate change often defy belief. But more importantly, the law seems to be no object to a man that obsessed.

Personal Corruption

Many of the most highly discussed political scandals to shake the Obama administration during his tenure have been bureaucratic failures, failures of leadership, the incompetence of government agencies, or corruption that could not be linked to Obama alone. We'll talk much more about those examples of government corruption and bloat in later chapters, but, first, we'd like to focus on Obama's personal corruption and greed – much of which has flown largely under the radar. Obama, more than any past President, has lived a life of privilege, opulence, and self-involved petulance that Americans view with increasing disgust as his time in office nears its end.

We've tracked down some of the finest examples of corruption, greed, and abuse of power initiated by the President directly. This is far from exhaustive, and there will be other examples as the book progresses, but this group should give you a feel for the quality of Obama's character once he got a seat at the golden banquet table. We trust you'll agree with us – it isn't pretty.

24. An Opaque Administration

We'll start by discussing the tone Obama set for his administration. It is from his personality that his senior advisers and handlers take their cues, and a keen observer can tell a lot about a leader's character by how he chooses to run his affairs. In 2007, then-U.S. Senator Barack Obama said that as President, he would have the most transparent and accountable administration in history – a promise that liberty-minded Americans dearly hoped he'd keep. He even promised that he would post all bills online for five days prior to signing them. This would allow the American people to see what is being proposed and to comment on it, thus giving the President greater input on whether a particular bill should be signed. It would have been a great precedent to set for the presidency, but Obama managed to break this promise a mere nine days after assuming office. On January 29, 2009, President Obama signed the *Lilly Ledbetter Fair Pay Act*, which had been passed by Congress only two days earlier. When Obama broke his promise the second time (on the signing of an expanded S-CHIP law on February 4, 2009), administration officials were asked why. The explanation was that it was "too difficult" to get the legislation up online for five days prior to signing and that they were working on the problem. Apparently, they are still working on this, because bills *still* aren't posted five days prior to signing.

Obama's broken promise on transparency doesn't end there. On his first day in office, Obama issued a presidential memorandum instructing federal agencies "to usher in a new era of open Government."[149] He also issued an executive order reversing changes to the Presidential Records Act made by the previous administration, claiming to hold himself and his records "to a new standard of openness."[150] In retrospect, this seemed to have more to do with implying that his predecessor ran a secretive government than with making his own government transparent. A 2012 analysis by *Bloomberg News* found that the Obama administration failed to meet his own alleged standard of transparency.[151] Despite that seemingly sincere call on his first day for a more open government, the Obama White House also spent years fighting the release of the White House visitor logs from his inauguration to September 2009.[152]

Obama also doesn't let the media photograph certain events, preferring instead to have the White House release official photos. According to the White House Correspondents

Association, this practice sets "a troubling precedent with a direct and adverse impact on the public's ability to independently monitor and see what its government is doing."[153] When the President of the United States is requiring the press to use propaganda in its reporting on White House business, we're in a heap of trouble already. And we're just getting started.

25. Excessive and Lavish Taxpayer-Funded Vacations

The presidency is probably the most stressful job in the world and each president has found the need to vacation while in office. No one complains about that and everyone understands that if a president doesn't sometimes decompress and renew his energy, he will not be an effective leader. But, with Obama, vacations have become so frequent and lavish that we must question whether Obama views the presidency as the most important job in the world, or as a way to live a swank lifestyle.

By March 2015, Obama and his family had taken 38 vacations, according to one estimate. This, of course, does not include Obama's hundreds of golf outings. George W. Bush was an avid golfer but, by the end of his presidency, but he'd only hit the links about 100 times, most of which were in his first year in office. Obama is well over 300 now. But that's petty time-wasting compared to the Obama family travel schedule. Those vacations have not only been numerous, but also costly to the taxpayers. While average Americans have struggled in the Obama economy, tens of millions of tax dollars have funded Obama's lavish vacations.[154]

Obama's defenders are quick to point to Obama's predecessor, George W. Bush, for his frequent trips to his ranch in Crawford, Texas. Of course, they neglect to mention that Bush consistently conducted White House business there, including hosting foreign dignitaries and members of his cabinet, a stark contrast to the lavish vacations of the Obamas.

Some of the more notable vacations include Michelle Obama's luxury trip to Spain in the summer of 2010, which cost taxpayers $467,585,[155] and the African safari in June 2011 that cost $424,000.[156] The Obama family went on a 20-day vacation in Hawaii in December of 2012 that cost American taxpayers a whopping $4 million dollars.[157] Showing his complete contempt for the American taxpayer, during the height of the "fiscal cliff" negotiations, Obama spent taxpayer dollars flying back from his Hawaii vacation to DC and then spent more flying back to Hawaii after Congress enacted the "fix" to the fiscal cliff. The estimated cost of all this jet-setting: $3 million.[158]

In 2013, Obama averaged more than one vacation per month,[159] including trips to Hawaii and Martha's Vineyard, and a Jay Leno appearance – those extravagances cost taxpayers $7.4 million.[160] As Obama's days in the White House are closer to their end, the pace of Obama's vacations hasn't shown signs of slowing down. Between November 2014 and February of 2015, the Obamas took another *three* vacations.[161] Another $12 million Martha's Vineyard mansion was booked for the First Family for the summer of 2015.[162]

The worst aspect of the Obama family's frequent and expensive vacations is the insensitivity shown towards Americans that are still struggling to get by because of Obama's inability to fix the economy. In 2009, the term 'staycation' was added to Merriam-Webster's Collegiate Dictionary due to the popularity of local day trips or home vacations in lieu of longer trips away from home because of the bad economy.[163] Perhaps Obama should have shown a little more empathy for his fellow Americans?

26. Campaigning On Taxpayer Money

Presidents of the United States are provided taxpayer-funded security and the use of Air Force One – both are job necessities.

But, when a president runs for reelection, their campaigns are expected to pay the costs of campaign trips, including those costs borne by local governments to provide security. But, there is a gray area. By combining campaign trips with official business, the costs can be shared, or even completely covered by taxpayers.

Past presidents running for reelection have combined official White House trips with campaign events (thus sharing the cost of the trips between their campaigns and taxpayers), but Barack Obama made this practice an art form during his reelection campaign.

When Obama attended a lavish celebrity-studded fundraiser in Manhattan, which raised $4.5 million for his campaign, the trip was partially funded by taxpayers because Obama made a short visit to Ground Zero for an official event.[164] It was one of many such instances in which Obama had the taxpayers share the burden of paying for him to campaign around the country.

When George W. Bush ran for reelection in 2004, he held a mere 57 fundraisers. In the year following the launch of his reelection campaign, Barack Obama held 124, or about one every three days.[165] A formal complaint by the Republican National Committee noted that alleged government-business events were occurring in battleground states and often resembled campaign rallies.[166]

Often, neither Obama's campaign nor the Democratic National Committee would pay struggling cities for the costs they incurred for extra security provided for Obama. Some examples:

- In the city of Westport, CT, Obama held a $35,800 per-person fundraiser in August of 2012. This resulted in additional costs to the city of $14,812 in overtime payments for police officers and firefighters. The Obama campaign refused to pay these costs.[167]

- In December 2012, the Obama campaign refused the request by the city of Portsmouth, NH to reimburse $30,000 in costs for a campaign stop in September.[168]

- When both Barack Obama and Mitt Romney held separate fundraisers at Newport Beach, California in

2012, both campaigns were billed for the security costs for those political events. Romney's campaign paid their bill. Obama's campaign did not.[169]

So, when Obama wasn't having all taxpayers share the cost of his campaigning, he was sticking it to small cities and towns that have been struggling on his watch. These sorts of "perks" are hardly necessary for the functioning of government, and hardly becoming of a man who rails against the largesse of corporate CEOs.

27. Giving Classified Information To Filmmakers

Another handy way to up your reelection chances is to puff up your image in the entertainment media by bragging about your accomplishments, even if it means releasing classified information to Hollywood. Prior to the 2012 election, it was revealed that the Obama administration might have provided classified information to filmmakers behind *Zero Dark Thirty,* a film on SEAL Team Six's raid on Osama bin Laden. The Obama administration originally denied providing director Kathryn Bigelow and screenwriter Mark Boal classified information. It wasn't until after the election that the Obama administration admitted giving those details to the filmmakers, and that it could have caused an "unnecessary security and counterintelligence risk."[170]

Ironically, when some Senators and Obama administration officials were given an advance screening of the film, there were objections to the portrayals of enhanced interrogations (which Obama opposes) playing a key role in finding bin Laden. But no matter. The film was a critical flop – but a fantastic way of showcasing Obama's role in the death of Osama bin Laden, and that's all that mattered at the time.

28. Taxpayer Dollars for Obama Donors

Let's not forget the time-honored custom of bribery when we talk about ways to gain that key electoral advantage. Selling access and influence has become the rule of the Obama administration. If you want Obama's support, or a nomination, the best way to get it is to write a check. Since taking office, Obama has shown that the best way to get something done is to buy his support. Here are just a few examples that have come to light since Obama's inauguration:

- Donors to Obama's campaigns have received back $21,000 in taxpayer money for each dollar they gave to Obama.[171]

- Obama's donors have been awarded major government contracts for their firms and were given positions to advise the government on where government money should be spent.[172]

- Obama donors were literally given a seat at Obama's table during the "fiscal cliff" meetings at the end of 2012.[173]

- Major corporations lobbying the American government were permitted to donate at least $283 million to Obama's second inauguration.[174]

- Obama established a permanent campaign group, Organizing for Action, to give corporations and individuals access and influence in exchange for donations.[175]

- Top donors and fundraisers were getting plum government jobs, frequently without any of the credentials needed to hold the position on offer. Ambassadorships, czarships, leading advisory roles and other appointments have become like feudal titles for loyal vassals of the king.[176]

- 80 percent of Obama's "green energy" loans went to his own donors.[177]

This hasn't stopped Obama from speaking out against the very practice that has become the norm of his administration. During his 2012 State of the Union address, Barack Obama criticized the "corrosive influence of money in politics."[178] He would know.

29. Pay to Play

Pay-to-play refers to a system where a government official hears requests and accepts the influence of those people who are willing to pay for the privilege. In a dictionary definition of this phrase, Obama's picture should appear. According to a *New York Times* analysis, about 75 percent of Obama donors who gave $100,000 or more got to visit the White House.[178] Some of them were first-time donors to Obama or the Democratic Party, and their donations sometimes coincided with their visits. [179]

One such donor was Sanjiv Ahuja, the CEO of LightSquared, a Virginia-based satellite broadband company. Ahuja donated more than $30,000 to the Democratic Party.[180] His White House meetings often coincided with his attendance at Obama fundraisers.[181] The donations also coincided with Obama's Federal Communications Commission giving "favorable regulatory decisions and other special treatment, while driving its competition out of business," according to the *Daily Caller,* which obtained documents and communications on the matter.[182]

This kind of inappropriate pay-to-play scheming has been a common occurrence in the Obama administration. Even though the U.S. government has stockpiled $1 billion in smallpox vaccines at $3 a dose, the Obama administration aggressively pushed through a no-bid contract for Siga Technologies to provide 1.7 million unnecessary experimental smallpox vaccine doses costing taxpayers $255 per dose. No one knows if the experimental vaccine even works, but the controlling shareholder of Siga, Ronald O. Perelman, is a long-time Democrat party donor. Andy Stern, the one-time boss of the Service Employees International Union (SEIU), which has donated about $27 million to Obama's political campaigns, also sits on the Siga board. [183]

The Pritzker family of Chicago have been long and generous donors to Obama. In 2011, they got a very sweet deal from the FDIC essentially forgiving them $144 million owed after one of their banks failed in 2001. 1,400 depositors of that bank—who were owed more than $10 million—were stiffed.[184]

Given all of this pay to play activity in Obama's Administration, it appears that Obama's 2011 executive order requiring government contractors to disclose their political donations was just a means of making it easy for Obama officials to identify those who have paid the price to gain influence or receive favors. [185]

30. Organizing for Campaign Finance Laundering

Shortly before his second inauguration, Obama made the stunning announcement that his presidential campaign was not going to disband. Instead, it would be relaunched as a non-profit group called Organizing for Action (OFA), which would mobilize supporters of his agenda during his second term.

Organizing for Action is run by former Obama White House and campaign staffers, with Obama's 2012 campaign manager, Jim Messina, serving as national chairman. Despite claims that the organization would be the next step of a grassroots movement, there is clearly something more sinister going on. With OFA not subject to campaign finance laws, the organization can accept unlimited personal and corporate donations.[186] And big donations were rewarded with big influence. Giving or raising at least half a million dollars would earn a donor a spot on a national advisory board, which would hold quarterly meetings with Obama at the White House.[187]

While technically legal, this group enables Obama to skirt campaign finance and ethics regulations designed to prevent outside influence from corrupting government officials. Obama may claim to be an advocate for the little guy, but it's the folks who can write the big checks who get a ticket to Obama's inner circle, and the ability to influence the White House agenda. Obama's rather blatant pay-to-play activities have become too much even for some Democrats to stomach, with such liberal Democrat stalwarts as Senators Al Franken (D-MN) and Elisabeth Warren (D-MA) complaining when Obama's pick to head up the Treasury Department ended up being Antonio Weiss, one of Obama's major campaign donation bundlers.[188]

31. Obama's Unqualified Ambassadors

Presidents commonly give ambassadorships to big donors and bundlers, and Barack Obama is no exception. Some donors outright expect such assignment as a reward for their loyalty. Just before Obama's second term began, so many fundraisers were expecting appointments that rules were set up for Obama's big donors who wanted plum ambassadorships: volunteer for more than one country and be ready to serve for only two years so Obama can award the post to someone else who has donated big money.[189]

According to an analysis by American Foreign Service Association, 30.7% of Obama's ambassadorships have gone to political appointees.[190]   Many of these have been campaign bundlers who collectively have raised millions of dollars for Obama's campaigns.[191] But the problem with these nominations wasn't that they were political, it's that many of his political picks have been grossly unqualified for the posts they were given. Here are some gems from Obama's second-term ambassadorial nominees:

- **Caroline Kennedy** - nominated as ambassador to Japan, despite having no foreign policy experience, and having little knowledge of the country and not knowing the language.[192]
- **George Tsunis** - Obama bundler nominated as ambassador to Norway; he proved, during his nomination

hearing, that he didn't know what system of government the country had.[193]

- **Noah Bryson Mamet** - Obama bundler nominated as ambassador to Argentina; he'd never even visited there.[194]

- **Max Baucus** - the retired Democratic Senator was nominated by Obama to be ambassador to China. He painfully admitted to the Senate Foreign Relations Committee that he was "no real expert on China."[195]

- **Colleen Bell** - Obama bundler and soap opera producer was nominated as ambassador to Hungary; she had no knowledge about the country.[196]

According to Christian Whiton, a former State Department adviser in the Bush Administration, while sending donors to be ambassadors is nothing new, sending people "that have no idea what they're doing or about the regions they're going to" is.[197] Henri J. Barkey, a former State Department official in the Clinton Administration, was also critical of Obama's ambassadorial picks. "The Obama administration's appointments suggest that the president isn't being honest when he says that diplomacy is important to him."[198] It's certainly not as important to him as his campaign coffers.

32. An Administration of Radicals

During his first presidential campaign, Obama buried his decades-long friendship with the racist Reverend Jeremiah Wright and domestic terrorist Bill Ayers. Obama may have distanced himself from Ayers and Wright during the campaign but, as president, he openly embraced individuals just as radical and out of the American mainstream as his former pastor and political mentor, and appointed or nominated them for high positions in his Administration. That is what happens when those who support your candidacy with contributions get the plum assignments, and those who are close to you are far outside the mainstream. Here are just some of them who are not mentioned elsewhere in this book:

- **Charles Freeman** - This nominee for director of the National Intelligence Council (NIC) was so bad that even Nancy Pelosi objected to the pick.[199] His ties to Saudi and Chinese interests and his anti-Israel positions, as well as his prior criticism of "America's lack of introspection about September 11" regarding "what might have caused the attack,"[200] aroused so much opposition that Freeman had to withdraw his name from consideration.

- **Donald Berwick** - Appointed by Obama in 2010 as Administrator of the Centers for Medicare and Medicaid Services (CMS), Berwick was controversial, not only because he got the position via a recess appointment after it was clear his nomination wouldn't get the consent of the Senate, but also for his forthright advocacy of health care rationing, and for his admiration of the way the British national health system denies care to people whose quality of life (as determined by bureaucrats) isn't worth spending money on.[201]

- **Nawar Shora** - This member of the fanatically anti-Israel Arab-American Anti-Defamation Committee was appointed by Obama, in 2010, as senior advisor to the Transportation Safety Administration (TSA) on civil rights and civil liberties matters.[202] What justification is there for putting such a person in a position to advise the TSA (which is charged with protecting us from, among other bad actors, Islamist jihadists) on protecting civil rights? There isn't any.

- **Debo P. Adegbile** - This former NAACP Legal Defense Official, nominated by Obama to head the Civil Rights Division at the Department of Justice, is an unapologetic supporter of convicted cop-killer Mumia Abu-Jamal and was involved in his defense, which spared him the death penalty.[203] His controversial nomination was blocked by the U.S. Senate in March 2014.[204]

- **Jeh Johnson** – This man was nominated by Obama to be his new Secretary of Homeland Security after the departure of Janet Napolitano under suspicious circumstances. After his nomination in 2013, it appeared that his main qualification was the fact that, over the course of a decade, he donated more than $100,000 to Obama and Democrat candidates and groups.[205] Johnson's lack of experience on immigration was particularly concerning.[206] But his experience in other areas was also troubling. As general counsel of the Department of Defense, he proposed changes for military tribunals that gave captured terrorists *more* protections.[207] In November of 2012, he falsely (or ignorantly) claimed that "the core of Al Qaeda is today degraded, disorganized and on the run."[208] In January of 2014, Johnson said that illegal immigrants currently in America had "earned the right to be citizens."[209]

33. Czars Everywhere, and All of Them Radicals

Beyond executive appointments to head up established federal departments, the modern president will also surround himself with, in theory, subject-matter experts that can help him respond to issues properly. Despite his original campaign promise of unprecedented transparency, Obama's Czars took on a much greater significance than in any previous administration as a group, and most of them completely bypassed the nomination process, which would have provided the transparency that Obama had promised. Without the advice and consent of the Senate, Obama was free to place some of the most radical individuals in high positions of the government, and many of them knew virtually nothing about the subject on which they were hired to advise the President. Here are a few of Obama's most radical czars, most of whom got their positions without the Senate's consent:

- **Van Jones, Green Jobs Czar (2009) (appointed without Senate approval)** - An admitted radical communist with connections to black nationalism and anarchism, Van Jones was appointed as Obama's Green Jobs Czar but was forced to resign six months later when he was unable to deflect questions into his radical history. His use of crude language to describe Republicans in a speech prior to taking his post, and his signature on a petition alleging the U.S. government had a role in the 9/11 terrorist attacks didn't help matters.[210]   Jones is also a supporter of convicted cop-killer Mumia Abu-Jamal.[211]
- **Cass Sunstein, Regulatory Czar (2009-12) (nominated, confirmed by Senate)** - Sunstein has advocated for the government to outlaw hunting and the consumption of meat. In a book published in 2004, he wrote that animals should have to right to sue in a court of law.[212]
- **Kevin Jennings, Safe Schools Czar (2009-11) (appointed without Senate approval)** - Obama's safe schools czar from 2009 to 2011, Jennings is a radical homosexual activist who founded the Gay, Lesbian and Straight Education Network (GLSEN) in 1990, which has promoted radical homosexual lesson plans and curricula in K-12 schools.[213] Jennings was the keynote speaker at a GLSEN conference in Boston, MA in 2000, where young children (as young as 12 years old) were given graphic instruction on various homosexual sex acts.[214]
- **John Holdren, Science Czar (2009-Present) (nominated, confirmed by Senate)** - Holdren was a 1960s radical whose writings have shown support for forced abortions and sterilizations to combat overpopulation and for a

massive campaign to de-develop the United States and other Western nations for the sake of the environment.[215]

- **Adolfo Carrion, Urban Czar (2009-10) (appointed without Senate approval)** - Prior to being appointed as Obama's Urban Czar, Carrion served as Bronx Borough president, and pocketed thousands of dollars in kickbacks from developers in exchange for getting projects approved or funded with taxpayer dollars.[216]

- **Vivek Kundra, Information Czar (2009-11) (appointed without Senate approval)** - Obama nominated the 34-year-old Kundra despite his criminal history. At the age of 21, Kundra was convicted of misdemeanor theft for stealing shirts from J.C. Penney. Kundra even attempted to evade arrest by running from police. Soon after starting his position at the White House, the D.C. technology office, where he had just left as Chief Technology Officer, was raided by the FBI, and two of his former aides were arrested on a slew of charges, including bribery and taking kickbacks.[217]

- **Carol Browner, Global Warming Czar (2009-11) (appointed without Senate approval)** - As the former head of the EPA under Bill Clinton, Browner was involved in the illegal destructive of the agency's computer files and email backups on her last day in office.[218] In January 2009, it was revealed that Browner was a member of the Commission for a Sustainable World Society, the climate change action arm of Socialist International.[219]

- **Mark Lloyd, FCC Diversity Czar (2009-12) (appointed without Senate approval)** - While working for a left-wing think tank prior to joining the Obama administration, Lloyd encouraged activists to harass conservative and Christian radio stations by filing complaints with the FCC in the hopes of possibly shutting them down.[220] Lloyd has also advocated for white media executives be *forced* to step down from their positions so that blacks, gays and other minorities can have power.[221]

- Ron Klain, Ebola Czar (2014-2015) (appointed without Senate approval) – In the summer and fall of 2014, a massive outbreak of the Ebola virus killed thousands of people in West Africa. Because it struck heavily in Nigeria, a nation very active in trade with the west, cases of the virus made their way to the United States and Obama tabbed Klain with formulating a strategy to contain an outbreak at home. The problem? Klain was not a medical professional nor someone with any expertise in infectious diseases and epidemiology. He was, essentially, a money moving Democrat operative.[222]

- Rob Malley, ISIS Czar (2015-?) (appointed without Senate approval) - In December 2015, Obama appointed Rob Malley as his administration's ISIS czar. Malley is a terrorist sympathizer who had been previously been fired from the Obama administration for meeting with the Palestinian terrorist group Hamas.[223]

It's hardly surprising that Obama didn't even try to get the advice and consent of the Senate for most of these individuals. Do these people sound like they represent American values? Not even close. Are these the kind of people a uniter brings into his Administration? Hardly. Are these the kind of people we want a president *choosing* to belong to his Administration? Most certainly not. But Obama's goal is to fundamentally transform America, and these are most definitely the kinds of people who can help him do just that.

34. The Worst Record with The Supreme Court

But enough about Obama's machine politics—a natural product of his political activism in Chicago, no doubt. What about Obama's lack of respect for the limitations of the executive branch? We've got plenty to say there as well. This is the sort of corruption that is more overt, yet less recognized as a character failing. While running for president in 2007, then-Senator Barack Obama said: "I was a constitutional law professor, which means, unlike the current president, I actually respect the Constitution."

There are many examples of Obama clearly *not* respecting the Constitution and the vast majority involve his tendency to bypass Congress to legislate via executive action, which we delve into elsewhere. But few things really drive home Obama's lack of respect for the Constitution better than the slew of unanimous rebukes he's been handed by the United States Supreme Court.

In *NLRB v. Noel Canning,* the Supreme Court ruled that Obama had made three unconstitutional appointments when the U.S. Senate was not in recess. In *McCullen v. Coakley,* the Obama administration had filed an amicus brief in favor of a Massachusetts law banning free speech within 35 feet of any abortion clinic. The law was unanimously found to be unconstitutional. The Obama administration also filed an amicus brief supporting warrantless searches of cell phones of American citizens in *Riley v. California*—and lost. In *U.S. v. Jones,* Obama's Justice Department failed to convince the Supreme Court that the federal government doesn't need a warrant to secretly put GPS tracking devices on citizens' cars for any reason.[224]

Obama's record with the United States Supreme Court, is the "worst record of any modern presidency," according to Ilya Shapiro of the CATO Institute. "In the first 6.5 years of Obama's presidency (January 2009 to June 2015), the government lost unanimously at the Supreme Court 23 times, an average of 3.62 cases per year." Obama's unanimous defeats are double that of George W. Bush, and one-and-a-half times as many as Bill Clinton. Historically speaking, the government has an average winning percentage of 70 percent before the Supreme Court, whereas the Obama administration, as of February 2016, won less than 50 percent.[225]

It says a lot when the highest court in the land, which is so often split ideologically on cases, reaches unanimous decisions so frequently *against* Barack Obama's extremist positions. Obama may fancy himself a president that "actually respects the Constitution," but the Supreme Court (and even two of his own Supreme Court nominees) clearly thinks otherwise.

35. Unconstitutional Recess Appointments

Let's get a bit more specific regarding one of the cases listed above where Obama was aggressively rebuked by the Supreme Court. Presidents have the power to nominate and appoint individuals to various federal positions, with the advice and consent of the U.S. Senate. Presidents can, however, temporarily fill federal positions on their own while the Senate is in recess.

When Obama's controversial nominees to the National Labor Relations Board (NLRB) and Consumer Financial Protection Bureau were met with significant opposition, he decided to bypass the Senate's constitutional role and declare his nominees appointed via recess appointment, even though the Senate was technically not in recess, but conducting "pro forma" sessions. These "pro forma" sessions were previously used by Harry Reid to prevent George W. Bush from making recess appointments towards the end of his second term.

Experts expressed sincere concern over the precedent Obama could establish by his actions, which could potentially end the Senate's constitutional role of advice and consent.[226] So much for constitutional checks and balances.

Obama's appointment of Richard Cordray as director of the Consumer Financial Protection Bureau was later approved by the Senate in a confirmation deal, but the legitimacy of his three "recess" appointments to the NLRB have since been battled out in the courts.

Just days after his second inauguration, a federal appeals court overturned those appointments, stating, "Allowing the president to define the scope of his own appointments power would eviscerate the Constitution's separation of powers."[227] A second federal appeals court agreed in May 2013.[228] A third federal appeals court also agreed a couple months later that Obama violated the Constitution with his three NLRB "recess" appointments, effectively invalidating all the decisions made by the NLRB with the illegally appointed nominees.[229]

The U.S. Supreme Court took up the case in 2014, but even one of Obama's own nominees, Justice Elena Kagan, found herself questioning Obama's abuse of power, saying "It really is the Senate's job to determine whether they're in recess or whether they're not," during oral arguments.[230] In the end, they ruled unanimously against Obama and rejected those appointments as invalid.

36. The Executive Order on Overtime Pay

But what about those executive actions we mentioned above? There are many from which to choose, and some of them will appear elsewhere in this book, but we'll give a few examples now – just a taste of the gall of this Imperial President. We'll start small.

In a move which stunned the business community, in March of 2014, President Obama unilaterally changed the regulations in the Fair Labor Standards Act of 1938 to move as many as 10 million "executive and professional" employees into a category which requires their employers to pay them overtime for working more than a certain number of hours per week.[231] There was no congressional debate. No congressional vote. No checks and balances. It was another blatant abuse of executive power that didn't just raise the ire of Republicans, but also of business groups who warned that these changes would vastly increase the cost of doing business.

As Marc Freedman of the Chamber of Commerce put it, "changing the rules for overtime eligibility will, just like increasing the minimum wage, make employees more expensive and will force employers to look for ways to cover these increased costs."[232] These increases in the cost of labor are typically offset by having fewer employees and/or increasing prices for consumers.

Since the new regulations would need a year to be written and for any changes to be implemented, this executive order was clearly just a political move aimed at trying to gin up the liberal base for the 2014 midterm elections. Still, if partisan politics are so important to Obama that the Constitution carries no weight with him when deciding to take unilateral actions on this scale, we would seem to have crossed a few too many bridges to hold much hope for a more functional Washington anytime soon.

37. Potential Executive Tax Increases

It didn't matter how clear the Constitution was about a particular issue; if Obama wanted to do something, he made every effort to do it, properly or not. In March of 2015, White House Press Secretary Josh Earnest stated that Obama was "very interested" in raising taxes via unilateral executive action. "The president certainly has not indicated any reticence in using his executive authority to try and advance an agenda that benefits middle-class Americans," Earnest explained.

What should make Obama reticent is Article I, Section 7, Clause 1 of the Constitution, which states "All Bills for raising Revenue shall originate in the House of Representatives; but the Senate may propose or concur with Amendments as on other Bills." In other words, the president does *not* have the power to unilaterally raise taxes.

Hans von Spakovsky, the manager of the Election Law Reform Initiative and senior legal fellow at The Heritage Foundation, said that Obama's consideration of executive tax hikes is another sign of how arrogant and dangerous Obama is. "He believes he can rule by executive fiat and that the restrictions and limitations in the Constitution on the executive can just be ignored or shrugged off. The president has no authority to raise taxes whatsoever. Only the House of Representatives can originate bills for raising taxes, and this would be just the latest unilateral, abusive and unconstitutional action of the president."[233]

As of this writing, Obama has yet to take any executive action on raising taxes, but the fact that he even entertained the idea is more proof of just how little he thinks of the Constitution and the rule of law.

38. Wanting Unilateral Power to Raise the Debt Ceiling

On March 16, 2006, then-Senator Obama said the debate over raising America's debt ceiling was a sign of leadership failure. "It is a sign that the U.S. Government can't pay its own bills. It is a sign that we now depend on ongoing financial assistance from foreign countries to finance our Government's reckless fiscal policies."

Congress's reckless spending was certainly a sign of failure, but it was hardly an act of kindness when Obama decided that Congress shouldn't have the power to raise the debt ceiling, but that *he* should.[234] Obama requested this unilateral power to raise the debt ceiling indefinitely as part of a deal he offered to House Republicans during the fiscal cliff negotiations. This request was a clear indication that he wanted unlimited spending power, not fiscal restraint, all while subverting the Constitution's system of checks and balances. The proposal was so absurd that it was met with laughter by Republican leaders when presented on Capitol Hill.[235] But there's nothing funny about a president who continually seeks to increase his own power.

39. Selective Enforcement of The Law

Sometimes it isn't Obama's crafting of a new law by executive order that smacks of the worst corruption. Sometimes it's his refusal to enforce laws already on the books. The President of the

United States doesn't just sign new bills into law. He also has to enforce existing laws. Unfortunately for the rule of law, this President has a hard time enforcing laws he doesn't like.

In February of 2011, Barack Obama unilaterally decided that the Defense of Marriage Act (DOMA), signed by President Bill Clinton in 1996, was unconstitutional and instructed his Department of Justice to stop defending the law in court.[236] Obama decided that, instead of working with Congress to repeal it, or passing a new law, he'd simply instruct his administration not to enforce it.

In August of 2011, the Obama administration announced that it would start using its discretion in enforcing the country's immigration laws, by suspending deportation proceedings against illegal immigrants "who pose no threat to national security or public safety." According to the *New York Times*, "The new policy is expected to help thousands of illegal immigrants who came to the United States as young children, graduated from high school and want to go on to college or serve in the armed forces."[237] Obama's actions, the *New York Times* conceded, would improve his image with Latino voters before Election Day. A week prior this announcement, Obama was criticized by Hispanic organizations for not doing enough on issues important to Latino voters, particularly immigration.[238] Obama's refusal to fully enforce immigration laws helped him win reelection. According to exit polls, Obama won 71 percent of the Hispanic vote,[239] up from 67 percent in 2008.[240]

It may be easy for some to excuse Obama's selective enforcement of the law simply because they feel the ends justify the means. Selective enforcement of the law can only lead to trouble. Dr. Milton R. Wolf, a *Washington Times* columnist and cousin to Barack Obama, called selective enforcement of the law "the first sign of tyranny."[241] If tyranny is what Obama wants, he's clearly done his part to set us down that path. If Obama can pick and choose what laws to enforce, all future presidents will see no reason not to do the same, to the great detriment of all Americans.

40. Violating His Own Laws

In 2015 during a speech at the African Union Headquarters in Addis Ababa, Ethiopia, Obama reckoned—if not lamented—that he couldn't run for a third term. "Under our Constitution, I cannot run again. I can't run again. I actually think I'm a pretty good President -- I think if I ran I could win. But I can't. [...] And no one person is above the law. Not even the President."[242] Two of those statements are laughable. The first one being when he said he thinks he's a pretty good president, the other being when he said that not even a president is above the law, because not only has Obama blatantly violated the Constitution and the rule of law many times in his presidency, his respect for the rule of law is so low that he has violated laws that he personally signed.

According to Section 1513 of Obama's economic stimulus, the executive branch was required to submit quarterly reports on the impact of the stimulus. These reports, which were meant to prove just how unprecedentedly transparent the Obama administration was, were to be submitted quarterly until the third quarter of 2013, but the last report ever submitted came in 2011, after the reports were showing just how poorly the stimulus was performing.[243]

Of course, Obamacare was another law signed by Obama that he often violated. According an analysis by the Galen Institute in January of 2016, 43 changes have been made to Obamacare without congressional approval, including multiple delays of the employer mandate, delaying the individual mandate, delaying the online insurance marketplace, expanding subsidies, covering abortions, delaying and eventually canceling Medicare cuts, and many others.[244]

In 2012, Barack Obama signed the Magnitsky Act, a bipartisan bill sanctioning human rights abusers in Russia. Eighteen Russian officials were sanctioned under the law in 2013, and the Obama administration promised to expand the list later that year. Unfortunately, it turned out to be yet another example of Obama's promised second-term flexibility with Russia, as

Obama effectively refused to enforce the law—a law he signed—by not adding as many as 20 new human rights abusers (as vetted by the Treasury and State Departments) to the list of those banned from traveling into or doing business in the United States.[245] One Obama official thought this might be a payoff to Russian President Putin for his "help" brokering a deal for Syria to give up its chemical weapons.[246] A deal that hasn't worked out too well.[247] Human rights abusers worldwide can breathe a sigh of relief that the United States' foreign policy for promoting human rights can be so easily manipulated.

Even Obama's terrible nuclear Iran Deal (which was not approved by Congress) violated an existing law he signed.[248] A provision in the Iran Deal allows for foreign subsidiaries of U.S. parent companies to do business with Iran. This directly violates the Iran Threat Reduction and Syria Human Rights Act of 2012, which specifically closed a loophole enabling foreign subsidiaries of U.S. parent companies to do business with Iran.[249] So, not only did Obama not get Congressional approval for his Nuclear Deal with Iran, he broke one of his own laws in order to enrich a terror sponsoring state.

41. Obama's Slush Fund for Liberal Groups

President Obama's 2008 campaign leaned heavily on promising that Wall Street would be held accountable for their misdeeds. For years, big lenders were issuing mortgages to people who couldn't really afford them—these mortgages featured higher than normal interest rates, low monthly payments that caused debt to *increase* rather than fall as payments were made, and payments that ballooned suddenly after a few years. When struggling homeowners inevitably began defaulting on these loans in ever-increasing numbers, the resulting pressure on the entire lending market culminated with the subprime mortgage crisis during The Great Recession.[250] The crisis had been brewing for thirty years thanks to initiatives aimed at helping the poor achieve home ownership, but these predatory lending practices were jaw-dropping in their brazenness.

Obama and his Justice Department aggressively worked to sue the major lenders for these unscrupulous practices, claiming they were scoring victories for minorities and the poor. Bank of America's settlement alone was $16.6 billion and just about every major lender had hefty settlements to pay.[251] But Obama's concern for the little guy seemed to evaporate when he and his allies in Washington realized that these settlement deals could be used to fund left-wing activism without congressional approval.

As early as 2010, it was reported that the Obama administration was funneling leftover money to various groups, some of which were clearly partisan, political groups allied with the Obama administration.[252] By 2013, Obama's Justice Department was actually *instructing* defendants to pay to liberal political groups directly, by including language in the settlement agreements that forgave two or more dollars owed for every one dollar given to groups approved by Obama administration officials. Bank of America got $194 million reduced from their penalty by donating $84 million to groups on Obama's approved non-profit list.[253] Other lenders such as Citigroup, Morgan Stanley, and Goldman Sachs had settlements with similar language. And Obama's allied groups profited significantly as a result. For example, $1.5 million that should have gone to predatory lending victims went instead to the National Council of La Raza. Another $1.1 million went to the National Urban League. Dozens of other similarly left-aligned groups also received hefty payouts at the expense of the victims.[254]

The reason we have a civil justice system is to resolve disputes and make victims of fraud, defamation and other financial violations whole again. When a court found big lenders guilty of damaging and predatory lending practices and awarded billions of dollars in compensatory damages, it did so intending to give the victims justice, not to shake down businesses for political protection money and fund left-wing activism of the most extreme sort. It would be equally wrong for a conservative

President to offer companies a sweetheart deal if they would only pay protection money to conservative groups like the Family Research Council, LiveAction, the Heritage Foundation, the Foundation for Individual Rights in Education and Americans for Prosperity and the left would never stand for it. Look all you want through the pages of this book; you will not find a more blatant example of racketeering for political purposes in it.

The Economy

There are three major economic indicators we tend to analyze with determining whether our government has had a positive or negative impact on the economy: annual government deficits and long-term debt, the status of employment and claims on the entitlement state, and the infrastructure that empowers consumption and investment, and thus, the growth of our gross domestic product (GDP). Note: we're not just talking about the physical infrastructure when we talk about the government's role in providing a scaffolding for the economy. This scaffolding includes: the demand for manufacturing, the status of the lending industry, the price of energy and other goods, the inflation of those prices, and the liquidity of the markets. Keep those factors in mind, because we'll be exploring the impact that Barack Obama had on each of them shortly.

On Election Day 2008, the biggest issue was the economy. With the economic meltdown of September fresh in everyone's memory, many Americans voted for Obama because he promised change from what a majority believed to be the Republicans' failure on the economy.

Obama promised to get our economy back on track. Obama would later claim that actions he took prevented a second Great Depression, but the record proves otherwise. The changes Obama delivered included: higher gas prices, spending increases, tax increases, record-breaking deficits, historic debt, stubbornly high unemployment and low workforce participation, and a slew of other failures at home.

By the end of 2013, Obama had already "pivoted" his focus back to the economy more than twenty times, without success.[255]

The unfortunate reality was that his constant need to announce that he was returning his attention to the economy came from the undeniable fact that, to most Americans, his policies didn't seem to be making things better. Let's tackle of few of his biggest-ticket items and discuss their efficacy.

42. Federal Takeover of Student Loans

As you'll see throughout this chapter, Barack Obama has responded to nearly every economic problem with a declaration that it is a national crisis demanding an immediate federal response and an attempt to centrally manage the problem either by a direct takeover of the government or by stiff regulations on the affected market or a manipulation of the forces governing that market. We begin our exploration of Obama's economic legacy with one of the leading issues for millennial voters who helped to propel him to prominence in 2007 and 2008: the cost of a college education. The young supported his presidential bid by a larger than two to one margin, but it seems like they've actually been punished, rather than be rewarded. Under Obama, the cost of going to college has increased faster than ever before. On Obama's watch, the average student loan debt for an undergraduate has roughly doubled. How did this happen?

On March 30, 2010, President Obama signed a law taking over the student loan program from private lenders. He did this under the guise of safeguarding students from the predatory lending practice of issuing loans with unfairly high interest rates and, in the short term, this move did lower student loan interest by one or two percent. The reality of the situation, though, is that by federalizing student loans, the government, actually profits immensely from both interest on loans it makes directly to students, and defaults, all while shackling America's young people in the bonds of government dependency and blocking any hope for more innovative methods of financing a college degree. According to Alan Collinge, founder of StudentLoanJustice.Org,

"To say that the federal government now sits atop the most predatory lending system in our nation's history is not an understatement."[256] In order to maximize profits for the federal government, the Obama administration fought vigorously against bankruptcy safeguards for student loans. Collinge added, "This all happened on Obama's watch. He cannot avoid accountability for what is shaping up to be among the largest financial catastrophes this country has ever seen."[257] Total outstanding student loan debt in the United States is over $1.2 trillion, making it second only to mortgage debt. The average student loan debt for college graduates in 2009 was $24,000.[258] In 2016, it exploded to $35,000.

On top of that mountain of debt, students now face an economy that is not eager to hire young people. Due to an increasing number of college graduates that can't find a job after leaving school in the Obama economy, student loan delinquency rates are higher than ever before; 11 percent of all student loans were 90 days or more delinquent, nearly double the rate it was in 2003.[259] Gone are the days when young people could expect to gain their independence and make their own way in the world after they finished college. The phenomenon of degreed adults returning home after finishing school and staying there for years or even decades is now so common that it has a culturally accepted name: boomerang syndrome. Millennials now boomerang as often as 30% of the time, and that number is on the rise.[260] For all of his big talk about the injustice being done to young people at American colleges, Obama has managed to make things far, far worse.

43. Federal Takeover of Community College

Lest you imagine that Obama was satisfied with handing the college lending industry over to federal managers, he outdid himself in 2015. With his support among millennials dropping as they struggled to enter the workforce and pay off their debts, Obama proposed a takeover of the community college system. To be precise, he proposed that community colleges should be free to attend (at taxpayer expense) nationwide.[261]

The argument went that funding the entire community college infrastructure would actually cost less than driving many youths into four-year colleges for the entire term and forcing them to take on large student loans and accumulate debt. There are several problems with this line of reasoning, however. First, the average student who completes a two-year degree, and then finishes completing a four-year degree thereafter, takes about three semesters longer to finish both degrees than the students who just complete a four-year degree. In other words, completing a two-year degree only saves you about one semester of tuition at a more expensive four-year institution.[262] This is because the credits don't always transfer well, the students who begin at a community college tend not to be the high-achievers who will advance quickly through a full bachelor's degree, and the students who start at community college also tend to join the workforce during or after their experiences. Second, the vast majority of people who complete a two-year degree never finish a four-year degree, and already tend to avoid having debts as a result of paying for community college. Third, community colleges vary wildly in quality and tend not to prepare students all that well for four-year degrees or the workforce unless they offer programs directed at a specific trade.

When you add up the particulars, this proposal amounts to a multi-billion-dollar speculative investment in a system that is much, much weaker and less equipped to educate our youth and prepare them for the workforce than the four-year college system. In fact, the non-partisan American Action Forum released a report late in 2015 that suggests the community college subsidy plan will be a perverse incentive and will have the opposite impact that Obama intends. Rather than improving access to post-secondary education, it would have the effect of reducing graduation rates, and squandering over half of the dollars invested in students who do not go on to obtain degrees.[263] On top of that, the debt the federal government would accumulate to promote this program would be the tip of the iceberg. This is an idea floated with the intention of leaning on the electorate to support the full takeover of the post-secondary educational establishment. At a time when the government is struggling to keep paying their own employees and their interest charges on outstanding debt, attempting to fully manage the college and university system is folly.

44. Cash for Clunkers

Speaking of speculative investments with little in the way of upside potential, this one was a doozy. Many of Obama's attempts to stimulate the economy were probably well-intentioned, but they were definitely not, generally, well thought out. Government programs often have unintended consequences and ultimately, do more harm than good. The *Car Allowance Rebate System* (more commonly known as Cash for Clunkers) was a program meant to stimulate the auto industry by enticing car owners to purchase newer, more fuel-efficient vehicles by offering a rebate on their older, less fuel-efficient vehicle. The program was such a "success" that the original $1 billion allocated for the program wasn't enough, and another $2 billion had to be approved to keep the program going.[264]

Based on the results, Cash for Clunkers was not worth the hefty price tag. According to an analysis by Edmunds.com, 690,000 vehicles were purchased during the program, but "only 125,000 of the sales were incremental. The rest of the sales would have happened anyway, regardless of the existence of the program."[265] Despite the environmental justification for the program, it actually hurt the environment. Vehicles traded in were destroyed, not resold, creating a huge amount of waste.[266]

Obama called Cash for Clunkers "successful beyond anybody's imagination."[267] If spending $3 billion to fail at stimulating the auto industry and hurting the environment was a success, we would prefer not to see what failure looked like.

45. The Biggest Government Spender in History

Speculative spending like the above is really just a minor symptom of a much bigger problem with Obama's economic policy. There is a firm fascination in the far-left with spending our way out of problems. How best to treat skyrocketing college costs? Buy out the college system and manage it. How best to revitalize manufacturing? Buy out the debts of manufacturers and spend on perverse incentives to get consumers back into consuming goods made in the United States. How shall we fix a healthcare system overwhelmed with increasing costs and declining access? Buy out the insurance system and force all Americans to participate (more on this one later). When your answer to every fiscal issue is to get the government into the business of managing businesses, at taxpayer expense, you're going to rack up a big bill.

While running for reelection in 2012, Obama claimed: "federal spending since I took office has risen at the slowest pace of any President in almost 60 years." It's a deliberate deception based on a widely held belief that a new president has no control over spending during his first year in office because that year's budget was approved by the previous president and Congress. It's a very convenient axiom that enables Obama and his defenders to distort his spending record. It also couldn't be more wrong.

The truth is, Obama's first year in office was by no means constrained by the budget approved by President Bush. In fact, only three of Fiscal Year 2009's twelve appropriations bills were passed under Bush because the Democrats in Congress, confident that Obama would win in 2008, waited until Obama took office before going on a spending binge. So, most of the spending that took place in 2009 was, in fact, approved by President Obama. This spending, which included Obama's failed stimulus and bailouts, resulted in a 17.9 percent increase in spending over Fiscal Year 2008 compared to the 3 percent increase proposed by Bush.[268] This increase in spending was the highest annual spending increase since the Korean War. By the end of his first year in office, Obama's spending as a percentage of GDP was 25.2 percent, the highest in history, except for during World War II. Obama's reckless spending could have been a short-term aberration following the financial crisis of 2008, but instead, Obama maintained that higher level of spending. Obama's spending has far outpaced his predecessors, and the historical post-WWII average.[269]

By ignoring his first year in office, Obama and his defenders can claim he merely maintained the status quo, conveniently hiding the fact that he is shirking responsibility for his record deficits, and for skyrocketing the nation's debt. No matter how much he tries to pass the buck, Obama is the biggest government spender in history.

46. Largest Deficits In History

If you spend as much as Obama has, the deficit will skyrocket without a big surge in economic growth. Not only did it skyrocket, but Obama has given us the top six highest U.S. deficits in history: $1.4 trillion (FY2009), $1.3 trillion (FY2010), $1.3 trillion (FY2011), and $1.1 trillion (FY2012), $680 billion (FY2013), and $483 billion (FY2014). Obama's first deficit was more than triple George W. Bush's largest deficit of $455 billion in FY2008.[270]

When adjusted for inflation, Obama's deficits (2009-2015) are the seven highest deficits in history, surpassing even the spending of World War II.[271] Yet, since Obama doesn't take responsibility for the cost of doing business in 2009, he claims that he has reduced the annual deficit by two-thirds. *Politifact* gives this claim a stamp of "mostly true", but they yield some important caveats, notably that he's comparing his performance now to his dreadful performance in 2009 when he added a huge stimulus package to the budget whose impacts we'll discuss at greater length shortly. The bottom line – cutting the deficit to levels in line with the worst years of your predecessor is not an accomplishment.

47. More Debt Than All Past Presidents ... Combined

As a presidential candidate in 2008, Obama called President George W. Bush "unpatriotic" and "irresponsible" for adding $4 trillion to the national debt during his two terms. But, here are the facts about our nation's debt from the day Obama took office, to the start of his second term, to the start of his last year in office:

Publicly Held Debt
January 20, 2009: $6.31 trillion
January 22, 2013: $11.57 trillion (+83%)
January 20, 2016: $13.61 trillion (+116%)

Gross Federal Debt
January 20, 2009: $10.6 trillion
January 22, 2013: $16.43 trillion (+55%)
January 20, 2016: $18.94 trillion (+79%) [272]

The national debt passed $19 trillion on February 1, 2016. At this pace, by the time he leaves office is 2017, it will pass $20 trillion, and Obama will have accumulated more gross federal debt than all previous U.S. presidents in history *combined*. How patriotic and responsible is that?

He often blamed Republican obstruction for slowing his plans for deficit reduction by blocking tax increases on the wealthy. There's just one problem. If every penny were taken from the wealthy above, say, $250,000 per year, the deficit reduction, even assuming no one fled the country to protect their assets, would be smaller than the rate of mandatory spending increases forced on the budget by the three largest entitlement programs: Medicare, Social Security, and Medicaid. To get enough tax revenue to make a real dent in the debt without cutting spending – something Obama has never suggested doing in any of his budgets, many of which were unanimously rejected in the Senate – he would have to tax the middle class and the wealthy to such levels as to make everyone rather poor.

48. Passing 100 Percent Debt/GDP Ratio

As bad as Obama's spending record is, it's made worse by the fact that, in August 2011, America's Debt-to-GDP ratio exceeded 100 percent.

The last time this happened was during World War II, which only happened because of temporary increases in spending to fund the war effort. Obama's exploding debt, however, shows no signs of relenting, as the current deficits are driven significantly by entitlement spending, which has gone up on Obama's watch.[273]

This unsustainable growth of America's debt continued unabated and, by the end of 2012, the Debt-to-GDP ratio had risen to 103.8 percent.[274] By the end of FY2013, the Debt-To-GDP ratio was 106 percent.[275] Most economists agree that, if it weren't for the fact that U.S. dollars back the entire global lending industry, such levels of debt, relative to GDP, would lead to super-inflation and economic ruin.

49. Credit Rating Downgrade

In modern history, many nations have had their credit ratings downgraded; nations like Argentina and Zimbabwe who have a long history of struggling economically and lack the influence of the United States on global monetary policy. But, on August 5, 2011, Standard & Poor downgraded US credit rating from AAA to AA+. This was the first time in its history at the United States had its credit downgraded.[276] Here again, Democrats have been quick to blame conservatives, claiming that our downgrade was as a result of uncertainty over whether the US would increase its arbitrarily-defined debt-ceiling or shut down the government, rather than accepting 'compromises' dictated entirely by Obama and Harry Reid. Of course, compromise isn't compromise if you don't give up something in return for getting something. And S&P's report lists multiple causes for the downgrade, including the above Democrat talking point and the lack of seriousness by

Washington's leftists in tackling entitlement deficit spending (more on this point shortly).

What did this mean? It meant that the financial world was starting to doubt whether the United States, under Obama, could generate enough money, long-term, to pay down the massive and rapidly rising US debt. With Obama's record high annual deficits, the questions remain: will we be able to repay Obama's debts? Will there be future downgrades to America's credit rating?

50. Explosion of Military Food Stamp Usage

Now, let's talk about entitlements. We can raise concerns over the price of Obama's many boondoggles, his economic stimulus plan (more to come on that one), and his experimental attempts to give the government more control over business, but the biggest source of debt, by far, is entitlement spending. So why, at a time when a sensible politician would be looking for ways to "bend the cost curve down" on these social safety net programs, would Obama cut military benefits and force able-bodied, working Americans who've volunteered to defend our freedoms and way of life onto the Supplemental Nutrition Assistance Program (colloquially, food stamps).

At the end of 2013, Defense Secretary Chuck Hagel warned of looming cuts to military pay and benefits. Our brave men and women in the military already make much less than civilian federal employees, yet these cuts, according to Hagel, were necessary for "military readiness."[277]

It comes as no surprise, then, that the cost of providing active and retired military families with food stamps has increased dramatically under Obama, nearly doubling from $52.9 million in 2009 to $103.6 million in 2013, largely because veterans were flocking to the food stamp program.[278] The right thing to do would be to increase compensation for our military, not cut it. While the Obama administration sees nothing wrong with cutting military pay and benefits while the number of military families using food stamps explodes, civilian federal employees have typically seen their wages and benefits increase annually.[279]

The least any nation can do for their warriors (who have volunteered to be put in harm's way in service of their country) is to make sure their families don't have to endure financial hardships that make them dependent on government support.

51. The Food Stamp President

If you want to understand why Obama would throw our military into SNAP, have a look at the bigger picture. By Election Day, 2012, the number of Americans on food stamps rose to a record-high 46.7 million people.[280] While most Americans share a desire to help those who are in poverty, the fact remains that being a government dependent is a demoralizing condition. Quite often, people who become dependent upon government for a long time lose the incentive to work and improve their own lives, especially since, the moment they get a job, their benefits will be cut, and it often doesn't pay as well to work as it does to collect from Uncle Sam.

The numbers are truly frightening. The number of food stamp recipients grew roughly 11,113 per day during Obama's first term.[281] By November 2012, for each person who managed to find a job in the Obama Economy, seventy-five went on food stamps.[282] On the day Obama took office, there were 31.94 million Americans participating in the food stamp program.[283] At the end of FY2015, there were 45.77 million – a 43 percent increase.

Further aggravating the problem is the cost of the program, which has skyrocketed. In FY2008 the cost of the food stamp program was $37.6 billion. Under Obama, the costs have doubled, coming in at $73.98 billion in FY2015 after peaking at $79.87 billion in FY2013.[284]

How did this happen? We need to look no further than Obama's 2009 "Stimulus," which increased the benefits of the program and relaxed eligibility. The "Stimulus," which was supposed to encourage economic growth, actually encouraged government dependency. According to Robert Rector, senior research fellow at the Heritage Foundation, able-bodied adults without dependents (ABAWDs), are the fastest-growing category of new food stamp users under Obama. Rector told *Breitbart News* "In 2008 there were about a million [ABAWDs] now [in 2015] they're at about 4.7 million."[285]

But it gets better! As one can imagine, when there's a nearly a five-fold increase in ABAWDs getting food stamps, there's also a massive increase in food stamp fraud. Compared to other federal programs, SNAP has one of the lowest rates of fraud, but when the program is running around $75 billion annually, even a small amount of fraud translates to millions of dollars.[286] The cost of food stamp fraud more than doubled during Obama's first term, costing taxpayers $750 million in 2012–despite the fact the Obama administration planned to crack down on food stamp fraud back in 2011.[287]

52. The Disability President

Unemployment benefits only last for a finite period of time, but many Americans that have been unable to find work have instead discovered an alternative to unemployment checks: Social Security Disability.

Under Obama, Social Security Disability claims have been rising at a 4.5 percent annual rate, even though the incidences of workplace injuries have been declining for many years now.[288] As of September 2012, there were nearly 8.8 million Americans receiving Social Security Disability payments, an increase of about 16 percent since Obama took office.[289] By the end of 2013, the number of Americans receiving disability benefits grew to a record 10.98 million.[290] The average monthly benefit also increased to a record $1,146.43.[291]

Because dependent people are more easily controlled, the government is making it easier for people to become dependent. One way the government is doing this is by no longer carefully checking those who are claiming Social Security Disability. According to a staff report from the Senate Permanent Subcommittee on Investigations, a large percentage of disability claims are not properly reviewed. Without proper reviews, it is hard to know how many people are getting Social Security Disability when not eligible for it.[292]

53. Killing The Welfare Work Requirement

Our history with entitlement reforms has involved many choices that led to increased costs, increased dependency, and increased complexity of the safety net, but few choices that actually improved the viability and effectiveness of such programs. There is, however, one shining example: the Republican-led *Welfare Reform Act* of 1996. Few people would claim that this landmark legislation was anything but a huge win in the fight against poverty, as well as the battle against government deficits. Welfare caseloads declined, child poverty declined, and the poverty rate for black children fell to its lowest level ever.[293] In spite of all these great benefits of reform, Obama filled the Department of Health and Human Services with opponents of welfare reform. In July of 2012, Obama quietly announced a plan that would effectively end the work requirement from welfare, a key element of its success.[294]

Obama and his supporters vehemently denied that his plan would gut Welfare Reform or end the work requirement. But, even Ron Haskins—the de-facto author of the bill as a congressional staffer in 1996—conceded that, if there was any way to undermine the work requirement, Obama's plan was the "way to do it."[295]

But does Obama even have the legal authority to make these changes? The Government Accountability Office says no. Rep. Dave Camp (R-MI), chairman of the House Ways and Means

Committee, and John Kline (R-MN), chairman of the House Committee on Education and the Workforce, explain that the Temporary Assistance for Needy Families (TANF) program created by the 1996 welfare reforms, which include the work requirements, can't simply be overridden:

> A Ways and Means Committee summary of the 1996 reforms issued shortly after the law was signed is explicit on this point: "Waivers granted after the date of enactment [of the 1996 law] may not override provisions of the TANF law that concern mandatory work requirements."
>
> The president's plan to waive the work requirements is not only illegal, it also is being implemented through an unlawful end run around Congress. The GAO determined the Obama administration's proposal to waive work requirements should have been submitted to Congress for review and possible disapproval. The administration didn't do that and said it does not need to.[296]

It takes a lot of chutzpah to gut welfare reform... and it takes even more to do so illegally.

54. Record Poverty

It amounts to one of our greatest recent tragedies that, despite our refusal to reduce the long-term costs of various social programs, poverty is a larger problem now that it has been in many decades. In a statement honoring the fiftieth anniversary of the war on poverty, Obama said that more work needs to be done, lamenting that "far too many children are still born into poverty, far too few have a fair shot to escape it."[297] Obama spoke about progress, but not the ugly truths of his own record on poverty. This omission is hardly surprising since, on his watch, poverty in America has reached record levels. In 2009, Obama's first year in office, the poverty rate was 14.3 percent. The poverty rate then held at or above 15 percent for three years for the first time since the mid-1960s.[298]

The poverty rate did fall to 14.5 percent in 2013, but was still higher than the 12.5 percent poverty rate from before the Great Recession.[299] And child poverty has been catastrophic under Obama, with UNICEF reporting 1.7 million more American children were living in poverty in 2012 than in 2008 (a two percent increase), bringing the total to 24.2 million—nearly a third of America's children.[300] Nearly forty percent of African-American children live in poverty.[301] As of December 2014, sixty-five percent of American children live in households receiving federal aid.[302]

55. Obama's Income Inequality Record

In looking for an issue to resonate with his base for the 2014 midterm elections and take some attention away from the botched Obamacare rollout, Obama started talking about income inequality—which he described as the "defining challenge of our time." In a speech at an event hosted by a liberal think tank, Obama declared that the "combined trends of increased inequality and decreasing mobility pose a fundamental threat to the American Dream, our way of life, and what we stand for around the globe."[303] Such rhetoric makes for great talking points to energize his base, but his actual record on income inequality proves that he's the real threat to the American Dream.

While the so-called "income gap" was pretty stable under President Bush, under Obama, the richest 20 percent of Americans have gotten richer while the bottom 80 percent have gotten poorer every year. An even more stark contrast is with the years of Ronald Reagan when everyone, rich and poor, got richer every year.[304] Even the liberal *Huffington Post* admitted that, under Obama, the wealthy have taken home a greater share of the nation's income than they did under President Bush.[305]

Obama routinely decried the so-called Bush tax cuts "for the wealthy" but the fact is that Obama's policies have been more pro-rich than any Republican's (and the Bush tax cuts were better for the middle class than the wealthy). Since Obama became president, the richest one percent have seen their share of America's wealth skyrocket to twenty-five percent of all income while the bottom ninety percent have seen theirs drop below fifty percent of the nation's income for the first time.[306] In Obama's America, the middle class is disappearing, while the very rich and the very poor are becoming completely isolated from each other.

To understand why, we not need look further than the median household income. Normally, if an economy is in recovery, median income, even adjusted for inflation, should rise over time, at least during the recovery from a recession/depression. But, "The Obama Recovery" actually saw a net *reduction* in worker pay. The American median annual household income declined for six years straight under Obama, despite the end of the recession in 2009. Even those Americans fortunate enough to be gainfully employed weren't seeing the benefits of the recovery!

The only people who've reaped the benefits work on Wall Street. Stock prices are doing just fine, fueled by speculation and the success of the wealthiest Americans under Obama. While the average pay of the American worker fell for six straight years, the incomes of the top five percent went up.[307] If Obama is concerned about income inequality, he certainly doesn't show it by supporting policies that are demonstrated to cause the gap to widen.

56. Record Long-term Unemployment

Now that we've demonstrated that Obama's economic policy was no good for our deficits and debts, and failed to address the looming hard times we'll face attempting to pay for entitlements that are expected to get more costly with time, we must ask: did his policies create jobs or improve the scaffolding of America's economy? We'll begin by taking a closer look at employment figures.

The definition of "long-term unemployed" is those persons who are unemployed for twenty-seven weeks or longer. When Obama first took office, the number of long-term unemployed was 2.6 million. That number more than doubled during the recession, peaking at 6.8 million people in April 2010, but it has since declined. By December 2014, the number of long-term unemployed was still 2.79 million.[308]

When Obama took office in January of 2009, the average (mean) duration of unemployment was 19.8 weeks. It continued to climb even after the recession ended, peaking at 40.6 weeks in July of 2011. By December of 2014, it was 32.8 weeks, still significantly above pre-recession levels.[309] Under Obama, the long-term unemployment rate is the highest it's been since World War II.[310]

And it's no wonder – he pushed for, and got, reforms to unemployment insurance and welfare that extended the maximum claim time from 24 to 99 weeks. He argued, at the time, that this was necessary to protect those impacted by the recession. There's just one problem: the recession, by his own claims, is over, and those reforms remain in place, as well as executive actions which defanged the bipartisan *Welfare Reform Act* of 1996 and prevented states from forcing welfare recipients to prove that they were looking for work. As the old saying goes: if you want more of something, incentivize it. Obama's actions suggested that he wanted more people trapped in long-term unemployment and collecting benefits. Well, they worked. In the Obama economy, long-term unemployment has become the new norm.

57. Decline in Labor Force Participation Rate

Context is vital when assessing economic figures. The official unemployment rate, the U3 rate, measures only people who are both out of work and actively looking for work. This unemployment number does not include those underemployed, or those who have given up looking for work. So while Obama has long trumpeted a slowly falling U3 unemployment rate as progress, when considering the workforce participation rate, this falling rate was anything but progress.

The workforce participation rate is calculated by the Bureau of Labor Statistics and indicates the percentage of Americans sixteen years of age and older who are working or looking for work.

In December 2007, when the most recent recession began, the labor force participation rate was 66 percent, and was down to 65.7 by the end of it. The labor force participation rate did not improve even after the recession ended. By May 2015, the participation rate was 62.9 percent, the lowest since Jimmy Carter's presidency.[311] The decline in the labor force participation rate has been the most significant factor in the decline of the official unemployment rate during Obama's presidency.[312] Even though the official unemployment rate for May 2015 was 5.5 percent, the seasonally adjusted U6 unemployment rate (which includes discouraged workers who stopped looking for work and part-time workers who want full-time work) was 10.4 percent, which is significantly higher than it was before the recession.[313] While the economy has slowly been recovering jobs since the recession, by May 2015, the economy still had 550,000 *fewer* full-time workers than it did before the start of the recession.[314]

58. Stimulus Failure

Let's take a look at Obama's signature employment bill – the omnibus spending appropriation that was targeted at halting the recession and creating jobs. To hear Obama tell it, in 2009, the passing of the American Recovery and Reinvestment Act would usher in a new era of American prosperity. Obama promised the American people that by spending hundreds of billions of dollars we would keep unemployment low, reduce poverty, create a new green economy, and provide shovel-ready projects that would rebuild our crumbling infrastructure.

None of that happened. All we got for our huge investment was a mountain of new debt,[315] a long list of failed "green energy" companies,[316] more poverty,[317] and infrastructure that is still crumbling.[318] Of course, there was a recovery, but it was a "recovery" marked by fewer new jobs than were needed to keep up with population growth and record low levels of workforce participation. As for those shovel-ready projects, even Obama had to painfully admit they didn't exist.[319]

Despite Obama administration forecasts of robust GDP growth of 4.3 percent in 2011 and 2012, GDP actually only grew 1.3 percent in 2011 and 2.4 percent in 2012.[320] Anemic GDP growth would continue for five years before showing real, however brief, signs of improvement.[321] As of the summer of 2016, GDP growth is again slumping, returning to immediately-post-recession levels around 1.5%.

The stimulus failed miserably when it came to getting Americans back to work as well. The Obama administration had predicted that the official unemployment rate would be five percent by January 2014—*without* the stimulus. But, the unemployment rate was actually 6.6 percent. Of course, the only reason the unemployment rate got that low was because the labor force participation rate kept declining. Despite Obama's stimulus, it wasn't until May 2014—a whopping seventy-seven months after the start of the recession—before non-farm employment returned to pre-recession levels, making Obama's economic recovery the slowest since the failures of the last massive community investment projects, more common known as the alphabet soup pushed forward by FDR.[322] Even after six years of Obama's economic policies, the official unemployment rate in December 2014—5.6 percent—was still above pre-recession levels.[323] To say Obama's stimulus failed to deliver is a huge understatement.

And no wonder! Richer blue states with lower poverty, unemployment, bankruptcy, and foreclosure rates received the bulk of Obama's stimulus money while poorer red states got shafted.[324] It is difficult to provide shovel-ready jobs when you're rebuilding the infrastructure in places where most of the people are already employed or possess significant personal wealth. Perhaps that is why unemployment stayed above eight percent for an unprecedented forty-three months.

59. Decline of Entrepreneurship

Few people, not even Barack Obama, would argue that entrepreneurship is not critical for the American economy. "Entrepreneurs embody the promise of America," Obama said in January 2011. "In fulfilling this promise, entrepreneurs also play a critical role in expanding our economy and creating jobs."[325] And you would think that, with Obama investing billions of federal dollars in startups and scientific research, there would be a surge in entrepreneurship. After all, Obama often called his stimulus bill an investment in the future.

Not so much. In January 2015, Jim Clifton, the CEO of Gallup, revealed that America now ranks "12th among developed nations in terms of business startup activity. Countries such as Hungary, Denmark, Finland, New Zealand, Sweden, Israel and Italy all have higher startup rates than America does."[326] Clifton also noted that "for the first time in 35 years, American business deaths now outnumber business births."[327] Unsurprisingly, the last time that was true was under Jimmy Carter.

Small businesses were forced to freeze hiring, cut jobs, even scale back growth because of Obamacare, and Obama's financial regulations have dried up startup capital.[328] Despite Obama's lip service to entrepreneurs, his policies have been killing America's entrepreneurial spirit.

60. Tax Hikes After Promised Tax Cuts

As a candidate for president in 2008, Barack Obama promised to cut taxes for the middle class. He promised that "no family making less than $250,000 a year will see any form of tax increase. Not your income tax, not your payroll tax, not your capital-gains taxes, not any of your taxes." It was a lie, of course. No politician, no matter their intentions, can keep tax rates low, increase government spending by roughly twenty percent, and keep deficits even remotely under control. Indeed, according to an analysis by Americans for Tax Reform, Obama's budget proposals from FY2010 through FY2015 included a total *442 tax increases!*[329] Even the left-wing fact-checking site *PolitiFact* had to concede that Obama's promise to cut taxes on the middle class was not kept.[330]

Despite his love for tax increases, Obama often claimed he was a tax *cutter*. He claimed that his stimulus bill cut taxes for 95 percent of Americans. It was a lie oft repeated, and rarely challenged by the media. The truth is that Obama's "stimulus" package didn't cut taxes, as veteran journalist and blogger Robert Stacy McCain explained, it merely included: "a temporary two-year tax credit that reduced payroll withholding by — brace yourself — a whopping $8 a week."[331] That didn't stop Obama from claiming it was "the biggest middle-class tax cut in history," a claim that was quickly debunked by the *Washington Post's* fact checker, who called the claim "ridiculous."[332]

Obama may want history to remember him as a friend to the middle class, but every single budget Obama has proposed included significant tax hikes. From his expensive climate policies, to tobacco taxes, to limits on tax deductions, Obama has proposed tax increases amounting to trillions of dollars, many of which hurt the middle class.[333] And we haven't even discussed the biggest tax hike of them all: the *Affordable Care Act.*

61. The First President Without 3 Percent GDP Growth

If you thought Obama's economic record couldn't get any worse... there's more.

GDP is perhaps best gauge of the strength of America's economy, and when you look at Obama's economy in terms of GDP, there is no way to sugarcoat how awful it has been. Despite seven years of Obamanomics, economic growth in the first quarter of 2016 was a dismal .5%, the slowest in two years.[334]

As of this writing, the CBO forecasts an annual GDP growth for 2016 to be 2.67%, which also means Obama would be the only president in U.S. history to have never had a year of 3.0% or greater GDP growth.[335] According to entrepreneur and *Forbes* contributor Louis Woodhill, if the economic growth in 2016 performs as projected, "Obama will leave office having produced an average of 1.55% growth. This would place his presidency fourth from the bottom of the list of 39* [*There have been 44 presidents, but only 39 presidencies. Some terms were shared by two people, as a result of death or resignation.], above only those of Herbert Hoover (-5.65%), Andrew Johnson (-0.70%) and Theodore Roosevelt (1.41%)."[336]

62. The Worst Economic Recovery

So let's total this all up for you, readers. What was the net result of increased taxes, increased spending, decreased labor force participation, a hobbling GDP growth rate, increased dependence, and serial attempts to hand the government more control over business?

If you listen to Obama, you'd think he was the first president ever to inherit an economy in recession. But both George W. Bush and Ronald Reagan inherited recessions. There have been eleven recessions since World War II, each of which was followed by a recovery. Even Obama has experienced economic recovery... it just happens to be the worst one.

All jobs that were lost in post-World War II recessions were recovered, on average, after about twenty-five months. It took seventy-seven months for non-farm employment to return to pre-recession levels, making Obama's recovery the slowest recovery of them all (by a wide margin!).[337]

The labor force participation rate has trended downward for the entirety of Obama's presidency.[338] The employment-population ratio has yet to recover either, having remained virtually flat since the end of the recession. In December 2007, the employment-population ratio was 62.7 percent. By the time the recession ended in June 2009, it had dropped to 59.4 percent. In December 2014 it was even lower, coming in at 59.2 percent, which is also below the average Employment-Population Ratio for the entire 18-month recession, and the 60.6 ratio when Obama took office.[339] Jim Clifton, the CEO of Gallup, said in early 2015, "The number of full-time jobs, and that's what everybody wants, as a percent of the total population, is the lowest it's ever been. [...] In the recession we lost 13 million jobs. Only 3 million have come back."[340]

As we noted earlier, wage growth hasn't been good either. Prior to the recession, annual wage growth was above 3 percent, but has averaged about 2 percent since 2010.[341] GDP growth has also hovered in the tepid two-percent range since the so-called recovery.[342] According to Steven Ricchiuto, the chief economist at Mizuho Securities USA, "there is no acceleration in underlying economic activity."[343]

The middle class has been hurt the most in the Obama economy. After six years of Obama's economy, the middle of the road wage earners still made less than they did before Obama took office, and have a lower net worth.[344] Median income in 2013, down 8 percent from 2007, still hadn't recovered from the 2008 recession.[345] While most of the jobs lost in the recession were medium or high wage jobs, nearly half of the jobs created in the Obama recovery have been low-wage jobs.[346] Home ownership has declined and, in 2014, reached a 19-year low.[347] Long-term unemployment is still at a record high.[348] Nearly two-thirds of Americans live paycheck-to-paycheck with no emergency fund to cover unexpected expenses.[349]

The Obama recovery has been particularly hard on women and minorities. Even though women make up 46.8 percent of the workforce, only 38.6 percent of all new jobs added under Obama have gone to women.[350] According the Bureau of Labor Statistics: "women have experienced weaker job growth after the end of the 2007-2009 downturn than they had experienced in the previous three recessions."[351] The wealth gap between whites and minorities has also gotten worse since the end of the recession.[352]

America's young people are also "experiencing hardships like never before under the Obama administration," according to an analysis by Young America's Foundation. The Youth Misery Index (YMI), which is calculated "by adding youth unemployment, student loan debt, and national debt (per capita) numbers," reached a record high in 2014. The Youth Misery Index increased 53.7 percent under Obama, which is "the highest increase under any President, making Obama the worst President for youth economic opportunity."[353]

Of course, Obama has often claimed that he inherited "the worst recession since the Great Depression," but even that's not true. The economy Ronald Reagan inherited was in rougher shape after the disastrous Carter years.[354] The slow recovery is not because the recession he inherited was "the worst recession since the Great Depression," but because his approach to getting the economy back on track failed miserably. And while some jobs have been created under Obama, he can't claim responsibility for them. The oil industry created more jobs in the United States than all other industries combined between 2008 and 2013 despite Obama's war on oil (more on this later).[355] Making Obama's job record even worse, job growth in just one state accounts for the nation-wide net gain in jobs since the recession. From December 2007 to December 2014, Texas added 1,444,290 jobs, while the 49 other states and the District of Columbia were still 275,290 jobs below pre-recession levels.[356]

Obama thinks—or at least claims—that he *saved* the economy. And while he may cherry-pick numbers that give the appearance of an economy that bounced back, the Obama Recovery is not one worth bragging about. Millions of people lost jobs and never got re-hired. Those who were able to find work mostly got lower wage jobs. Household wealth is still below its 2007 peak. In fact, Obama's economic growth gap topped two trillion dollars in GDP in the summer of 2015. According to *Investor's Business Daily*, Obama's so-called economic recovery "is far worse than all the previous 10 stretching back 70 years."[357]

The Great Divider

A person has to be at least a bit self-absorbed to run for president. But most presidents manage to balance this with at least a bit of humility. Obama doesn't possess this quality. Time after time, when he had the chance to insert himself into a situation that garnered extensive media coverage, he did so. Time after time, when America looked to Obama for leadership, he gave them only self-aggrandizing words and cold partisanship. Time after time, when the world extended a hand to this once-great nation, Obama shoved it aside and greedily took that hand for himself. And time after frustrating time, when Obama had an opportunity to put his personal feelings aside and show his opponents that he really did care about representing them, and not just his ardent supporters, he turned it aside. Let's list off a few examples of this tendency that, by themselves, would be splitting hairs to list as entries on our final listing of Obama's largest failures, but that, taken together, show a pattern of narcissism and self-involvement not becoming of the White House.

- In April of 2009, Obama chose, as a gift to the Queen of England, an iPod loaded with his inauguration speech and his speech to the 2004 Democratic National Convention.[358] She reportedly already owned an iPod.[359]
- When Hawaii senator Daniel Inouye died in December 2012, Obama eulogized the senator and war hero by talking about himself, constantly referring to Inouye's life through his own, even devoting some time to talk about his own family vacation.[360]

- When Neil Armstrong, the first man to step on the Moon, died in 2012, President Obama "honored" him by posting a picture of Obama looking at the Moon.[361]

- When it came time to honor the great civil rights pioneer Rosa Parks, Obama "honored" her by posting a picture of himself sitting in the bus in which Parks bravely refused to give up her seat.[362]

- Obama similarly "honored" President John F. Kennedy on the 50th anniversary of his assassination with a photo of himself gazing at Kennedy's portrait.[363]

- Obama couldn't stop himself from doing the same thing a few weeks later when Nelson Mandela died, tweeting a picture of himself hugging his daughter in his prison cell.[364]

- Obama would again use a picture of himself to "honor" those who died during the attack on Pearl Harbor. The picture showed Obama in the foreground descending the stairs of the USS Arizona Memorial, but didn't fit the full name of the memorial in the background.[365]

- And, of course, Obama also had the biographies of past Presidents on the White House website updated to include references to himself and his policies. For instance, in the biography of Calvin Coolidge, the first President to address the nation via radio, it was added that Obama was the first to use Twitter at a town hall meeting.[366]

This has gone beyond just odd—it's Cult of Personality stuff, unworthy of a President of the United States. Is it really much of a surprise that White House staffers have given Obama the nickname "Obam-me?"[367] The thing is, this stuff is minor, even if it is a bit creepy. What's coming in this chapter will make you wonder just how much Obama cared for America compared to how much he evidently cared for himself.

63. An Overtly Partisan Inaugural Speech

Obama's personality is actually very well characterized by his most famous public speeches after the 2008 campaign (wherein he put forward a false identity sprinkled with only hints of the truly divisive figure he'd become). Elections can be bitter, poisonous contests, but inaugurations are times to put all that partisan bitterness behind us and come together for the good of the country. Barack Obama, having just been reelected with fewer votes than his first election, started his second term with a country more divided than when he first took office. But, instead of signaling a shift towards the center, and a willingness to bring the two major parties together to address the country's problems, he gave what many described as the most partisan inauguration speech in our country's history.[368]

Republicans may have still been licking their wounds after the election just a couple months earlier, but the first step in breaching the partisan divide is for the country's chief executive to reach out to the opposition. Instead, as Senator John McCain noted, this was the first inauguration speech where such a call for both parties to work together was absent.[369]

Sarah Tanksalvala of the *Washington Examiner* called the speech, "an ode to collectivism while quoting the founding fathers and documents. It was partisan while claiming to speak for the identity of the American."[370] *National Review*'s Yuval Levin described it as follows:

The president probably didn't even quite see that his second inaugural was almost certainly the most partisan inaugural address in American history — more partisan than one delivered on the brink of civil war, or in the midst of it, or after the most poisonous and bitterly contested election in our history. He accused his political opponents of rabid (even stupid) radical individualism, of desiring to throw the elderly and the poor onto the street, of wanting to leave the parents of disabled children with no options, of believing that freedom should be reserved for the lucky and happiness for the few, and of putting dogma and party above country.[371]

Ron Fournier of the *National Journal* wrote, "What happened to the idealistic young politician who argued against dividing the country into red and blue Americas? It seems we're not going to see him again."[372]

The *Washington Post*'s David Ignatius called Obama's speech "flat, partisan and surprisingly pedestrian—more a laundry list of preferred political programs than a vision for a divided America and a disoriented world."[373] Ignatius continued:

> *[Obama] gave a progressive speech that Democrats will like; he affirmed the importance of climate change and gay rights, defended by name the sanctity of Medicare, Medicaid and Social Security, and made a pitch for infrastructure and education spending.*
>
> *All worthy causes, but the speech lacked the unifying or transcendent ideas that could help Obama do much more than continue the Washington version of trench warfare during his second term. If you were hoping that the president would set the stage for a grand bargain to restructure America's entitlement programs and fiscal health for the 21st century, you wouldn't have found much encouragement.*
>
> *Missing from the speech was the first inaugural address's perhaps naïve dream of uniting America. This second speech seemed to accept that America is divided and, as Obama put it, "progress does not compel us to settle centuries long debates about the role of government for all time." He called out those who would "treat name-calling as reasoned debate"—I wonder who that could mean?—but Obama's plan seemed to be to roll the negativists, rather than try any longer to reason with them.[374]*

It's telling that Obama spoke of unity in 2009, when his party controlled both Houses of Congress, but did not in 2013, when he had divided government. It's a stark contrast to the attitude of his predecessor, George W. Bush, who had majorities in both the House and Senate at the start of his second term, but still made extraordinary efforts to include Democrats on big issues, such as his goal to reform Social Security.

Obama signaled an unwillingness to compromise, or even work with the Republican Party in his second term. It's extremely unfortunate. America is more divided now than ever, and Obama apparently wants to keep it that way.

64. Equal Pay Deception

All presidents lie or spin statistics at least a little to make their points and push their agendas, but Obama's particular brand of lying is uniquely corrosive and narcissistic. As president, Barack Obama has championed the cause of equal pay. In fact, the first bill Obama signed as president was the *Lilly Ledbetter Fair Pay Act.* In his 2014 State of the Union address, he said, "women make up about half our workforce. But they still make seventy-seven cents for every dollar a man earns. That is wrong, and in 2014, it's an embarrassment."

Based on the standard he holds for the national workforce, his passionate rhetoric on pay equity doesn't match his record. According to a *Washington Post* analysis in 2014, "The average male White House employee currently earns about $88,600, while the average female White House employee earns about $78,400 [..] That is a gap of thirteen percent."[375] This gender-based gap has remained unchanged since Obama's first year in office.

The White House naturally fought back against the accusation, revealing that "men and women in equivalent roles earn equivalent salaries."[376] This explanation makes sense, so much sense that it also explains the alleged gender pay gap nationally: men and women working similar jobs make similar pay. The "gap" only exists when you compare all men with all women without considering all the facts. Obama's claim that women only make seventy-seven cents for every dollar a man makes is false, and the explanation from the White House demonstrates that Obama clearly knew he was perpetuating a falsehood. That didn't stop him from continuing to champion a battle against a non-existent problem. If Obama were honest, he'd concede that, just as in his White House, the national statistic he cited doesn't account for differences in education, occupation, position, or even hours worked. But the rules of fair debate do not apply to Obama, and the truth matters far less than the cause. Obama's deliberate deception and "war on women" rhetoric was the real embarrassment.

65. Opposing School Choice (while Private Schooling his Kids)

There are principled, if potentially misguided, reasons to oppose government programs that enable parents to choose schooling options other than the public system. We would also never pillory a man for choosing to pay out of pocket to send his kids to a private school, hoping it will be better for their future. But it strikes us as more than a bit hypocritical and elitist for the President of the United States to use his wealth and influence to secure, for his daughters, the finest private school he can find (Sidwell Friends School – a private Quaker institution with a yearly tuition of $37,500), while at the same time lecturing Americans on the need to focus their desire for educational reforms on the public school system. It feels, to the average resident of the inner city, a bit like Marie Antoinette explaining that they should just eat some cake.

It is factually undeniable that many private, charter, and parochial schools get far better results than public schools, nationwide, and especially in the inner cities. So why, in 2015, has Obama claimed that public schools do better than their alternatives? His argument is based on a book, published in 2013 by Sarah and Chris Lubienski, called *The Public School Advantage: Why Public Schools Outperform Private Schools*. It turns out that the Lubienskis published this "study" with a conclusion in mind, purposefully ignoring performance metrics like graduation rate, employment rate, SAT scores, and college admission that favor all other schooling types and focusing on two national math tests that are geared toward the particular way in which math is taught in public schools (the *bad* way: focusing less on facts and more on exploration of concepts).

Given that Obama feels it is worth the tuition to evade the D.C. public school system when raising his own daughters, one must ask the question: why would he promulgate what is, at best, a hotly disputed claim as the truth while speaking at a summit on poverty? It seems, to us, that if the public option is so solid for the poor of D.C., Obama would have no qualms with sending his own children to the public system. But even if we want to be charitable and say that Obama believes the public option is good, but not quite as good as the very expensive top-of-the-line private options, we can't ignore the reality that, when objective analysis is done, the public schools just don't measure up. The very people for whom Obama claims to speak at poverty summits are clamoring for charter schools, school choice vouchers, and other alternatives, as seen in the emotional documentary *The Lottery*, while he ignores their wishes to push a special interest group (the public teacher unions) to the fore. Here again, Obama's preference for the cause, and for his own beliefs, trumps any sense of sensitivity for the needs of the poor and disadvantaged or any desire to seek out the truth.

66. Selective Respect

Sometimes, the disrespect that Obama displays isn't down to specific actions or language, but to inaction. For example, on July 16, 2015, a Muslim gunman opened fire at two U.S. military installations in Chattanooga, TN, eventually killing four Marines and one sailor. We'll talk more about the absurdity of military "gun free zones" later in this book, but, for now, let us focus on Obama's response to this tragedy. Presidents have a certain responsibility to maintain morale and command the respect of those that serve them in the U.S. military. The Commander-in-Chief has always taken great pains to pay homage to the fallen, and Obama was responsible for the five dead service members. Certainly, he would immediately take some note of these terrible deaths at the hands of our enemies? Well, not exactly.

Obama was swift to decorate the White House in gay pride colors once the Supreme Court legalized same-sex marriage throughout the United States. Obama ordered flags flown at half-staff to honor the victims of the Newtown massacre on the same day of the tragedy. Oddly, it took Obama's White House five days before they decided to lower the White House flag to half-staff in honor of the dead in Chattanooga. Even then, it appears that it was only ordered because just about everyone else in the country was flying their flags at half-staff: State governors, businesses, the U.S. Congress, and private citizens. It can only be assumed that someone in Obama's political machine suddenly woke up to how bad it looked politically to have the White House flag flying high while everyone else was in mourning. It looks like if you want to be honored by Obama, you'd better be politically useful. We recognize that events happen at the speed of light these days, but there are some things that should take precedent over ideology, over agenda, and over time constraints – this is one of them. Obama's failure to show reverence for the fallen on a consistent basis is disturbing and in stark contrast to his predecessors.

67. Missed Budget Deadlines

Here is another classic example of Obama's warped priorities. As a presidential candidate and as president-elect, Obama promised to "go through our federal budget – page by page, line by line – eliminating those programs we don't need, and insisting that those we do operate in a sensible, cost-effective way."[377] This promise suggested Obama was very serious about the nation's budget, and getting the country's fiscal house in order, as the President is charged with doing above all other priorities but national defense.

But as president, the budget became such a low priority for him that, not only did he break his promise to go line-by-line to eliminate waste (not that anyone really believed he'd do that anyway), but he couldn't even manage to submit his yearly budget proposal on time. According to the Budget and Accounting Act of 1921, the President of the United States is required to submit his annual budget by the first Monday in February. Since it was signed into law, most presidents submitted their budget on time, but no president ever missed the legally mandated deadline more than once. That is, until Barack Obama became President.

Obama's budget for FY2011 and FY2016 were both on time, but the others were all late[378]:

FY2010: 98 days late
FY2012: 7 days late
FY2013: 7 days late
FY2014: 66 days late
FY2015: 30 days late[379]

While hardly the worst of his offenses while in office, his repeated violation of the law regarding the budget is yet another example of Obama's tendency to care more about crafting a narrative and pushing his larger agenda than about the hard work of managing the nation.

68. Hypocrisy on No-Bid Contracts

As a presidential candidate in 2008, Obama promised that he would end the practice of awarding contracts over $25,000 without bidding. This was in response to the leftist complaint, during the Bush Administration, that Halliburton—once run by Vice President Dick Cheney—had received no-bid contracts for work in Iraq. Obama broke his promise here for much the same reason he broke his promise to close Guantanamo Bay prison camp: reality.[380] While it is often in the public's interest that government contracts be bid upon by various firms, sometimes certain types of jobs can only be done by certain firms. Obama, living in a liberal fantasy world and anxious to fire up his leftwing base, made the promise to end no-bid contracts without thinking the matter through.

As a candidate, Obama may have just been ignorant of how things work. As president, though, his ignorance became hypocrisy when he awarded a $433 million no-bid contract to Siga Technologies, the maker of an experimental smallpox vaccine that also happens to be a major donor for Democrats. The conflict of interest was so blatant that Claire McCaskill, a top Democrat in the Senate, called for an investigation into a potential conflict of interest and possible waste of tax dollars.[381]

69. Removing God and Jerusalem from his Party Platform

Let's move away from Obama's priorities and delve into his obsession with crafting a narrative that casts him in the best possible light at all costs. We would never argue that Obama is the only politician in our history to do some of this, but, for Obama, this seems to be the very top priority, above people, above policy, above all else. The next several entries on our list will illustrate the lengths to which Obama will go to make himself the hero, and the harm such tactics have done.

It is a staple of American politics to call upon the blessings of God for our efforts. Even today, the overwhelming majority of Americans express belief in God and a majority of them adhere to the Judeo-Christian concept of God. So, honoring God is, in practical terms, generally considered uncontroversial in American politics. But, at the 2012 Democrat National Convention, God was explicitly removed from the party platform, as was any mention of Jerusalem, and Democrats in attendance booed an amendment proposal to reinsert both statements, leading former L.A. Mayor Antonio Villaraigosa to cram them into the platform using an up or down vote and some very generous estimates of the yea votes. The "bad optics" of the Democratic Party delegates booing God and Jerusalem, however, are not the point of this entry.

Once the media reported the story, the Democratic National Committee went into full damage control. The media aided and abetted, and the bad situation was quickly spun into a positive for Obama, suggesting he personally intervened to get the mention of God and Jerusalem as Israel's capital back in the party platform. Of course, the truth is that Obama had already been aware of the change. *Politico* reported that Obama "had seen the language prior to the convention [...] but did not seek to change it until after Republicans jumped on the omissions..."[382]   Obama seems incapable of admitting that he approved of this change and then got caught by a disapproving public. When the citizens deem his positions out-of-line, Obama refuses to own them and make the case in their defense.

70. Exploiting Disaster and Tragedy to Push his Agenda

If there's any time to put politics aside, it's in the wake of a national tragedy. But Barack Obama has seen fit, more than once in his presidency, to take a national tragedy and use it to push his own agenda. Obama used the BP Oil spill as cover for banning offshore drilling. He even compared the situation to the 9/11 terror attacks.[383] The memorial service for the victims of the Tucson shooting where Rep. Gabrielle Giffords was severely wounded was turned into a quasi-political rally and an opportunity to rail against tea party extremists and call for better gun control measures to boot.[384]

During a press conference several days after the shooting in Newton, CT at the Sandy Hook Elementary School, Obama invoked the massacre *and* Hurricane Sandy in a shameful plea for Republicans to agree to raise taxes. "After what we've gone through over the past several months," Obama said regarding the hurricane and the shooting, "the country deserves the folks to be willing to compromise for the greater good."[385] Not that Obama ever showed any desire to compromise on taxes or entitlement reform during the fiscal cliff negotiations. We'll get to some of these issues again before we're done, but here, we're simply highlighting the reality that Obama seems preoccupied with messaging, even when cramming in that political talking point is in the poorest of taste or carries the whiff of exploitative opportunism at the emotional harm of the victims of tragedy.

71. Unprecedented Attempts to Influence the Supreme Court

The judiciary is independent of the executive under our system of government, and for good reason. A free nation must have a legal system which is beyond the control of the executive in order to guarantee the people against executive tyranny. While the President enforces the law, it is the Judiciary that decides which laws are Constitutional and whether or not they are enforceable. Given Obama's routine disregard for the law, it is no surprise that he has tried to pressure the Judiciary to rule in his favor on political matters.

According to Josh Blackman, a constitutional law professor at the South Texas College of Law, "Very few Presidents have spoken about pending Supreme Court cases after arguments were submitted. Even fewer discussed the merits of cases. Only a handful could be seen as preemptively faulting the Justices for ruling against the government. President Obama, however, stands alone in his pointed and directed arguments to the Supreme Court."

His public comments about two cases involving the constitutionality of key aspects of Obamacare serve as fine examples of this tendency. Those cases were: *NFIB v, Sebelius*, which addressed the individual mandate, and *King v. Burwell*, which addressed federal subsidies.

Of *NFIB v. Sebelius*, Obama said, "Justices should understand that, in the absence of an individual mandate, you cannot have a mechanism to ensure that people with preexisting conditions can actually get healthcare." He also said that it would be "unprecedented" for the Court to overturn the law. In *King v. Burwell*, Obama, in preemptively faulting the Court, said the case "shouldn't even have been taken up."[386] In both cases, the Supreme Court ruled in Obama's favor. Regardless of whether or not Obama's preemptive public attacks on the Court influenced any Justices, it is not the job of any president to try to influence the Supreme Court. Obama's own college law professor, Laurence Tribe, pointed out that, "[p]residents should generally refrain from commenting on pending cases during the process of judicial deliberation. Even if such comments won't affect the justices ... they can contribute to an atmosphere of public cynicism."[387] For Obama, though, such risks are worth it – the good of his legacy matters more than the good of the nation.

72. Politicizing the National Endowment for the Arts

Brace yourselves – this is where it starts to get *really* creepy. In the summer of 2009, Patrick Courrielche, a contributor at *Breitbart*, participated in a conference call by the National Endowment for the Arts (NEA) that called on up-and-coming and well-known artists "to help lay a new foundation for growth, focusing on core areas of the recovery agenda - health care, energy and environment, safety and security, education, community renewal."[388] The call was run, in part, by NEA Director of Communications, Yosi Sergant; Buffy Wicks, Deputy

Director of the White House Office of Public Engagement; and Nell Abernathy, Director of Outreach for Obama's United We Serve campaign:

> Backed by the full weight of President Barack Obama's call to service and the institutional weight of the NEA, the conference call was billed as an opportunity for those in the art community to inspire service in four key categories, and at the top of the list were "health care" and "energy and environment." The service was to be attached to the President's United We Serve campaign, a nationwide federal initiative to make service a way of life for all Americans.
>
> [...]
>
> We were encouraged to bring the same sense of enthusiasm to these "focus areas" as we had brought to Obama's presidential campaign, and we were encouraged to create art and art initiatives that brought awareness to these issues. Throughout the conversation, we were reminded of our ability as artists and art professionals to "shape the lives" of those around us. The now famous Obama "Hope" poster, created by artist Shepard Fairey and promoted by many of those on the phone call, and will.i.am's "Yes We Can" song and music video were presented as shining examples of our group's clear role in the election.[389]

There has been plenty of debate over the appropriateness of the government funding art, particularly when it's controversial or obscene. But there's something completely un-American about the Obama administration actively calling on the art community to generate propaganda for their agenda with government grant money. It is also illegal, as the conference call violated six federal laws, including the Anti-Lobbying Act and the Hatch Act.[390]

73. Telling Media How to Report his Positions

On April 27, 1961, President John F. Kennedy said, "Without debate, without criticism, no Administration and no country can succeed--and no republic can survive."[391] Times certainly have changed. Instead of extolling the virtues of freedom of the press, Barack Obama instead has sought to minimize debate and criticism from the press.

While speaking at the Associated Press luncheon, on April 3, 2012, Obama told an audience of journalists how to report his positions. He said, "So as all of you are doing your reporting, I think it's important to remember that the positions I'm taking now on the budget and a host of other issues, if we had been having this discussion 20 years ago, or even 15 years ago, would have been considered squarely centrist positions."[392]

Obama influences his media coverage in other ways as well. While running for re-election, Obama granted many interviews to local media. By August 2012, Obama had done 58 local media interviews, but only 8 national media interviews.[393] It was revealed that Obama was doing this to set ground rules for his local media interviews, something that he wouldn't be able to get away with as easily with the national media. With local media, Obama could often dictate the topics that would be discussed, allowing him to control the conversation, and avoid criticism and accountability.[394] Kennedy's words, spoken more than 50 years ago, seem like an ominous warning now.

74. The Know-Nothing President

One way that Obama tries to spin events to fit a picture of him as a heroic crusader besieged by unreasonable adversaries is to deflect blame when things that should be under his purview go haywire. His skill in this area is epic, as you'll see. We know that the President of the United States has information resources that are available to no one else in the world. A veritable army of people in the Executive branch is on hand to provide Obama with information on any conceivable issue. Despite this, Obama seems to be grossly unaware of what's going on in the world, or even with his own Administration.

Whenever a scandal arose within his administration, Obama *claimed* to have found out about them the same time everyone else did, the exact same way: through the media. This is how it was for Fast and Furious, the NSA spying on world leaders, the IRS targeting conservative groups, the Department of Justice secretly acquiring phone records from the Associated Press, the VA waiting list scandal, and many other events that would surely have toppled any Republican presidency. Obama, we're supposed to believe, was just as shocked and surprised as the rest of us.[395] Even the Hillary Clinton email scandal was claimed to have been first revealed to Obama when the media broke the story in March 2015.[396] Of course, in that case, we have incontrovertible proof that Obama's claims of ignorance were boldfaced lies, since we have records of more than 20 emails sent by Hillary Clinton to Obama from her private email address. We're forced to wonder: just how many emails did Obama receive from Hillary Clinton while she was the Secretary of State? Did he never see the address of the sender? In all of these cases, the official White House explanation for what Obama knew and when is clearly suspect. In the case of Hillary's email, according to a report from *Politico*, the White House was aware of Hillary Clinton's private email scandal six months before the *New York Times* broke the story.[397]

It's doubtful that anyone really believes Obama was unaware of the scandals brewing in his administration. But denying involvement in, or foreknowledge of, scandals is expected of politicians. However, there's no excuse for how Obama was repeatedly blindsided by consequential events worldwide, including the Arab Spring,[398] the North Korea rocket launch,[399] the rise of ISIS in Iraq, Russia's invasion of Ukraine,[400] and the collapse of the U.S. backed government in Yemen[401]. A dangerous world is made even more dangerous when the President of the United States and his administration are repeatedly caught off-guard by world events. Unfortunately, Obama's detachment from foreign policy has made America less safe, and less respected worldwide.

75. Blaming Bush and Congress

Every president casts at least some blame upon his predecessor. It is a natural inclination to ascribe any particularly thorny issue to the policies of the man who came before. But, for President Obama, blaming his predecessor has become an exercise in the absurd and fits a pattern of deflecting blame and criticism that extends to an inconceivably huge range of issues.

Over the course of Obama's first term, he blamed Bush for the economy, for the botched Operation Fast and Furious, for the massive deficits, for our plummeting national wealth, for our problems in the Middle East – for just about everything which has gone wrong. At one point, President Obama was blaming President Bush for things while standing right next to President Bush.[402] It must have become so reflexive that he didn't know what else to say. Regardless of whether it was his first day, or the end of his first term, Obama hasn't taken responsibility for the outcomes of his policies. Obama's administration even tried to blame the Solyndra scandal on Bush, even though Bush's Energy Department *denied* Solyndra's loan application two weeks before Obama took office.[403]

Obama rarely took responsibility for his failures, but often took sole credit for accomplishments he should not have, like healing one of the victims of the theater shooting in Aurora, Colorado who had been shot through the head.[404]

Obama likes to talk about the bad economy he inherited, but he never credits Bush for the military and intelligence agencies he inherited that were far more able to fight terror and analyze threats effectively than they had been before 9/11.

When Obama wasn't blaming Bush for his problems, he was blaming Congress—particularly the Republicans in Congress. When Obama first took office, he inherited impressive advantages for Democrats in both the House and Senate, meaning that he saw no need to court Republican support to achieve his agenda. Obama could have done whatever he wanted, and the Republican Party was nearly powerless to stop it.

And yet, four years later, while running for reelection, Obama spent lots of time blaming the GOP for his own lack of accomplishments, particularly on domestic issues. The economy was still limping along, despite his stimulus and Obamacare, both of which were supposed to stimulate the economy and create jobs. According to Obama, there was progress made on the economy, but he needed more time to accomplish more because Republicans were blocking his agenda.

He blamed the Republicans for his failure to pass immigration reform.[405] He blamed the Republicans for his unwillingness to compromise with Republicans.[406] He blamed Republicans for his plans to ignore Republican desires.[407] He even threatened to blame Republicans for the failure of the fiscal cliff negotiations in his 2013 State of the Union address, despite the fact he was the one not willing to compromise.[408] And, of course, he blamed the GOP for not funding critical parts of the government during the brief shutdown that occurred in October of 2013, even though Republicans in the House of Representatives passed piecemeal funding bills that Harry Reid refused to even bring to the floor for debate. While the left was busy tormenting would-be national monument visitors and demagoguing the shutdown, Republicans were being turned away even when they attempted to fund such benign things as cancer research initiatives.

76. Worsening the Partisan Divide in Congress

Leaders lead – they do it by owning their beliefs and ideas, by working hard to convince people that their ideas are good ones, by compromising with those who oppose them to get something done, and by striving to listen to the objections of their peers and consider them. They certainly do not lead by ignoring critics, demonizing their would-be partners and then shaming them when they inexplicably do not see eye to eye. Unfortunately, a man who cannot accept responsibility for his own mistakes, own his ideas in the face of popular opposition, or see things from the perspective of anyone but himself is going to be a polarizing figure if he is placed in a leadership role. Those character traits are the definition of narcissism, and Obama embodies them fully.

Despite his left-wing record, Obama campaigned, in 2008, on a theme of bipartisanship and a promise to end partisanship in Washington by bringing "Democrats and Republicans together to pass an agenda that works for the American people."[409] Unfortunately, Obama forgot the definition of bipartisanship when he took office without needing a single Republican vote to pass his agenda.

The fact-checking site *PolitiFact* reported in August of 2012 that, rather than bringing Congress together in a bipartisan fashion, under Obama, Congress was more divided than ever before.

The House, led by a Republican majority that includes a slate of tea party members elected for the first time in 2010, set a record for the frequency of these party-line votes.

The Senate, where Democrats were in charge, held far fewer partisan votes, but the average Democratic senator fell in line with his or her party's majority more than any time in the last five decades -- another record.

[...]

"I don't think Obama ever brought the Republicans up to the White House in the way that (President Bill Clinton) would," said Sean Theriault, a political scientist from University of Texas at Austin. "It's unlikely it would have helped, but he didn't try as hard as he could have."[410]

Obama has put virtually no effort into working with Congress to achieve a bipartisan agenda. By comparison, George W. Bush had many bipartisan successes on big issues like tax cuts, the Patriot Act, No Child Left Behind, Medicare reform, pension reform, and even the 2008 Stimulus and TARP. Obama, however, got one Republican vote in the House and zero in the Senate for Obamacare, and zero Republican votes in the House and only three votes from Republicans in the Senate for his 2009 stimulus bill.

77. Threatening to Veto Bills that Would Force him to follow the Law

Every president, when taking the oath of office, swears to "preserve, protect and defend the Constitution of the United States." Even though Obama has taken this oath twice, he has repeatedly chosen to violate the Constitution for the sake of his own agenda.

All through Obama's two terms in office, his unconstitutional actions and power grabs have outraged growing numbers of American citizens, as well as members of Congress. Lawmakers have tried nearly everything they can, short of impeachment, to reign in Obama and stop his excesses. After a long train of usurpations and abuses by Obama, two separate pieces of legislation were drafted to curtail the President's unconstitutional actions. The Faithful Execution of the Law Act of 2014 would require that Congress receive an explanation from the U.S. Attorney General every time an executive branch agency unilaterally decides not to enforce a law. The Enforce the Law Act would give Congress the power to sue the president when he unilaterally changes a law or doesn't enforce the law.[411]

While neither of these laws would stop a Presidential action, Obama was so unwilling to surrender the unbridled power he has assumed, that he threatened to veto both bills. It's hard to believe that a U.S. President could have such disdain for the Constitution and the laws of the land that such bills were even necessary to write, let alone veto.

78. Threatening to Defund Homeland Security Over Executive Amnesty

The Department of Homeland Security (DHS) was created after the September 11 terrorist attacks with the purpose of protecting the United States from terrorism and other domestic threats and emergencies. Since the department was established, it has been the focus of much criticism, particularly with regards to violating Americans' 4th Amendment Rights. Still, it's hard to imagine a circumstance where the sitting President of the United States might threaten to block funding for an agency created with the purpose of protecting the homeland. Yet, Barack Obama made such a threat.

In December of 2014, Obama advisor Dan Pfeiffer told *The Huffington Post* that Obama "would veto a bill to fund the Department of Homeland Security if it included a rider that nullified his executive action on deferred deportation."[412] In other words, Obama would block funding for the Department of Homeland Security if the Republican Party defied his unilateral and unconstitutional executive amnesty. This is yet another example of Obama putting politics ahead of the security of the United States—which includes border security—so that he can get everything he wants without compromise. In this case, Obama didn't even have to use his veto power. A bill funding DHS that defunded Obama's executive amnesty had passed the House but was blocked by Democrats in the Senate. House Republicans, in order to prevent a shutdown ultimately caved and passed a clean DHS funding bill in early March 2015, leaving Obama's executive amnesty intact.[413]

79. Refusal to Compromise on the "Fiscal Cliff"

After he was reelected, Obama decided that compromise was no longer necessary; even when Republicans gave him something he wanted, he wasn't going to give them something back in return. Obama has oft repeated that he wants to see "the rich pay their fair share," and had promised to end exemptions and deductions for high-income earners. He was unable to fulfill this promise before the election, but with the "fiscal cliff" looming at the end of 2012, Obama was offered precisely this by Republican House leaders, who had hoped Obama would accept their concession and offer one of his own to complete the deal.

The GOP had offered a balanced compromise: reduce or eliminate various exemptions and deductions for high-income earners; in exchange for making all of the Bush tax cuts permanent.[414] With this deal, Obama could finally keep his promise, and could do so with bipartisan support! But this wasn't good enough for Obama, who rejected the deal because he still wanted an increase in tax rates.[415] There would be no halfway with him. No compromise. No concessions. Just *his* way or the highway. Obama may have been re-elected, but he was reelected with divided government, and instead of being the unifying politician he claimed he would be, he established, once and for all, without any ambiguity, that compromise just wasn't a word in his vocabulary, despite his rhetoric for a "balanced approach" to solving the country's fiscal problems.

80. Jumping to Race-Based Conclusions

Another unfortunate characteristic of Obama's public rhetoric has been his tendency to use race as a wedge to divide Americans. When asked about the Secret Service prostitution scandal back in 2012, White House press secretary Jay Carney said "it would not be appropriate" for Obama to comment on it while the investigation was ongoing.[416] And he was right. Unfortunately, there have been times where Obama has inappropriately commented on ongoing investigations, and perhaps not coincidentally, each case has alleged racial components.

Less than a month before the Secret Service prostitution investigation, Obama felt it was proper to weigh in on the ongoing investigation of the shooting death of Trayvon Martin. Obama claimed that the nation needed some "soul searching" over the shooting death of the young African-American. He added, towards the end of his statement, "If I had a son, he'd look like Trayvon,"[417] essentially giving credence to the unfounded allegations that Trayvon's race was a factor in his being shot and killed.

This was not the first time that Obama jumped to conclusions about a racial motive in an ongoing investigation. In July of 2009, Obama spoke out about the arrest of Harvard University Professor Henry Louis Gates Jr., who had been mistakenly arrested while he was trying to enter his own home. Gates had been struggling with his door and a 911 call had been placed by a neighbor who thought they were witnessing a break-in attempt. Sgt. James Crowley of the Cambridge Police Department responded and, when the officer arrived, Gates initially refused to provide identification and so was ultimately arrested for disorderly conduct.

A week later, Obama said that Crowley "acted stupidly" by arresting Gates, who is African-American and cited "a long history in this country of African-Americans and Latinos being stopped by law enforcement disproportionately." Obama said all of this despite admitting that he didn't know all the facts or "what role race played."[418] His comments brought further controversy to the situation, prompting him to invite Gates and Crowley to the White House for a "beer summit," in an attempt to diffuse the controversy he made worse.

Obama has been very selective in what cases he finds it appropriate to comment on and make hasty judgments about. It's extremely unfortunate that the nation's first black president would so irresponsibly jump to race-based conclusions, even when he admitted that he didn't have all of the facts. The same story would be repeated following the death of Michael Brown in Ferguson, MO. Here again, Obama was quick to call for a "national discussion" on racial biases in law enforcement, long before the facts were in regarding whether Officer Wilson's actions were justified. And what is the result of this tendency of America's first black President to view everything through the prism of racial politics and social justice? Some polling indicates that Americans are more racially divided now than they were when Obama took office.[419]

81. The Race-Baiting President

The 2008 election of Barack Obama was seen by many as a turning point in race relations in America. In fact, even Obama's opponents could not help but feel a surge of pride in the United States that we had so far buried our racial past that we had elected our first black President. As it has turned out, the election of Obama has proved a watershed in the history of American race relations, but not in the way most had hoped. Rather than being the unifying force he pretended to be, Obama has repeatedly used his position to drive wedges between American ethnic groups.

From *de-facto* condoning voter intimidation by the Black Panthers[420] to his words and actions on the Trayvon Martin case,[421] Obama has taken every opportunity he can to increase racial animosity in the United States. Obama is quite egregious in his efforts to inject racial hatred into issues which have little or nothing to do with race.

Obama went out of his way to erroneously claim that the illegal immigration law passed by Arizona in 2010 would cause harassment of Hispanic-Americans because of what they "look like."[422] In an interview with the *New York Times*, he even claimed that, if Congress didn't support his economic agenda, racial tensions "may get worse."[423] In an interview with *The New Yorker*, published in January of 2014, he implied there was a racial component to his low approval ratings, claiming: "There's no doubt that there's some folks who just really dislike me because they don't like the idea of a black president."[424] When it came to the legalization of marijuana, Obama made a race-based argument to justify his support, "African-American kids and Latino kids are more likely to be poor and less likely to have the resources and the support to avoid unduly harsh penalties..."[425]

His Administration has done virtually everything it can to racialize every issue. Health and Human Services Secretary Kathleen Sebelius equated opponents of Obamacare with opponents of civil rights legislation in the 1960s during the 2013

NAACP convention. She even equated the fight for Obamacare to "the fight against lynching and the fight for desegregation."[426]

Under the leadership of Obama's Attorney General Eric Holder, the Department of Justice has selectively enforced laws on a racial basis. According to whistle-blower J. Christian Adams, Holder's belief that he is the arbiter of racial justice has led him to perceive many cases through the ideological lens of racial politics and critical race theory, ultimately biasing the entire Obama administration.[427]

After exploiting tragic events in Ferguson, MO and New York City involving young black men being killed by white police officers and claiming that racism is deeply rooted in American society,[428] Obama had the nerve to tell NPR that he felt race relations had improved during his presidency.[429] Of course, polls have shown otherwise. According to a Bloomberg Politics poll at the end of 2014, a majority of Americans felt race relations have gotten worse since he took office.[430] Americans don't just believe they have gotten worse, they genuinely are worried about it. According to a Gallup survey released in April 2016, more than a third of Americans are worried "a great deal" about race relations, more than doubling since 2014, and the highest ever recorded.[431]

82. Officially the Most Polarizing President... Ever

We can now take this opportunity to summarize Obama's impact on the nation's political discourse. He has proved to be divisive, unwilling to compromise, willfully deceptive, unable to accept responsibility for any negative outcome or any position he has taken that proved unpopular, too quick to place blame, to look for reasons to place us into groups and too obsessed with crafting a story about himself as a hero. It all adds up. Obama campaigned on a promise to unite the country, and began his first term with approval ratings over 60 percent.[432] Unfortunately, he quickly squandered the goodwill of those who took him at his word, and would have the largest partisan gaps in approval of any president.

The partisan gaps for Obama, as measured by Gallup and reported in a 2015 article on the subject:

Year 1:	65 points
Year 2:	68 points
Year 3:	68 points
Year 4:	76 points
Year 5:	71 points
Year 6:	70 points.[433]

Obama's first four years in office "were the most polarized for any president's first, second, third, or fourth years." All of Obama's years in office to date rank in Gallup's top ten most polarizing years.[434]

Of course, this isn't just a reflection of Obama's job performance, but also of the political environment in the United States, since the partisan gaps have been consistently above 60 points since 2004, and presidential approval ratings have become increasingly polarized. According to Gallup, "there has been an average party gap of 70 points in Obama's approval ratings, which, if it continues, would be easily the highest for any president to date. Bush is second with a 61-point gap throughout his presidency, followed by Clinton (56) and Reagan (52)."[435]

Still, Obama certainly deserves a huge chunk of the blame. He started his first term with high *bipartisan* approval, but his party had majorities in both Houses of Congress, so he didn't need Republican support for his agenda, and didn't bother seeking it out. After Republicans gained control of the House in 2010, he still didn't seek bipartisan support, and after Republicans regained the Senate in 2014, he showed even more defiance, stating that, though he heard the voices of the Americans that voted, he also heard the even louder voices of the ones that stayed home – suggesting that the outcome of the 2014 midterms was not a repudiation of policies, but a rejection of "business as usual" in Washington.[436] Perhaps if he entered office in 2009 with divided government he would have learned about the concept of compromise and been a less divisive president.

Foreign Policy: General

At the G20 Summit in London, England in 2009, the first international summit of his presidency, Obama was asked about previous comments he made regarding America's "diminished power and authority" over the last decade. He was hardly humble in his explanation on how to solve that problem. He said, "I would like to think that with my election and the early decisions that we've made, that you're starting to see some restoration of America's standing in the world." [437]

Despite coming into office with virtually no foreign policy experience, Obama believed he would arrive on the scene, restore the world's faith in the U.S. as a reliable partner, convince die-hard enemies of the west to negotiate in good faith, and end the many regional wars and seemingly intractable ideological differences that divide the world, or, at least, begin the healing process. The reality, however, looked much different. His lack of foreign policy experience opened him up to many embarrassing, insulting, or otherwise inexcusable gaffes. In one such example, in September of 2012, Obama said of Egypt, "I don't think that we would consider them an ally, but we do not consider them an enemy." White House aides and the State Department had to scramble to correct the record that Egypt is, in fact, a major non-NATO ally, and has been since 1989. [438]

But the mistakes ran much deeper than confusion over America's complex relationships around the world. His vanity and naiveté would come back to hurt him most when he applied a warped, backward strategy of befriending our adversaries and holding our friends at arm's length. This frightful combination emboldened our enemies, damaged our friendships, and destabilized the entire world, from the Middle East to South America.

We'll deal with radical Islam, the Middle East, and the global fight against terrorism in a later chapter; but first, we will review Obama's general approach to matters of foreign policy and discuss his evident confusion as to the difference between a friend and a foe, as well as his often disrespectful and dictatorial management of the U.S. Armed Forces. By the time you've read through this chapter, you might just be as confused as we were in trying to decipher Obama's strategy for safeguarding America's interests and fostering peace.

83. The Global Apology Tour

When Obama first became president, he went on what was dubbed by some as the "Global Apology Tour."[439] Essentially, the purpose of this series of summits, international speeches, and diplomatic gatherings was to rebrand the United States in a manner that Obama believed would be more acceptable to the rest of the world. In his view, the U.S. had acquired a bad reputation under George W. Bush and other prior administrations, and the way to fix it was to announce that he would govern differently. The various appearances were generally met with favorable reactions from around the world. There was just one problem; they accomplished nothing, other than to show weakness and brand America as unreliable and lacking in a consistent moral vision.

While in France, in April 2009, Obama said that, in America, there is "a failure to appreciate Europe's leading role in the world." He followed that up with: "America has shown arrogance and been dismissive, even derisive."[440] A week later, while speaking to the Turkish Parliament, Obama claimed that America is still "working through some of our own darker periods in our history," citing slavery and segregation as legacies we still struggle with.[441] At the Summit of the Americas later that same month, he did concede that America has played a key role in promoting peace and prosperity, but that "we have at times been disengaged, and at times we sought to dictate our terms."[442]

Obama's apologizing for the United States continued through his final year in office. In 2016, just before Memorial Day weekend, Obama became the first U.S. president to visit the Hiroshima Peace Memorial, and, while not making a direct apology, called the United States' use of atomic weapons on Japan, the same ones that resulted in the Japan's surrender and the end of World War II, "mistakes of the past."[443] Similarly, when he toured Havana on his diplomatic mission to Cuba, he went out of his way to praise Castro's regime for getting it right on healthcare and education and say America could learn from the Cuban example on human rights, all while sidestepping Castro's dubious claim that Cuba held no political prisoners.[444]

There are many similar examples, all proving Obama's negative view of America and its history. What they share in common is an apparent belief that you can sell your brand as reliable by claiming it's been terrible up until today. In reality, people don't tend to think a bad neighbor will become a good one overnight, or that a liar will become honest today, simply because he declares that he is. We would question just what, precisely, Obama hoped to accomplish with such a dreary, slanted portrayal of America's past? It certainly isn't good branding, and it certainly gained us nothing diplomatically to do it.

Even if a President of the United States takes a dim view of America's place in history, when acting as the commander and chief of the armed forces, he cannot use his influence to denigrate the nation without expecting negative consequences throughout the world. As you'll see, negative consequences weren't far off.

84. Cutting Funding to Fight AIDS

Obama did not enter the White House facing a situation where America had no political capital around the world. Despite his conviction that George W. Bush had left us without a friend in sight, America had many allies and ran many successful programs to fight the world's most pernicious problems. Somehow, Obama managed to turn many of those advantages into old memories, and many of our longstanding friends into neutral observers. Let's look at a few examples.

George W. Bush's initiative to fight AIDS around the world, the President's Emergency Plan for AIDS Relief (PEPFAR), has saved millions of lives, particularly in Africa. From the program's launch in 2003 to the time Bush left office, the number of HIV-infected people in Africa that were getting proper treatment went from less than 50,000 to 2 million.[445] His efforts didn't go unnoticed by the people of the African continent either. When President Bush took a farewell tour of Africa near the end of his second term, massive crowds of grateful Africans cheered for him.[446]

Despite the massive amounts of spending increases that have occurred on Obama's watch, he has cut funding for PEPFAR.[447] Obama's cuts put as many as 640,000 people around the world at risk of no treatment, with an outsized, devastating effect on Africa where most AIDS deaths occur.[448] The AIDS Healthcare Foundation was highly critical of Obama's cuts, which came after he had promised to expand the fight against AIDS months earlier:

"This latest action merely confirms what people with HIV/AIDS and their advocates have long suspected – the President simply is not committed to fighting global AIDS. Coming on the heels of the President's flowery rhetoric last December, the cynicism is simply breathtaking," said Michael Weinstein, President of AIDS Healthcare Foundation, which provides free HIV/AIDS medical care to over 125,000 people in 26 countries abroad.[449]

It's hard to imagine why Obama would choose to cut funding to fight AIDS around the world when he's given millions of dollars to terrorist groups, but he did. And doing so convinced who knows how may Africans that the United States had no interest in coming to their aid.

85. Hurting our Special Relationship With Britain

Since the American declaration of war against Imperial Germany in 1917, Britain has been America's most consistent and staunch ally around the world. While there have been differences, when the United States found itself in difficulties, we could always rely upon the support of Britain. This friendship was forged by common priorities, shared values, and bloodshed in joint military missions for nearly a century.

In spite of this long-standing friendship, almost as soon as Obama took office, he set about cutting ties by offering insults to our British friends. After the 9/11 terrorist attacks upon the United States, the British government loaned a bronze bust of Winston Churchill to the U.S. as both a pledge of British friendship and an invocation of resolve in the face of adversity. This bust of the greatest Briton of the past century—and the first foreigner ever accorded honorary American citizenship—stayed in the Oval Office during President Bush's term. Weeks after taking office, Obama had packed up the bust and sent it back to Britain.[450]

And the insults didn't stop there. Obama has made a series of gaffes and insults at the expense of our ally. In March of 2009, Obama gave Prime Minister Gordon Brown a most lackluster presidential gift: a box set of classic American films. This uninspired gift managed to be doubly insulting since the discs were incompatible with British DVD players.[451] Obama also repeatedly snubbed Prime Minister Brown throughout the year, at one point forcing Brown to settle for an impromptu chat in a kitchen at the United Nations building.[452]

In May of 2011, while a guest at Buckingham Palace, Obama continued toasting the Queen as the orchestra began playing "God Save the Queen."[453] A major faux pas on his part, that left a thick air of awkwardness in the room. Obama clearly abandoned the once-special relationship with Britain when he boldly declared, in 2011, "We don't have a stronger friend and stronger ally than Nicolas Sarkozy, and the French people."[454] Obama sure found a great way to insult Britain and dishonor the memories of fallen British soldiers who died in defense of America.

Because of the continued deterioration of America's relations with Britain during Obama's presidency, in March of 2012, a panel of British lawmakers wanted to end the "special relationship" with the United States because the phrase is no longer an accurate description of reality.[455] White House officials were also reportedly dismissive about the "special relationship". According to the London *Telegraph*, "the reality, right now, is that, in the White House's eyes, Britain is not so much 'special' as rather annoying."[456]

In March of 2016, Obama, rather than accept responsibility for the destabilization of Libya, blamed British Prime Minister David Cameron for allowing the country to become a "shit show."[457] Even *TIME* described the relationship between the US and the UK as "less special than ever."[458] And Obama clearly has no interest in repairing the damage done. When the British government decided they would hold a vote on whether or not to stay in the European Union, Obama went to Britain threatening dire economic consequences if they voted against staying in the Union.[459] This threat resulted in significant backlash.[460]

Obama may have promised to "restore America's standing in the world," but his actions suggest he was really more interested in alienating our allies.

86. Betraying Poland

To say that relations with our ally Poland have gotten worse under Obama is an understatement. On September 17, 2009, Obama, a longtime opponent of missile defense, killed plans for joint missile defense with Poland and the Czech Republic. These countries, once under Soviet rule, still fear Russia today. Obama had pledged support for the program just six months earlier.[461] According to Dr. Paul Kengor, author and political science professor at Grove City College, "Obama's action was a shocking betrayal of these two allies, and it was done to mollify Vladimir Putin and the Russians."[462] According to Kengor, "Poles and Czechs were stunned. Poles especially were aghast at the timing of Obama's decision," which was announced on the 70th anniversary of the day Stalin's Red Army invaded Poland. "Back then, too, in September 1939, Poland was virtually defenseless, and Uncle Sam didn't help."[463]

It is also fitting that Obama's infamous hot mike moment with Russian President Dimitri Medvedev (when he told him he'd have more flexibility to accommodate Russia's demands on the issue of missile defense) came almost 29 years to the day after Ronald Reagan announced his Strategic Defense Initiative in 1983. Obama's misguided attempts to "reset" relations with Russia have come at the expense of a close ally and our own national security.

Given that Obama's priorities seemed to be in working with Russia, rather than containing Putin's ambitions and securing Eastern Europe, perhaps we shouldn't be surprised that Obama played golf on the day of the funeral of the Polish President, First Lady, and nearly 100 senior officials who died in a plane crash. It shouldn't shock us that, when he awarded the Presidential Medal of Freedom to a Polish resistance fighter, he caused much outrage by calling a Nazi death camp a "Polish death camp."[464] These seem like minor slights until you ask: has Obama ever gaffed and insulted Russia or China in this manner?

87. The First Anti-Israel President

Since the establishment of the State of Israel in 1948, each President has reinforced the United States' commitment to the safety and liberty of the Israeli people. But, under Obama, the United States has taken a different direction in its policy towards Israel. With Obama in the White House, America has aligned itself more with Israel's enemies. In 2009, during a meeting with Jewish leaders, Obama acknowledged that his administration's policies would put "daylight" between America and Israel.[465] And he's certainly done a good job keeping his word here. Obama's anti-Israel record practically speaks for itself. Here are a few examples:

- He called on Israel to return to the "1967 borders," which Israel considers indefensible.[466]

- He called on Israel to stop all Jews from moving into the West Bank without a reciprocal request that Muslim populations stay out of the region.[467]

- He legitimized the U.N. Human Rights Council, which has called Israel the world's worst human rights violator, while ignoring nations that literally behead people for having the wrong faith, being homosexual, or choosing the wrong Muslim sect.[468]

- He refused to accept Jerusalem as the capital of Israel.[469]

- He let Iran know that if Israel defends herself and strikes at Iran's nuclear facilities, then Israel is on her own and we had nothing to do with it.[470]

- He snubbed and insulted the Prime Minister of Israel when he was visiting the United States.[471]

- He met with representatives of the Hamas terrorist group, which is responsible for launching missiles into Israel, but frequently dodges Prime Minister Netanyahu.[472]

- He nominated anti-Israel Chuck Hagel as his Secretary of Defense for his second term.

- He never visited Israel during his first term, despite visiting several of its Middle East neighbors.[473]

- He excluded Israel from his Global Counter-Terrorism Forum. However, eleven Muslim countries were invited to join.[474]

- While Palestinian Authority President Mahmoud Abbas has stated in no uncertain terms that he will not accept any "peace" deal which recognizes Israel as a Jewish State, Obama and Secretary of State John Kerry have pressured Israel into accepting a new "framework" which forces Israel to recognize the Palestinian State with an implied threat of America abandoning Israel if they don't go along.[475]

- His second Secretary of State, John Kerry, absurdly claimed that Israel risks becoming "an apartheid state" without a two-state peace deal with Palestine.[476] Despite the uproar that followed the revelation of this offensive comment, Obama did not immediately repudiate Kerry's remarks.

- Obama's State Department used insulting language to describe Prime Minister Netanyahu's speech before a joint session of Congress.[477]

- He sent campaign operatives to Israel in January of 2015 to lead an effort to defeat Netanyahu in Israel's elections.[478]

- He exposed top secret information about Israel's nuclear program to the world.[479]

- He ended a forty-year-old program which guaranteed Israel oil supplies in case of a cutoff.[480]

- Obama's Federal Aviation Administration (FAA) attempted an unjustified ban on American flights to Israel following a rocket strike by Hamas. The ban—which was criticized by Israeli and American leaders as unjustified and possibly punitive—was quickly reversed due to widespread criticism.[481]

- He even spied on Israeli Prime Minister Benjamin Netanyahu during the ongoing nuclear negotiations with

Iran, reportedly using information obtained from private conversations to influence public debate about the treaty.[482]

American Jews have traditionally supported Democrats, and despite Obama's undeniably anti-Israel record, he has maintained that support. The late Ed Koch, former mayor of New York City and lifelong Democrat, supported Obama's reelection despite acknowledging that he knew, in his second term, Obama "would renege on what he conveyed on [sic] his support of Israel."[483]

88. Nominating Chuck Hagel as Secretary of Defense

Now let's turn our attention to Obama's management of the U.S. Armed Forces. Over the next several entries, you'll see that our servicemen have plenty of reasons to be skeptical about Obama's commitment to national security or to the wellbeing of our men and women in uniform. We begin with his choices for who would head up the Departments of Defense and State and implement his vision for foreign affairs.

In a time when America's budget is strained and when our military is stressed by more than ten years of active operations, Obama needed to find a clear thinking and effective nominee to head up the Defense Department. Unfortunately, he opted for an organizational spear carrier without the necessary credentials when he selected Chuck Hagel to succeed Leon Panetta for the position in 2013.

Hagel's positions have been consistently inconsistent. He co-sponsored a resolution to give then-President Clinton retroactive approval for the Kosovo War, but later called President George W. Bush (who got Congressional approval before going to war) "reckless."[484] He flip-flopped on both the War in Iraq and the PATRIOT Act. During the 2008 presidential campaign, he said he'd be happy to serve in either a McCain or an Obama administration, yet has denounced Republican lawmakers backing McCain's aggressive foreign policy positions on a regular basis.

He has often been on the wrong side of foreign policy issues. He called the ultimately successful "surge" of troops in Iraq our worst mistake since Vietnam. He was one of only two senators to oppose sanctions against Iran in 2001.[485] In August of 2006, he refused to sign a bipartisan Senate letter calling on the EU to declare Hezbollah a terrorist organization.[486]

Hagel has also managed to be consistently wrong in his positions regarding Israel over the years. In October of 2000, he refused to sign a Senate letter in support of Israel. In November of 2001, he refused to sign a letter to President Bush urging him not to meet with Yasser Arafat until his forces stopped attacking Israel. In March of 2007, he claimed that there is a "Jewish lobby" which intimidates American government officials into doing Israel's bidding.[487] In March of 2009, he signed a letter urging Obama to open direct talks with Hamas leaders. When Israel tried to stop Hamas from firing rockets from Lebanon into Northern Israel, Hagel condemned President Bush for not stopping Israel. In April of 2010, he made the absurd accusation that Israel is becoming an apartheid state.[488]

When Hagel testified before the Senate for his confirmation, he revealed himself ignorant of the workings of the Department of Defense and woefully unprepared to take on one of the hardest jobs in government. Hagel was confirmed, but had an unprecedented forty-one Senators voting against him. Prior to Hagel, no other Defense Secretary has ever been confirmed with so many votes in opposition.[489] In picking Hagel for Secretary of Defense, Obama endorsed his faulty foreign policy and an anti-Israel mindset many consider anti-Semitic.

Hagel would eventually be forced out of the Pentagon in November 2014. According to David Sedney, the deputy assistant secretary of defense for Afghanistan, Pakistan and Central Asia from 2009-2013, Hagel was forced out "because of criticism the administration has faced over its national security policies and because of the overall weakness of those policies."[490]

89. Obama's Secretaries of State

There have been some excellent Secretaries of State in American history and, indeed, a wise and strong President picks a person for that post who will be a vigorous advocate of sound policy and someone who can help a President sort out the problems of an increasingly complex world. For President Obama, however, strong and wise have not been qualifications for his Secretaries of State.

Obama's first Secretary of State was Senator Hillary Clinton, A person with zero experience in foreign affairs whose time in the U.S. Senate resulted in few legislative achievements and zero chairmanships. Clinton left the State Department after Obama's first term and was replaced by Senator John Kerry. On paper, he, at least, had great foreign policy experience, but his record doesn't withstand closer scrutiny. Kerry has been on the wrong side of history entirely too often, from his adherence to the disgustingly anti-American "Winter Soldier" program of the far left during the Vietnam War, to his well-documented serial mistakes about how to thwart the USSR during the Cold War to his 2003 no vote against a campaign in Iraq that he once voted for.[491]

Without a doubt, the Obama-Clinton-Kerry foreign policy record has been disastrous. Clinton's tenure lacked achievements, but was rife with setbacks. Clinton, herself, appeared pleased with the mere fact that she flew around the world a lot, but diplomatic relations with Syria, Venezuela, and all of our allies, even Canada, suffered on her watch.[492] The Russian "reset" was a complete failure.[493] Relations with Israel deteriorated, Britain became alienated, Japan and South Korea fear that we won't honor our alliances, and America's enemies see no reason to fear us. Perhaps one of the biggest stains on her record as Secretary was the Benghazi attack of September 11, 2012. A bipartisan Senate

Intelligence Committee investigation faulted the State Department for not providing enough security.[494] We'll discuss this in much greater detail in a later entry.

Under John Kerry, there have been ample crises around the world, but little progress. From failed ceasefire negotiations between Israel and Hamas, to the rise of the Islamic State in Iraq, it's been one bad headline after another.[495] The Obama administration policy on Syria has also been a continuing disaster, with some indications that U.S. policy in Syria has evolved toward helping Iran to restore their ally in Syria: Bashar al-Assad.[496] In early 2014, Kerry failed miserably to bring Russia and Ukraine to the negotiating table and has made no major initiatives to resolve that growing crisis.[497] While the world is burning around us, Kerry wishes to make one of his top priorities the negotiation of a climate change treaty.[498] Whatever your position on global warming, it is difficult to understand the connection between international relations and global warming unless your objective is to create global economic controls in the name of mitigating it.

What does Obama have to show for his foreign policy record? According to a September 2014 poll, Americans felt less safe six years into Obama's presidency than they did a year after the 9/11 terrorist attacks.[499] It is astounding that Obama's policies have made Americans feel less secure than they did in the immediate aftermath of the largest terrorist attack on U.S. soil in history. But this is likely the American people understanding better than Obama that weakness invites enemy action. This is the legacy Obama-Clinton-Kerry foreign policy.

90. Cutting Military Healthcare Benefits

Aside from cutting our country's defense budget, Barack Obama has proposed cuts that would cause higher premiums for Tricare, the health care program for active and retired military and their families. The White House estimated that the higher fees would generate $6.7 billion in revenues over a decade.[500] Premiums would increase by as much as 345 percent after five years. Pentagon officials are concerned that this change would hurt military recruitment, as health benefits are a key incentive to joining America's military.[501] Interestingly enough, Obama's cuts didn't affect unionized civilian defense contractor benefits.[502]

One of the more popular provisions of Obamacare is a rule change that allows young adults to stay on their parents' coverage until the age of 26. However, this provision does *not* apply to military families under the military health care plan. For those families to extend their coverage to dependents under 26, it will cost an extra $200 a month in premiums, while private plans have no such fee. By August of 2012, only 9 percent of eligible young-adult dependents of service members that were eligible for the Tricare extension had signed up. [503]

91. Political Correctness in the Military

Given that our military is continually asked to risk everything in our defense, maintaining the highest possible standards is just common sense. America's armed forces must be the best fighting force in the world, equipped to outfight, outwit, and outlast any who would oppose them. With Barack Obama as Commander-In-Chief, the military has instead become the latest place where the most bizarre and absurd ideas of liberal political correctness are to be applied with no thought to how such actions might affect our ability to fight and win a war.

In 2013, Obama lifted the ban on women serving in combat, despite undeniable biological differences that make women less likely to meet the existing physical demands.[504] Case in point: in January 2014, more than half of female Marine recruits were unable to meet the minimum fitness standards for combat duty. Rather than just admit that not all women can meet the standards, the requirement was delayed, probably to allow some means to modify the standard so more women may qualify.[505]

In the same year, the Obama administration announced plans to make the Marine Corps uniforms gender-neutral.[506] The first major changes to the uniforms in over 90 years, it is hard to understand why resources were wasted on such a proposal, especially given the announced military budget cuts in 2014.

Barack Obama's military has also become far more hostile toward God and Christianity, in order to make sure a select few are not offended. In 2013, the Pentagon recruited Mikey Weinstein, an anti-Christian extremist, to develop a religious tolerance policy for the military.[507] Soon afterwards, new regulations were announced that service members who proselytize their faith may be subjected to a court martial.[508] And in 2015 it happened. Lance Cpl. Monifa Sterling was court-martialed for posting a bible verse on her desktop computer.[509] It appears that being openly Christian isn't encouraged in Obama's military--hardly surprising given that the U.S. Army now defines Christian ministries as hate-groups, comparable to the Ku Klux Klan, Neo-Nazis and the Nation of Islam.[510]

With Obama as Commander-In-Chief, our armed forces are abandoning time-honored traditions in favor of a politically correct agenda, all at the expense of morale and military readiness.

92. Keeping Military Bases and Facilities "Gun-Free Zones"

Military bases have been "gun-free zones" since 1993. Regardless of the intentions of the ban, the disarming of soldiers on military bases has had terrible consequences. After the 2009 shooting at Fort Hood—when Nidal Hasan killed 13 people and injured 31 others—this absurd policy should have been instantly reevaluated by Obama administration. It wasn't.

In 2011, Congressman Peter King (R-NY), House Homeland Security Committee, warned that military bases, recruitment stations, and other armed services facilities "have become the most desirable and vulnerable targets for the violent homegrown

Islamist extremists seeking to kill Americans in their homeland."[511] According to a counterterrorism and security report released during the hearings, "at least 33 threats, plots and strikes against U.S. military communities since 9/11 have been part of a surge of homegrown terrorism." The report also noted "serious gaps" in the "military's preparedness for attacks against its personnel, dependents, and facilities -- such as a lack of adequate and clear training in spotting indicators of violent Islamist extremism in individuals who wear the same uniform as those they may target." Yet, military facilities remained "gun-free zones."

They remained "gun-free zones" even after the Washington Navy Yard shooting on September 16, 2013, when lone gunman Aaron Alexis killed twelve and injured three. Alexis was, according to the FBI, under "the delusional belief that he was being controlled or influenced by extremely low-frequency electromagnetic waves."[512] Military facilities were still "gun-free zones" on April 2, 2014, when there was another deadly shooting at Fort Hood, and soldiers were once again needlessly defenseless during the presence of a deadly threat. More than a dozen soldiers were shot, and three were killed before the gunman shot himself. The shooter, Ivan Lopez, an Iraq war veteran, reportedly "snapped" after being denied his request for leave, and the shooting may have been connected to Post-Traumatic Stress Disorder.[513] And, when a Chattanooga, TN military base was shot up by an Islamic Jihadi, it too was "gun-free".

There is no excuse for our military facilities to remain vulnerable. Barack Obama should have done something to make sure that soldiers in the most powerful military in the world were no longer reliable "soft targets" for crazed gunmen or terrorists. Obama may not have been responsible for military facilities becoming "gun-free zones", but he is responsible for keeping them that way when there were many reasons not to.

93. Purging Dissent In The Military

The Obama administration isn't content to reduce morale in the ranks of the military by slashing their benefits, making them bow to a political correctness doctrine that often defies common sense, and disrespecting them by failing to honor their service and sacrifices. He also wishes to change military culture by force, if necessary. Since Obama took office, there has been a noticeable number of senior military officers who have been fired. According to J.D. Gordon, a retired Navy commander and former Pentagon spokesman, by mid-November 2013, 200 military leaders had been let go, or one every 8.8 days, despite decades of loyal service and experience.[514] This extraordinarily high number of military brass firings has led many to speculate that Obama has been purging commanders he doesn't agree with, and threatening those that are still serving into submission.[515]

According to Retired U.S. Army Maj. Gen. Paul Vallely, Obama is "intentionally weakening and gutting our military, Pentagon and [sic] reducing us as a superpower, and anyone in the ranks who disagrees or speaks out is being purged."[516] An anonymous source in the Pentagon said that even "young officers, down through the ranks, have been told not to talk about Obama or the politics of the White House. They are purging everyone and if you want to keep your job — just keep your mouth shut."[517]

Further confirmation came in March of 2014, following the release of a video obtained by BuzzFeed. In the video, Coast Guard Commandant Admiral Robert Papp revealed that, in 2010, Obama had called all five service chiefs into the Oval Office, and presented them with an ultimatum: support the repeal of "don't ask, don't tell" (DADT) or resign. "If any of us didn't agree with it — we all had the opportunity to resign our commissions and go do other things," Papp says in the video.[518]

As a presidential candidate, Obama claimed he wanted members of the Joint Chiefs of Staff to make decisions "based on what strengthens our military and what is going to make us safer, not ideology."[519] Back then, Obama claimed that he didn't want to surround himself with yes-men telling him what he wants to hear all the time. "That's part of what happened with George Bush," he claimed. "He surrounded himself with people who were of the same mind."[520] Unfortunately, as president, his ideology and agenda became far more important than military strength and readiness.

94. Assassinating U.S. Citizens without Due Process

Drones have proven to be an effective weapon in fighting terrorist groups around the world. The advantages of speed and stealth in attacking the enemy with the absence of American lives being put at risk are undeniable, even if controversial. Drone strikes often come with collateral deaths of non-combatants. Further adding to the controversy are the deaths of American citizens by drone attacks overseas.[521]

But what of their use inside the United States, against American citizens? Obama's Attorney General Eric Holder asserted, in Congressional testimony on March 6, 2013, that, under "extraordinary" circumstances, the President has the legal authority to use drones to kill Americans *inside* the territory of the United States.[522]

Drones are risky enough as a tactic overseas, but to use them on Americans on American soil is a denial of a whole series of rights we are guaranteed by the Constitution, including the vital right to due process.

How can it possibly be constitutional for the President of the United States to kill Americans without giving them due process? John Brennan, Obama's CIA Director and the architect of Obama's drone policy, argued that due process is *not necessary* to kill Americans if they are being targeted for potential future acts of terrorism against the United States.[523] *Potential future acts?*

Holder eventually stepped back from his claim after Senator Rand Paul filibustered Brennan's confirmation.[524] But given Obama's record of indifference to the law and the Constitution, it

THE LEGACY OF BARACK OBAMA

is reasonable to assume that Obama may act upon the authority he believes he has in order to kill Americans on American soil without due process before the end of his presidency. Even if he doesn't, he claimed he could, and that should chill you to the core. Imagine a scenario where a future president claims that a political actor is similar to terrorists (already happened!) and has them blown away by drone strike to rid himself of an adversary?

In light of this, it is truly frightening to learn that President Obama has given himself the power, without any Congressional oversight, to order the death of American citizens not only overseas, but far from any battlefield. *The Guardian* reported, in February of 2014, that Obama has weekly meetings with his national security team to approve a "kill list" from among suspected terrorists.[525] Obama has refused to provide any details of this, other than his assertion that he has the legal authority to do it. We don't know who gets targeted, or why. Once again, given the routine resort to illegality on the part of Obama, one cannot help but shudder at the thought that Obama believes he has the right to kill American citizens without legal sanction or military necessity.

95. Cutting Weapons Programs

In order to ensure that our service members go into battle with the very best weapons and equipment possible, the U.S. budgets a significant amount of discretionary spending toward the development and procurement of equipment and weapons. Because we didn't do this during the years prior to World War II, when we went into the war, we had torpedoes that wouldn't explode, aircraft that were sitting ducks, and ammunition that was corroded and useless. We paid in blood for that lack of foresight. Because of this, each post-World War II President has ensured that the budget for new weapons and equipment met the needs of the moment.

But Obama is taking a different approach. He wants to cut defense because he needs the money elsewhere, but he also doesn't want to reduce the number of personnel in the military and civilian defense establishment (at least he didn't during the 2012 campaign, as that would have swollen the ranks of the unemployed). So, Obama chose to make the bulk of his defense cuts in development and procurement. All told, 40 percent of Obama's defense cuts come from this area which means we'll spend $110 billion less than needed between now and 2017.[526] It seems that, when Obama's not tormenting our troops with his personal agenda or putting them at risk with bad foreign policy, he's defanging them and stealing their capability to defend themselves in combat.

96. Killing Successful Missile Programs

If you aren't yet convinced that Obama has been determined to turn the U.S. Military into a small-time operation, we have more evidence for you. In 2014, he announced his intention to eliminate two successful Navy missile programs. Obama's 2015 budget proposed to cut the Tomahawk missile program budget, before ultimately eliminating it in 2016. The Hellfire missile program would also be canceled in 2015. So what will replace them? Unfortunately, the answer to that makes the situation even worse. The Obama administration proposed investing in a different missile system that won't be combat-ready for at least ten years.[527]

Obama's proposal came as a shock to Congress and military experts. Former Pentagon staffer Mackenzie Eaglen, who analyzes military readiness, called the move "short-sighted, given the value of the Tomahawk as a workhorse." Seth Cropsey, the director of the Hudson Institute's Center for American Seapower, said Obama's proposal doesn't make sense. "This really moves the U.S. away from a position of influence and military dominance." According to Cropsey, depriving the Navy of Tomahawks is the best way to "reduce the U.S. [sic] ability to shape events" in the world.[528] Obama may be quick to remind the public that he is the Commander-in-Chief, but he certainly doesn't embrace the role and advocate for the needs of his armed forces.

97. Proposing Massive Military Cuts

If all of the above comments on the state of the military under Obama weren't enough, we offer his 2014 military budget. In his February, 2014 announcement of proposed military budget cuts, Secretary of Defense Hagel said, "this is the first time in 13 years we will be presenting a budget to the Congress of the United States that's not a war-footing budget."[529] In this, Hagel declared that, to the Obama administration, not only were there no wars for us to fight, but we had no enemies out there threatening us and our allies. To Obama, it would seem, the world is at peace. Others can look at the chaotic and violent state of the world and wonder just where Obama got that idea. We can never know when or in what form a military threat will arrive and so our military must be instantly prepared for all possible contingencies.

This is hardly a time to be cutting our military budget. There's civil war in Syria and chaos in Libya. Conditions in Afghanistan and Iraq are deteriorating, and al Qaeda is growing in the Middle East and Africa. ISIS has risen and declared themselves a Caliphate in the heart of the region. Iran is still determined to develop nuclear weapons. There are growing threats to America and America's allies and interests all over the globe. According to Ben Shapiro, then a journalist with *Breitbart*, the proposed 30 percent cut in the military budget is historically very large— comparable to the post-Soviet defense cuts, except that those cuts took place over an 11 year period, as opposed to a 3 year period like the Obama military cuts. The post-Soviet defense cuts also "paved the way for the rise of al Qaeda," which ultimately led to the 9/11 terror attacks.[530]

Despite the many potential national security threats that we face, our army will shrink in size to as low as 440,000 thousand personnel, the smallest army we've had since 1940, just before it was forced to fight a war it wasn't prepared for.[531] Not only will our military get smaller, it will get less effective. Under this budget proposal, military benefits are slashed, too.[532]

The world is practically on fire thanks to Obama's miserable foreign policy failures. There is more danger today of major war than any time since World War II. After damaging America's alliances, encouraging America's enemies and helping turn the world into a melting pot of hatred, fear and resentment, Obama's coup de grâce would be to hollow out the military.

98. Trips To Tyrannical Regimes

When Obama wasn't busy distancing himself from allies or savagely curtailing our military battle readiness, he was cozying up to long-time enemies of the U.S., of human rights, and of liberty. The next few entries include just a few examples of this disturbing trend.

Shortly after winning his second term, Obama made trips to Burma and Cambodia – two nations long run by brutal, tyrannical regimes. People who care about human rights were appalled by the action. Though Democrats have been hard-pressed to criticize Obama, several House and Senate Democrats, including Senator Dick Durbin from Obama's home state of Illinois, criticized Obama's actions in a letter to the White House.

By taking a strong and public stand in support of human rights and democracy during this first-time visit by a U.S. President to Cambodia, your words would encourage and embolden the Cambodian people and send a clear message to the entire region about American values and expectations, particularly in the wake of the Arab Spring. However, failure to speak out will serve to undermine America's narrative of support for Asian democrats. [533]

When the United States mutes its support for human rights and gives legitimacy to tyrants by treating them as rational, civilized members of the world community, then freedom fighters get discouraged – and tyrants are more apt to be brutal, as they become convinced that the United States won't interfere.

99. Condoning The Use of Child Soldiers

In 2008, President George W. Bush signed the *Child Soldiers Prevention Act*, which imposed sanctions on countries whose governments used child soldiers. Despite the law, several countries using child soldiers have continued receiving military assistance under Obama.

The law, which went into effect in 2010, gives the president the power to waive the penalties as he sees fit. While this seems like a simple human rights issue with no gray area, Obama considered these waivers in "the national interest."[534] The Obama administration claimed that the law would have penalized countries that were crucial to the fight against al Qaeda. So, several countries in northern and central Africa have continued using child soldiers, with the effective blessing of Barack Obama.

And what did Obama get out of condoning the use of child soldiers in those countries? If the fight against al Qaeda was the justification, then apparently these waivers were all for naught. Al Qaeda's influence in the region has increased on his watch.

100. Illegal Scientific Exchanges with China

It took twenty-two years for the United States to develop and deploy the new F-22 Raptor. The F-22 is a superb aircraft which looked likely to maintain U.S. aerial superiority for a decade or two into the future. But, in September of 2012, China unveiled two new fighter jets which bear an uncanny resemblance to the American F-22.[535] How did China do it? They got the technology from us.

China gets technology like this by any means necessary. They'll buy it when it's for sale and steal it when it's not.[536] Congress has said our military technology is not for sale. Obama, by his actions, said that it was.

It turns out that Obama has facilitated *illegal* scientific exchanges between the United States and China.[537] In 2011, Congress, as part of a spending bill, prohibited using government funds to pay for scientific exchanges between the United States and Chinese governments. Obama's Administration ignored Congress, claiming that a prohibition on the use of federal funds for something does not prohibit federal employees from doing it, so long as no funds are allocated expressly for that purpose. Obama may not be above using faulty logic to get what he wants, but that doesn't mean the Obama administration didn't break the law. But it's even worse knowing they broke the law to help China—and there is no good explanation for wanting to do that.

101. Unilaterally Normalizing Relations with Cuba

Communist Cuba is a bankrupt, oppressive regime that the United States has kept at arm's length for more than half a century. Given that the government of Cuba talks a lot about social justice—while imprisoning and killing anyone who steps out of line—plenty of American liberals have a soft spot for that antique Communist regime. In line with starry-eyed theories about what Cuba is like, Obama decided, without any notice and with no political debate, to restore American relations with Cuba. It began when, in a secret deal, Obama leveraged the swap of some Cuban spies in return for an imprisoned American aid worker as an initial means of starting negotiations with Cuba over normalization of relations. The deal was so secret that members of Congress were neither informed about the decision, nor given a justification for the release of the Cuban spies, claiming executive privilege.[538]

Even Senator Robert Menendez (D-NJ) slammed Obama over the deal. "President Obama's actions have vindicated the brutal behavior of the Cuban government," he said in a statement. "There is no equivalence between an international aid worker and convicted spies who were found guilty of conspiracy to commit espionage against our nation." Menendez also said the swap set "an extremely dangerous precedent."[539]

Having tested the waters with Cuba, in a surprise announcement in mid-December 2014, Barack Obama announced that the United States would be restoring full diplomatic relations with Cuba, including opening an embassy in the communist country. True to form, Obama's strategy for reversing over a half-century of U.S. foreign policy did not include going through Congress. The move followed the aforementioned spy swap and formalized the Obama administration's stance that Cuba was to be accepted and embraced. Senator Menendez again protested, saying that Obama's actions "vindicated the brutal behavior of the Cuban government."[540]

Despite Obama's desire to act unilaterally, much of American policy towards Cuba is codified in U.S. law, such as the economic embargo, and thus can't be changed no matter how powerful Obama's pen and phone have become.[541] So, while Obama could not immediately change all aspects of U.S. policies towards Cuba, he did whatever he could, including going out of his way shake hands with Cuba's dictator Raul Castro, and nixing Cuba from the U.S. list of state sponsors of terrorism. Obama justified his decision by saying that Cuba had not provided any support to terrorists in the prior six months, and he also guaranteed that Cuba would not support terrorism in the future.[542] Naturally, a day after the announcement, Cuban-backed FARC terrorists in Colombia murdered ten Colombian soldiers.[543]

Normalizing relations with Cuba, including weakening the trade embargo and allowing for tourism, has had one other significant, negative impact in the Western Hemisphere. Cuba and Venezuela have been small-time trading partners for decades,[544] but the infusion of cash Cuba has gained from America has allowed them to step up purchasing oil from Venezuela at prices set by a brutal Maduro regime that has overseen the near-total collapse of one of the wealthiest nations of South America.[545] In short, Obama's actions in Cuba have helped to temporarily prop up Maduro in Venezuela and, in so doing, have prolonged the suffering of the Venezuelan people, many of whom now live without any access to food, water, electricity or basic sanitation. Cuba and North Korea have even sent elite forces to aid Maduro in Venezuela, with no comment from the Obama administration on Cuba's role.[546]

Obama claims that we have to change our policy towards Cuba because our policy hasn't worked. This is an odd way to look at it. The policy may not have brought down the Cuban regime, but it certainly crippled the Cuban economy and prevented them from exerting much, if any, influence on global political matters. The Cuban government is an evil, brutal regime, but a small one, thanks to the embargo. In the past, both Presidents Carter and Clinton, going along with this belief among some that Cuba is enlightened, tried to improve relations with Cuba, and, each time, the Cuban government accepted the U.S. favors and then committed acts directly against U.S. interests.[547] Cuba has sponsored terrorism, been connected with international drug trafficking, and has always worked to thwart the United States and our allies. Opening up to Cuba is a foolhardy act, carried out in purblind obedience to progressive propaganda. It is, in a way, the perfect capstone to Obama's foreign policy of turning us away from friends and towards our enemies.

102.Russia's Invasion of Ukraine

Next, we present the ultimate example of what happens when you try to accommodate your enemies while holding your allies at bay. Let's talk about the increasing aggression of Vladimir Putin. Obama's weakness on the world stage was foreseen back in 2008, when Sarah Palin pointed out that then-Senator Obama's reaction to Russia's invasion of the Republic of Georgia was so weak and indecisive that it might encourage Putin to invade Ukraine.[548] She was mocked for her statement, but the whole world would come to see that she was right when, in 2014, soon after the Winter Olympics in Sochi concluded, Russia did, in fact, invade Ukraine.

And why not invade? What had the Russians to fear from the United States, after all? Obama had, of course, warned Putin to keep out of Ukraine, but what of it? What had Obama ever done in the world that would convince Putin, or any other world leader, to pay heed to his empty bluster? As Putin was unwilling to lose total control of the Ukraine (especially the east of the country with its large ethnic Russian population), Russian troops were swiftly sent into the Crimea and other parts of eastern Ukraine to secure Russia's interests.[549]

According to Charles Krauthammer, Obama showed "weakness" in his statement on the developing situation in Ukraine, and implied that "we're not really going to do anything" about it. Krauthammer observed that Putin: "knows he has nothing to fear from the west, because it's not led by anybody. It used to be led by the United States."[550]

Because of Obama's weakness in world affairs, the world knows Obama won't do anything that requires a long-term military commitment and the buy-in of the American people. Putin had Russian troops in Ukraine within days of his allies being forced out of power there. And the reason Putin was able to act so quickly and decisively is because he knows, as does the whole world, that under Obama, the United States will do nothing. In fact, Obama skipped a national security team meeting on the situation with Russia and Ukraine on March 1, 2014.[551]

As "punishment" for the invasion, Obama imposed small, targeted sanctions against a small number of Russian and Ukrainian officials. Those sanctions were quickly mocked by Russia's deputy prime minister—a rather unfortunate reminder of just how weak Obama is perceived to be by the rest of the world.[552]

As Russian troops started to arrive in Ukraine, the world was also reminded that, during the 2012 presidential campaign, Mitt Romney asserted that Russia was America's "number one geopolitical foe," because Putin's Russia was always willing to side with the bad actors on the world stage.[553] But Palin and Romney likely take no comfort in being proved correct about Putin's ambitions because Obama's weakness may result in a new Cold War between Russia and the West. Considering Obama's plans for massive military cuts, a new Cold War may not end as well for the United States as the first one.

103. Declining Respect for America's Power

Obama has been described in foreign media as an "embarrassing amateur on the world stage," with a "weak-kneed, confused, and strategically incoherent" foreign policy.[554] Between his foreign policy fumbles and leadership failures, it is no surprise that respect for American power has declined significantly on his watch.

Obama may think he's restored America's standing in the world, but the American people disagree. In 2013, the Pew Research Center found that, for the first time in 40 years, a majority of Americans, 53 percent, believe the United States has less power and prestige in the world—more than double the amount measured in 2004. A majority also believe that the United States is less respected internationally than it was ten years ago.[555]

This decline of respect for America's power has manifested itself in alarming ways on the global stage. According to British defense advisor Sir Hew Strachan, Obama has "devalued the deterrent effect of American military capability."[556] Unfortunately, he is right.

Obama's repeated snubbing of Israel and his apparent lack of concern with containing Iran's nuclear program resulted in Israel and Saudi Arabia, two enemy nations, devising a contingency plan for a joint strike on Iran.[557]

In December 2013, a U.S. Navy guided missile cruiser in the South China Sea was forced to take evasive action after a Chinese warship on a collision course refused to stop. The Chinese ship refused to stop despite a radio warning. Sources told CNN this was "a highly unusual and deliberate act by China."[558]

In February 2014, Iran, possibly emboldened by their perceived victory over America after Obama's 2013 nuclear agreement, sent warships close to American maritime borders for the very first time in response to U.S. naval deployments in the Persian Gulf.[559] While there was no real threat to the United States, John Bolton, former U.S. ambassador to the United Nations, argued that Iran is building up its capabilities for the future and could one day be a real threat. "It shows they could put a weapon on a boat or freighter, and if (Iran) has ballistic missiles it could put it anywhere on the U.S. coast."[560]

The weakness of Obama's foreign policy is visible in all corners of the world. For the first time since the collapse of the Soviet Union, Russia has moved aggressively to capture and annex territory in the Ukraine.[561] This is despite Obama's much advertised "reset" of relations.[562] At the same time, a burgeoning arms trade is taking shape in North Korea.[563] China is also now flexing its military muscle against the Philippines, another U.S. ally in the Asia-Pacific region.[564] There are serious fears of war in that area, with some drawing a parallel between Southeast Asia in 2014 and Europe in 1914, on the eve of World War I.[565] U.S. relations with Afghanistan have also deteriorated, threatening the gains we made there in stopping the spread of international terrorism and ousting the Taliban, who are now massing along the Western border and preparing to advance at the first sign of our withdrawal.

Since taking office, Obama has been gradually surrendering the position of the United States as the ultimate peacekeeper of the world, a position won by the United States through the heavy expenditure of blood and treasure during World War II. In just a few short years, Obama has undermined the long-established power and authority of the United States on the world stage. That is what happens when your foreign policy consists of befriending tyrants and mullahs, abandoning your promises to allies, and disrupting or destroying your own military at every level.

Bully Tactics

The last thing Americans expected, when they elected Obama, was a government run rather like a mob outfit. His campaign touched on the general concern people felt for the overreach of George W. Bush's Department of Homeland Security, that sense that they were at the mercy of their government, rather than in command of it. He seemed to have a sunny, charitable disposition. Even his criticism of Bush was tempered by a tone of disagreement, but not hatred.

But, once he took office and settled in, Obama said, time and again, "That's a fine looking business you've got there. It'd be a shame if something happened to it." Substitute government agency, monument, park, lifestyle, healthcare plan or some other cherished American value or privilege for business and the line worked just as well. When Obama didn't get his way in Washington, the American people paid the price. His temper frequently erupted into bursts or irrational saber rattling and bitter rhetorical spasms that left even his supporters a little mystified.

After just three full years of being forced to attempt to work with a Republican-controlled House of Representatives, Obama was prepared to air his dirty laundry on national television during the 2014 State of the Union address, when he declared that, if Congress didn't play ball, "I have a pen, and I have a phone." Perhaps we should add the Constitution to the list of items it would be a shame to lose for not acquiescing to his demands. We've tallied a few of his latest and greatest attempts to use the levers of power to bully the nation to his way of thinking for your perusal.

104. Decline of Economic Freedom

In order for there to be economic growth, there has to be economic freedom. Just look at the nations that have none—in the communist dictatorship of North Korea, the people reportedly eat tree bark to survive.[566] Zimbabwe, which used to be self-sufficient in food, has suffered a 70 percent reduction in food production since dictator Robert Mugabe gained power.[567] Venezuela, until recently run by the late dictator Hugo Chavez, sits on an ocean of oil, and is also blessed with other, abundant natural resources. Yet, the country now suffers from food and power shortages.[568] The common denominator in these examples is a government which has taken control over the economy. Every time this is tried, economic disaster results.

Economic freedom allows people to start and expand businesses as they see fit. It allows people to take risks and earn rewards. People decide for themselves what is in their best interests. Freedom and ingenuity create more success than top-down attempts to increase national wealth. It's basic human nature – we do not strive to improve ourselves without incentives.

Under Barack Obama, the United States has experienced a significant decline in economic freedom. According to the 2015 Economic Freedom of the World report by economists James Gwartney, Robert Lawson, and Joshua Hall, the US has slipped from 7th to 16th in the world in economic freedom from 2008 to 2013.[569]

There was a similarly sharp decline during the Obama years according to the Heritage Foundation's Index of Economic Freedom. As they see it, the United States had the 6th freest economy in the world when Obama took office, but came in at 11th place in 2016. "The U.S. score declined repeatedly during the Obama years thanks to dramatically increased government spending and regulations, a failed stimulus program that enriched the well-connected but left average Americans behind, and laws such as the Affordable Care Act, which denied the right of individuals to keep the health plans they already had, and as the president had promised."[570]

105.Massive Increases in Federal Regulations

We began with a summary of the state of America's economic freedom because it is tied to Obama's first and best tool for intimidating, controlling, and otherwise dominating detractors in the private sector – regulatory burden. According to a report compiled for the Small Business Administration, complying with federal regulations cost the United States economy $1.75 trillion in 2008[571], $2.038 trillion in 2012[572], and $1.9 trillion in 2014[573] To put those number into perspective, they are about 50 percent greater than the price paid privately by American citizens for their health care. To be sure, some regulations add a net benefit to the economy. If we didn't regulate against dumping raw sewage into our drinking water, then the follow-on costs of cleaning up the water (as well as treating those harmed by the contaminated water) would probably be much higher than the cost of regulating. But at a cost of $2 trillion, an economy producing only about seven or eight times that much in GDP cannot possibly be net-benefiting.

Many, perhaps most, regulations have some redundancies, or are too broad in scope to be worth the cost of enforcing them. For example, did you know that an American citizen who owns a cow cannot sell milk from that cow to their neighbor without violating federal regulations on the sale of milk?[574] That regulation comes from an ill-conceived government effort to regulate the price of milk to the benefit of big agribusiness in crucial primary states like Iowa and Wisconsin.

But, Barack Obama loves regulations. In Obama's first five years in office, 157 major new regulations were imposed—

more than double the number of regulations imposed at the same point in the George W. Bush Administration. These regulations cost more than three times as much as those put forward under George W. Bush. Obama can claim the dubious distinction of having four of the five highest Federal Register page counts in history.[575] Obama may be proud of this honor, but the rest of us have to pay for it. In 2014, 75,000 pages of new regulations were added by the Obama administration, at a cost of over $200 billion.[576] In 2015 alone, another $22 billion in new regulations were added.[577] This madness is creating a climate where no one knows the law, and yet everyone is paying the price for keeping up with it.

106.Unions over Workers

The second weapon at Obama's disposal has always been big labor. Obama has always been able to count on the support of unions, and unions have also been able to count on Obama to support their efforts to increase their power and influence, even at the expense of liberty and our country's economy.

Typically, in order for a company to unionize, there is a secret ballot election among the workers. When their ballots are secret, workers are more likely to vote their conscience, which may or may not be in favor of joining a union. Hence, Democrats put forward the fabulously misnamed Employee Free Choice Act, commonly referred to as "Card Check." The argument goes that, in a secret ballot, voters may be fed misinformation by coordinated anti-union forces from company management, robbing them of their freedom to form groups and associate as a union. But what Card Check actually does is eliminate secret ballot elections and potentially expose employees to intimidation and misinformation by union organizers before and after elections!

A voter's right to a secret ballot is a core American value – no citizen should ever have his or her political viewpoint held against them by people with opposing views. One would think that support for secret ballot voting would be universal, but it is not so. Barack Obama supports Card Check. This opposition to secret ballot elections goes against America's traditional, democratic process. It is unfathomable that an American president would support it, especially given the negative economic impact of forced unionization. But with union participation on the decline (down nearly 50 percent from 1983 to 2011), Obama has seen plenty of pressure to help out this traditionally liberal voting bloc, since unions give massive amounts of campaign cash to Democrats. Aside from his support of a federal Card Check law, Obama also opposes state-level right-to-work laws.

Right-to-work laws make it illegal for a company to force union membership and the payment of union dues as a condition of employment. Any worker can belong to any union he likes, but he cannot be *required* to belong to a union in order to be employed at any firm. Obama opposed this basic protection of workers, dubbing them "right to work for less" laws.[578] Despite his rhetoric supporting forced unionization, by 2012, states with right-to-work laws created four times as many jobs as forced-unionization states.[579] From 2009-2012, right-to-work states accounted for 72 percent of the new jobs created, even though they only account for less than 40 percent of the population.[580]

If putting people to work transcended politics for Obama, he'd support right-to-work laws because they actually *encourage* job growth. And if he supported liberty, he'd be in favor of workers doing as they wish, rather than being forced, against their will, into unions that are no more than campaign arms of the Democratic Party. Instead, he supports the right of unions to harass and intimidate some workers and exclude others from good jobs, simply because they disagree on politics.

107.White House Snitch Line

In August of 2009, a rather Orwellian blog post on the official White House blog called on Obama's supporters to submit "scary chain emails and videos," "rumors," "emails," and even "casual conservation" to a specific White House email address so the Obama administration could "keep track of all of them."[581] This is Obama's third weapon of mass intimidation – the three Ds of silencing debate, as chronicled by Kirsten Powers in her recent bestseller: *The Silencing: How the Left is Killing Free Speech.* Those three Ds are: delegitimize, divide, and dehumanize. Trust us, Obama has used them all to perfection. The snitch line divides Americans into tribes and calls on his supporters to rat out their illegitimate opposition, for example.

Later, Obama's reelection campaign would follow suit with an "Attack Watch" page, on which registered Obama supporters could denounce their fellow Americans for expressing anti-Obama opinions.[582] This was not a clearinghouse where Obama supporters could obtain talking points to refute attacks against Obama – it was a page for Obama supporters to report on fellow citizens who were speaking ill of the President, and it was overrun with grotesque depictions of inhuman caricatures that supposedly represented conservatives and Republicans, all with the approval of the White House.

This kind of thing might be typical in countries ruled by dictators, but it is completely contrary to American values and succeeded, in this case, only in making Obama look tiny, thin-skinned and imperial. After the conservative media got wind of the story, Obama's campaign aides apologized and the site was removed. Treating American citizens like children who need a chaperone or criminals who need to be reported for thought crimes is not becoming of any politician, let alone the President of the United States.

108.Obama's Enemies List

Believe it or not, Obama's 2012 campaign team actually stooped to even uglier tactics than "Attack Watch". It's scary to think that, despite the chilling aura surrounding Richard Nixon's so-called "enemies list", any President would repeat this behavior. Unfortunately, Barack Obama did just that by using a campaign fact-checking microsite to identify and vilify several private citizens who were donors to Mitt Romney's campaign in 2012.

The donors on Obama's "enemies list" were identified on Twitter and disseminated via email to his supporters. One such Romney donor was Sheldon Adelson. In the summer of 2012, the Obama campaign emailed supporters vilifying Adelson and his wealth—the same day Obama's Justice Department began an investigation of alleged money laundering by several executives of the Las Vegas Sands Corporation, which is owned by Adelson.[583]

Obama also tweeted a call for his supporters to demand that the Koch brothers make public the names of donors who had joined them in setting up political action committees for the 2012 campaign.[584] Obama attempted to intimidate not just the Koch brothers, but anyone who wanted to work with them by urging his most rabid supporters to denounce the donors and attempt to cast them as pariahs to be excluded from polite society.

Even Democratic pollster, strategist, and commentator Douglas E. Schoen called this a "misuse of government power to vilify private donors" which "diminishes the prestige of the Oval Office and damages our social consensus."[585]

109.Military Labeling of Christians and Conservatives as Extremists

Back in the 2008 campaign, Obama was caught referring to his opponents as people who are bitterly clinging to guns and religion.[586] With an attitude like that, it should come as no surprise that Obama's Defense Department classified

Catholics and Evangelical Christians as religious extremists in their training manuals, lumping them in with groups like al Qaeda, Hamas, and the Ku Klux Klan.[587] A Defense Department teaching guide, obtained by Judicial Watch via a FOIA request, also labeled the Founding Fathers and conservatives as extremists, and equated conservative values with the Ku Klux Klan. "Nowadays, instead of dressing in sheets or publicly espousing hate messages, many extremists will talk of individual liberties, states' rights, and how to make the world a better place."[588] Who wouldn't hate to be exposed to something as dangerous as someone talking about how to make the world a better place?

Tom Fitton, the president of Judicial Watch, criticized the Obama administration for having "a nasty habit of equating basic conservative values with terrorism."[589] But, really, it isn't even right to classify these as "conservative" values; they are just bedrock *American* values. As Commander-In-Chief, how does Obama explain why the military is classifying groups that typically oppose him politically as "extremists"? All Americans should be worried about an Administration that appears to view people in favor of individual liberty as a potential threat. A political threat to Obama, they most certainly were. We suppose that's enough to deploy the three Ds.

110.Threatening Gallup for Unfavorable Polls

Every politician seeks to control the debate; to set up coverage in the most favorable light to himself and the worst for his opponent. But when the Obama administration was faced with a series of negative polls from Gallup during the 2012 campaign, they decided to teach Gallup a lesson.

Initially, David Axelrod, one of Obama's senior advisors, had contacted Gallup to complain about Gallup's polling methods. When Gallup defended their methods, the Department of Justice joined a lawsuit which had initially been filed against Gallup in 2009 by a disgruntled former Gallup employee.[590] The screws were turned; Gallup, and all other organizations, were being taught that if they didn't do what Obama wanted, then the full power of the United States government would be directed against them. Not long after the DOJ got involved, Gallup changed their polling methods and, miraculously, Obama moved up in favorability and in head to head match-ups at the national and state levels against Mitt Romney.

111.Threatening S&P for Credit Rating Downgrade

Barack Obama hasn't just used his Justice Department to target political enemies, sometimes he just uses it for payback. In February of 2013, the Justice Department accused credit rating agency Standard & Poor for an allegedly fraudulent ratings system, which the government claimed was not objective. The Justice Department sought $5 billion in damages. No other credit rating agencies were included in the lawsuit.[591]

In January of 2014, court filings showed that the Obama administration had angrily warned Harold McGraw, the chairman of Standard & Poor parent company McGraw-Hill Financial, that they'd be held accountable for their 2011 decision to downgrade the United States credit rating from AAA to AA+. According to McGraw's deposition, then-Secretary of Treasury Timothy Geithner told him the government would look at S&P's conduct very carefully. "Such behavior could not occur, [Geithner] said, without a response from the government," McGraw said, in his deposition. The government had been investigating all three major credit rating companies, but focused solely on S&P after the 2011 downgrade of the United States credit rating.[592]

112.Bypassing Congress to Mandate "Black Boxes" in all Vehicles

When Obama wants something, he gets it by any means necessary. The final tool at his disposal when intimidation, rhetorical weaponry, and regulatory burdens approved by Congress don't get the job done is executive discretion regarding the execution of existing laws. He used this power often enough during his first term, but after the 2012 election, he has engaged in a campaign to expand the accepted limits of executive discretion and crafted all sorts of creative new laws without congressional oversight. For example, a new regulation imposed by Obama's Department of Transportation requires that all automakers install event data recorders (EDRs) to collect data on passenger vehicles starting on September 1, 2014.[593]

The alleged intent of EDRs (commonly referred to as "black boxes") is to understand how drivers respond in a crash, and give the federal government the "critical insight and information" they need to save more lives, according to Obama's Transportation Secretary Ray LaHood.[594] But, Horace Cooper of the National Center for Public Policy Analysis called the requirement "an unprecedented breach of privacy for Americans."

"Contrary to what is now being claimed, EDRs can and will track the comings and goings of car owners and even their passengers," Cooper said. "EDRs not only provide details necessary for accident investigation, they also track travel records, passenger usage, cell phone use and other private data. Who you visit, what you weigh, how often you call your mother and more is captured by these devices. Mandating that they be installed and accessible by the DOT is a terrible idea."[595]

Cooper explained that, since the system will be running whenever the engine is on, there is no guarantee that the information that would be collected from it would only be relevant to an auto accident. The AAA auto club and the Alliance of Automobile Manufacturers have also expressed privacy concerns.

If this wasn't disturbing enough, Congress *rejected* this mandate in 2011, but Obama has consistently refused to let Congress get in the way of imposing his agenda. So he bypassed Congress again, and subverted the Constitution, imposing the mandate through Department of Transportation.

113.Alarming Changes to the Freedom of Information Act

The Freedom of Information Act (FOIA), which was signed into law on July 4, 1966, by President Lyndon Johnson, empowers private citizens to request the disclosure of government documents, as long as they are not deemed as too sensitive for release. There have been changes to the law since it was first enacted, but Obama's Justice Department proposed a disturbing change to the law. Historically, when FOIA requests are denied, a reason for the denial is supposed to be given. But the new rule, proposed by the Obama administration, would "direct government agencies who are denying a request under an established FOIA exemption to 'respond to the request as if the excluded records did not exist,' rather than citing the relevant exemption." Both left and right leaning government transparency advocates called the proposed rule change "Orwellian."[596] Outcry over the mere suggestion of such changes caused the Obama administration to backtrack, but they later proposed new rules which simply allowed them to deny FOIA requests for trivial reasons.

Obama's track record regarding FOIA requests has been bad from the start, it turns out. Documents released in 2014 revealed that, back in 2009, the Obama White House secretly rewrote a portion of the *Freedom of Information Act* (FOIA) to suppress politically sensitive documents. Any documents involving "White House equities," now had to first be reviewed by White House officials before being released, allowing the White House to indefinitely delay the release of documents it prefers remain hidden.[597] This explains why a 2014 analysis by the Associated

Press found that the Obama administration has denied, censored or stonewalled FOIA requests at record rates.[598] But even this wasn't enough to satisfy Obama's need for secrecy. In March of 2015, the White House formally exempted itself from FOIA requests entirely.[599] One can only wonder what Obama wanted to hide during his last two years in office.

114.Using the EPA to Bypass Congress

To say Obama's environmental agenda has been a disaster is an understatement. From 2009-2012, it was estimated that one-fifth of the nation's coal plants were shut down.[600] Obama's coal regulations are estimated to cost the U.S. economy 1.65 million jobs between 2012 and 2020.[601]

The negative impacts of these regulations aren't the whole story. Obama's Environmental Protection Agency (EPA) has been imposing these regulations entirely without Congressional oversight or review. The coal industry has been crushed, jobs are being lost, energy prices are going up, and the Constitution has been thoroughly ignored. In his 2012 State of the Union, Obama promised even more "executive action" on the environment.

But if Congress won't act soon to protect future generations, I will. I will direct my Cabinet to come up with executive actions we can take, now and in the future, to reduce pollution, prepare our communities for the consequences of climate change, and speed the transition to more sustainable sources of energy.[602]

There's nothing ambiguous about it. Obama considers Congress's role in passing legislation irrelevant, especially when it comes to the environment. If he wants to destroy you, he'll find a way.

115.Unilateral Implementation of Cap-And-Trade

In the aftermath of the 2010 elections, Obama's climate change agenda suddenly was dead on arrival. No longer in possession of a Democrat-controlled, rubber-stamp legislative majority to drastically cut greenhouse gas emissions, it was clear that more modest proposals were the only chance for Obama to advance his climate change agenda, especially since Democrats weren't able to take back the House in 2012. So, what did Obama do? He decided not to bother with Congress at all.

With the potential for a Republican-controlled House and Senate after the 2014 midterm elections, Obama decided not to accept political realities by working on a compromise solution that could achieve bipartisan support; instead, he bypassed Congress altogether. In spring of 2014, Obama's Environmental Protection Agency proposed new rules and regulations to do what he wanted.[603] These new rules included a cap-and-trade policy, which sets limits on emissions but also allows companies to "trade allowances or credits for emissions as a way of staying under different benchmarks the EPA sets for each state."[604]

No debate. No congressional approval. No checks and balances. Obama wanted to impose cap-and-trade no matter what the cost, and regardless of whether the Congress approved. According to a study by the Chamber of Commerce, "the EPA's climate rule could cost $50 billion annually and about 40 percent of the U.S. coal fleet could be retired by 2030."[605] But Congress was denied the opportunity to do their job and debate the merits and faults of the proposal.

Obama abandoned a legislative approach to his climate agenda in favor of executive fiat to avoid compromise once Congress no longer was able to give him a blank check. If every president acted this way, the Constitution would be irrelevant.

116. Making the Sequester as Painful as Possible

The last desperate refuge for anyone who cannot get their way is to throw a fit. It usually doesn't work, but Obama has allies who can be relied upon to call a fit a principled stand, hide the evidence of his immaturity, and generally provide cover. The last two entries in this chapter are as puerile, ugly, and pathetic as it gets – locked in battles with Congressional Republicans who were placed there by the American people to slow him down, he collapsed into two separate fits of rage where the victims were ordinary people, and the outcome would have been completely different if the bad actor had been conservative.

It became clear in the early months of Obama's second term that even though the election was over, the campaign was not, and that governance was a lower priority than politics. Hoping that the American people would blame Republicans for the sequester cuts, he instructed various agencies to ensure that the cuts would be as painful as Obama promised they would be. The *Washington Times* reported:

> *The Obama administration denied an appeal for flexibility in lessening the sequester's effects, with an email this week appearing to show officials in Washington that because they already had promised the cuts would be devastating, they now have to follow through on that.*

> *In the email sent Monday by Charles Brown, an official with the Animal and Plant Health Inspection Service office in Raleigh, N.C., Mr. Brown asked "if there was any latitude" in how to spread the sequester cuts across the region to lessen the impacts on fish inspections.*

> *He said he was discouraged by officials in Washington, who gave him this reply: "We have gone on record with a notification to Congress and whoever else that 'APHIS would eliminate assistance to producers in 24 states in managing wildlife damage to the aquaculture industry, unless they provide funding to cover the costs.' So it is our opinion that however you manage that reduction, you need to make sure you are not contradicting what we said the impact would be."* [606]

A whistleblower in the National Parks Service also revealed that supervisors denied plans to deal with budget cuts in a manner that would minimize the impact on the public, and were instead instructed to cancel special events, tours, and educational services provided by park rangers.[607]

There were also reports that several hundred immigrants who had been detained by Immigration and Customs Enforcement (ICE) were released, and that their release was "to ensure detention levels stay within ICE's current budget," according to an ICE spokeswoman.[608] Many saw the move as politically motivated to increase public opposition to sequestration, with the hope that Republicans would be blamed. Is this what an administration does when it's looking out for the best interests of the American people?

117.Making the Government Shutdown as Painful as Possible

From 1976 to 2009, there have been 17 government shutdowns: one time during Ford's presidency, five times during Carter's, seven times during Reagan's, once under George H.W. Bush, and twice under Clinton.[609] Whether the issue at the heart of the shutdown was abortion funding, congressional spending, education funding, military spending and foreign aid, deficit reduction, or balancing the budget, each time the President and Congressional leaders negotiated until a solution was found to end the impasse. But, when a government shutdown occurred on Obama's watch, he actually *refused* to negotiate with Congress in order to end it. The issue at the center of this shutdown was Obamacare. Republicans wanted to defund it, but the Democrat majority in the U.S. Senate, following Obama's dictate, would not allow for it.

As the October 1st budget deadline approached, Congressional Republicans had essentially retreated to one, single demand on the President: in return for a one-year delay in the implementation of the Individual Mandate, Congress would provide a continuing resolution to keep the government open. This was merely to provide average Americans a similar delay to the one Obama had unilaterally and illegally granted to big business.

Obama refused to agree to this very reasonable demand, and when the government officially shut down, he constantly blamed *Republicans* for it, rather than work with both sides (like past presidents have) to negotiate a compromise. Who caused the shutdown may be debatable, but Obama's lack of leadership to end it is not.

The American people were instead treated by Obama and congressional Democrats (with the help of the mainstream media) to a childish blame game. Republicans were called "terrorists", "hostage takers", and were said to have "a gun pointed at the head" of the country. Vile language which one would be wary of using against avowed, foreign enemies of the United States was poured out from Obama upon Republicans once the shutdown started. And when not brazenly generating hatred and anger towards his fellow Americans who happen to disagree with him, President Obama was doing whatever he could to make the shutdown "as painful as possible," as he'd also done with the sequester.

National Parks and war memorials were unnecessarily closed, barricaded, and guarded by U.S. Park Service Rangers to prevent access. A supposedly shuttered government had money to print up signs and rent fences to close off parks that are normally open twenty-four hours a day, seven days a week. Aged veterans were actually barred from visiting the open-air World War II and Vietnam War Memorials by the Obama administration. The veterans eventually resorted to breaking through the barriers to pay their respects.[610] According to leaked emails obtained by *National Review Online*, the National Park Service knew the Veterans were coming, but decided to put up the barricades anyway.[611] Similarly, a tour group of senior citizens who were not only kicked out of Yellowstone National Park, but also treated to frightening, brutal police intimidation until they left the park.[612]

Never missing a chance to be vindictive, Obama also forced the shutdown of national parks that the federal government doesn't even fund, including the Claude Moore Colonial Farm in

Virginia, privately funded campgrounds in Arizona, the Ford Theatre, and Mount Vernon.[613]

Private property owners within the Lake Mead National Recreation Area in Nevada were also forbidden to go to their own homes because Lake Mead was shut down.[614] In service of Obama's goal of causing pain, citizens of the United States were treated worse than enemies. Obama, once again, chose to inflict pain on U.S. citizens rather than work in their best interests. It got so bad and so absurd that even ultra-liberal House delegate Eleanor Holmes Norton (D-DC) confronted Obama about the absurdity of his actions.[615]

Obama made the shutdown out to be an existential crisis, and then set about hurting the American people in the hopes that he could direct their anger at the Republican Party. After a bit more than two weeks of watching Obama throw a childish temper tantrum, Congressional Republicans eventually gave Obama everything he wanted for the good of the country. Funding was provided, Obamacare rolled forward and Obama had to give not an inch.

As bare-knuckl political brawling, Obama's actions might impress the ill-informed, but there is a delicious irony in all this for those who believe in justice: The Obamacare roll-out (which also started on October 1st, 2013) was such a disaster that Obama would have been better served had he agreed to the one-year delay of Obamacare as Congressional Republicans had demanded.

Administration Corruption

Throughout American history, until very recently, its citizens have, correctly, held the chief executive accountable for the corrupt actions of his cabinet and the executive branch agencies under his command. He is, after all, the one that hires and fires cabinet officers, appoints leaders to departments and agencies, and directs their mandates. The leader sets the tone and accepts responsibility for his entire branch of government. Richard Nixon was forced to resign when it came to light that members of his campaign team were trying to dig up dirt on his opposition during the 1972 election. Today's leftists, including Obama himself, were quick to hold George W. Bush accountable when allegations of corrupt backroom deals over the military supply chain between Cheney and Halliburton came to light, even though Bush was not directly implicated. It has, quite rightly, been asserted that the man at the top must take responsibility for the doings of his underlings and must treat corruption harshly or stand accused of being complicit.

There have been strong leaders in the White House who have confronted real, systemic corruption in high places – who have taken on the responsibility of ensuring that the business of running the country remains above board and beaten back the crooks and scoundrels of their age. One fine example is Herbert Hoover. For all of his failings on the economy, Hoover was a fierce and successful trench warrior in the battle against government corruption, owing to his staunch Quaker upbringing. Even Bill Clinton, a man with a rather dubious personal morality, managed to confront corruption in the Pentagon and among military contractors and streamline government military spending.

In contrast, there is the Obama administration, widely recognized as one of the most corrupt of all time. The men and women he chose to form the backbone of his executive branch have, to a degree not seen since U.S. Grant or Andrew Johnson, been found to be abusing their authority, creating all manner of havoc, and trampling all over the American people in their quest to fundamentally transform the American political landscape. And, perhaps even worse than their corruption, they've also proved to be spectacularly inept. Everywhere we look, today, we find examples of the government failing to serve its constituents, either by stupidity or wicked intent.

In some cases, the connections tie directly to Obama, in some cases, they stop short of the Oval Office, but in every case, someone that Obama hired was responsible; and in just about every case, Obama took no action to punish those responsible and even denied that any corruption had taken place. We reject the notion that Obama was merely "in over his head" – though, if he were, it would be a stinging indictment of his Presidency anyway – and insist that he be held accountable for choosing a bevy of corrupt, far-left, utopian thugs and gave them marching orders that led directly to scandal after scandal on his watch. This chapter will give a full accounting of these scandals of administrative failure and abuse.

118.Taxpayer Dollars For Hired Trolls

There are four basic ways an administration can be corrupt. The person at the top can hire grossly incompetent people to do the work out of political favoritism. The administration can become embroiled in scandals of intent (they tried to do something illegal or unethical and were caught). The leader can use the power of government to shield his or her allies from prosecution for criminal wrongdoing or stop them from coming under scrutiny for ethics violations. And, of course, as was the case with Nixon, a leader can improperly use the power of government to aid in his reelection. Obama's administration was so corrupt, so consistently, that he managed to do all of those things repeatedly. We'll start where Nixon's career ended; let's discuss where Obama weaponized his incumbent advantage to get himself and his allies in Washington reelected.

The first example may seem minor but stop and think about what it implies. You probably never thought your tax dollars would be paying for bloggers to anonymously troll websites. But the Obama administration did just that. In 2009, it was revealed that Obama's Justice Department, under the leadership of Attorney General Eric Holder, was hiring bloggers to participate in a secret propaganda campaign by anonymously posting comments on newspaper websites with stories critical of Obama, Holder, and the Justice Department.[616] This was a gross misuse of taxpayer dollars for an agency that is supposed to enforce the nation's laws without political influence or motivation. Of course, we would be remiss if we didn't also mention Obama's White House backed attack site "attackwatch.com" – a website that his administration advertised as a way to report on the untruths being spread by your friends and coworkers. It wasn't just Holder who was spending government money to pester conservatives in cyberspace.

119.Delayed Release of Food Stamp Usage Report

It is hard to argue that an economy is improving when the number of people getting food stamps is at a record high. News of America's rising food stamp dependency, coming right before Election Day, could have had a negative effect on President Obama as he fought hard for reelection in 2012. Of course, an honest government, working for the American people, would just release the data as scheduled and let the chips fall where they may. Not on Obama's watch.

Food stamp data is usually released around the end of the month. This means we should have received our last pre-election food stamp report around the end of October, but we didn't get it until November 10th, four days *after* the election.

It's pretty clear why the report was delayed. According to the report, food stamp usage had risen in the United States to a record high of 47.1 million people.[617] The American people didn't learn the full truth when they were supposed to, which meant Obama conveniently didn't have to answer new tough questions about his economic record before the election.

120.Delaying Regulations until After the Election

Incumbent presidents running for reelection have a special advantage over their opponent in that they have greater ability to influence current events and control the narrative of the election. In the 1997 movie "Wag the Dog," the President's spin-doctor enlists the help of a Hollywood producer to stage a fake war to distract the public from a sex scandal.

In 2012, the real-life Obama administration, in the spirit of the movie, "systematically delayed enacting a series of rules on the environment, worker safety, and healthcare to prevent them from becoming points of contention before the 2012 election."[618]

Naturally, the Obama administration denied any political motivation behind the delays, but was contradicted by seven current and former administration officials involved, and a report by Administrative Conference of the United States (ACUS), which found that internal reviews of proposed regulatory changes "took longer in 2011 and 2012 because of concerns about the agencies issuing costly or controversial rules prior to the November 2012 election."[619]

On the campaign trail, Obama proudly promoted Obamacare and questioned the motives of the law's opponents, all while regulations that specifically impacted health coverage, costs, and qualifications for subsidies were kept quiet. By waiting until after

Obama was safe from electoral consequences of his signature legislation to publish the final regulations, voters were denied the opportunity to know exactly how the law would affect them before they voted. This scandalous lie of omission by the Obama administration succeeded in giving him political cover in order to win a second term before millions of Americans would find out just how bad Obamacare really was.

121.Illegally Telling Companies to Postpone Layoffs Until after the Election

When running for reelection, it helps when bad news that could hurt your chances isn't reported until after the voters have already spoken. Desperate to hold onto power, Obama wasn't about to let bad news stand between him and four more years as the most powerful man on the planet, even if it meant breaking the law to do so.

A month before the presidential election, Virginia-based defense contractor Lockheed Martin announced that, in response to a White House request, they were delaying layoff notices until *after* the election. *ABC News* reported:

Lockheed, one of the biggest employers in the key battleground state of Virginia, previously warned it would have to issue notices to employees, required by law, due to looming defense cuts set to begin to take effect after Jan. 2 because of the failure of the Joint Select Committee on Deficit Reduction — the so-called Super-committee, which was created to find a way to cut $1.5 trillion from the federal deficit over the next decade.

Such massive layoffs could have threatened Obama's standing in the state he won in 2008 and is hoping to carry again this November.

On Friday, the Obama administration reiterated that federal contractors should not issue notices to workers based on "uncertainty" over the pending $500 billion reduction in Pentagon spending that will occur unless lawmakers can agree on a solution *to the budget impasse, negotiations over which will almost definitely not begin until after the election.*[620]

As *Breitbart's* Mike Flynn explained, the law requiring notices of layoffs was "passed in 1988 by a veto-proof Democrat Congress. It went into effect without President Reagan's signature. It was an urgent matter for Democrats, until, apparently, they didn't like the consequences of it."[621] The consequence of *violating* this federal law was more favorable, since Obama won Virginia by only 116,000 votes.[622]

122. Obama's 2010 Census Takeover

When he wasn't busy attempting to manipulate the twenty-four-hour news cycle with government power, Obama was busy trying to reorder the government to be more advantageous to progressives, even down to its most central functions. The decennial census of the United States is one of the few government actions actually commanded by our Constitution. Every ten years there is to be an enumeration of the people of the United States so that representation in our House of Representatives can be properly apportioned among the states. Given his record, it's hardly surprising that Obama tried to politicize this process.

Population shifts have resulted in increases in representation to states favoring Republicans and decreases in states favoring Democrats. For example, in 1980, New York (a blue state) had 41 electoral votes, and Texas (a red state) had 26 electoral votes. Today, Texas has 38, while New York only has 29 electoral votes.

Even the recent shift over the past decade shows a potential electoral problem for Democrat candidates. According to Michael Medved, "if the epic Bush-Gore battle of 2000 played out on the new Electoral College map, with the two candidates carrying precisely the states they each won 11 years ago, the result would have been a far more clear-cut GOP victory margin of 33 electoral votes (instead of the five-vote nail-biter recorded in history books)."[623]

While the census is apolitical, the results have political implications with regard to the redrawing of congressional districts, reapportionment, and the Electoral College.

So, why would Obama want the census to be moved from the Commerce Department to the White House, under the supervision of Obama's then-chief of staff, Rahm Emanuel? The results of the census play a significant role in the allocation of federal funds, potentially enabling a political party to deliver a disproportionate amount of tax dollars to areas represented by members of their own party.[624] The White House was not forthcoming about what Emanuel's role in overseeing the census would be, but the conflict of interest was clear:

> [...] critics say the White House chief of staff can't be expected to handle the census in a neutral manner. Emanuel ran the Democratic Congressional Campaign Committee in the 2006 election, and he was instrumental in getting Democrats elected into the majority. [625]

According to reports, the census, under the supervision of the White House, sought to reach out to gays and lesbians, in order to tally the number of same-sex marriages. Same-sex couples in states where same-sex marriage was not, then, legal were even advised to consider themselves married on the census form.[626] There were also efforts to get as many illegal immigrants as possible to participate in the census.[627] These manipulations of the numbers would be convenient for Obama's domestic agenda.

The census also provided Obama with another opportunity to boost the country's employment numbers during a very politically convenient time for him. Census workers reportedly were directed to slow down and extend their work unnecessarily.[628]

123.Sestak Job Offer Scandal

If that wasn't bad enough for you, Obama also attempted to manipulate the election process itself. When Senator Arlen Specter sought re-election to the United States Senate in 2010 as a Democrat, Congressman Joe Sestak felt compelled to challenge Specter for the Democratic nomination, thinking that the Democratic Party's best interests weren't served by having a recent convert to their party in the U.S. Senate.

Apparently, the Obama administration felt that Specter's chances of being reelected were better. According to Sestak, he was approached by a White House official with an offer for a high-ranking job in exchange for dropping out of the race. The White House eventually admitted that they had former President Bill Clinton approach Sestak with the job offer.[629] The White House claimed it did nothing wrong, and that no laws were violated. But, according to 18 U.S.C. § 600, the job offer was absolutely illegal. The Heritage Foundation explains:

The statute makes it unlawful for anyone to "promise any employment, position, compensation, contract, appointment, or other benefit" to any person as a "consideration, favor, or reward for any political activity or for the support of or opposition to any candidate or any political party...in connection with any primary election." As the OLC opinion says, § 600 "punishes those who promise federal employment or benefits as an enticement to or reward for future political activity, but does not prohibit rewards for past political activity." Future political activity would arguably include dropping out of a contested primary in order to benefit the White House-endorsed candidate (here, Sen. Specter).[630]

Further, 18 U.S.C. § 211 states that "whoever solicits or receives" such an offer shall be fined and/or imprisoned for no more than a year.[631] Sestak (who ultimately won the Democratic primary, but lost the general election to Republican Pat Toomey) may not have accepted the offer, but Bill Clinton, at the urging of the Obama administration, did break the law. And if Obama ordered the offer to be made, it would be an impeachable offense.

Of course, Obama's Justice Department rejected a request by Congressman Darrell Issa (R-CA) for a special counsel to investigate, and the scandal was effectively swept under the rug.[632] No one in the Obama administration was ever held accountable for breaking the law.

124.Obama's Tax Cheats

So we know that Obama thought that the electoral process was his to game as he pleased, but how else did he give cover and support to his political allies? We can begin by marveling at the safe haven that his White House gave to tax code violators. Even though Obama says he wants the rich to pay "their fair share" of taxes, he made a habit of nominating tax cheats to serve in his administration, and then stuck by them when the truth of their tax evasions came out.

After Obama nominated Timothy Geithner to be his Treasury Secretary, it was revealed that Geithner failed to pay payroll taxes over a number of years on income he made working for the International Monetary Fund. He called the omissions careless, even though he had been made aware, at the time, that he was responsible for paying those taxes. During his confirmation hearings, Geithner blamed TurboTax software for his failure to pay those taxes. Geithner would end up paying $42,702 in back taxes.[633]

Obama originally nominated Tom Daschle to be his Health & Human Services Secretary. But, Daschle was forced to drop out after it was revealed that he failed to pay over $100,000 in income taxes. Kathleen Sebelius was then nominated for the position. Shortly after she testified before the Senate Health, Education, Labor, and Pensions Committee, it was revealed she owed over $7,000 in back taxes.[634] The confirmation vote for Hilda Solis to be Obama's Labor Secretary had to be postponed after it was revealed that her husband had just paid $6,400 in tax liens from sixteen years before.[635] Nancy Killefer had to withdraw her nomination to be Obama's Performance Czar after it was revealed she had a nearly $1,000 lien on her property for failing to pay property taxes in 2005.[636]

It would be natural to think that President Obama – who is forever demanding we tax "the rich" - would at least ensure that all of his people are square with the tax man. Natural, but not accurate. In early 2012, it was revealed that thirty-six Obama aides owed $833,000 in back taxes.[637]

But he didn't just employ his tax-evading allies, he fed private citizens with bad tax records using stimulus grants. Perhaps even more shocking than the program's inability to stimulate the economy is the tax money that was given to people who were tax cheats. By law, tax cheats were not eligible to receive any money from the government's mortgage insurance program. But, the Federal Housing Administration (FHA) had no means to determine which applicants owed back taxes and should have their applications denied. In the end, $1.4 billion in stimulus loans and $27 million in tax credits were given to tax delinquents.[638]

125.Partisan Cover

As Americans, we believe in the idea that, in the eyes of the law, we should be equal. In fact, it is clearly stated in the Constitution that the President shall see to it that the laws are faithfully enforced. Not just some laws; not just the laws the President likes but all the laws, all the time and with complete impartiality. Sadly, under Barack Obama, justice has been far from blind... in fact, it has, at times, been overtly partisan. That partisanship revealed itself two ways: through selectively ignoring valid cases for prosecution, and by selectively targeting political enemies for prosecution.

In 2009, Obama's Justice Department, led by Attorney General Eric Holder, made the controversial decision to drop the voter intimidation case against the New Black Panther Party (NBPP) that had begun under the Bush Administration. On

Election Day in 2008, NBPP members were videotaped wearing paramilitary clothing and carrying clubs in front of polling places, intimidating potential voters from entering polls. The Obama administration refused to explain the refusal to prosecute, and this blatant violation of civil rights went unpunished.[639] By the summer of 2010, the U.S. Commission on Civil Rights declared that there was evidence of "possible unequal administration of justice" by the Justice Department.[640] Holder denied there was a racial motivation during a House Appropriations subcommittee hearing in March 2011, justifying the decision to not prosecute by citing the roadblocks African American endured when trying to vote 50 years prior in the South.[641] In short, he made the case that there was no racial bias by invoking a racial motive.

Along with selective enforcement of the law, Obama has also used the Justice Department to protect his political allies from criminal and ethical probes that would likely have resulted in convictions or at least bad press for Obama allies.

When Harry Reid was still Senate Majority Leader, and had the power to obstruct any legislation that came from the Republican-controlled House, or amendments that originated in the Senate that didn't conform to Obama's agenda, Obama prevented a federal investigation of a corruption probe that implicated Harry Reid as one of two U.S. Senators who may have taken money and benefits from political donors in return for political favors.[642]

During the Fast and Furious investigation in 2012, Obama protected Attorney General Eric Holder by asserting executive privilege (for the first time in his presidency) over thousands of requested documents just before the House Oversight and Government Affairs Committee was expected to vote to hold Holder in contempt for withholding those documents from the committee.[643]

Later that year, Obama's Department of Homeland Security also requested that Immigration and Customs Enforcement (ICE) delay the arrest of a campaign intern of Senator Robert Menendez (D-NJ) until after the 2012 elections, when

Menendez was up for re-election, saving him from a potentially damaging pre-election scandal.[644]

Obama's Justice Department did not see fit to investigate New York City's Sanitation Department after whistleblowers revealed that union bosses ordered drivers to botch snow cleanup after a major blizzard in 2010 in order protest budget cuts.[645] Nor was there a federal investigation started after the new mayor Bill de Blasio was accused, by residents of the affluent Upper East Side of Manhattan, of deliberately leaving the neighborhood unplowed as retribution for not supporting him.[646] We wouldn't ordinarily expect there to be a federal investigation for a city scandal under normal circumstances, but, as you'll see shortly, Holder's Department of Justice made a long habit out of pursuing political adversaries that were involved in local or personal imbroglios that should never have involved the feds either.

But none of the above obfuscations of justices compares in audacity with the lengths to which Obama and his surrogates have gone to defend his heir apparent, Hillary, Rodham Clinton. In March of 2015, the New York Times reported that Hillary Clinton may have broken several serious federal laws by maintaining a private email server during and after her time with the State Department and failing to turn over all of those records properly at the close of her tenure.[647] As the weeks and months unfolded, Clinton passed through several excuses. First, she claimed that she did nothing improper. Then she called her decision to host her own emails while on the job a mistake, but repeated her claim that she'd sent no classified information with that email. Then she claimed that no messages marked as classified at the time were sent passed through that email when they discovered classified material in her released and heavily redacted email set. Then her aides and the media rallied around a shaky defense that she did nothing different than former Secretary of state Colin Powell. Finally, she fell back on amnesia, saying that she was unaware that what she was doing was against the rules even though the rules are explained to all personnel in great detail when they obtain security clearance.[648] All the while, Clinton campaigned for the Democratic nomination for President with much media fanfare and support from within the Obama administration.

As evidence mounted that Hillary had stored and transmitted classified and top secret information on her private email server, and that emails were deliberately erased to avoid accountability, the Obama administration has done what it can to protect her, and perhaps himself right along with her. Even though Obama had previously claimed to have been unaware that Hillary was using a private email server, Obama and Hillary exchanged at least 18 emails that the State Department refused to release.[649] Obama's Justice Department is not cooperating, rendering the FBI investigation virtually impotent. According to Andrew McCarthy at *National Review,* "The FBI routinely conducts major investigations in collaboration with Justice Department prosecutors — usually from the U.S. attorney's office in the district where potential crimes occurred. That is because the FBI needs the assistance of a grand jury. The FBI does not have authority even to issue subpoenas, let alone to charge someone with a crime. Only federal prosecutors may issue subpoenas, on the lawful authority of the grand jury. Only prosecutors are empowered to present evidence or propose charges to the grand jury. And the Constitution vests only the grand jury with authority to indict — the formal accusation of a crime. In our system, the FBI can do none of these things."[650]

Obama's State Department has also done its part to protect Hillary. In March of 2016, it was revealed they would put off completing their review of classified information on Clinton's secret email server until *after* the election in November.[651] A month later, the State Department admitted that a key Benghazi email of Hillary's was withheld from watchdog group Judicial Watch since 2014. The disclosure of the email would have exposed Hillary's private server before Hillary had thousands of her emails deleted.[652] This pattern of protection Obama's allies received extended to dozens of other administration operatives involved in multiple other scandals too numerous to list here, though a few of them will be highlighted below. But what of the second method of engaging in corrupt, partisan justice?

126.Partisan Prosecution

When not selectively enforcing the laws or giving his friends a pass from law-breaking, Obama has also has used the Justice Department to target his political enemies. Senator Menendez learned this the hard way when, in 2015, the Department of Justice suddenly decided to move forward with criminal charges against Menendez on a five-year-old case. Washington D.C. insiders believe the decision was politically motivated, as Menendez had been speaking out against Obama in recent months on foreign policy matters like Obama's plan to normalize relations with communist Cuba, and his nuclear deal with Iran.[653]

Given Obama's willingness to use his law enforcement powers to punish his fellow Democrats who step out of line, it is no surprise that Republican critics of Obama have also been in the crosshairs. In 2014, when staffers and political appointees of New Jersey Governor Chris Christie were accused of closing toll lanes in order to cause a major traffic jam on the George Washington Bridge as political retaliation against the Democratic Mayor of Fort Lee, New Jersey, it received immediate national attention… not just by the media, but by the Obama administration, which quickly started a federal investigation.[654] He was eventually cleared, but "Bridgegate" dogged him even unto his 2016 presidential campaign.

In January of 2014, Dinesh D'Souza, the conservative author and speaker who has written books critical of Obama, and produced the widely popular anti-Obama documentary *2016: Obama's America*, was indicted for campaign finance violations for having orchestrated $20,000 in straw donations to the campaign of a friend who ran for U.S. Senate.[655] The motivations behind the indictment weren't merely questioned by conservatives, but by liberals and legal experts as well.

Legal experts slammed the Obama administration for what appeared to be a partisan selective prosecution. Harvard Law School professor and Obama supporter Alan Dershowitz said, in an interview with *Newsmax*, "This is an outrageous prosecution and is certainly a misuse of resources. It raises the question of why he is being selected for prosecution among the many, many people who commit similar crimes." Dershowitz also believes that the indictment came from high up in the Obama administration. "This sounds to me like it is coming from higher places. It is hard for me to believe this did not come out of Washington or at least get the approval of those in Washington," he said.[656]

National Review's Andrew McCarthy also noted that the Obama administration was effectively prosecuting D'Souza twice for the same crime by charging him with making illegal donations and making false statements to the government, in order to maximize his punishment. According to McCarthy, "by gratuitously piling on another felony, Obama and Holder portray D'Souza as a serious crook and subject him to the onerous potential of seven years in prison — all for an episode that ordinarily would not be prosecuted at all."[657]

Unfortunately, D'Souza was the not the only conservative activist that Obama targeted for selective harassment. James O'Keefe, founder of the undercover journalism outfit known as Project Veritas, has long been an outspoken opponent of open-border immigration policies and videotaped himself, dressed as a terrorist, crossing from the United States to Mexico, and reentering the country unchecked, as a part of a video series on the complete lack of security along the U.S. – Mexico border and the risks that it poses. The video went viral and fueled Tea Party-backed demands to scuttle all talk of further discussion of any immigration reform bill in 2014. The border crossing was, technically, illegal, however. US Customs officers were quick to detain O'Keefe and, incredibly, place him on a terrorism watch-list that exposed him to intense scrutiny each time he traveled internationally. If this seems a bit excessive to you... brace yourselves. It's going to get a lot worse as you read on.

The way Obama has pulled the blindfold off of Lady Justice should be troubling to all Americans. If a president thinks he can choose the winners and losers to suit his political needs, then equal protection under the law no longer exists.

127.Illegal Firing of an Inspector General

When Gerald Walpin, the Inspector General of the Corporation for National and Community Service, was abruptly fired by Barack Obama in mid-2009, it raised many questions. Walpin, a Republican who had been appointed to the position by President George W. Bush, had a long and distinguished career devoid of partisanship.

As it turns out, the firing was illegal. According to the 2008 Inspector General Reform Act (a bill then-Senator Barack Obama co-sponsored), Walpin was entitled to 30-days' notice and a written explanation to Congress for the dismissal. Neither was provided.[658] Walpin was informed of his firing by a phone call from the White House counsel's office, and was given an hour to resign or be fired.[659]

Naturally, one can't help but be curious as to why Obama would want to remove Walpin so quickly, in violation of a law Obama himself co-sponsored. Well, Walpin had been investigating the misuse of AmeriCorps grant money by St. HOPE, a nonprofit organization of Sacramento Mayor Kevin Johnson, the former NBA star and a friend and supporter of Obama's. Walpin's investigation exposed an apparent cover-up of sexual abuse accusations against Johnson, and he subsequently pressed for Johnson's criminal prosecution.[660] Walpin was fired before he could report his findings, and Johnson was offered a deal by the White House to avoid prosecution. The White House then began a smear campaign against Walpin.[661]

128.Refusal to Punish Sebelius for Breaking the Law

And, of course, when the buck stopped at Obama's desk regarding the meting out of discipline for a cabinet member who broke the law, Obama opted to take no action at all. On February 25, 2012, Health and Human Services Secretary Kathleen Sebelius publicly endorsed Barack Obama for reelection during a taxpayer-funded event. Her political position wasn't surprising, but, by making a partisan political remark at such an event in her official capacity as a member of the Cabinet, she was in violation of the Hatch Act of 1939. The Hatch Act prohibits federal employees from engaging in partisan political activity.

Less than two months before the presidential election, the Office of Special Counsel (OSC) issued a report that found that Sebelius was indeed in violation of the Hatch Act. Matthew Boyle, an investigative reporter at *The Daily Caller,* said such a violation "normally results in the offender's termination from government employment," and suggested that the Obama White House was offering special treatment to Secretary Sebelius.[662]

According to the OSC report, Sebelius was very much aware of the Hatch Act when she made her violation.

Secretary Sebelius stated that she knew that the Hatch Act restricts political speech during official events. She was given written materials after her initial ethics briefing in 2009 (which included material on the Hatch Act), received trainings and updates at least once a year that included information about the Hatch Act, and received copies of Hatch Act reminders that HHS sent to employees via email. In addition, through her Chief of Staff, the Secretary received White House memoranda that discussed the Hatch Act. Secretary Sebelius stated that she knew at the time of the HRC appearance that when speaking in her official capacity she could not encourage attendees to vote for particular candidates. Subsequent to the HRC speech, the Secretary stated that she sought additional guidance regarding her obligations under the Hatch Act.[663]

According to the OSC, "An employee who violates the Hatch Act shall be removed from their position, and funds appropriated for the position from which removed thereafter may not be used to pay the employee or individual."[664] Of course, Obama never fired her for breaking the law. She resigned in 2014 soon after Obamacare's open enrollment period ended. This was an opportunity for Obama to show that he had little tolerance for lapses in ethics – the sort of character he claimed to possess that George W. Bush did not – and he declined.

129. The Pigford Scandal

There's one other way to use the power of government to give aid to your allies. You can make it easier for them to sup at the government money trough. *Pigford v. Glickman* was a 1997 lawsuit that alleged that the United States Department of Agriculture (USDA) had discriminated against 91 African-American farmers by denying them loans. The farmers won the case and each were to be paid $50,000 from a judgement fund originally set at $120 million. Over time, the number claimants subsequently grew to the thousands.

Fraudulent *Pigford* claims didn't start under Obama, but he did everything in his power, starting from his days as a U.S. Senator, to use it to his advantage in what would become a huge taxpayer-funded vote-buying scheme costing billions.[665]

In 2010, the Obama administration increased the judgement fund another $1.15 billion, clearly expecting a huge influx of new filers, and potential votes that could be bought. The Obama administration was instrumental in expanding *Pigford* settlements to include Hispanic, Native American, and women farmers who claimed discrimination—groups he needed support from in order win reelection.

With Obama and Attorney General Eric Holder managing the *Pigford* judgement fund, the number of discrimination claimants exploded even further, most not needing any evidence to make their claim or receive a payout. Boiled down, the Obama administration set up a system in 2012 which allowed anyone (of the right ethnic group or gender, of course) to make a *Pigford* claim even if they'd never farmed before, or had no evidence of having been discriminated against by the government.[666]

The *New York Times* exposed evidence of all sorts of fraudulent claims, including multiple claims by the individual, claims on behalf of children, and claims made by people on behalf of the deceased.[667]

If that wasn't bad enough, the Obama administration went so far as to remind thousands of people to submit their claims before time ran out.[668] Thanks to the efforts of the Obama administration, the cost of *Pigford* payouts exploded to $4.4 billion,[669] and all we got for it was another four years of Obama in the White House.

130. Federal Energy Loan Scandal

Where this government feeding trough really becomes problematic, though, is when it leads directly to incompetence or the mishandling of taxpayer funds simply because money was awarded based on political favoritism, rather than qualification or viability. And that brings us to the utter incompetence of the Obama administration. The next few entries will be dedicated to documenting the ineptitude of government service on Obama's watch. We assure you, this will not be an exhaustive list since, if we were to attempt that, we would need to write an entirely new book on the subject. Let's begin with Obama's green economy.

To propel us towards a "green energy" future, Obama used federal loans as carrots for development. The trouble was that those carrots were given out in a highly politicized process that produced abysmal results as a direct result of Obama's meddling. The 2009 Stimulus earmarked $80 billion to be used for clean energy loans, grants, and tax credits. On October 31, 2012, previously undisclosed emails revealed that the White House pressured Department of Energy officials into approving many of these government loans.

The emails, made public by the House Oversight and Government Reform Committee, showed personal involvement by President Barack Obama and Vice President Joe Biden. Obama had claimed, in a television interview less than a week earlier, that the decisions on the loans had been made by the Department of Energy, and were not influenced by politics. The emails also revealed that loan money was used to help Senator Harry Reid's 2010 reelection campaign.

A May 2010 email shows that Reid requested a meeting with Jonathan Silver — the Obama bundler who resigned his post at DOE after the Solyndra bankruptcy — to discuss green energy projects in Nevada.

Silver interpreted Reid's request in light of the campaign. "Reid is constantly hit at home for not bringing in the federal dollars," he wrote. Silver's task, according to the DOE memo prepared for his meeting, was to assure Reid that "we anticipate a good number of projects to be approved in the coming months."

The House Oversight and Government Reform Committee notes that "throughout 2010 LPO emails indicate that projects in Nevada were prioritized because they were 'high profile,' 'tied to larger events,' or because they had Senator Reid's support." [670]

Officials at the Department of Energy were concerned that Obama's personal involvement was putting taxpayer dollars at risk. Still, that didn't stop Obama from repeatedly claiming that the process was not politicized. One lawsuit against the DOE, filed in January of 2013, alleges that, not only were these loans granted to donors of Obama and other Democrats, but the DOE transferred proprietary technology from these companies and handed it off to the Obama cronies who were awarded the loans.[671] But, the loans weren't just politicized; they were also extremely bad investments. At least fifty Obama-backed clean energy companies went bankrupt or found themselves in major financial trouble. One such company was Solyndra.

Solyndra, a solar energy company, went bankrupt on September 6, 2011, and 1,100 workers were laid off. Solyndra received a $535 million DOE loan in 2009 that had been advocated by the White House, despite concerns by the DOE that the company was on track to go belly up.[672] Why would the White House push for a loan of more than half a billion dollars to a start-up that DOE officials knew was heading towards bankruptcy? Solyndra employees were Democratic donors, and one of Solyndra's largest investors, billionaire George Kaiser, had been a campaign fundraiser for Obama in 2008.[673]

Like so many other things, the Obama administration tried to blame the Bush Administration for the failed Solyndra loan.[674] Solyndra had applied for government loans as early as 2007, but the Bush Administration actually denied their loan request two weeks before Obama took office.

131.Stimulus Jobs Saved or Created in Phantom Districts

But there's more regarding the stimulus! Despite a weak economy still suffering from high unemployment, Obama argued that his 2009 Stimulus worked. Regularly referring to jobs "saved or created" by the stimulus, Obama painted a picture of himself as the man who single-handedly saved our economy. To help document the success of the stimulus, a government website, recovery.gov, was set up as part of the stimulus bill. This site tracked how and where the stimulus money was spent, and how many jobs were "saved or created."

There was, however, a major problem. The website was reporting on money spent and jobs "saved or created" in congressional districts that did not exist.[675] According to Watchdog.org, there were 440 non-existent congressional districts that received $6.4 billion in stimulus funds, to "create or save" nearly 30,000 jobs.[676] There were other problems with the website as well: According to recovery.gov, a single lawn mower purchased with stimulus funds to cut grass at an Arkansas cemetery "saved or created" fifty jobs. *Really?*

Despite the absurdity of the data, the Obama administration had been using the recovery.gov stats to prove that the stimulus bill was a success. Stimulus recipients were blamed for input errors, but the site could have easily been designed to prevent inaccurate data from being inputted, a feature the Obama administration apparently didn't think was necessary.[677]

There were also questions about how stimulus money recipients can know how many jobs were "saved or created" because of the money they received. Instead of being a beacon of government transparency, recovery.gov became a huge database of faulty data used by the White House to overstate the success of the stimulus bill.

132. The OPM Hack

The Office of Personnel Management (OPM) may sound like a government agency so dull that no one should care about it, but it is an agency every American should be aware of. OPM, as its name implies, is responsible for managing the personnel of the United States government but more importantly is also stores a great deal of highly sensitive, personal information on government employees and, in some cases, their families. This information is gathered and retained in order to provide the basis of employee security clearances. In short, what OPM has in its database is precisely the sort of information two different sorts of people would love to have: those who in engage in identity theft and those engaged in espionage against the United States. This information should be provided the highest possible security by our government. But this is the Obama administration and so, naturally, the information at OPM was hacked by Chinese operatives.

In typical Obama administration fashion, when the story first broke in June of 2015, it was claimed that about four million people were affected.[678] A month after the story first broke, the figure had been revised upward to thirty-two million Americans whose personal information were stolen by China.[679]

How was the hack done? Surely it was the work of a specialized group of super-hackers who had to work desperately for years to crack our security, right? Wrong. OPM hired contractors to manage their security and some of the people working for the contractors were, incredibly, physically located within the borders of the People's Republic of China.[680] These contractors had access to every line of data in OPM's system. All the Chinese government had to do - if they weren't the actual contractors hired in the first place - was just ask their own citizens to give up the data.

Naturally, Obama's administration tried to claim that the hack was discovered during their aggressive and effective attempts to beef up cyber-security. Just as naturally, that claim was false. The reality is that the hack was only discovered by chance.[681] No one yet knows precisely how long the hackers had access to our data, but it appears long enough for them to get everything they wanted.

As it turns out, this hack wasn't a surprise. As early as 2010, U.S. intelligence agencies were expressing concerns about OPM's cyber-security. So much concern was, in fact, expressed that the intelligence agencies didn't want their personnel records merged with those held by OPM, fearing that, if hackers could get into one part of the database, they could then use that ability to crack the security in other parts. Eventually, the merge of information was apparently carried out, in spite of security fears. Michael Adams, who spent decades working for U.S. Special Operations Command said, "Based on my understanding of U.S. government databases and networks, as well as recent conversations with U.S. government officials, I have high confidence that the agencies do not have a clear understanding of the architecture of their systems and how they're interconnected."[682] In short, those who know believe that our government hasn't a clue about cyber security.

Given the nature of the hack and what it involves, it will be many long years before we, the American people, are fully advised of how bad it was. One thing we do know is that, already, victims of this hack are getting fake emails designed to fool them into giving up even more information.[682]

How does something like this happen? According to Paul Conway, who served as Chief of Staff of OPM during the Bush Administration, it was "a devastating example of the poor personnel judgment exercised by President Obama" in appointing Katherine Archuleta as OPM director.[683] Archuleta, a political appointee, was grossly unqualified for the position. Archuleta, in turn, "ignored repeated written warnings from OPM Inspector General Patrick McFarland regarding the vulnerability to cyber attack of key personnel IT systems." Archuleta was eventually forced to resign, but, according to Obama's spokesman, she still had the confidence of the president.[684]

While Obama's failures are manifold over his term of office, there is something particularly outrageous about this one. The victims of this hack are just average, everyday Americans trying to do their jobs. Obama put the wrong person in charge of the agency, and the direct result of that mistake was largest breach of government data in America's history.

133.Politicizing FOIA

It's now time to move beyond incompetence, beyond electioneering, and beyond cronyism. Now we enter the realm of the scandalous. The thing that separates scandalous behavior from other forms of government mismanagement and abuse is that the bad actor knows that what they're doing is illegal, unethical, or inexcusable and does it anyway. There is an old joke that periodically makes the rounds on social media along the lines of: "Is he evil or incompetent? Why can't he be both?" These next several entries confirm that Obama and his cronies in Washington are indeed both.

The Freedom of Information Act (FOIA), as described by FOIA.gov, is a law that "gives you the right to access information from the federal government. It is often described as the law that keeps citizens in the know about their government." The Obama administration clearly only wants their political allies "in the know" because its compliance with the law is highly politicized. According to documents obtained by *PJ Media* in 2011, "FOIA requests from liberals or politically connected civil rights groups are often given same day turn-around by the DOJ. But requests from conservatives or Republicans face long delays, if they are fulfilled at all."[685]

This trend of politicizing continued unabated into Obama's second term. In 2013, it was revealed that Obama's EPA was waiving FOIA fees for environmental groups, but not conservative groups.[686] According to AP Washington Bureau Chief Sally Buzbee, the Obama administration uses FOIA requests "as a tip service to uncover what news organizations are pursuing. Requests are now routinely forwarded to political appointees. At the agency that oversees the new healthcare law, for example, political appointees now *handle* the FOIA requests."[687] Even political appointees in the Department of Homeland Security were handling FOIA requests, according to an investigation by the House Committee on Oversight and Government Reform.[688]

Obama claimed that he was committed to creating "an unprecedented level of openness" in government. Instead, we got an unprecedented level of partisanship in government, with selective "transparency" given only to those whom Obama considers political allies.

134. Obama's Scandal-plagued EPA

There were many scandals in the Obama administration, but one agency that has been constantly plagued by scandal and abuse of power is the Environmental Protection Agency (EPA), which became increasingly corrupt, politicized, thuggish and secretive under Obama.

Obama's EPA ruled, in December of 2009 (without any act of Congress), that carbon dioxide, the gas exhaled by human beings, was a pollutant that "may endanger public health or welfare," and thus subject to government regulation.[689] But this was just the beginning of Obama imposing his environmental agenda without congressional approval. After the 2010 midterm elections, when Republicans took back the House of Representatives, Obama hinted, during a press conference, that he was willing to bypass the newly divided Congress to impose even more environmental regulations via the EPA.[690]

The Environmental Protection Agency's philosophy of enforcement under Obama was described by Al Armendariz, a former EPA regional administrator, as "kind of like how the Romans used to conquer little villages in the Mediterranean: they'd go into little Turkish towns somewhere, they'd find the first five guys they'd run into, and they'd crucify them." As Armendariz explained it, "That town was really easy to manage for the next few years."[691] Armendariz also improperly colluded with left-wing activists to go after Range Resources, a Texas-based natural gas firm, for allegedly contaminating private water wells, despite there being no evidence. The EPA's Office of Inspector General would later cover up the fact that the EPA had violated its own policies to protect Armendariz and the agency's new oppressive tactics.[692]

Given this, it's hardly surprising that, in November of 2012, after the presidential election, it was revealed that Obama's EPA Administrator Lisa Jackson was illegally using several secret alias email accounts to conduct official business, in order to avoid potential exposure and scrutiny of the EPAs activities via FOIA requests.[693] One such email account used by Jackson to thwart transparency laws was for the fictional Richard Windsor. Jackson's efforts into creating this fake identity for Richard Windsor were so extensive that EPA records indicated he was awarded certificates for completing various training courses required by the agency, and Windsor was even awarded the "scholar of ethical behavior" three years in a row from 2010 through 2012.[694] Jackson announced her resignation soon after these allegations surfaced.[695]

The scandals involving Obama's EPA didn't end there. In May of 2013, on the heels of the scandal involving the IRS illegally targeting conservative groups during the 2012 election cycle, it was also revealed that the Environmental Protection Agency was giving preferential treatment to environmental groups over conservative groups attempting to obtain government records under the Freedom of Information Act (FOIA). According to the Competitive Enterprise Institute, of the 82 FOIA requests made by environmental groups, 92 percent, were granted fee waivers, while of the 26 requests made by conservative groups, 81 percent were *rejected*— effectively stopping the requests.[696] As if that wasn't enough, the EPA took a page out of the IRS' playbook and illegally leaked the personal information of over 80,000 private farms and ranches to various left-wing environmental groups, which prompted a bipartisan group of senators to demand answers, not only about why this private information was released, but also why it had been collected in the first place.[697]

It's clear, given the stained record of the EPA on Obama's watch, that he has turned the Environmental Protection Agency into a device for enforcing his radical environmental agenda without congressional approval or oversight.

135.Testing Deadly Pollutants on Americans

One of the most shameful episodes in American history was the so-called Tuskegee Syphilis Study (1932-1972) where African-Americans, who thought they were getting free treatment for syphilis from the United States government, were actually left untreated so that doctors could study the natural progression of the disease.[698] The infamous study resulted in the establishment of the Office of Human Research Protections (OHRP) and new laws and regulations to protect people involved in studies involving human subjects. Unfortunately, protecting human subjects has since taken a back seat to Obama's political agenda. This event stands as the icing on the poison cake that is the EPA under Obama.

According to a report obtained by the *Daily Caller* on the Environmental Protection Agency's particulate matter experiments, it was revealed that the EPA exposed people with health problems to particulate matter 50 times above what the EPA recommends as safe, and did this without fully informing all the participants of what they were being exposed to and the possible risks involved.[699] As the EPA director put it in 2011, "particulate matter causes premature death. It doesn't make you sick. It's directly causal to dying sooner than you should." Despite this, Obama's EPA sought out Americans with underlying health problems and lured them into the experiments with promises of payment.[700] In addition to particulate matter, subjects were exposed to diesel exhaust and ozone. This gross irresponsibility on the part of the EPA is just astounding.

So, why would the Obama administration deliberately expose American citizens to substances they knew could kill them? They sought to justify more stringent clean air regulations, as the EPA has long asserted that particulate matter is deadly.[701]

To complete the horror of the Obama administration's actions, Obama's EPA defended the study by claiming "the exposure risk for healthy individuals is minimal."[702] Even if this didn't contradict previous statements made by the EPA, the people being used as test subjects were not healthy individuals. Apparently, the risk of death by particulate matter depends on the political convenience of the Obama administration, which sees nothing wrong with using American citizens as expendable guinea pigs to advance its agenda.

136.The Veterans Affairs Scandal

There is no one in America who is owed more than our veterans, especially those who have been injured in connection with their service. Obama promised to end the horrendous backlog in Veteran's Administration benefit claims (some claims can languish for years without resolution) and promised that he would be a President who would fight for veterans, "every hour of every day."[703]

Unfortunately, the backlog of VA claims has increased massively on Obama's watch, with unprocessed claims often exceeding 900,000, and around two-thirds of all claims backed up more than 125 days.[704] The length of time for claims to be processed was an average 272 days in 2013, up 40 percent from 2011.[705] The number of veterans who die waiting for care and benefits has also skyrocketed on Obama's watch.[706] The surge in claims resulting from aged Vietnam veterans, and the wars in Afghanistan and Iraq have gone unaddressed by the Obama administration.

It wasn't until April of 2014, when it was revealed that as many as 40 veterans in a VA hospital in Arizona had died while spending a long period on a hidden waiting list, that this issue started to gain the attention it deserved. Senior officials at the hospital deliberately tried to hide the fact that veterans were waiting long periods for care and that as many as 1,600 veterans were kept waiting for months for an appointment. Outraged, several Senators called for a full investigation into the fraud and mismanagement (and the resulting deaths) plaguing Veterans Affairs Hospitals.[707] Whistleblowers have since come forward alleging similar problems and deceptions at no less than seven other VA hospitals around the country.[708] Sadly, though not unexpectedly, Obama's Justice Department showed no interest in launching their own investigation.[709] Instead, whistleblowers have found themselves targets of retaliation by the agency.[710]

In response to the growing scandal, the Obama administration went into damage control mode with the resignation of a top Veterans Affairs official, Under Secretary for Health Robert Petzel. But it was an empty gesture, considering Petzel planned to retire in 2014 anyway. Even more insulting is that Obama's pick to replace Petzel, Dr. Jeffrey Murawsky, managed a VA hospital in Chicago that, at the time of this writing, is under investigation for keeping secret lists to conceal wait times for veterans seeking health care.[711]

Like with other scandals that have plagued his presidency, the White House claimed Obama was unaware of the problems in the Department of Veterans Affairs, allegedly learning about them "on the news" when the scandal exploded in May 2014.[712] But the truth is that, after winning his first election, Veterans Affairs officials informed his transition team of the problems in the department with veterans seeking care.[713] Obama had ample opportunity to work out a plan to improve the care of our veterans. But instead of making things better, as he pledged to do during his campaign, he moved on to his real priorities, yielding no action on behalf of veterans in need. According to an internal Veterans Affairs report, released in July 2015, nearly three years after the scandal broke, 238,647 veterans waiting for VA healthcare had died before receiving treatment.[714] This is far worse than a broken promise, this is a national disgrace, and a complete betrayal of the men and women who volunteered to serve our country.

137. Operation Fast and Furious

Project Gunrunner was a project of the Bureau of Alcohol, Tobacco, Firearms and Explosives (ATF) designed to track and interrupt the flow of American firearms to Mexican drug cartels. Operations began under the Bush Administration and were continued under the Obama administration. Operation Fast and Furious (2009-2011) was the largest gunwalking operation under the project, delivering roughly 2,000 firearms across the border. But, the operation was seriously compromised; the ATF lost track of hundreds of firearms, and an unknown number of these firearms would later be linked to various crimes, including the murder of U.S. Border Patrol Agent, Brian Terry.[715] The Mexican government claims that at least one hundred and fifty Mexicans have been killed or wounded with "Fast and Furious" weapons and that not a single cartel leader has been caught using one.[716]

Naturally, the Obama administration tried to cover it up. They even tried blaming President Bush for the operation, even though Operation Fast and Furious started nine months into Obama's term.[717] Attorney General Eric Holder even claimed to have no knowledge of the operation. When a congressional investigation took place, Obama asserted executive privilege and refused to provide any documents about it, resulting in an historic vote by Congress to hold the Attorney General in contempt, which passed with bipartisan support.[718]

The first congressional report on the investigation released in July of 2012 faulted five ATF employees for the botched operation.[719] The Justice Department claimed vindication; but a second report, released at the end of October, found several failures of the Justice Department as well.[720] A third report on the Justice Department's obstruction of the investigation has yet to be completed.

Over a hundred people, including Border Patrol Agent Brian Terry, were murdered with firearms provided by the U.S. Government. Obama and Holder have not only lied about the operation, but have done whatever they can to stonewall the investigation. So much for transparency.

138.The IRS Scandal and Cover-Up

On May 10, 2013, the former Director of the IRS Exempt Organizations division, Lois Lerner, revealed, during an American Bar Association meeting, that Tea Party and other conservative groups had been improperly scrutinized by the IRS between 2010 and 2012.[721] Ms. Lerner did this hoping to control the narrative about the brewing scandal (an Inspector General report on the matter was about to be made public) but outrage immediately followed. A huge scandal was now born.

The Obama administration was forced into damage control mode, and quickly blamed rogue "low-level" employees in one office for targeting the conservative groups. But, it was later revealed that twelve different IRS offices across the country had targeted conservative groups in the two-year period leading up to the 2012 election.[722] There was also evidence of White House involvement. One IRS employee testified that the directive to target Tea Party groups came from Washington, D.C.[723] Proof of this came in May of 2014, following the release of IRS documents pursuant to a FOIA request by Judicial Watch. These documents showed that the DC headquarters of the IRS orchestrated the crackdown on Tea Party groups. The documents also showed that top IRS officials were strongly urged by Democrat Senator Carl Levin to go after the Tea Party.[724]

Some IRS employees even said that they believed that Obama wanted a crackdown on Tea Party groups.[725] IRS Commissioner Douglas Shulman was at the White House at least 157 times while the IRS targeting was ongoing. That's more visits than any of Obama's Cabinet members.[726] Emails obtained by the House Oversight and Government Reform Committee also revealed that the IRS exchanged confidential taxpayer information with the White House in 2012.[727]

According to the Treasury Department's Inspector General, two hundred ninety-two Tea Party groups were targeted by the IRS, compared with only 6 liberal groups that were similarly scrutinized.[728] But none of those liberal groups were given the same scrutiny as any Tea Party group.[729] According to the House Committee on Oversight and Government Reform, ten percent of Tea Party donors were audited by the IRS—ten times higher than the average annual rate of Americans who are audited.[730] Two pro-life nonprofit groups were also denied tax-exempt status by the IRS. One of these groups, the Coalition for Life of Iowa, was told by an IRS agent that their application would only be approved if they signed a letter promising not to protest outside of Planned Parenthood, the nation's largest abortion provider which endorsed Obama both in 2008 and 2012.[731]

It appears that the IRS didn't just target conservative groups, but also private individuals who had been critical of Obama, GOP candidates, and Romney donors. Some examples include:

- Businessman and Romney SuperPAC donor Frank VanderSloot was audited twice by the IRS after appearing on the Obama reelection campaign "enemies list."[732]
- There was a suspicious audit of Eric Bolling, co-host of the Fox News Channel's The Five.[733]
- A major Romney fundraiser and her extended family were subjected to audits that, according to the agent, were the result of an "administration directive."[734]
- Former GOP Senate candidate Christine O'Donnell's private tax records were reportedly leaked.[735]
- Renowned neurosurgeon Dr. Ben Carson was audited after giving a speech critical of Obama while Obama was in attendance.[736] The White House had demanded an apology from Dr. Carson for offending the president, but he refused.[737]

As a result of congressional hearings, it was also discovered that the IRS covered up the scandal until after the 2012 election. When Barack Obama was asked about when he knew about it, he dodged the question.[738] An analysis by the American Enterprise Institute suggests that the IRS's actions may have influenced the results of the election.[739]

The Department of Justice promised their own investigation into the scandal. However, a year and a half later, Congress had not yet been briefed on the progress, and groups victimized by the IRS had not yet been interviewed—hardly surprising, considering that Barbara Bosserman, an Obama donor, had been secretly chosen by the Obama administration to lead the investigation.[740] In an additional attempt to delay the investigation, Congressional

Democrats demanded an investigation of the IRS Inspector General who had discovered the illegal activity.[741]

Jay Sekulow, chief counsel of the American Center for Law and Justice (ACLJ), said the appointment of Bosserman was disturbing, and "puts politics right in the middle of what is supposed to be an independent investigation to determine who is responsible for the Obama administration's unlawful targeting of conservative and tea party groups."[742] Of course, the Obama donor's sham investigation allegedly found no criminal activity by the IRS. The widespread targeting of conservative groups was instead absurdly blamed on "a mismanaged bureaucracy enforcing rules about tax-exemption applications it didn't understand," and announced, on January 13, 2014, that no criminal charges were expected to be filed.[743]

The Obama administration clearly has no interest in holding anyone accountable. In fact, they were so undeterred by the scandal that they not only felt they could hire an Obama partisan to run the investigation, but the IRS *continued* using similar tactics to target conservatives and conservative groups several months after the scandal:

- In November of 2013, a cancer patient, interviewed on Fox News about the cancellation of his health insurance policy due to Obamacare, was informed, soon after his appearance, that he was being audited.[744]

- During the Thanksgiving recess in 2013, the Obama administration quietly introduced new IRS rules governing nonprofits that many agree were designed to silence Tea Party groups before the 2014 midterm elections.[745]

- In January of 2014, the *New York Times* revealed that the IRS was reviewing the activities of Friends of Abe, the entertainment industry's only conservative group. The group's application for tax-exempt status had been under review for two years, and at one point, the IRS

demanded access to the group's membership list, which
is not normally required, according to tax experts.[746]

Naturally, Obama told Fox News' Bill O'Reilly that the scandal had "not even a smidgen of corruption."[747]

On March 11, 2014, the House Committee on Oversight and Government Reform issued a report indicating that Lois Lerner not only "created unprecedented roadblocks for Tea Party organizations" but that she had worked to advance Obama administration desires to curtail the activities of organizations critical of the President. According to emails obtained during the investigation, it was also clear that she gave false statements to the House Oversight committee during their investigation.[748] Emails uncovered during the investigation showed that Lerner gave confidential tax information on the anti-voter fraud group True The Vote to Democratic Congressman Elijah Cummings (the ranking Democrat on the House Ethics Committee, which is responsible for investigating the IRS), and that she colluded with Obama's Justice Department regarding possible prosecution of conservative tax-exempt groups.[749] Lerner's refusal to testify resulted in the House of Representatives voting to hold her in contempt.[750]

Then, in June of 2014, it was discovered that the IRS had "lost" two years' worth of Lerner's and other IRS officials' emails.[751] While the IRS blamed a crash of Lerner's hard drive for the lost emails, IRS regulations required Lerner to keep printed copies of her emails; and the IRS is now being as obscure as possible as to whether or not Lerner followed the rules on this matter.[752] The IRS also cancelled a contract with an email-storage contractor a few weeks after the potentially damaging emails were "lost."[753]

Despite all the evidence of illegal activity, and the blatant attempts to cover up the scandal with a phony internal investigation, all the evidence pointing to a large, tangled web of corruption, cover-ups, and abuse of power, Obama and his allies in the media have repeatedly tried to label this a phony scandal.[754] But the fact that the very heavy hand of the IRS has been used to harass and oppress Obama critics is downright frightening. What sort of America does Obama want? We don't want to find out.

Civil Liberties

If there was one place – one small slice of Obama's campaign agenda – where progressives and libertarians could find common cause in 2008, it was their common concerns regarding the decline of civil liberties under the George W. Bush administration. Republicans, under Bush, pushed for and passed the Patriot Act, a law that seriously increased the power of the executive branch and began the modern era of government spying and data mining. They engaged in some actions with suspected terrorists that made even Bush's staunchest supporters nervous: enhanced interrogation techniques, indefinite detention of potential combatants, broader wiretapping efforts, and the like. Bush asserted executive privilege to protect an ally of his from an investigation. The consensus in the media and among leftwing politicos was that Republicans in the Bush administration were doing enormous harm to our civil liberties in order to expand the power of the executive branch.

Obama campaigned as a Constitutional scholar who was alarmed at the overreach of Bush and his Republican allies. He painted himself as someone who would fiercely defend the Bill of Rights, roll back executive overreach, and return Washington to the sense of balance we felt that it had in the 1990s. His campaign was, to our chagrin, one big fantasy.

The Obama we got instead launched a full-on assault on the first, second, fourth, and tenth amendments, massively expanded the power of the executive branch, governed from the top down, and guaranteed that Washington would remain completely divided and dysfunctional. The real Obama was a scholar of the Constitution insomuch as he learned the best ways to warp it to suit his agenda. He expanded the abuses of the Bush administration against terrorism targets and extended them to American citizens. He criminalized his political opponents without good cause. In short, he ruled like a tyrant. And few seemed to notice.

We noticed.

This chapter is dedicated to our once-proud defense of civil liberties and to Obama's total failure to uphold them.

139. Punishing Anti-Islamic Speech

Is our right to free speech in jeopardy? Perhaps you should ask Nakoula Basseley Nakoula, the man behind the anti-Islamic video that the Obama administration tried to blame for inciting the attack on the U.S. consulate in Benghazi.

While it is now clear that the Obama administration knew al Qaeda was connected to the attacks early on, they made a strong effort to blame Nakoula's little-seen YouTube video "Innocence of Muslims" for inciting the violence. On September 12, 2012, Egyptian President Mohamed Morsi called on the U.S. government to arrest Nakoula. Three days later, he was brought in for questioning by federal authorities. He was arrested on September 28, 2012, for allegedly violating the conditions of his probation.[755]

Nakoula's arrest caused alarm for some who believe Nakoula was unfairly targeted so that the Obama administration could make an example of him.

"As someone who has had clients accused of violating conditions of probation, this is not standard operating procedure for these violations. It is relatively rare to see people incarcerated on relatively minor violations," said George Washington University law professor John Turley.

"There were great suspicions raised by the speed and intensity of investigation of the filmmaker. Many people viewed it as something of a pretext investigation," he said. "It seemed obvious

to many of us that the administration wanted a picture of this man being handcuffed and put in the back of a cruiser so it would play around the world and in the Arab street."[756]

The day after Obama was reelected, after spending months in jail without due process in violation of the Fifth Amendment to the Constitution, Nakoula was sentenced to spend a year in jail.[757] Those actually responsible for the attack on the consulate that killed four Americans have yet to be brought to justice.

140. The Gibson Guitar Raid

On August 24, 2011, armed federal agents raided the Gibson Guitar headquarters in Tennessee. They shut down production, sent employees home, and confiscated wood. Gibson was accused of illegally importing woods from India, but Gibson had not violated any American law. The Department of Justice was enforcing the laws of India, even though the Indian government approved the exports. According to Gibson, the government of India did not support or consent to the actions of the Justice Department.[758]

Gibson had fully complied with foreign laws, and the wood seized by the government conformed with industry-recognized, independent standards for "responsible management of the world's forests."[759] But that didn't stop the Obama administration from going after Gibson.

If the Justice Department's use of foreign laws to pressure and extort money from American businesses that have not broken any American laws isn't disturbing enough, there is evidence that the raid was politically motivated. Both C.F. Martin Guitars and Fender use wood from the same source as Gibson, but neither has been raided by the government, or forced to pay any fines. Martin and Fender both contribute money to Democrats. Gibson's CEO is a Republican donor.[760]

Regardless of the motive, the raid on Gibson fits a pattern of the Obama administration being openly hostile to non-union companies, or union companies that have moved their operations to right-to-work states.[761] In fact, Seattle's largest employer, Boeing, nearly lost an opportunity to expand into South Carolina – a right to work state – when the National Labor Relations Board voted to disallow the company's deal to construct a $2 billion manufacturing plant in the state. Obama's appointees to the NLRB were the difference in the vote.

In 2012, Gibson settled its case with the federal government for $300,000. This amounted to a forfeiture of $262,000 in seized wood and $50,000 in the form of a donation to promote the conservation of protected tree species.[762]

The wood was eventually returned to Gibson, who in turn made it into Government Series II Les Paul special edition guitars in a glorious act of defiance of the Obama administration.[763] Nevertheless, for breaking no laws and for having their fourth amendment rights violated, Gibson had the luxury of a lengthy legal battle and the loss of $50,000, shaken down to promote a left-wing cause. The moral of this story: be a conservative business owner at your own risk.

141.Indefinite Detentions of American Citizens

But let's spend some time analyzing Obama's management of the war on terror from the perspective of civil liberties. As a candidate, Obama spoke out against not just the indefinite detention of American citizens, but even against the indefinite detention of foreigners caught supporting terrorist groups. Obama promised that he would "restore" habeas corpus, the provision in American law that no one may be detained by the government without being formally charged with a crime.[764] The election of Obama to the Presidency was to be an end to the allegedly unconstitutional acts of President Bush. And, so, one would think that, when a federal judge ruled the provision for indefinite detention in the National Defense Authorization Act

(NDAA) to be unconstitutional, that would be the end of it. [765] Not quite.

As soon as that federal judge had ruled that indefinite detention was out of the NDAA, Obama administration attorneys filed for an emergency stay on the order, and got it.[765] That they got the order is no surprise: the courts are usually willing to give a lot of leeway on national security matters to the Executive branch, at least until a final ruling has been made. What is shocking is that Obama would seek an emergency stay on the order throwing out indefinite detention of American citizens. What does he want that power for when he campaigned against such tactics as a violation of the civil liberties of suspected terrorists?

142.Increase in Electronic Government Spying

Obama, like many Democrats, was a loud and vocal opponent of the Bush Administration's efforts to intercept communications between persons inside the United States and suspected terrorists overseas. According to them, this was a sinister attempt to eavesdrop on American citizens at random, and thus a gross violation of civil liberties. Alas, once Obama became president, he started to sing a different tune.

In 2010, the *New York Times* reported that the Obama administration wanted to make it easier for the government to monitor domestic internet communications.[766] According to the American Civil Liberties Union (ACLU), there has been a 64 percent growth in electronic spying by the United States government since Obama took office in 2009.[767]

In September of 2012, the Obama administration argued in federal court that the public has no "reasonable expectation of privacy" in cellphone location data, and that the government can obtain these records, which can detail a person's movements as recorded by wireless carriers, without a warrant.[768]

Further blemishing Obama's record on civil liberties, his Administration green-lighted a giant government database of information on millions of citizens, even ones not suspected of terrorism or any crime at all. The *Wall Street Journal* first reported on this in December 2012:

> *Top U.S. intelligence officials gathered in the White House Situation Room in March to debate a controversial proposal. Counterterrorism officials wanted to create a government dragnet, sweeping up millions of records about U.S. citizens—even people suspected of no crime.*
>
> *Not everyone was on board. "This is a sea change in the way that the government interacts with the general public," Mary Ellen Callahan, chief privacy officer of the Department of Homeland Security, argued in the meeting, according to people familiar with the discussions.*
>
> *A week later, the attorney general signed the changes into effect.[769]*

Why does Obama want to make it easier to read your email, or listen to your phone calls? For someone who once taught Constitutional law, he seems to be awfully ignorant of the Fourth Amendment.

143.Monitoring Credit Card Transactions

Every time you use your credit card, the Obama administration knows about it. According to documents obtained by Judicial Watch in 2013 via a Freedom of Information Act (FOIA) request, the Consumer Financial Protection Bureau "has spent millions of dollars for the warrantless collection and analysis of Americans' financial transactions."[770]

The Consumer Financial Protection Bureau (CFPB) was formed in 2011, as authorized by the Dodd–Frank Wall Street Reform and Consumer Protection Act of 2010. It was supposed to protect consumers from predatory lending practices, but, instead, it's following in the footsteps of Obama's National

Security Agency, and is treating all Americans like criminals without due process. According to a (CFPB) strategy document, the agency's goal is to monitor 80 percent of all credit card transactions—about 42 billion transactions a year, as well as 95 percent of mortgage transactions. But this never was the intention of the Dodd-Frank Act—which specifically prohibits the CFPB from collecting personally identifiable financial information on consumers.[771]

Given Obama's poor record on civil liberties, it's not surprising that an agency created for consumer protection actually became another agency of surveillance. Making this financial data mining even worse is the fact that Obama's CFPB Director, Richard Cordray, could not guarantee that the data being collected by the government was secure from fraud. The CFPB expects to collect 51 terabytes of financial information on the American people, or enough to fill up 50 public libraries, by 2017. Included in this data trove will be information on personal FICO credit scores, credit balances, and borrowers' income and payment history.[772] Of course, this is for our "protection." How exactly does the government monitoring our credit card transactions "protect" us?

144.Data Mining the American People

Even if you weren't an Obama supporter in 2012, depending on your online activity, you may have been flagged by his campaign as a potential voter, and unwittingly provided them with personal data. According to *Politico* in March of 2012:

Obama for America has already invested millions of dollars in sophisticated Internet messaging, marketing and fundraising efforts that rely on personal data sometimes offered up voluntarily — like posts on a Facebook page— but sometimes not.

And according to a campaign official and former Obama staffer, the campaign's Chicago-based headquarters has built a centralized digital database of information about millions of potential Obama voters.[773]

There was enough concern about this data-mining operation that Obama's campaign data director had to pen an op-ed denying any Orwellian intentions.[774] Ironically, Obama was doing this while talking up the need to protect the privacy of the American people on the internet.[775] He is clearly more interested in protecting his power than your privacy.

145. The NSA Scandal

As a U.S. Senator, Barack Obama was a critic of domestic surveillance, and even worked to pass legislation which would have seriously reigned in the power of the government to collect data on the American people without a specific reason.[776] His position on domestic surveillance did not change during his first campaign for president—he vowed to fight such things as a renewal of the Foreign Intelligence Surveillance Act (FISA).[777] But, once Obama reached the White House, his position "evolved" like it had for many other issues. Under President Obama, Bush-era programs to intercept intelligence about foreign enemies of the United States "evolved" into a massive data collection free-for-all which scoops up masses of information from just about everybody—without cause or a warrant.

In April 2013, a top secret FISA court order was made forcing Verizon to provide the National Security Agency (NSA) information on all calls on its systems. Not just calls between the United States and other countries, but domestic calls as well. The details of the secret order were leaked by former NSA contractor Edward Snowden and revealed by *The Guardian* in June 2013—a month after the IRS scandal broke.[778] Sources familiar with the NSA's operations told the *Wall Street Journal* that other telecom companies and internet service providers were also covered by the program.[779]

The surveillance program, called PRISM, was created in 2007, but experienced "exponential growth" under Obama, according to the *Washington Post*. This expansion changed surveillance practices "away from individual suspicion in favor of systematic, mass collection techniques."[780] Under the expanded PRISM program, the NSA and FBI were "tapping directly into the central servers" of Microsoft, Yahoo, Google, Facebook, PalTalk, AOL, Skype, YouTube, and Apple, "extracting audio and video chats, photographs, e-mails, documents, and connection logs that enable analysts to track foreign targets."[781]

Even the *New York Times* editorial board couldn't hold back criticism of Obama:

The government can easily collect phone records (including the actual content of those calls) on "known or suspected terrorists" without logging every call made. In fact, the Foreign Intelligence Surveillance Act was expanded in 2008 for that very purpose.

Essentially, the administration is saying that without any individual suspicion of wrongdoing, the government is allowed to know whom Americans are calling every time they make a phone call, for how long they talk and from where.

This sort of tracking can reveal a lot of personal and intimate information about an individual. To casually permit this surveillance — with the American public having no idea that the executive branch is now exercising this power — fundamentally shifts power between the individual and the state, and it repudiates constitutional principles governing search, seizure and privacy.[782]

The Obama administration continued to defend the expanded program as a crucial tool in the fight against terrorism, though they could not cite a single instance where an imminent terrorist attack was prevented because of it. A federal judge ruled, in December of 2013, that the bulk collection of Americans' phone records was indeed a violation of the Constitution—though his ruling was stayed pending an appeal by the Obama administration.[783]

As Obama went from being a critic of domestic surveillance to becoming its most powerful advocate, our country ceased to look like the America envisioned by the Founding Fathers and became much more like China or Soviet Russia.

146. Proposing Government Monitors in Newsrooms

The next issue at hand is Obama's view on the value of our freedom of the press. It seems that, in Obama's America, the free press is only free to think like he does. Not content with the fact that nearly all of the mainstream media has been on their side, the Obama administration has made many efforts to ensure that their actions and policies are only viewed in the most favorable light. For instance, the Obama administration tried "very hard" to discourage Fox News from reporting extensively on the Benghazi attack in 2012.[784] The threat wasn't enough to stop the network from investigating and reporting on it, but the Obama administration didn't stop trying.

Less than a year later, a new FCC program called "Multi-Market Study of Critical Information Needs" (or CIN, for short) was proposed. This program would involve placing FCC agents in America's newsrooms to determine how stories were selected, whether there was bias in reporting, and whether "critical information needs" were being met.[785] And the FCC was not planning on just monitoring broadcast news, but also placing agents in print media outlets—over which the FCC has no regulatory authority.

The clear intent of CIN is to intimidate the news media. The FCC controls the licensing of broadcast media, and placing FCC agents to monitor the America's newsrooms would put immense pressure on the media to report news as the government wishes, or risk losing their FCC license. After the existence of the proposed program was exposed by Ajit Pai, one of the FCC's five commissioners, in February 2014, immediate outrage caused the FCC to back down... for now.[786]

147. Threatening Journalists for Bad Press

In 2013, when the so-called sequestration budget "cuts" were looming, Barack Obama tried to blame the cuts on Republicans. He'd been playing the blame game for months. It was during his third presidential debate with Mitt Romney that Obama first claimed it was not his idea, but that Congress had proposed sequestration.

Not so, according to legendary journalist Bob Woodward, who pointed out, both in his book, *The Price of Politics* and in an opinion piece in the *Washington Post*, that automatic spending cuts were proposed by the White House and personally approved and signed into law by Obama.[787]

Less than a week after that piece was published, Woodward revealed, during an appearance on CNN, that a senior White House official warned him that he would "regret" criticizing Obama for his true role in the genesis of the sequester.[788]

Soon after Woodward's story came to light, other journalists started coming forward with similar stories about threats and abusive treatment they'd received for merely asking tough questions of members of the Administration, or for unflattering coverage.

The *New York Post's* Maureen Callahan spoke with several reporters. David Brody, the chief correspondent for *CBN News* told her, "I can tell you categorically that there's always been, right from the get-go of this administration, an overzealous sensitivity to any push-back from any media outlet." Liberal journalist Jonathan Alter also said he'd been subject to similar abusive treatment from the Obama administration for writing something they didn't like. A young female reporter was called crude names in an email for merely asking important questions of an Obama Cabinet Secretary.[789]

Ron Fournier, editor-in-chief of the *National Journal*, also came forward, "I received several e-mails and telephone calls from this White House official filled with vulgarity, abusive language, and virtually the same phrase that Woodward called a veiled threat."[790]

Washington Times columnist Lanny Davis, a centrist Democrat and Obama supporter, was threatened with having his access to White House officials limited for being critical of the administration's policies.[791]

This kind of thuggery from the White House, which flies in the face of our First Amendment rights to freedom of the press, has been standard operating procedure in the Obama administration.

148.Assault on Free Press

When Barack Obama took office, he promised that his administration would create "an unprecedented level of openness in government."[792] What we got instead was what *New York Times* public editor Margaret Sullivan described as "unprecedented secrecy and unprecedented attacks on a free press."[793] According to Sullivan, the ability of the press to report freely on its government is "under siege," by the Obama administration.

In May of 2013, the Associated Press revealed that Obama's Justice Department had secretly obtained two months of phone records of AP reporters and editors. AP President and CEO Gary Pruitt said, "There can be no possible justification for such an overbroad collection of the telephone communications of The Associated Press and its reporters. These records potentially reveal communications with confidential sources across all of the newsgathering activities undertaken by the AP during a two-month period, provide a road map to AP's newsgathering operations and disclose information about AP's activities and operations that the government has no conceivable right to know."[794] The Obama administration wouldn't say why it had been secretly and illegally obtaining the records, but it may have been connected to a government investigation into the source for an AP story of a foiled terror plot.[795] As a result, longtime sources stopped talking to the Associated Press and other news organizations.[796]

Soon after the AP phone records story broke, the *Washington Post* reported that, in 2010, the Justice Department had secretly obtained *Fox News* reporter James Rosen's phone records, tracked his movements, and read his emails while investigating possible leaks of classified information to Rosen for an article on North Korea's nuclear program published in 2009. The Justice Department justified their actions by labeling Rosen a "co-conspirator" with Stephen Jin-Woo Kim, a State Department contractor, who was charged with violating the Espionage Act of 1917 for leaking the information to Rosen.[797] The secret warrant was approved by Attorney General Eric Holder.[798]

According to Michael Barone, senior political analyst for the *Washington Examiner*, "Presidents and attorneys general of both parties have been reluctant to use the Espionage Act when secret information has been leaked to the press because they have recognized that it is overbroad." But not Barack Obama and Eric Holder. "They have used the Espionage Act of 1917 six times to bring cases against government officials for leaks to the media -- twice as many as all of their predecessors combined."[799]

A report by the Committee to Protect Journalists, a nonprofit organization that promotes press freedom worldwide, was highly critical of Obama's aggressive and unprecedented attacks on the free press. "In the Obama administration's Washington, government officials are increasingly afraid to talk to the press. Those suspected of discussing, with reporters, anything that the government has classified as secret are subject to investigation, including lie-detector tests and scrutiny of their telephone and e-mail records," the report says.[800] Longtime *New York Times* reporter David Sanger called the Obama administration, "the most closed, control freak administration I've ever covered."[801]

149.The So-Called "People's Rights Amendment"

The ultimate endpoint for Obama's policy toward the First Amendment, and especially toward freedom of the press and of speech, is a radical shift in the way we perceive the first amendment. He wants the Constitution, through its amendments, to define protected speech as coming from an individual only. Many countries don't have free speech, freedom of the press, freedom of assembly, or freedom to petition, but these freedoms are fundamental American values. Barack Obama wants to eradicate these freedoms and replace them with a carefully defined, limited freedom only to speak as an individual.

This is no conspiracy theory. David Axelrod, Obama's top political adviser, promised that, in a second term, the Obama administration "will use whatever tools are out there, including a constitutional amendment" to overturn the landmark Supreme Court case, *Citizens United vs. Federal Election Commission*.[802] The Court held that the First Amendment prohibits the government from restricting the political spending of corporations and unions.[803] The "fix" to this problem is the so-called *People's Rights Amendment*, which explicitly declares that the First Amendment does not apply to "corporations, limited liability companies or other corporate entities established by the laws of any state, the United States, or any foreign state," and enables Congress and the states to regulate the free speech of those entities. Such entities include newspapers, magazines, television networks, even churches, but, notably, do not include labor unions. According to UCLA law professor and law blogger Eugene Volokh:

> If the People's Rights Amendment were enacted, Congress would have an entirely free hand to censor what is published in newspapers organized as corporations, what is published by book publishers organized as corporations, what is created by movie studios that are organized as corporations, what is distributed by music companies that are organized as corporations, and so on.[804]

That doesn't sound like something that would (or should) happen in "the land of the free," does it? But, this remains the fevered dream of the far left, including Obama, even now.

150.Assault on Religious Freedom

But what of the final freedom explicitly enumerated by the first amendment: the freedom of religious expression? Under Obama, you'd better hope that your religion aligns well with his domestic agenda. And even if it does line up most of the time, you'd better learn from the example of the Catholic Church should you stray even a little.

The Catholic Church has long held the position that access to healthcare should be available to everyone. This is in keeping with Catholic teaching, which holds that access to healthcare is so fundamental to human life that it cannot be denied due to inability to pay or other factors. So, many Catholics initially did support Obamacare.

But, when the healthcare law was passed, it was found to have provisions that would require institutions such as Catholic schools and hospitals to provide birth control and abortion services to their employees—in direct violation of Church teaching. Obama held that these mandates were required because things like birth control and abortion are "basic" healthcare and further claimed that requiring a Catholic institution to carry health insurance that includes abortion and birth control services was not the same thing as requiring the church to participate in those activities directly.[805] This is akin to believing pregnancy is a disease, that birth control is the preventative treatment, and abortion the cure. Whether you agree with this line of thinking or not, it certainly seems un-American to require religious institutions to ascribe to it.

Despite the fact that freedom of religious expression is guaranteed by the First Amendment to the Constitution, American businesses are finding themselves being persecuted by the Obama administration for standing up for their religious beliefs.

By February 5, 2013, The Becket Fund for Religious Liberty had filed forty-seven lawsuits on behalf of hospitals, universities, and businesses with religious affiliations over the birth control mandate.[806]

One of those businesses was the Christian-owned Hobby Lobby, a chain of arts and crafts retail stores. After an attempt to get an injunction against the mandate failed, Hobby Lobby announced that the company would refuse to provide birth control coverage and, also, would not pay the $1.3 million per day fine required by the Obamacare law.[807]

It's hard to believe that in the United States of America, standing up for your religious beliefs would have you fined by the government, but that was nearly the case here. In 2014, Hobby Lobby won their case before the Supreme Court with a narrow, five-to-four margin, as the court held that the state had not met its burden of proof to convince the justices that the HHS mandate was the least-invasive way in which the state could pursue their interest (that being their desired goal of granting free access to birth control and abortions to all women), and that closely-held corporations would be exempt from the mandate.

151.Executive Gun Control

We've tackled the Fourth Amendment. We've reviewed the First Amendment. But what of the Second? Obama *claims* that he believes in the Second Amendment to the Constitution, but he certainly doesn't act that way. Instead, he has chipped away at the rights of gun owners while simultaneously quashing the constitutional system of checks and balances.

When Obama's gun control agenda failed to pass Congress, Obama, true to form, chose to take unilateral executive actions to achieve his goals. In January of 2013, using the Sandy Hook shooting a month earlier for political cover, Obama signed 23 executive actions related to gun control.[808] These executive orders were never debated in Congress, and would never have passed in the normal way. Obama's executive orders were so egregious that many state leaders immediately announced plans to resist compliance with any executive action that violated the Second Amendment.[809]

Two more executive actions on gun control were also signed in August of that year[810], with still two more the following January.[811]

But, Obama still wasn't done. In 2015, plans to ban a widely-used bullet for the AR-15 semi-automatic rifle were announced. The Bureau of Alcohol, Tobacco, Firearms and Explosives (BATFE) justified the ban with the claim that the "armor-piercing" ammunition *could be* used in semi-automatic handguns, and thus they pose a significant threat to police— though no evidence of this ever happening was provided. The Obama administration was merely trying to ban the popular ammunition because his attempts to ban the sporting rifle itself through legislation had failed.[812] After a great deal of public outrage, the BATFE announced that they were backing off from the ammunition ban, at least for the time being.[813] But, it's safe to say that Second Amendment rights will remain a target of Obama through the end of his presidency.

One final attack against the Second Amendment was still to come, however. Following the ISIS-inspired terrorist attack in San Bernardino, CA in December of 2015, Obama took to the airwaves to decry the attacks as a sign that America needed tougher gun control. The folly of this plan to stop terrorist attacks by disarming law abiding citizens aside, Obama used the event to pressure Congress to pass legislation making it illegal for people on a terrorism watch-list to purchase firearms of any kind. When the GOP-led Congress refused to do so, he signed an executive order on February 8,

2016, which, though it lacked much in the way of legal teeth, was a set of guidelines suggesting the same sorts of measures he'd advertised the previous December, including a moratorium on terror watch list suspects buying guns, an end to the dubious "gun show loophole" and other measures opposed by gun rights lobbyists.[814]

Obamacare

We've gone through quite a remarkable list of transgressions, failures, and general malfeasance thus far, but we've stayed away from any serious discussion of Obama's most important, and most reviled domestic law – the *Affordable Care Act* (hereafter, Obamacare). This execrable chapter in American history exemplifies every... single... one of Obama's greatest flaws and dastardly impulses (other than his confused and misguided foreign policy agenda, which we have saved for last, and you'll see why when you reach our conclusion).

Perhaps there were good intentions when this legislation was crafted – we want to believe that Obama at least meant well by this bill, though the tactics he used and the people he employed in the service of the cause raise serious questions on even that attempt at charity on our parts, as you'll soon see. But, good intentions or not, this bill combines sheer government incompetence, overbearing nanny-state thinking, bad management, radical ideologies far outside the mainstream of American politics, violations of our most sacred civil liberties, the utter detonation of the Constitution and the rule of law, and a crippling economic impact unlike any other healthcare initiative to date into one sickening, blatantly dishonest, life-threatening package. No domestic policy, no single piece of legislation has ever so perfectly summed up an administration and a political movement as well as this, except possibly Roosevelt's New Deal (though, to be fair, the New Deal was a package of bills passed over a two year period, not a single omnibus nightmare 2500 pages in the making and passed in the dead of night).

Not only does Obamacare perfectly describe Obama's presidency, but Americans' reactions to it, from supporters and dissenters alike, perfectly describe the state of civil discourse in this polarized nation, this victim of Saul Alinsky's *Rules for Radicals*. We are, now, what progressive radicals have made of us, in our laws, and in our collective consciousness. What was laughingly called "debate" on this bill, though it dragged on for over a year, was an exercise in team sports with one side demanding that the other side shuts up (guess which side was which!). When Obama held a summit to discuss the economic impact of Obamacare, he blithely told Republicans, who were attempting to warn him that the bill would bend the cost curve on healthcare up, not down, "I won. Elections have consequences." And when concern over the bill gave the GOP a rare U.S. Senate victory in Massachusetts, elections suddenly stopped having consequences.

As we walk you through the horrendous details of Obamacare, be on the lookout for the misbegotten themes you've seen throughout the rest of this book – they're all represented. It is a testament to what a man like Obama can accomplish when he sets his mind to the task of "fundamentally transforming" the country.

152.A Partisan Health Care Bill

When Barack Obama won the presidency in 2008, he promised to make health care reform a bipartisan effort. If he'd been genuine, he would have been following in the footsteps of fellow Democrats like Franklin D. Roosevelt and Bill Clinton who understood that, for changes to stick, both sides of the aisle must have partial ownership of them and, therefore, interest in maintaining those changes in perpetuity. But there was nothing bipartisan about how Obamacare became law.

In fact, Democrats were so desperate just to get it passed and signed that when Scott Brown won a special election to fill Ted Kennedy's former seat—and end the Democrats' filibuster-proof majority—Democrats used a legislative process called reconciliation to limit debate in order to fast track the bill's passage in both chambers. But, according to the Heritage Foundation, reconciliation "was not intended to be the procedure of last resort when other means fail, and to do so would be a complete abuse of reconciliation rules."[815] Despite his campaign promise to bring Democrats and Republicans *together* in the process of reforming healthcare, Obama signed a trillion dollar government takeover of one-sixth of the United States economy that passed with zero Republican votes in the Senate and only one Republican vote in the House.[816]

But it's actually worse than it sounds – not only did Obama get the bill passed with essentially no GOP support, but he refused to include GOP legislators and conservative analysts when designing, drafting, and proofing the bill. The end result of this sort of exclusivity and baldly partisan ramrodding was that Republicans felt betrayed and powerless, thus guaranteeing that conservatives would make repealing the bill a central plank in election platforms and galvanizing the grassroots against Obamacare.

Even if you think Obamacare is a good idea—and if you do, we advise you to keep reading—this is a spectacularly short-sighted failure of leadership, and it cost his party dearly. Democrats suffered two of the worst shellackings in modern political history at the ballot box in 2010 and 2014, costing them the entire Southern US, many of the gains they'd previously made in the Midwest, and even some ground in the Northeast. Much of this pushback was centered on the failure of Obamacare and conservative opposition to the bill (though there were, of course, other factors).

153.The Obamacare Co-Op Debacle

An obscure provision in Obamacare allocated $2.4 billion in taxpayer-funded, tax-free loans to establish twenty-three Obamacare co-ops nationwide to compete with private health insurance providers. The Obama administration had to approve each loan, and one would think that when it comes to our nation's health care, some standard would apply to which companies got loans.

The *Washington Examiner's* Richard Pollack reported on some of the loans the Obama administration approved:

- $62 million to Maine Community Health Options; the company's President had been molesting teenage boys for more than three decades.[817]

- $65 million to Louisiana Health Cooperative; CEO Terry Shilling was sanctioned by the Securities and Exchange Commission for insider trading.[818]

- $112 million to CoOportunity Health; CFO Stephen Ringlee had at least three businesses fail since 2009.[819]

- $129 million to Florida-based Community Health Solutions of America, for an Obamacare co-op in Ohio. The principals of this co-op have histories of failed companies, bankruptcy, and tax problems.[820]

But the largest loan, $340 million, went to Freelancers Insurance Company, which is based out of New York, run by Sara Horowitz, an old friend of Obama's from back when he was a state senator. This might not seem so terrible if her company had a reputation for quality service, but they didn't. Freelancers Insurance Company has an extremely high rate of consumer complaints, and, for two consecutive years, was rated the "worst" insurer by state regulators.[821]

Why did these companies get so many of our tax dollars? Apparently, the Obama administration doesn't want us to know how these companies are selected, as the agency that awards the loans, the Center for Consumer Information and Insurance

Oversight (CCIIO), hasn't made their selection criteria public. Due to gross mismanagement, by January 2016, more than half of Obamacare co-ops had failed, costing a quarter of a million Americans their insurance, and leaving the taxpayers $1.2 billion in unpaid loans.[822] The outlook for the remaining co-ops isn't much better. According to a Government Accountability Office report released in March 2016, four of the eleven remaining co-ops did not meet enrollment projections.[823]

The Obamacare co-ops may very well be the health insurance version of the Solyndra boondoggle, but bigger.

154.Fudging the Enrollment Numbers

Despite the fact that millions have had their existing plans canceled and millions more will eventually share the same fate, Obama called his health care law a success, and no longer up for debate when he announced that by end of open enrollment, the Obamacare exchanges had allegedly signed up 7.1 million people.[824]

But who, exactly, counted as a successful Obamacare enrollee? That is a question that even the White House didn't want to answer. For starters, there were a significant number of duplicate enrollments (from consumers who were advised to create new accounts and re-enroll because of problems with the health exchange website) that were counted.[825] Various studies have raised serious doubts about the number of enrollees touted by Obama. According to a study by the RAND Corporation, there were only 3.9 million legitimate exchange enrollees. And then there's the question of how many people who signed up for Obamacare didn't have insurance before. Only 1.4 million enrollees were previously uninsured, according to the RAND study.[826] Another study by McKinsey & Company in 2014 found that of those signing up for Obamacare, only 26 percent were previously uninsured.[827]

A very large number of people signing up for Obamacare either previously had insurance plans which were cancelled because of Obamacare, or were merely signing up for Medicaid. And future plan cancellations still loom for millions more Americans even though Obama repeatedly promised it would never happen, which will surely be counted as new enrollees when their time comes.

155. Do-Nothing Obamacare Contractors

In the summer of 2013, the British firm Serco was awarded a five-year contract worth over a billion dollars to process Obamacare paper applications.[828] The Obama administration must have figured they'd be pretty busy. But in the spring of 2014, whistleblowers came forward from Serco offices in four states admitting that they were being paid taxpayer dollars to do nothing.

One employee reported that, over a six-month period, he processed only forty applications. Another, who quit her job in frustration, said that she processed only six applications in the entire month of December. She reported being kept on the clock from 9 pm to midnight while being forbidden to make any calls or do any work. In a Serco office in Arkansas, workers are required to be on the clock and get paid, but not make any calls. That office was *still* hiring, too.[829]

Where are the oversight and accountability? Why are taxpayer dollars being wasted so frivolously? The nonpartisan, nonprofit Sunlight Foundation may have the answer. Of the forty-seven contractors awarded contracts by the Obama administration, seventeen spent a cumulative $128 million on lobbying in 2011 and 2012. Twenty-nine of these contract winners had employees or PACs that contributed a total of $32 million to federal candidates and parties during the same period. Barack Obama's reelection campaign received nearly $4 million from employees and PACs of Obamacare contract winners. Serco spent more than $1 million on lobbying and donations prior to being awarded its Obamacare contract.[830] Money certainly does talk.

Making matters worse, Serco came under investigation by Britain's Serious Fraud Office a few days after being awarded the Obamacare contract. An audit revealed Serco and another company had over-billed the United States government by more than $80 billion.[831] Despite this, the Obama administration defended their decision to award the contract to Serco.[832]

156. The Obamacare Thought Police

As Obamacare took effect, the realities of the law put a significant squeeze on businesses across the country, forcing employers to lay off workers in order to reduce cost and stay afloat. To minimize the political fallout of the implementation of his signature healthcare law, Obama twice delayed the employer mandate for businesses with fifty to ninety-nine employees, once in 2013 and again in 2014.[833] Of course, delaying the onset of the mandate did nothing to convince businesses that they shouldn't try to keep their workforce below those benchmark levels. Those very benchmarks became a perverse incentive to lay off employees to get ready for its implementation. James Taranto of the *Wall Street Journal* explains:

> *One problem with the employer mandate is that it creates perverse incentives. Businesses with fewer than 50 employees aren't subject to the mandate, which means that for a company on the cusp, the marginal cost of hiring the next employee could run into the tens of thousands of dollars--or, for one just above the threshold, the marginal savings from firing a worker can be considerable. Employers can also reduce their liability by replacing full-time workers with part-time ones.*
>
> *[...]*
>
> *By adding a new threshold--100 workers as well as 50--the new delay creates an additional perverse incentive. At least until 2016,*

a company that doesn't offer insurance is better off not hiring the
100th worker--or firing him.[834]

Realizing this, but unwilling to risk political fallout from these layoffs in the crucial midterm election year, the Obama administration did what any totalitarian regime would do: he wrote new regulations making it clear that employers could not lay off workers to get below the 100-employee threshold and qualify for exemption from the mandate. Employers who did lay off workers were required to certify to the IRS—under penalty of perjury—that avoiding the costs of Obamacare was not a motivating factor in those layoffs.[835]

Obamacare has utterly failed to provide the promised benefits and has become destructive of economic activity. And it now appears that the Obama administration is trying to silence Obamacare's critics with threats of jail time unless they remain silent about how Obamacare has hurt their business.

157. Waivers For Obamacare's Proponents

If Obamacare is great, why would anyone want a waiver, and why would the government grant them one? It's a fair question, seeing as 1,231 companies (affecting just under 4 million people) received waivers, according to the Department of Health and Human Services.[836] Oh—and many Federal employees got waivers too.

The majority of the waivers granted were given to Obama's allies in Big Labor—which overwhelmingly supported the law.[837] It's not just Obama's Big Labor allies getting Obamacare waivers either. An Obama cabinet nominee also received an Obamacare waiver.

Sally Jewell, the CEO of REI, has always been a supporter of Obamacare. In 2009, she participated in an Obama administration roundtable on health care reform. That didn't stop her from seeking and receiving an Obamacare waiver for REI's health coverage back in 2011.[838]

158. Obamacare Causing Americans to Delay Medical Care Over Costs

The higher premiums and deductibles experienced because of Obamacare naturally had negative consequences. According to a Gallup poll released in November 2014, one in three Americans reported that they have "put off getting medical treatment that they or their family members need because of cost."[839] In the fourteen years that Gallup had been asking the question, this was the *highest* number ever reported.

How is this possible? Obamacare was supposed to *increase* access to health care. Unfortunately, for too many people, particularly the middle class, health care premiums and deductibles increased because of Obamacare. According to Gallup:

Those who indicate that they have put off medical treatment in the past 12 months are asked to rate the seriousness of the underlying condition or illness. This year, 22% of Americans say they have put off medical treatment for a "very" or "somewhat serious" condition. This is double the 11% who say they have put off treatment for a non-serious condition. Furthermore, the percentage who have put off treatment for a serious condition has increased slightly since 2013.[840]

Only low-income families with less than $30,000 annual household income saw a decline in delaying health care over costs, according to the survey. When it comes to access to healthcare, Obama didn't spread the wealth, he redistributed it. With a third of Americans delaying health care because they can't afford it after paying for insurance under Obamacare, it's impossible to claim that Obamacare was a success. In fact, it's quite obvious that it made the problem it was trying to solve even worse.

159. Funding Abortions under Obamacare

Even with large majorities in both Houses of Congress, getting enough *Democrats* on board to pass Obamacare wasn't very easy. Corrupt deals and promises had to be made just to secure an essentially party-line vote on the controversial legislation. When quite a lot of support had at last been purchased there remained one, final roadblock for Obamacare's passage in the House of Representatives: Congressman Bart Stupak's coalition of pro-life Democrats who could not support Obamacare because of language allowing for taxpayer-funded abortion medications under the law.

Stupak, under pressure from both sides of the abortion issue, negotiated an Executive Order that effectively banned public funding of abortions in Obama's healthcare law.[841] Without this compromise, Obamacare would have never passed the House of Representatives. Less than a month after Obamacare was signed into law, Bart Stupak, seeing the writing on the wall, announced his retirement.[842]

Stupak paid a huge political price for his support for Obamacare and, ultimately, the compromise he made in good faith with President Obama would be all for naught. Obama would later abandon his promise to Stupak. Language in the Obama administration's final regulations for the law requires coverage of medications which cause abortions.[843] At the 2012 Democratic National Convention, Stupak, speaking to a Democrats for Life panel, said, "I am perplexed and disappointed that, having negotiated the Executive Order with the President, not only does the HHS mandate violate the Executive Order but it also violates statutory law."[844]

160. Illegal Unilateral "Fixes" to Obamacare

The Obamacare rollout was an undeniable disaster—not just for Obama, but for the entire Democratic Party. When millions of Americans discovered they were to lose the plans they had and would now have higher premiums and higher deductibles, it was clear that something had to be done in order reduce the political fallout.

On November 14, 2013, Obama announced that insurance companies could continue to offer plans that violated the requirements of his signature health care law for an additional year. Such a delay was previously labeled as "terrorism" by congressional Democrats, and was the issue at the center of the government shutdown debate.[845]

Obama's need to do something to ease the fears of Democrats up for reelection in 2014 came at the expense of the Constitution, and had even Democrats, like former DNC Chairman Howard Dean questioning whether Obama had the legal authority.[846] Eugene Kontorovich, a constitutional law professor at Northwestern University School of Law, said Obama's fix "exceeds the president's discretion in implementing the law and amounts to legislation from the White House. The president has no constitutional authority to rewrite or unbundle statutes, especially in ways that impose new obligations on people, as the fix does."[847] UC Berkeley law professor John Yoo wrote that Obama's fix "amounts to a suspension power that the Framers consciously rejected by including the Take Care Clause in Article II of the Constitution."[848] The "Take Care" clause is that bit which instructs the President to ensure that all laws are faithfully enforced; whether the President likes the law, or not. Whether it's politically expedient, or not.

In response to Obama's clearly illegal action, House Republicans announced the Keep Your Health Plan Act, which would have accomplished the same thing Obama called for, just in a constitutional manner. But, Obama, not wanting Republicans to benefit politically from the situation, announced he would veto the bill.[849]

Obama's illegal fix was neither his first or last, having already unilaterally delayed the employer mandate. By the end of 2013, Obama had made 14 changes to Obamacare without consultation or approval from Congress, with the last change of the year making it possible for people to sign up for bare-bones "catastrophic" health coverage via a so-called "hardship exemption."[850]

As 2014 came in and polling started to indicate that Obamacare may lead to electoral disaster for the Democrats in November, Obama went even further in trying to delay the effects of the law. Obama delayed the employer mandate for medium-sized businesses—again, without congressional approval.[851] But that didn't go far enough to ease electoral concerns.

Eventually, someone in the Obama administration must have figured out that the original one-year delay to allow consumers to keep existing health care plans that don't comply with Obamacare wasn't long enough to prevent cancellation notices being mailed out prior to the 2014 midterm elections. So, in March of 2014, Obama officials announced—as usual, without congressional approval—that this provision of the law would be delayed for *two* more years.[852]

Aside from the fact that all of these changes prove that Obamacare is incredibly flawed and was hastily passed and signed without proper examination or consideration of its impact, the means by which Obama has insisted on "correcting" its many flaws (purely for political cover) have been gross abuses of a president's power.

At a House Judiciary Committee hearing, Jonathan Turley, a professor of public interest law at George Washington University stated, "The problem with what the president is doing is that he's not simply posing a danger to the constitutional system. He's becoming the very danger the Constitution was designed to avoid. That is the concentration of power in every single branch."[853]

161. Threatening Drug Makers to Support Obamacare

Thanks to a yearlong investigation by House Republicans, the truth behind the pharmaceutical industry's support for Obamacare was discovered. Despite Obama's promises of transparency, these deals were kept secret, without the public or members of Congress knowing. The investigation revealed that the nation's top drug companies were threatened with higher taxes if they didn't publicly support the law. Internal documents from the investigation were released on May 31, 2012. According to the *Washington Times*:

> *The documents show that former White House Chief of Staff Jim Messina and health care reform point woman Nancy-Ann DeParle told drug company representatives in June 2009 that if they didn't cooperate on the initiative, Mr. Obama would demand a 15 percent rebate on Medicare drugs and push to remove the tax deduction for direct consumer advertising — items that could cost the industry $100 billion over the next decade.*
>
> *The threats appeared to work, and the parties met the next month to hammer out a final deal. The drug companies agreed to pay higher Medicaid rebates and a new health care reform fee to raise $80 billion for the legislation, and promised to run positive television ads about it.*[854]

Obama claims his administration "is committed to creating an unprecedented level of openness in government."[855] It strikes us as odd, then, that his administration raised the institution of the backroom deal secured through extortion to an art form.

162.Obamacare Hospital Layoffs and Closures

If the true goal of Obamacare was to make healthcare more accessible, then clearly something is wrong. In addition to higher premiums and deductibles, cancelled plans, and a website that didn't work, Obamacare found other ways to be an obstacle to getting access to healthcare.

The world-renowned Cleveland Clinic announced in September of 2013 that they would be cutting their annual budget by five to six percent and cutting jobs to prepare for Obamacare reforms.[856] Hospitals across the country cut thousands of jobs in 2013 because of Obamacare, with even more expected in 2014. The healthcare sector has typically been a reliable source of job growth, even when the economy is in recession. But now, thanks to Obamacare, it is entering into a recession of its own.[857]

In some cases, hospitals simply closed. In Georgia alone, four hospitals closed over a two-year period because of Obamacare-related payment cuts.[858] In addition to closed hospitals and reduced staffs, a lot of doctors are simply refusing to take patients enrolled in Obamacare programs for fear of increased costs and reduced payments for medical services.[859] Under Obamacare, healthcare is not only less affordable, it is less accessible.

163.Lack of Healthcare Transparency

Healthcare represents one-sixth of the entire US economy and affects Americans of all walks of life. At current rates of inflation, the cost of healthcare to the Federal Government, and to the taxpayers, will soon become so large that conservative and liberal economists all agree it will amount to a national crisis. Unfortunately, there is no clear consensus on how to fix this burdensome issue. There have been a variety of ideas on how to fix the system's shortcomings. America is a large and diverse nation with varied healthcare needs. It is also the central hub for the world's most promising medical research, and Americans shoulder much of the cost of developing new drugs and therapies by paying higher prices than the developing world. That being the case, there are many competing interests in the healthcare market and they all need a seat at the table when we discuss major reforms. The only chance for a rational solution for our health care system is if everyone has input and all negotiations are done in an above-board manner without secrecy. And this is what Obama had promised—in fact, he promised to broadcast the final negotiations live on C-SPAN.

Sadly, that was just another broken Obama promise. Because of an alleged need to "fast-track" the final Obamacare bill (which wouldn't go into full effect until four years after passage), Obama agreed with then-House Speaker Nancy Pelosi that the final negotiations would be held behind closed doors.[860] While the administration claimed that failures of the healthcare system demanded immediate action, there's a good chance that Obama feared losing his filibuster-proof majority in the Senate before the final bill could be passed.

It was this lack of transparency that was crucial to Obamacare getting passed, according to Obamacare architect Jonathan Gruber, because the details would have been politically unpopular. "Lack of transparency is a huge political advantage. And basically, call it the stupidity of the American voter or whatever, but basically that was really, really [sic] critical for the thing to pass..."[861] Nancy Pelosi put it best when she infamously said, "We have to pass the bill to find out what is in it."

164.A Bill That Hurts Businesses

Obama promised to lower health care costs on his watch, but they've actually gone up. In 2012, for the first time ever, employer-provided health insurance costs for a family of four exceeded $20,000.[862] A survey by the Mercer consulting firm found that nearly two-thirds of employers expected their health care costs to *increase* in 2014 when Obamacare became fully implemented.[863] These higher costs will force some employers to change their health coverage and/or require their employees to pay more. Other companies will have to pass the costs on to customers. After Obama was reelected, Papa John's CEO John Schnatter said that Obamacare would force his company to raise the price of pizza.[864] This may not sound like much, but Papa John's is not alone.

According to the National Restaurant Association, which represents nearly 13 million employees in the restaurant and food service industry, the extra costs imposed by Obamacare are a threat to the already slim profit margins on which most restaurants operate. Dawn Sweeney, President and CEO of the National Restaurant Association, said that restaurant owners "cannot be saddled with excessive costs and regulatory burdens that threaten their very business."

Obamacare doesn't just force businesses to make their employees or customers to pay more to offset the extra costs. It also means that smaller businesses that can't afford to provide coverage as mandated by Obamacare will be forced layoff or cut the hours of their employees in order to avoid heavy penalties. Florida restaurant owner, John Metz, who runs roughly forty Denny's Restaurants and owns the Hurricane Grill & Wings franchise, decided, after Obama was reelected, to add a five percent surcharge to customers' bills and cut hours of employees to under 30 hours a week to avoid the $2,000 per employee penalty for not offering a government-approved insurance plan, as required under Obamacare. According to Metz, the cost of covering employees under the law would be more than most of his restaurants make in a year.[865]

165. Cutting Medicare To Pay for Obamacare

Medicare benefits were not supposed to change, according to Obama. But it's hard to explain how benefits will stay the same and the program will remain solvent when Obamacare actually *cuts* $716 billion from Medicare. Medicare actuary Richard Foster said these cuts "will not be viable" in the long term.[866] Foster also projected that more than 7 million Medicare recipients enrolled in private Medicare Advantage plans would have to find other coverage because of the cuts, a reduction in enrollment of about half.[867] These cuts will ultimately force seniors to pay higher premiums and see a reduction in benefits.

Obama's raiding of Medicare also brings the program along on the fast track to insolvency. According to the 2011 Medicare Trustees Report, Medicare will be bankrupt by 2024, five years earlier than previously estimated.[868]

166. Rationing Health Care

If there is any part of Obamacare with bipartisan agreement, it is opposition to the Independent Payment Advisory Board

(IPAB), the fifteen-member government agency created by Obamacare with the stated purpose of finding savings in Medicare without compromising coverage or the quality of care. By design, this board of unelected bureaucrats is protected from Congressional review.[869]

It wasn't just members of Congress raising objections to IPAB either. Even the American Medical Association, which was influential in getting Obamacare passed, has called for IPAB's repeal.[870]

While there has been plenty of debate over charges that the IPAB would amount to so-called "death panels," many Democrats have recognized that the IPAB will reduce access to care. Julie Reiskin, who was nominated to serve on the Legal Services Corporation Board of Directors by Barack Obama, said that the IPAB will "ration care or increase consumer cost sharing."[871]

167.Obamacare-Caused Layoffs

Many American business owners, struggling under the Obama economy, held out for the results of the 2012 presidential election before making major decisions about the future of their companies. They were hoping for a change in administration that might give them some hope of relief, but they were denied. When Obama won reelection, the chances of Obamacare being repealed became nonexistent. With new regulations and higher taxes looming, businesses across the country started announcing future layoffs. Here are just a few:

Boeing: 30 percent of executives.[872]
Energizer: about 1,500 employees.[873]
Murray Energy: 156 employees.[874]
Groupon: 80 employees.[875]
Stanford Brake: 75 employees.[876]
Rocketdyne: 100 employees.[877]

According to the Bureau of Labor Statistics, in November 2012 there were 1,759 "mass layoff actions" from firms with more than 50 employees, affecting nearly 165,000 workers.[878] This was not merely the continuation of a trend, since mass layoffs had actually been *declining* for three years.

Some companies didn't even wait until the election to make their moves. Medical companies like Boston Scientific, Medtronic, Abbot Lams, Covidien, Kinetic Concepts, St. Jude Medical, Welch Allyn, Hill-Rom, and Stryker, Smith & Nephew had previously anticipated massive layoffs in 2013 because of new taxes in Obamacare.[879] It appears that the negative impact of Obamacare on jobs won't end there either. The Congressional Budget Office estimated in early 2014 that Obamacare will push roughly 2 million workers out of the labor market by 2017.[880]

168.The Obamacare Rollout Disaster

On October 1, 2013, millions of Americans were now, in theory, able to shop for their new "affordable" government-approved healthcare plans by visiting HealthCare.gov or their states' insurance exchange sites. Massive system failures not only prevented access to the sites, especially at HealhCare.gov, but prevented people who did manage to get access from properly signing up for a new plan. Sources in the insurance industry said that, because of software problems, as few as one percent of applications contained enough data to successfully enroll the applicants in a plan.[881]

A mere six people succeeded in signing up for Obamacare on its launch day.[882] According to the nonpartisan research firm Millward Brown Digital, less than half of one percent of the visitors to the federal healthcare website were able to complete enrollment in the first week.[883]

The early sign-up numbers were awful. At times, it looked like it would be nearly impossible for the Obama administration to meet its goal of 7 million enrollees during the six-month enrollment period.

To call the Obamacare rollout a disaster is an understatement. But the most shocking part is that the Obama administration was aware that the site was not ready to handle the anticipated load. According to a confidential report obtained by CNN, the Obama administration "was given stark warnings just one month before launch that the federal healthcare site was not ready to go live."[884] Why, then, did the Obama administration let the rollout (which was destined to be a total failure) occur at all, especially after refusing the House Republicans' compromise to delay Obamacare for a year–a delay which could have helped prevent the debacle from happening in the first place?

Not only was the site not ready for launch, the site was also determined to have major security flaws, putting the private information of millions of Americans at risk of being stolen. The Obama administration knew of these flaws and vulnerabilities, but did nothing, according to documents provided to the House Committee on Government Oversight and Reform.[885] One top Obamacare official had recommended the site be shut down over the security risks—but was overruled—directly contradicting the Obama administration's claims that they were not aware of any security concerns prior to the site's launch.[886]

Obamacare enrollees also discovered that it was nearly impossible to add a newborn baby to an already purchased plan. Other common life changes affecting premiums (marriage, divorce, death of a family member, etc.) couldn't be handled by the website.[887]

Considering that HealthCare.gov was clearly not ready for its public launch, and a major security risk, one can't help wonder why the company that built the site, CGI Federal, was given a $678 million no-bid contract, even though there were several companies qualified to perform those services. It could be that a Princeton classmate of First Lady Michelle Obama's is a top executive at CGI, or that the president of the company's North American operations became a donor for Obama's reelection campaign after receiving the contract to build HealthCare.gov.[888] The $678 million no-bid contract may have worked for getting Obama a new campaign donor, but was too big a price for a site that simply did not work.

169.Mass Policy Cancellations

"If you like your health-care plan, you will be able to keep your health-care plan, period."

Obama repeatedly made this claim while making the case for Obamacare. Unfortunately, Americans would learn, the hard way, that this promise was a lie, as millions of Americans discovered that their current health plans were not compliant with the law, and were no longer available.

To call this a broken promise would be inaccurate. It was, in fact, a deliberate deception meant to ensure the law's passage and, eventually, his own re-election. Obama administration officials estimated back in 2010 that 93 million Americans would *lose* their health care plans under the new law.[889] By the end of February 2014, just five months after the Obamacare rollout, 6.3 million people had already had their existing plans cancelled.[890] Obama has also quietly pursued new regulations to make "fixed benefit" plans—which are less expensive than more comprehensive plans—illegal. This, of course, would result in another wave of policy cancellations.[891]

Knowing that millions would lose their plans didn't stop Obama from regularly promising the opposite while running for reelection. It turns out, if it wasn't for that one big lie, the 2012 election would have turned out differently. According to a Wilson Perkins Allen Opinion Research survey, when voters were asked if they would still have voted for Barack Obama knowing they'd actually lose their health care plans, nearly 1 out of 4 said they would not have. An *ABC/Washington Post* poll conducted a month and a half after the botched Obamacare rollout found that if voters had an election do-over Romney would have won with 49 percent to Obama's 45 percent.[892] Simply put: Obama's big lie helped him get reelected.

As millions of Americans started receiving cancellation notices, Obama began denying he ever made that promise. "What we said was you could keep it if it hasn't changed since the law was passed," was Obama's absurd claim. Caught in one of the most brazen lies in American history, Obama's recourse was to present another lie to cover up the first. Unfortunately for Obama, video recordings prove he made the unequivocal promise that Americans could keep their plans no matter what at least 29 times.[893] An investigation by CNN revealed that insurance company executives were actually threatened by the Obama administration to keep quiet about the cancellations.[894] Liberal pundit Bob Beckel was also scolded by the Obama White House for advocating a year-long delay of Obamacare in order to address the problems.[895]

All the problems with the rollout of Obamacare may have been worth it had people found that they were getting the better, more affordable coverage Barack Obama had promised. But that turned out to not to be true either. Millions of Americans actually found that the new plans they'd now have to buy were *more* expensive and had *higher* deductibles than what they had before. College students, who had previously been able to purchase cheap health insurance through their college or university, can't anymore because of Obamacare.[896] Cancer patients have lost their existing plans, and found themselves paying more than double for their new Obamacare-compliant plans.[897] Even a single mother whose story was cited by Obama as an Obamacare success story after buying insurance off her state's exchange website would find the plan she picked wasn't actually affordable.[898]

There were many stories of real Americans losing their coverage and finding out they had to pay higher premiums for plans with higher deductibles. It's the sad epilogue of Obama's lie. A lie millions of Americans have to pay for. So egregious was Obama's lie about keeping your plan that the left-wing fact-checking site *PolitiFact* crowned Obama's claim, "if you like your health care plan, you can keep it" the Lie of the Year for 2013.[899]

170. Higher Healthcare Premiums and Deductibles

When first running for president, Obama promised his health care reform would lower insurance premiums by $2,500 per family per year. It sure sounded good on the stump but the reality of Obamacare doesn't even come close to lowering premiums by that amount. In fact, according to the Congressional Budget Office, Obamacare actually *raises* annual premiums per family by $2,400 as of 2014, making health insurance premiums $4,900 higher than what he promised.[900] In 2015 and 2016, a number of insurers have announced still further spikes in premiums and deductibles, and those increases are happening at faster rates than ever.

After the Obamacare rollout in 2013, consumers began to experience the sticker shock predicted by the CBO. Not only were their new premiums much higher than promised, but their new deductibles were simply unaffordable.[901] Despite the promises by Obama that health care costs would go down, Jonathan Gruber (Obama's health care advisor and the architect of Obamacare) said back in 2009 that Obamacare would *not* be affordable, and said in 2012 that Obama was fully aware of that fact.[902] The hardest hit, of course, are the middle-class, since they won't qualify for subsidies.

171. The Largest Tax Increase on The Middle Class in History

Aside from being a government takeover of health care, Obamacare is also the largest tax increase on the middle class in history. When the Supreme Court upheld the law by declaring that the individual mandate was constitutional only as a tax, the *Wall Street Journal* explained the implications of the decision:

It is now undeniable that Mr. Obama has imposed the largest tax increase in history on the middle class. Individuals who don't buy insurance will have to pay several hundred dollars, depending on income. The Congressional Budget Office says that 76% of those who pay the mandate tax will make less than 500% of the federal poverty level, estimated to be $24,000 for a family of four in 2016. That means 76% of the payers will earn less than $120,000 a year.

So much for Mr. Obama's promise not to raise taxes on anyone earning less than $200,000. And this initial mandate tax will only be a teaser rate when it becomes clear it isn't nearly enough either to finance the bill or drive individuals to buy insurance. Millions will wait to buy insurance until they need expensive treatment, knowing they can always buy it when they show up at the hospital.[903]

Whether you want to call it a tax or a mandate, the middle class will pay *more* because of Obama's policies. Yet, during a *60 Minutes* interview, Obama not only insisted he hadn't raised taxes, but he had the nerve to claim he had *cut* taxes.[904] For the record, Obamacare has eighteen new tax hikes, with $36.3 billion in taxes hitting the American people in 2013, alone, not counting the penalties some will pay due to not complying with the individual mandate.[905] That value understates the problem as well. Many in the middle class, including the biggest unions, have health plans that are considered "Cadillac coverage" and, beginning in 2017, will be taxed at a very high rate. In fact, the vast majority of people with top-of-the-line insurance are middle class, not wealthy, and will pay the price either in the transfer to the more expensive Obamacare exchanges or through the movement of more of their compensation from untaxed healthcare plans to taxed salary. On top of everything else we're about to endure with this albatross, it is the ultimate progressive coup and the saddest irony that they should win an argument in court by claiming that a penalty was a tax, and then turn around and claim that they didn't raise taxes. There can be no better representation of the filthy deceit of the far left in America.

Radical Islam

An honest study of Obama's actions and stated goals in the fight against international terrorism and theocratic, illiberal violations of human rights around the globe reveals a man who either does not grasp the potential scope of the threat posed by Islamic Jihadism, or has willfully chosen to ignore the threat in deference to a personal belief that the United States shouldn't be a leader on the global stage. In either case, the results on the ground have proven utterly disastrous for freedom and American security.

With a dismal record on the economy, Obama needed to pump up his foreign policy record while running for reelection. In addition to constantly claiming credit for killing Osama bin Laden, he often repeated the claim that "al-Qaeda is on its heels." You didn't have to be a supporter of Obama to *wish* that were true, but the facts proved otherwise. Still, Obama propagated this falsehood as long as he could. But after al-Qaeda was linked to the attack on the U.S. Consulate in Benghazi, and reports of a comeback of al-Qaeda in Iraq[906] and North Africa emerged,[907] he had to drop it from his speech.

Whether or not he honestly believed his own propaganda, Jihadist sentiments have grown from the start on his watch. According to Gen. Jack Keane, a retired four-star General, and former vice chief of staff of the U.S Army, in testimony before the Senate Armed Services Committee in January 2015, radical Islam has "grown fourfold in the last five years."[908] According to Keane, the Obama administration "became paralyzed by the fear of adverse consequences in the Middle East after fighting two wars."[909]

Obama may not be able to admit we are at war with radical Islam, but that refusal won't change the fact that radical Islam has exploded, and engulfed most of North Africa, the whole of the Middle East, and parts of Southeast Asia, Europe, and the Pacific Islands. Former allies of the United States in the affected areas have tumbled and fallen, or been driven into the arms of the most powerful Islamic theocracies, Iran and Saudi Arabia. Muslim factions are quickly taking sides in what may soon become a regional war powered by weapons of mass destruction, including nuclear bombs. We believe that, ultimately, this is Obama's greatest failing – he pursued a badly incoherent, morally timid, and illogical strategy in the fight against radicalism and terrorism, and we may soon pay for it with our freedoms or even our lives.

172. Foreign Policy Flip Flops

If we had to select one word to describe Obama's policy toward terrorism, and we were forced to pick something other than a synonym for "idiotic" or "cowardly", we would choose "incoherent". We're leading off this chapter by shining a light on his tail-chasing and lack of conviction because we think it really underscores everything else that will follow on the list.

As a candidate for president, Barack Obama campaigned loudly against such Bush Administration policies as renditions and indefinite detention for terrorists. But, as president, he didn't just retain these policies, he expanded them.[910] Obama's previous position may have been out of naiveté, or just a ploy to garner support from the Democratic Party's liberal base, but, apparently, the realities of being Commander-in-Chief have trumped his rhetoric. Other times, unfortunately, his foreign policy flip-flops have not been in the best interests of our country, or our allies. Here are a few examples:

- Obama forcefully promised, as a candidate, to recognize the 1915 Turkish genocide against the Armenian people,

240

but, as president, Obama squashed congressional efforts to pass a resolution recognizing the genocide.[911]

- In 2007, Obama stated that the president does not have the power to unilaterally authorize military action, but did not seek congressional approval for sending our troops to Libya.[912]

- Early in his administration, Obama called Egyptian President Mubarak an ally and a "force for good."[913] When it became clear that Mubarak was in trouble, Obama did an about face and called for Mubarak to surrender power.[914]

- Obama said that he would not turn a blind eye to the ongoing genocide in the Darfur region of Sudan, but has done absolutely nothing about it as President.[915]

- He publicly claimed, in a speech to the American Israel Public Affairs Committee, that the United States "will always have Israel's back" but effectively retracted the statement a couple of days later during a press conference.[916]

We're just scratching the surface here – this is but a taste of the total chaos that has been Obama's foreign policy. The point to keep in mind is that these sorts of flip-flops happen routinely in every administration, but when they cluster like this, they have an impact much more important than any individual issue. They tell the world that we don't know what we're doing – they give credence to the Islamist propaganda that the United States is a blind, petulant empire indiscriminately killing innocent people and destabilizing nations for no reason and leaving nothing but misery behind.

173. Nominating John Brennan as CIA Director

John Brennan served as Obama's Homeland Security Advisor during his first term. He had been Obama's original pick for CIA

Director back in 2009, but was forced to withdraw because of Democrat opposition. Liberated by his reelection, Obama nominated him for the position again in 2013. But Brennan's road to heading the CIA would still not be easy. Brennan, the architect of Obama's controversial drone program, also "helped construct and justify the administration's claim that it can kill people, including American citizens, abroad, on its own authority, even when those people are not in countries with which we are at war."[917] During his Senate Committee Hearing, Brennan claimed that due process is not necessary to kill Americans for their potential future acts.[918]

There are other reasons why Brennan was a bad choice for the job. According to Steven Emerson, the executive director of The Investigative Project on Terrorism, Brennan has "shown a tendency to fall for the bait from radical Islamists."

Globally, [Brennan] repeatedly expressed a hope that "moderates" within Iran and its terror proxy Hezbollah would steer their respective constituencies away from terrorism.

Domestically, he claims that radical Islam does not pose its own, unique threat to American security. He has helped strip language about "radical Islam," "jihad" and similar terms from government vernacular, choosing instead to refer to "violent extremism" in an attempt to deny terrorists religious credibility.

When it comes to jihad, he stubbornly maintains the word does not belong in conversations about terror, no matter what terrorists themselves say.

Likewise, he also yielded to demands from American Islamists to purge law enforcement and intelligence training material of the terms "jihad" and "radical Islam."[919]

Brennan has also claimed that terrorists are motivated by economic and political factors, not religious ones, despite plenty of evidence to the contrary.[920]

Brennan's political correctness has undoubtedly blinded him to potential threats. In 2010, Brennan allowed a sheik linked to Hamas to participate in an FBI-hosted "Citizens Academy" which gave him a tutorial on the National Counterterrorism Center and

THE LEGACY OF BARACK OBAMA

other secure government facilities.[921] Brennan was confirmed by the Senate, but received a record breaking 34 votes *against* his confirmation for the position.[922]

174. Skipping the Paris Anti-Terrorism Rally

George W. Bush famously said, in his 2002 State of the Union Address, in which he laid out a vision for his response to the 9/11 Terror Attack, "To all nations who have sponsored terrorists or given them safe harbor, I have a simple message. You are either with us, or you're against us." He was roundly mocked by leftists for his "simplistic" worldview, but there are certain times when a question arises for which there must be a simple answer or no answer at all. This is one of those questions: does the United States stand opposed to terrorism in the name of religion or not?

In the aftermath of the Islamic Jihadist massacre conducted in the offices of the French satirical paper *Charlie Hebdo* for running cartoons of the Islamic prophet Muhammad, the world united in outrage against the attack and in solidarity with the French people. On January 11, 2015, an historic rally against terrorism and in support of free speech took place in Paris, bringing together 1.3 million people, including 44 heads of state from around the world. One very glaring absence from the event was Barack Obama.

Obama's muted response to the shooting at the *Charlie Hebdo* offices, where 12 people were killed, stands in sharp contrast to his remarks following the death of Michael Brown, killed resisting arrest in Ferguson, MO in 2014. Obama sent three representatives to Brown's funeral.[923] But this rally against terrorism, a worldwide expression of solidarity, was not important enough to Obama for him to attend. What was Obama doing that kept him away from joining hands with other world leaders, including German Chancellor Angela Merkel, Israeli Prime Minister Benjamin Netanyahu, and British Prime Minister David Cameron?

According to an administration official, Obama had an open schedule, and spent part of the afternoon watching football on television.[924] With all the world leaders present, security could not have been a legitimate concern. Obama should have been there, or a high-ranking official in his administration. But, none were there. Vice-President Biden, whose public schedule was also open, did not attend. Secretary of State John Kerry was in India. Attorney General Eric Holder, who was actually in Paris at the time for a terrorism summit, did not participate either.[925]

Outrage over the snub forced the Obama administration to apologize and admit that it should have sent a high-ranking official to the event. Security concerns were blamed for Obama's absence—though, according to a former Secret Service agent, if Obama *wanted* to go, the Secret Service could have made it work.[926]

The snub wasn't surprising. In 2012, the Obama administration condemned *Charlie Hebdo* for featuring cartoons of Muhammad for being offensive and for potentially inflaming violence.[927] Obama also declared, in a speech to the U.N., that "the future must not belong to those who slander the prophet of Islam."[928] The Obama administration was even reluctant to call the attack "terrorism," and avoided any language associating violence with Islam.[929] Time and time again, when it comes to free speech and standing up against terrorism, Obama has been on the wrong side; and if you think complaining about a symbolic gesture not made is splitting hairs, we recommend you keep reading. This is just a symbol, but a symbol of an intellectual rot at the core of Obama's worldview that threatens everything we hold dear.

175. Double Talk on Lockerbie Bomber Release

On July 25, 2009, Abdelbaset al-Megrahi, the Lockerbie bomber, was released from prison on compassionate grounds. Al-

Megrahi was dying of prostate cancer. He was also responsible for the deaths of 270 people and, naturally, there was plenty of outrage. Of those 270 victims, 189 were Americans. Barack Obama denounced the decision. A year later, in a joint press conference at the White House with the British Minister, Obama reiterated that sentiment:

I think all of us here in the United States were surprised, disappointed, and angry about the release of the Lockerbie bomber. And my administration expressed, very clearly, our objections prior to the decision being made and subsequent to the decision being made. So we welcome any additional information that will give us insights and a better understanding of why the decision was made.[930]

But, less than a week later, it was revealed that the Obama administration had secretly advised Scottish ministers to free the Lockerbie bomber rather than jail him in Libya.[931] Not only did Al-Megrahi receive a hero's welcome upon returning to Libya, but also he lived for another two years, much longer than the short few months expected when he was released.

176. Hidden Drone Attack

On November 1, 2012, the Iranian air force attacked an unmanned U.S. drone aircraft in international airspace. News of Iran's deliberate act of war was not released to the American people until November 8th, two days *after* the presidential election.[932] The Pentagon dubiously argued that they couldn't tell us about the attack until after the election because of security concerns.

The Pentagon obviously denied political motivation for keeping the incident secret. However, key Republican leaders, who would normally be briefed about such an incident were not informed. Nor was Mitt Romney, who had been receiving intelligence briefings at the time.[933] Political expediency cannot be tolerated as an excuse for failing to respond immediately—and with conviction—to such acts by enemy combatants.

177.Islamic Radicals at the White House

According to the founder of the Muslim Brotherhood, Hassan al-Bama, "it is the nature of Islam to dominate, not to be dominated, to impose its law on all nations and to extend its power to the entire planet."[934] That is pretty clear and straight forward. Boiled down, it means that if you are non-Muslim, then the Muslim Brotherhood is your enemy. If any group should be watched and opposed by the United States – the champion of pluralist government and freedom of conscience in the world – then the Muslim Brotherhood is it. And, for the longest time, that is exactly how the United States treated the Muslim Brotherhood: as an enemy in practice. Until Obama became President – he seems incapable of telling friend from foe, especially in the battle against radical Islam.

In April of 2012, it was revealed that White House officials had met with members of Egypt's Muslim Brotherhood. The White House justified the meeting, saying that the Muslim Brotherhood would play a "prominent role" in Egyptian affairs going forward.[935] Indeed, they would. After all, the White House had played a key role in ousting the Mubarak regime, which had kept a lid on the Muslim Brotherhood.

But that's not all. According to an investigation by the Investigative Project on Terrorism, "scores of known radical Islamists made hundreds of visits to the Obama White House, meeting with top administration officials."

The IPT made the discovery combing through millions of White House visitor log entries. IPT compared the visitors' names with lists of known radical Islamists. Among the visitors were officials representing groups which have:

- *Been designated by the Department of Justice as unindicted co-conspirators in terrorist trials; Extolled Islamic terrorist groups including Hamas and Hezbollah;*
- *Obstructed terrorist investigations by instructing their followers not to cooperate with law enforcement;*
- *Promoted the incendiary conspiratorial allegation that the United States is engaged in a "war against Islam"— a leading tool in recruiting Muslims to carry out acts of terror;*
- *Repeatedly claimed that many of the Islamic terrorists convicted since 9-11 were framed by the U.S government as part of an anti-Muslim profiling campaign.*

Individuals from the Council on American-Islamic Relations (CAIR) visited the White House at least 20 times starting in 2009. In 2008, CAIR was listed as an unindicted co-conspirator in the largest terrorist money laundering case in U.S. history – the trial of the Holy Land Foundation in which five HLF officials were convicted of funneling money to Hamas.[936]

These are hardly the types of people that should be given access to the White House, meeting with top administration officials, and potentially influencing the administration's foreign policy.

178. Allowing Terror-Linked Refugees into the U.S.

Who wants to have someone with "limited burglary contacts" as their neighbor? There won't be too many takers on that. But that is what President Obama is doing with the United States, except worse. In Obama's very determined effort to be nice to people who hate us, in February 2014 he changed our immigration laws—without Congressional authorization—to relax restrictions on refugees and asylum seekers who have provided "limited" material support to terrorists and terrorist organizations. The Obama administration—which has denied asylum to oppressed Christians—called this law change "common sense."[937]

One of the excuses offered for waiving the restrictions is that some people might have helped terrorists under duress.[938] Apparently, Obama feels that the safety of Americans takes a back seat to giving possible terrorists the benefit of the doubt by laying down the welcome mat and letting them into the country. This is what Obama calls "common sense"? This level of incoherence was but a taste of what was to come, however.

In 2015, as millions of Syrian and Iraqi refugees – and by refugees, we mean able-bodied, fighting-aged young men, predominantly – poured into Europe and overwhelmed the EU's resources, world leaders began pressuring the United States to take some of them. Obama was all too happy to oblige, and he began making plans to order Immigration and Naturalization Services to drastically expand its program for refugees in order to accept ten thousand Syrians in 2016,[939] justifying the move on humanitarian grounds and claiming that they would be heavily vetted.[940]

The problems with this were threefold. First, the refugees pouring into Europe were, at the time Obama was pushing for this resettlement program, rampaging through the continent leading to huge spikes in rape rates,[941] armed robberies, and assaults and inspiring a nationalist political pushback throughout eastern Europe.[942] Second, his own security experts told him and the American people that the vetting process could not be thorough enough to screen out terrorists.[943] And third, Americans were overwhelmingly opposed to the idea and 31 state governors signed executive orders or bills passed by state legislatures declaring their refusal to accept them.[944] Whatever beef you may have had with his first decision to allow terror-linked refugees into the US, the lack of care he displayed then for the will of the American people and for their protection was dwarfed by this foray into ill-placed magnanimity.

179.Attempt to Prosecute Khalid Sheik Mohammed in the United States

Barack Obama had made it clear that he wanted 9/11 Mastermind Khalid Sheikh Mohammed and four co-conspirators to be tried in the U.S. Federal court system. This was a terrible idea on many levels: Security costs would have been enormous, it would give terrorists a public platform to denounce America, and it could have jeopardized intelligence sources. Despite these reasons, Obama, an outspoken critic of military tribunals, was determined to have a public trial in New York City.

The plan was so bad that there was bipartisan opposition from Congress. New York City officials were also opposed to the plan.[945] The administration did eventually reverse their policy. Not because they realized the error of their ways, but because Congress refused to provide the funds for a trial on American soil.[946] The bottom line can be summed up thusly: international terrorism is not a federal crime; it is an act of war. Federal authorities have no jurisdiction to prosecute Khalid Sheik Muhammed, and it reveals a stunning lack of common sense for Obama to make a public spectacle out of the handling of a war criminal.

180.Ignoring Worldwide Christian Oppression

In 2007, Obama promised, "As a president of the United States, I don't intend to abandon people or turn a blind eye to slaughter." They were fine, noble words but totally devoid of substance in the years that followed. According to a report by the bipartisan United States Commission on International Religious Freedom released in May 2014, the Obama administration has ignored the persecution of Christians worldwide.[947] This is particularly outrageous as, throughout his Presidency, Obama has been quick to condemn what he perceives as persecution, as long as the alleged victim fits certain criteria. It would seem that the only people he won't ignore are the ones that allow Obama to burnish his image among his core, liberal supporters. Whenever it appears that an American minority person is being ill-treated - even if the accusation of ill-treatment turns out, upon investigation, to be false - there is Barack Obama lavish with his condemnations. On the other hand, when it comes to the world's most oppressed religious group, Obama has been silent.[948] In 2012, Christian villages in Sudan were bombed during Christmastime by the country's own military.[949] In Pakistan, Christians are routinely accused of anti-Muslim blasphemy on trumped up charges—often resulting in death for the accused.[950] ISIS has forced the Christian population of Mosul, Iraq to flee for their lives.[951]

Christian oppression around the world is very real, particularly in Muslim nations, and has been getting much worse as time goes on. With the situation darkening, Obama makes no effort to even speak out forcefully against the evil. Obama even allowed his Administration to press forward with the deportation of a Christian German family that sought asylum in the United States so they can home-school their children,[952] while also denying refugee status for some of Egypt's Coptic Christian minority fleeing persecution.[953]

181.Tax Dollars for Terrorist Groups

On a Friday night in April of 2012, it was revealed that Barack Obama bypassed Congress in order to send $192 million in aid to the Palestinian Authority (PA). Funding for the PA had been frozen by Congress after PA president Mahmoud Abbas requested that the U.N. recognize a Palestinian state. Obama claimed his waiver was important to the national security of the United States. A bizarre claim indeed, since his actions came just months after the terrorist group Hamas became a partner with the PA. In other words, Obama bypassed Congress to give nearly $200 million of our tax dollars to a terrorist organization.[954]

Five months later, Obama informed Congress that he would provide $450 million in emergency aid for Egypt's new government, now controlled by the Muslim Brotherhood, a group with a history of supporting terrorism.[955] Left unexplained was just what "emergency" required the American taxpayer to fund a Muslim Brotherhood government. To put it into perspective, Osama bin Laden, his top deputy Ayman al-Zawahiri, and 9/11 mastermind Khalid Sheikh Mohammed all once belonged to the Muslim Brotherhood before bin Laden formed al Qaeda. Hamas considers itself to be the Muslim Brotherhood's Palestinian branch.[956] Indeed, prior to the fall of the old Mubarak regime in Egypt, the Muslim Brotherhood had been suppressed as a terrorist organization in Egypt. The left claims that the Muslim Brotherhood is more moderate than its affiliates, but their own charter makes clear that their goal is to spread Sharia Law throughout the world.[957] And in a sad finale to this story, the Muslim Brotherhood government in Egypt lasted less than two years and was deposed by the Egyptian military for being too radical and endangering Egypt's economic ties to the west.

With our national debt skyrocketing and Obama planning on gutting our military budget, it is impossible to understand why Obama believes our tax dollars should be given to foreign enemies of the United States.

182.Bypassing Congress to Give Aid to The Muslim Brotherhood

Ever since the 1979 peace deal between Egypt and Israel, the United States has supplied large amounts of military and economic aid to Egypt. This aid was predicated upon Egypt continuing to maintain peace with Israel, including ensuring that Israel would suffer no attacks from the Egyptian-governed Sinai Peninsula.[958] In the aftermath of the so-called "Arab Spring", the Egyptian government fell under the control of the Muslim Brotherhood, a terrorist group committed to violent action against both Israel and the United States. Because the old Egyptian regime had been overthrown and everyone was unsure what sort of government would finally emerge, Congress restricted aid to Egypt until the Obama administration certified to Congress that the Egyptian government is maintaining peace with Israel, is democratic, and is respecting the rights of all Egyptians.[959]

Despite increasing reports of Muslim Brotherhood actions to suppress opposition (as well as increasingly horrific attacks upon Egypt's Coptic Christian minority), President Obama unilaterally waived Egypt's requirements in order to release $1.5 billion in funds for Egypt's military.[960]

Obama dressed up the move by claiming that national security interests required us to give the aid, even though Obama could not certify that Egypt was meeting the requirements demanded by Congress. Obama argued that aiding the Egyptian military would help ensure a democratic future in Egypt. Even members of Obama's own party questioned his motives. Senator Patrick Leahy (D-VT) called Obama's actions a mistake, arguing that the restriction imposed by Congress were "intended to put the United States squarely on the side of the Egyptian people who seek a civilian government that respects fundamental freedoms and the rule of law, and to clearly define the terms of our future relations with the Egyptian military."[961]

But what happened when a revolution (backed by overwhelming numbers of the Egyptian people[962]) overthrew the Muslim Brotherhood government? Obama moved to cut aid to Egypt![963] Suddenly, our national security interests were no longer a factor. Suddenly the secular Egyptian military was a greater threat to peace than a terrorist organization at the levers of power in the most influential country in the Middle East other than Israel.

Obama's actions here are hard to explain, and impossible to justify. Going around Congress in order to provide aid to an enemy of America just doesn't sound like the actions of a president who has our nation's values and interests at heart.

183.Purging Gitmo

As a candidate in 2007, Obama promised that he was going to close the terrorist detention facility at Guantánamo Bay, Cuba (Gitmo) as soon as he was elected. He promised it so many times that it was a given: both Obama's supporters and opponents assumed that Gitmo was as good as closed as soon as a he could organize the closure. Opponents of this plan had many legitimate concerns and questions. Where would the prisoners go? How would they be tried? Where would we hold any terrorists captured after Gitmo was closed?

But, Obama was less concerned about the logistics and more concerned with fulfilling his promise. He signed an executive order on January 22, 2009 requiring Gitmo closed within one year.[964] But, he was not able to carry out his own executive order because of opposition from Congress. This Congressional opposition eventually led Obama, on January 3, 2013, to sign the National Defense Authorization Act (NDAA) which barred the use of federal funds to transfer Gitmo prisoners to the United States, despite a promised veto.[965]

Obama has been unable to close Gitmo as he promised, but he has been systematically purging the prison of its terrorist inmates, as a sort of end-run around Congressional opposition to closure. In 2003, there were 680 prisoners. By early January 2015, there were less than 130. According to the *New York Times*, Obama's goal for his last two years in office "is to deplete the Guantánamo prison to the point where it houses 60 to 80 people and keeping it open no longer makes economic sense."[966]

While the Obama administration claims only 6 percent of terrorists released from Gitmo have returned to fight for the enemy, retired CIA officer Gary Berntsen says it's at least 50 percent, and the purging of Gitmo is actually inspiring the growth of radical Islam. "Many of these people that we captured would tell us right to our faces: We're going to be released and kill you and your families when we get out. That's their attitude. Because they don't believe the United States is going to act harshly against them. They see the light at the end of the tunnel, they want to continue the fight against us."[967]

There is a massive element of unreality in the process of releasing these prisoners. So strong is Obama's desire to close Gitmo that out-going Secretary of Defense Hagel admitted that he felt pressure within the Administration to accelerate the release of prisoners against his better judgment.[968] The Obama administration claims that all those released are low-risk, but five Yemeni detainees were released in January 2015 even though they were all medium or high-risk detainees.[969] But Obama, after claiming for years that Gitmo is a Gulag-style cesspit of abuse, would sooner free them—giving them the opportunity to rejoin their jihad against America—rather than keep Gitmo open. The reality is that Gitmo houses some of the most evil and dangerous men in the world. They were given regular meals and exercise time. They were also allowed to freely practice their religion.

None of us know how many lives will be at risk just so that Obama could keep the most absurd of his campaign promises, but we do know—from testimony from Paul Lewis, Obama's Special Envoy for Guantanamo Closure—is that "there have been Americans that have died because of Gitmo detainees."[970]

184.Negotiating With Taliban Terrorists

In January of 2012, the *New York Times* reported that "Several Taliban negotiators [had] begun meeting with American officials in Qatar, where they [were] discussing preliminary trust-building measures, including a possible prisoner transfer[.]"[971] According to Judicial Watch, "As part of 'Taliban reconciliation efforts,' the terrorists would be transferred to Qatar, a Middle Eastern Arab state where [the Taliban] will soon open an office. The Obama administration sold the preposterous deal to Congress by saying that the prisoners wouldn't actually be released but rather transferred to the custody of the Qatari government and they will remain in jail."[972]

With bipartisan opposition in Congress to the plan, the Obama administration's negotiations failed. Eventual peace talks are still in consideration. It seems rather strange that the Obama administration would be willing to negotiate directly with a terrorist organization. Except that according to the State Department, the U.S. strangely does not consider the Taliban a terrorist group.[973]

185.The Bowe Bergdahl Swap

The Obama White House's habit of making deals with terrorists reached a new low in 2014 as five high-ranking Jihadi's were released into the custody of Qatar in exchange for the return of Army deserter Bowe Bergdahl. The U.S. military has long followed the admirable code: leave no one behind. No matter what the costs or risks involved, everyone comes home. This, of course, is in the nature of the honor of the men and women of our armed forces. But honor is a two-way street, and those who desert, especially in the face of the enemy, are often held in contempt. Given this, the circumstances surrounding Bowe Bergdahl's release from Taliban captivity came under immediate scrutiny.

Soldiers who had served with Bergdahl claimed that he had left his post in Afghanistan voluntarily, and that he had, in fact, deserted.[974] Subsequently, soldiers reported being threatened by the Obama administration to remain silent about what they knew about Bergdahl's disappearance.[975] According to reports by a private intelligence agency contracted by the Defense Department, Bergdahl also converted to Islam and declared jihad while in captivity.[976]

Adding together the increased jeopardy of Americans worldwide by negotiating with terrorists (and by the activities of the five terrorist leaders we released), the doubts over whether

Bergdahl was captured or had deserted, the lopsidedness of the swap, and not informing Congress of the details of the planned exchange, what was thought to be a political win for Obama was now a huge political liability. Responsibility (or blame) for the swap was directed away from Obama when Administration officials suddenly claimed that Secretary of Defense Chuck Hagel had actually been the one to make the final call on the swap.[977]

The Obama administration justified the swap by saying that the United States never leaves any of our service members behind —a justification that rings hollow given the four Americans left behind in Benghazi, or the U.S. Marine who had been held in captivity in Mexico, whom Obama didn't seem motivated to bring to freedom, or the servicemen still in Iran despite our sudden willingness to negotiate with Tehran. Bergdahl, according to members of his platoon, was a deserter, yet he was traded for five high-level Taliban members, who are likely to rejoin their fight against America. Was this really about Bergdahl, or emptying Gitmo? In January 2015, military and intelligence officials had already suspected that one of those released rejoined the fight.[978]

Obama clearly thought he would be considered a hero for securing Bergdahl's freedom, and would enjoy more political capital to spend on his agenda at home. Instead, it became yet another foreign policy blunder—a blunder that encourages our enemies and endangers all Americans. On March 25, 2015, ten months after his release, Sgt. Bergdahl was charged with desertion. If convicted, he faces life in prison.[979]

186.The Boston Marathon Bombing

As of the writing of this book, the Boston Marathon has been settled in federal court, with the conviction of Dzhokhar Tsarnaev and his subsequent death sentence. FBI probes into how the Tsarnaev brothers were able to carry out their plot and elude antiterrorism investigators are underway, but it will likely take some time to put all of the pieces together. What we do know at this time suggests that the Obama administration could have prevented the tragedy that occurred on April 15, 2013.

Less than two months before the bombing, Obama had issued a "National Policy for Countering Improvised Explosive Devices," in which he wrote "we must not become complacent," over the threats of improvised explosive devices (IEDs) at home and abroad.[980] However, the day after the bombing, it was revealed that the budget for domestic bomb prevention had been cut to $11 million by the Obama administration. The budget was $20 million during the Bush Administration.

Obama has argued that a mere two percent reduction in government spending due to the sequestration of government spending that followed the 2011 debt ceiling negotiation would have been devastating to our country, yet cutting 45 percent from domestic bomb prevention was apparently inconsequential to him. Had the Obama administration not made those cuts, would the bombing have been prevented? There's no way to tell, but it certainly appears Obama had become very complacent about the threat of terrorism here in the United States.

Unfortunately, Obama's complacency over the threat of terrorism manifested itself in other ways. Just a few days after the bombing, the FBI was able to identify two suspects in the bombing: Chechen brothers Tamerlan Tsarnaev, 26, and Dzhokhar Tsarnaev, 19, who came to America as refugees in 2002. Tamerlan had been arrested in 2009 for domestic violence. The Obama administration could have deported him after the arrest, but did not.[981] Why wasn't he deported then? Two years later, Tamerlan was interrogated by the FBI, at the request of the Russian government, regarding possible extremist ties.[982] Government spying on civilians has also been up under Obama, yet Tamerlan was *not* under surveillance by the federal government. Why not? We have someone with possible extremist ties and a police record that the Obama administration chose not to deport and was not keeping an eye on.

One explanation could be the Obama administration's unwillingness to link terrorism and Islamic extremism. On the evening of April 19, 2013, after Dzhokhar Tsarnaev was caught, Obama, speaking to the nation, devoted nearly twenty percent of his statement to talking about diversity and not rushing to judgment about the motives of the terrorists.[983] It had already been widely reported that Tamerlan had shared radical Islamic videos online in support of killing enemies of Islam, but Obama wanted us to turn a blind eye to the bombers' motives.[984]

A week after the bombings, it was revealed that the Russian government had actually warned the FBI "multiple times" about Tamerlan's radicalism, but the agency was "more concerned with al-Qaeda and other Middle Eastern terrorist groups," and overlooked the threat of Chechen terrorists.[985] A major intelligence failure appears to have taken place.

The Obama administration needs to answer a lot of questions about why the eldest brother wasn't on the FBI's radar, and why resources for preventing domestic terrorism were slashed.

187. Missing The Opportunity to Destroy Al-Qaeda

The death of Osama bin Laden in May 2011 was not only a great moment in the War on Terror, it was also the biggest missed opportunity. Had Barack Obama been less interested in getting credit for (and benefiting politically from) bin Laden's death and more interested in actually defeating al-Qaeda, the War on Terror perhaps would have turned out better in the years following the terror mastermind's death.

In addition to bin Laden's body, there were also papers, hard drives and thumb drives containing a treasure trove of intelligence removed from his lair. According to bestselling author and award-winning investigative journalist Richard Miniter, the potential to wipe out al-Qaeda was lost because "Obama ran to the cameras and raced to tell the world that bin Laden was dead." According to Miniter, the data collected included "the whereabouts of al-Qaeda's senior commanders, the secret sources of funds, its hideouts, its sleeper cells, its pending plots."[986] Had Obama waited a few weeks for U.S. intelligence agencies to translate and analyze the captured documents, they would have had actionable intelligence that "nearly every al-Qaeda leader could have been killed or captured."[987]

It gets worse. Not only did Obama miss the opportunity to wipe out al-Qaeda, but he deliberately misled America about al-Qaeda's supposed demise in order to get reelected. According to five senior U.S. intelligence officials "the documents (captured from bin Laden) sat largely untouched for months—perhaps as long as a year."[988] At that point, the 2012 presidential election was six months away, and Obama was going around the country repeating the claim that al-Qaeda was near its demise. Nothing could have been further from the truth, and the captured documents proved that. Al-Qaeda, the documents showed, was alive and well and growing. In order to keep Americans in the dark about this before the election, the Obama administration limited the Defense Intelligence Agency's access to the documents "and instructed DIA officials to stop producing analyses based on them."[989]

Obama covered up the truth about al-Qaeda so that he could use al-Qaeda's demise as a campaign talking point, even as al-Qaeda was growing and getting stronger. It is unfortunate that the most important aspect of bin Laden's death for Obama was the political consequences, because he failed to capitalize on the strategic benefits the United States secured from the documents that were recovered. Had Obama not rushed to take credit and taken advantage of the intelligence received, the demise of al-Qaeda may have become a factual talking point, instead of a fictional one.

188. Terrorist Attacks on US Soil (and Obama's Denialism)

At least six terrorist attacks on U.S. soil have been successful on Obama's watch. The Fort Hood shootings on November 5, 2009, the bombing of the Social Security building in Casa Grande, Arizona on November 30, 2012, the Boston Marathon bombing on April 15, 2013, the July 16, 2015 Chattanooga, TN attack, the shootings in San Bernadino, CA in December of 2015, and the June 12, 2016 mass shooting in Orlando, FL. There've been other potentially terror-related incidents, more limited in scope, including a pair of brutal murders of police officers in New York City, a beheading in Oklahoma City, the shooting that took place outside of Pamela Gellar's irreverent "Draw Mohammed" art contest in Garland, TX, and a drive-by shooting at a military base in Little Rock, AK. But even if you want to limit the count to the first six, that's a lot of bloodshed in the name of the prophet right here at home, and these are the attacks that succeeded. There were at least two others that could have been just as devastating and failed only because the perpetrators weren't competent in their execution of well-laid plans.

A plot by al-Qaeda leaders in Yemen to blow up a plane over Detroit on Christmas Day in 2009 was carried out by Abdul Farouk Umar Abdulmutallab, who had explosives sewn into his underwear. The attempt was nearly successful, but Abdulmutallab failed to detonate the explosives properly. He was subdued by passengers and arrested upon landing. This was a gross failure of the system. Abdulmutallab had been on a U.S. terror watch-list and his own father had recognized his son's radicalism and informed the U.S. Embassy in Nigeria alerting them that his son was a potential threat to the United States.[990]

Less than six months later, there was another close call with an attempted car bombing in Times Square. On May 10, 2010, two street vendors noticed smoke coming from a parked car in Times Square. The car bomb had been ignited but failed to explode. The bomb was disarmed and no one was hurt or killed. Faisal Shahzad, who had been trained at a Pakistani terror training camp, was arrested two days later. The plot was directed and financed by the Pakistani Taliban.[991]

The *Washington Times* reported, in May of 2010, that Shahzad "was on the Department of Homeland Security's Traveler Enforcement Compliance System list as late as 2008. The Obama administration *removed* him from that list. He also was under the scrutiny of the national Joint Terrorism Task

Force until the Obama administration waved it off the case." Had Shahzad been a more competent terrorist, the Obama administration would have had to answer a lot of question about their actions.

Adding insult to injury, while all of this bloodshed occurred, Obama steadfastly refused to acknowledge the source of the violence. In the run-up to his re-election effort in 2012, Obama couldn't risk the political ramifications of having successful terrorist attacks in the U.S. on his watch, and so the Fort Hood and Social Security incidents (which occurred during his first term) were *not* classified as terrorism, despite all the evidence that these were, in fact, acts of terror.

Nidal Malik Hasan, the U.S. Army major who shot and killed 13 people and wounded many others, had been in contact with Anwar al-Awlaki, a radical American-born imam who had been under investigation by U.S. intelligence agencies for years. In December of 2011, it was revealed that Obama's Department of Defense had classified the shooting as "workplace violence."[992] Even Obama would not describe the shooting as terrorism.[993]

Abdullalltif Ali Aldosary, the Iraqi refugee who created a homemade explosive and bombed a Social Security building, had previously been denied U.S. citizenship for "terror-related activity." Aldosary had planned the bombing in advance, and had researched terrorist bombs. According to the criminal complaint, documents on how to build bombs were hidden behind a picture in his home, and he also tried to obtain information on how to create RDX, a powerful military high-yield explosive, which has been used in many terrorist plots.[994] Despite all this, Aldosary was not charged with terrorism. Instead, he was charged with "maliciously damaging federal property by means of explosives," and with illegal possession of a firearm.[995]

After the election, and despite no serious risk to Obama or his party, Obama still refused to refer to the term "radical Islamic terrorism" or "Jihadist", and still insisted on calling the San Bernadino and Orlando attacks bouts of gun violence, as though they were common crime to be dealt with by our justice system and not acts of war. If the government doesn't recognize a terror attack as a terror attack, then Obama keeps his legacy free of terror attacks. But, calling it "workplace violence" or "damaging federal property" doesn't change the truth of Obama's record on domestic terrorism.

189.Whitewashing Islamic Terrorism

While Obama's refusal to link blatant acts of terrorism with radical Islam is well documented,[996] and, honestly, quite disturbing, his Orwellian attempts to censor references to Islamic terrorism from the public have far worse implications. On March 31, 2016, President Obama and President Hollande of France gave joint remarks to the press on terrorism. Video of the remarks were posted on the White House, then briefly removed, then re-posted. The re-posted video edited out portions of Hollande's remarks where he referred to "Islamist terrorism."[997] Suddenly, Obama's policy of not referring to Islamic terrorism now included altering audio and video to remove references to Islamic terrorism.

But perhaps the worst example came in the wake of the Orlando mass shooting. The public was already aware through earlier media reporting of eyewitness accounts that the gunman had pledged allegiance to Allah and ISIS, but that didn't stop the Obama administration from trying to frame the incident as a bigoted act of gun violence rather than an act of Islamic terror. But, their denialism eventually turned into full-fledged revisionism. A week after the shooting, the FBI released edited transcripts of the 911 calls made by gunman Omar Mateen, omitting all references to Islam and ISIS, which makes this blatant attempt to rewrite history even more baffling. Outrage naturally followed, and the FBI and Justice Department eventually released the full transcripts later the same afternoon.[998] Despite the fact Mateen's motives were crystal clear, the day after the full transcripts were released, Attorney General Loretta Lynch declared that Mateen's motives may never be known. Really? [999]

Why would the Obama administration try to whitewash the real motivations of Mateen from the public? If anything, keeping such information from the public can only make us less safe. With regular terror attacks on U.S. soil becoming a new reality on Obama's watch, he should be more concerned with protecting us than with protecting radical Islamists.

190. Intelligence Failures in the San Bernardino and Orlando Mass Shootings

As Obama's presidency draws to a close, the violence here at home seems to be on the rise. As previously mentioned, there have been two particularly bloody mass shootings since late 2015, one in San Bernadino, CA involving Syed Rizwan Farook and Tashfeen Malik, a married couple who'd been radicalized in Afghanistan and took to their Jihad at a Christmas party with their colleagues,[1000] the other a lone gunman who held an Orlando gay night club hostage and slaughtered fifty young men and women, then called police to declare his allegiance to ISIS.[1001] We do not blame Barack Obama for these incidents – even a well-oiled intelligence machine is going to miss a plot every now and then. Instead, we intend to highlight massive failures of the intelligence apparatus and demonstrate the connection of those failures to the Obama administration's politically correct policy toward radical Islam.

Following the San Bernardino attack, during which fourteen people were killed and twenty-two were injured, as Barack Obama took to the airwaves in a rare televised address from the Oval Office to denounce the 'gun violence' and insist that conservatives get behind 'common sense gun reforms', real questions about the effectiveness of our domestic terrorism prevention apparatus began to surface. In the wake of the chaos, it was revealed that Malik had been granted a green card despite the fact that her public writings and social media presence, while in Afghanistan, revealed a strong radical streak.[1002] On top of that, neighbors observed a host of deeply troubling behavior from the young couple– massive shipments of supplies to their garage, strangers coming and going at odd hours and the like – and chose not to report it to police for fear of being branded racists for engaging in 'profiling'.[1003] And following up on any leads they might have gained from Farook's cell phone became impossible when agents investigating the attack blundered into locking up the phone with no way to recover it.[1004]

Then, in the summer of 2016, following the grisly murder of fifty innocent people in Orlando, FL, the Jihadi attacker's history came to light, and cast further doubts on the seriousness of our security policy. The man responsible, Omar Mateen, had, twice before, been on the FBI's radar as a possible terrorist threat and no action was taken. They even interviewed him three times in 2013 and 2014 due to his having contacts who were known terrorists.[1005] In fact, the FBI dropped their investigation of Mateen after concluding that concerns over his terroristic threats were the result of anti-Muslim bigotry of his coworkers.[1006]

Indeed, Mateen had let plenty of clues about his radical leanings and mental instability in recent years, including harassing his colleagues, spewing racist and sexist slurs at work, being arrested for beating his ex-wife, and leaving an extensive social media trail between him and Jihadis. Oh, and did we mention that Mateen's father was, at the time of the shooting, running for the Presidency...of Afghanistan – as a pro-Taliban figure with years of social media propagandizing for the Taliban behind him? But the kicker, it would appear, is that Mateen was a member of a radical mosque in Orlando that some in the intelligence community have wanted to be investigated for its radical preaching and ties to terrorist affiliates, but Obama senior officials ignored the threat posed by this mosque.

We could forgive the intelligence community for missing one or two terrorists – they are doing their best under very difficult circumstances – but what we cannot forgive is an administrative climate that appears to slow the counter-terrorism forces' response to potential threats, interfere with their ability to investigate radicals, demand that agents err on the side of inaction rather than action lest accusations of profiling surface, and, in general, hold back our best people from effectively doing their jobs. When you compound this climate with the rapidly rising pace of ISIS and Al Qaeda-backed terror plots on U.S. soil and the culture of politically correct intimidation of the citizenry, what you get is a recipe for disaster.

191.The Benghazi Attack & Cover Up

There is much we don't know about what happened on September 11, 2012, when the American consulate in Benghazi, Libya was attacked, along with the U.S. Embassy in Cairo, Egypt. We know that, in Benghazi, four Americans were killed, including U.S. Ambassador to Libya, Christopher Stevens. Investigations are still ongoing and we don't have a comprehensive statement about what happened from Obama. But, there are some things about the Benghazi attack which cannot be doubted:

- The attack was clearly carried out by terrorists linked to al Qaeda and this fact was known in the administration within hours of the attack. [1007]
- The murdered Ambassador in Benghazi had called repeatedly for additional security for our diplomatic posts in Benghazi. [1008]
- Former Defense Secretary Leon Panetta has testified that he personally informed Obama that the consulate was under attack, and that they didn't speak again for another six hours, contradicting previous claims by Obama that he was fully engaged with the response. [1009]

- Obama's former Secretary of State, Hillary Clinton, has testified that she never read the cables from Libya insisting upon the need for greater security.[1010]

- Survivors of the attack are under federal gag order, preventing them from discussing or testifying about what happened.[1011]

- A Senate Intelligence Committee report found that the State Department failed to increase security, despite deteriorating safety conditions in the area.[1012]

- While early reports of a "stand down" order were determined to be false, a House Armed Services Committee report faulted the White House for not providing adequate security, and for ignoring or failing to comprehend "the dramatically deteriorating security situation in Libya and the growing threat to U.S. interests in the region." The Defense Department also knew that it was terrorist attack "nearly from the outset."[1013]

- The claim that an obscure, anti-Islamic video was the cause of a spontaneous demonstration that got out of hand was an outright lie, but the Obama administration used the video connection as a talking point anyway.[1014] This was proven in April 2014, when a declassified email revealed by Judicial Watch showed that the White House played a central role in falsely blaming the video in order to protect Obama. Charles Krauthammer called the email "a classic cover-up of a cover-up," and a "serious offense."[1015]

- State Department documents, released in June 2015, also confirmed that the White House was immediately involved in crafting the "blame the video" strategy.[1016]

With the attack occurring two months before the presidential election, it is quite clear that the White House cared more about getting Obama reelected than the four

Americans who died needlessly because of the Obama administration's incompetence. Protecting Obama trumped everything, especially the truth. The Obama administration was willing to deliberately deceive the entire country rather than risk political fallout. What happened in Benghazi was preventable, and the cover-up that followed was positively Nixonian.

192.Failures of Inaction

In addition to his failures in places like Iraq and Afghanistan detailed elsewhere in this book, Obama's intellectual blind spots in the Middle East and the surrounding countries have taken a significant toll on the entire region. The Middle East is difficult for any president, but the setbacks resulting from Obama's policies have been particularly severe.

In June of 2009, millions of Iranians took peacefully to the streets in the "Green Revolution", demanding democracy. Obama made no effort to back the Iranian people—claiming he didn't want to meddle in Iranian affairs—and ignored Iranian freedom fighters' request for aid.[1017] The Iranian government slaughtered those moderates and freedom fighters in the streets, crushing any hope America had of procuring an ally in the region and feeding into Islamic propaganda claiming that the U.S. is no friend to freedom, only intervening when they have something to gain.

While Obama didn't want to help the Iranians free themselves of a dictatorship, Obama was perfectly content to push former Egyptian President Hosni Mubarak, an ally of the United States, to step down in 2011 during the Arab Spring uprisings, thus ushering in a terrorist, Muslim Brotherhood government. Obama then helped the Muslim Brotherhood government by waiving human rights requirements, thus allowing for continued military aid to Egypt, despite horrific human rights violations. One could argue that, with or without American intervention, Mubarak's days were numbered, but the real failure here was one of inaction.

When the Muslim Brotherhood government was at risk of being ousted by popular revolt backed by Egypt's military, Obama first backed the Brotherhood, threatening to cut military aid in response to the uprising.[1018] Then, as chaos and violence erupted in the country, Obama chose to step back and wash his hands of it, declaring "America cannot determine the future of Egypt."[1019] Ultimately, the people of Egypt and their military joined hands to rid their home of the cancerous Muslim Brotherhood, with no help or encouragement from President Obama. Obama's incoherent strategy in Egypt has diminished America's standing and influence in the country, leaving the moderates now in control of the nation to wonder whether it's in their best interests to ally with the U.S., or whether they should join with Saudi Arabia instead.

As previously noted, Obama's inaction in Syria, following Assad's use of sarin gas on rebels in 2013, has led to the formation of an alliance between Iran and Assad, whilst simultaneously convincing many rebels to join with ISIS as their only viable ally against Assad, playing into the local belief that the U.S. is not a reliable ally. Leon Panetta, who had previously served as Obama's CIA Director and Secretary of Defense, said Obama damaged the credibility of the United States by drawing a red line then failing to follow through.[1020] According to Panetta, Obama's failures in Syria and his early withdrawal from Iraq (against the advice of his advisors) led to the rise of ISIS in both countries.[1021] In Afghanistan, Obama's 2010 troop surge failed to stop the Taliban's momentum there, as he wasn't committed to an aggressive military posture.[1022]

Obama's counterterrorism strategy in Yemen also collapsed with the fall of the U.S.-backed Yemeni government in January 2015. Months earlier, Obama had dubbed the strategy a successful model for fighting the Islamic State in Iraq and Syria.[1023] But here, again, we see that those who are so far emerging triumphant in Yemen are Iranian-backed Islamists. In fact, so threatening is this to Yemen's neighbors that Saudi Arabia has actually launched a military campaign to roll back the Iranian-backed forces.

Likewise, as the sectarian violence in Lebanon worsened in 2014 and 2015,[1024] spurred on by ISIS fighters in the region, Obama chose to take no action, resulting in the collapse of security in Beirut – one of the most economically crucial cities in the Middle East. This particular inaction is still ongoing, and the security of Lebanon is, as of this writing, still very much in doubt.[1025]

All these failures in the region have added up. James Jeffrey, Obama's former U.S. Ambassador to Iraq, said, in March 2015, that the Middle East is destabilizing faster under Obama. "The situation has gotten worse, and the recipes that we have tried to use to stem the violence and to stem the destabilization, the basic challenge to the nation states in the region, by one or another Islamic religious movement, be it the Iranians, be it ISIS and al Qaeda, have not been successful, and now we're at a crisis point."[1026] Robert Gates, who served as Obama's first Secretary of Defense, said, in an interview in May 2015, that he didn't think the Obama administration had any Middle East strategy. "We're basically sort of playing this day to day."[1027]

193. The ISIS Intelligence Scandal

As a U.S. Senator, Barack Obama joined the chorus of liberal politicians claiming that George W. Bush manipulated intelligence about Iraq in order to justify going to war in 2002. As president, he would find himself embroiled in an intelligence scandal of his own.

In the summer of 2015, it was revealed that the Pentagon inspector general was investigating claims that high-ranking military officials were manipulating intelligence assessments of the war against ISIS.[1028] According to a report by *The Daily Beast,* more than 50 CENTCOM intelligence analysts had formally complained that their intelligence reports regarding ISIS were being "inappropriately altered by senior officials." According to the analysts, intelligence reports were manipulated to portray ISIS as weaker than it really was, so that the intelligence mirrored the "the administration's public line that the U.S. is winning the battle both against ISIS and al Nusra, al Qaeda's branch in Syria."[1029]

Barack Obama's intelligence chief, James Clapper, was directly implicated in the scandal, for having had "frequent and unusual contact" with the military intelligence officer implicated in the investigation, Army Major General Steven Grove. Clapper — who, in 2013, gave false testimony to the Senate about the scope of domestic surveillance — was speaking daily with Grove, telling him the administration's perception on the outlook of the war, and questioning CENTCOM's assessments. All of this raises questions about how much Clapper's boss, Obama, knew about the manipulation of intelligence.[1030]

Obama, true to form, claimed he was unaware of the details of the investigation. During a press conference, Obama claimed, "What I do know is my expectation, which is the highest fidelity to facts, data—the truth." But, according to retired Lt. Gen. Michael Flynn, Obama's former top military intelligence official, the investigation of manipulated intelligence should focus on the White House. In an interview with Fox News, Flynn said, "Where intelligence starts and stops is at the White House. The president sets the priorities and he's the number one customer."[1031] Flynn also told CNN that in 2011 and 2012 Obama ignored intelligence reports warning about the rise of ISIS because they did not fit the narrative of his reelection campaign.[1032]

While pre-war intelligence about Iraq may have been incorrect, there is actual evidence that intelligence about ISIS was deliberately doctored to benefit Obama politically while he was running for reelection. While this may have prevented Obama from being held accountable for the destabilization of the Middle East before he was reelected, there's no telling what damage was done because of it.

During war operations, especially, the collection and analysis of intelligence is crucial. What sort of intelligence on enemy strength and intentions provided by the Commander in Chief guides the actions of the troops in the field. The lives of military personnel are risked based upon what the supposed best intelligence says. If intelligence is manipulated in order to paint a far more positive situation than the facts warrant, then lives may be needlessly lost and the enemy not hit where they are most vulnerable. It is one thing for a politician to spin a situation to obtain maximum political advantage or damage control, but to put the lives of the men and women of our armed forces at risk in order to support a political narrative is nothing short of criminal.

194. The Libyan Quagmire

The Arab Spring led to a series of protests through North Africa, from Somalia and South Sudan to Egypt to Libya to Morocco, varying in severity and violence primarily in proportion to the level of control the leaders of each nation were able to exert. Mubarak in Egypt was widely unpopular and, without any involvement from the US beyond rhetoric, that regime collapsed into a violent struggle between the Muslim Brotherhood and the moderates. In Libya, however, there was little indication that anything more than localized violence had erupted in the spring of 2011 when Barack Obama inexplicably decided that the regime of eccentric dictator Muammar Gaddafi must end. In fact, Gaddafi previously had the favor of the United States because he'd proven a strong ally in the fight against terrorist groups like Al Qaeda.

Despite no vital security threats to the United States and, counter to after-action claims by the left, no indication that Gaddafi's regime was in any danger of collapse, Obama chose to meddle in Libya.[1033] Rather than taking a leading role, he stepped back and let NATO handle the formulation of strategy in the region, though he was the driving force behind the plan, and the results were disastrous.[1034]   Gaddafi toppled alright, but, in his place, there was only a civil war between radicals and what was left of Gaddafi's military. Obama refused to help the military train soldiers and police to fight terrorists or provide material aid to them, leading to the rise of the Islamic State and Al Qaeda in the country.[1035] In short, Obama and then-Secretary of State Hillary Clinton took a stable, albeit repressive country that had been an ally in the fight against terrorism, and turned it into a breeding ground for the most radical of Jihadis in a feeble attempt at nation building. The Obama/Clinton Libyan misadventure was everything many disliked about the war in Iraq only much, much worse. Unlike Iraq, Obama committed U.S. forces for the intervention in Libya without a congressional declaration of war, violating the War Powers Act of 1973.[1036] Libya, like Iraq, suffered greatly at the hands of Obama's foreign policy decisions, turning the once stable and prosperous country into a terrorist haven.[1037]

Obama had defended the mission to the American people saying he acted to "prevent a massacre" and inaction would have been "a betrayal of who we are."[1038] It sure seems that, far from preventing a massacre, he created one; and that blood is on his hands.

195.Obama's Syria Debacle

During a press conference on August 20, 2012, President Obama asserted that, while he had no plan for a U.S. military intervention in Syria, engaged in civil war for over a year, that the "moving around" or use of chemical weapons would be a "red line" that would "change my calculus; that would change my equation."[1039]

Once Obama drew his "red line" he was caught in a bind: if chemical weapons were moved or used, he'd have to do something or look like the biggest fool and weakling in the world. The Assad regime in Syria clearly didn't consider Obama's threats to be serious, as there were continual reports of Syrian movement of chemical weapons and even reports of chemical weapons usage over the next year. In April 2013, Defense Secretary Chuck Hagel and Secretary of State John Kerry were all saying that the Assad regime had used chemical weapons, and Obama's "red line" had been crossed.[1040] Senate Intelligence Committee Chair Dianne Feinstein also said, "It is clear that 'red lines' have been crossed and action must be taken to prevent larger scale use."[1041] But, no action was taken. Obama's "red line" had become rather pink and blurred.

Finally, the White House acknowledged the use of chemical weapons by the Assad regime in various sites outside Damascus on August 21, 2013, a year and one day after Obama's "red line" speech, killing more than 1,400 people.[1042] Obama, by his own words, had to do something. What followed was nothing less than an embarrassing display of incompetence, with the entire world watching.

Obama was unable to garner enough global support for an attack on the Assad regime. Soon after attack plans were finalized, the British government backed out, putting Obama in the awkward position of having to go it alone, if at all.[1043] Obama would also find that he wouldn't find enough support for strikes against Syria at home either. A vote in Congress looked like it might even fail completely.[1044] Obama then claimed that he had a right, as commander-in-chief, to order a military strike against Syria without congressional approval, and backpedaled on his "red line" remarks, falsely claiming, "I didn't set a red line; the world set a red line." He also asserted, "My credibility is not on the line. The international community's credibility is on the line. And America's and Congress's credibility is on the line." Apparently, the credibility of everyone but the commander-in-chief, the man who set the "red line," was on the line.[1045]

Opposition for military action against Syria grew. Polls showed that the American people strongly opposed a strike.[1046] In order gin up support, Obama had Secretary of State Kerry "reassure" the public that a strike against Syria would be "unbelievably small."[1047] This did little to move public opinion, but certainly proved to Assad that any action by Obama would be relatively quick and painless. With the promised military strike in doubt, Obama waived a federal ban on arming terrorists in order to provide aid to Syrian rebels who were linked to al-Qaeda.[1048]

In the end, and to the detriment of American prestige and military might, Russia came to Obama's rescue and brokered a deal which got Obama off the hook for military action in return for a promise by Syria to surrender their chemical weapons.[1049] Of course, the deal, itself, was a humiliation for the United States. Obama's red line was crossed with no action from us; Russia got a massive increase in influence as they got their ally, Assad, out of a tight spot; Iran was able to continue funneling money, fighters and weapons to the Assad regime and all of this wreck and ruin for U.S. policy was bought with a paper agreement by Assad to surrender his chemical weapons. But, the Assad regime failed to honor the agreement, as the first deadline for the surrender of his stockpile of chemical weapons was not met. Naturally, Assad's non-compliance was downplayed by the Obama administration.[1050] In February 2014, Obama's own Secretary of State, John Kerry, admitted that Obama's Syria policy was a failure.[1051]

Obama was partially right, though. America's credibility worldwide was on the line, but, as President and Commander-In-Chief, the damage done to America's credibility was *his* fault and responsibility. It's hard to say if time will ever reverse the damage he's done as some of the very forces he armed have turned their weapons against free people in Iraq and Syria, and not against the Assad regime, helping to empower and supply ISIS.

196.Boko Haram

Ranked by the Global Terrorism Index as one of the world's most deadly terrorist forces,[1052] Boko Haram in Nigeria rocketed to international attention with the kidnapping of hundreds of schoolgirls in April of 2014.[1053] It swiftly became known that the fate Boko Haram had for these girls was either their sale into slavery or their forced marriage to Boko Haram fighters. The people of the world were justly outraged by this, but Boko Haram had been around for many years prior to this outrage.

While the origins of the group go back to the early 2000s, it was only in 2009 that Boko Haram was able to start cutting a bloody swath through Nigerian society, which is divided about equally between Muslim and Christian citizens. Between 2009 and 2014, Boko Haram murdered thousands of people in scores of terrorist attacks, with the targets very often being Christian churches while services were being held. For years, lawmakers, U.S. officials, and outside groups were calling on the Obama administration to label Boko Haram as a terrorist organization,[1054] but no action was taken until after the kidnapping outrage.[1055]

Why, did the Obama administration ignore Boko Haram and refuse to allocate any resources to its defeat? There are some in Nigeria who accuse Obama and his senior adviser David Axelrod of conspiring to harm the Nigerian economy and hand the northern part of the country to Boko Haram, in the hopes of ousting sitting Nigerian President Jonathan, whose challenger was backed by AKPD, a Nigerian consulting group funded by Axelrod.[1056] We concede that this theory is speculative, but what is not speculative is the blood-soaked cost of Obama's inaction on Boko Haram.

After ignoring the problem for years and only taking notice when the situation escalated enough to potentially embarrass him, Obama made vigorous statements about how the United States would react forcefully against Boko Haram.[1057] However, the whole action seemed to amount to First Lady Michelle Obama tweeting a photo of herself holding up a sign with "#BringBackOurGirls" printed on it in May 2014. But, other than that, not much has been done. In fact, Boko Haram's murders increased by 300 percent from 2014 to 2015, despite Michelle Obama's tweet.[1058] Indeed, our best experts believe it is beyond doubt that Boko Haram benefited significantly from the State Department's inaction.[1059]

A bloody price has been paid by Obama's inaction to confront the threat of Boko Haram. Boko Haram's death toll is now in the thousands and the organization is claiming enormous influence over Africa's most prosperous nation, and the best Obama can muster is hashtag diplomacy. Whether or not he had personal reasons to ignore this group, there is no justification for failing to act, refusing to provide arms and intelligence at the request of the Nigerian government, and sealing the fates of thousands of Christians.

197.Losing Afghanistan

Barack Obama has long referred to the war in Afghanistan as "the right war," but, as conditions in the country have shown, he messed it up badly.[1060] Fulfilling his campaign promise, as president, Obama shifted resources to and increased troops in Afghanistan, and completed the withdrawal of U.S. forces from Iraq. Unfortunately, Obama never really considered the war in Afghanistan his responsibility, and according to Secretary of Defense Robert Gates, Obama was more concerned with getting out of Afghanistan than a long term victory strategy. "The president doesn't trust his commander, can't stand Karzai, doesn't believe in his own strategy and doesn't consider the war to be his," Gates wrote in his memoir. "For him, it's all about getting out."[1061]

Despite Obama's shifted focus to Afghanistan, conditions in the country declined significantly after he became Commander-in-Chief. Nearly three-quarters of U.S. casualties in Afghanistan came after his troop surge.[1062] A burgeoning opium trade (despite U.S. efforts to curtail it) and government corruption threaten the country's long-term stability.[1063] Relations with Afghanistan also deteriorated under Obama, culminating with his threatening Karzai with full U.S. troop withdrawal by the end of 2014 due to an impasse over a security agreement.[1064] He made good on his threat and began withdrawal, only to reverse his decision in

October 2015 after "extensive, lengthy review." In other words, when it was clear that the Taliban was regaining influence.[1065] It is truly shocking that American policy in Afghanistan is so completely timid that Afghan elections and Obama's lack of seriousness when asked to compromise have led to this outcome.[1066]

Obama may not have wanted to be a wartime Commander-in-Chief, but he asked the American people to make him one in 2008 and again in 2012. It was his job to ensure American victory, but victory has never been his objective, and Afghanistan is worse off because of it. According to Elise Jordan of *The Daily Beast*, "Afghanistan today is much more violent than when Obama came into office. Fewer Americans may be dying. But many more Afghan civilians are being killed, according to U.N. statistics. More guns, more warlords, more militias—that's Obama's probable legacy. It's what happens when you can't deal with reality and commit one way or the other in wartime—you lose."[1067]

198.Losing Iraq

Obama may have sold himself to the liberal base of the Democrat party in 2008 as the candidate who most hated the war in Iraq, but by choosing to run for President, once he became Commander-In-Chief, Iraq became his responsibility. That he didn't start the campaign is no excuse for him letting Iraq be lost, but that is exactly what he did.

When Obama took over as Commander-In-Chief, things were looking up for Iraq. The country was relatively stable, thanks to the hard fighting of both American and Iraqi forces and the troop surge in 2007, which then-Senator Obama opposed.[1068] Various radical Islamist groups inside Iraq had been decimated and the level of violence was down to a place where Iraqi forces, backed up at need by American troops, could secure the peace. The war, for all intents and purposes, had been won. All Obama had to do was to maintain U.S. support for Iraq and things would be fine.

Obama's main anti-Bush promises in the 2008 presidential campaign had been to close the Guantanamo Bay prison and the get us out of Iraq. Failing almost immediately on the closing Guantanamo Bay, Obama became determined to at least get us out of Iraq at the earliest possible moment. Obama refused to view Iraq as "his" problem. It appears that in his mind, the war there was Bush's problem. But President Obama bungled the negotiations with Iraq over a "status of forces agreement" which would have allowed as many as 20,000 U.S. troops to remain in Iraq for training, support and (in an emergency) to fight.[1069]

When the Obama administration announced a full withdrawal of U.S. troops by the end of 2011, there was a promised commitment to Iraq's future stability.[1070] But, experts worried that, without American backup, the still-maturing Iraqi military and still evolving Iraqi government would not be able to handle a renewed attack by Islamist militants, especially if such militants were able to get backing from Iran. These fears were almost immediately justified as levels of violence in Iraq started to rise after the American withdrawal.[1071]

Massive sectarian violence started to erupt between all of Iraq's religious and ethnic groups. While it may have seemed senseless to an outside observer, those who had a plan for Iraq knew what they were doing: weakening the government, crippling the Iraqi military, making everyone hate and fear everyone else and setting the nation up to be taken in stages. In January 2014, the Islamic State of Iraq and Syria (ISIS) violently captured of the city of Fallujah, where U.S. forces had previously exterminated al-Qaeda in 2005.[1072]

The leader of ISIS, Abu Bakr al-Baghdadi, had previously been in U.S. custody in Iraq, but was freed by Obama in 2009.[1073] Since taking Fallujah, ISIS has made more progress. In June of 2014, ISIS acquired a stockpile of chemical weapons when they took over a military base in Northern Iraq, raising fears that those weapons could be used as dirty bombs.[1074] As of this writing, ISIS is stepping up terror attacks on Baghdad itself and has captured about 40% of Iraqi soil, including four of Iraq's six largest cities.

Iraq's fate is unclear but appears bleak. The ISIS incursion has split what remains of the state into sectarian regions, with the Kurds controlling the North of the country, and Sunni and Shiite Muslims battling for possession of the rest. With Obama having washed his hands of the situation, the progress made by our troops has been reversed, and their sacrifices have gone to waste. Iraq now appears to be falling apart into the same sort of vicious civil war as we have seen in Syria, and it may wind up as a satellite of Iran.

The United States lost 4,000 lives and spent around $800 billion in Iraq over an eight-year period in order to try to bring a bit of peace, stability and freedom to the region. Because President Obama did not take Iraq seriously, viewing it as no more than a Bush mistake, all the blood, treasure and effort we expended in Iraq has gone entirely to waste. In addition to our own losses, the people of Iraq now suffer under sectarian civil war and the brutal conquest of an apocalyptic horde of monsters whose reign of terror is unlike anything previously seen in the region.

199.Obama's Nuclear Deal with Iran

A terrorist-sponsoring nation with a burgeoning nuclear program, Iran is run by religious fanatics who execute homosexuals, women who have committed adultery, and converts from Islam to Christianity.[1075] Iran hardly seems like a nation Obama, or any president, would wish to offer friendly terms to in any negotiation. But, over a period from 2013 to 2015, Obama engaged in a series of negotiations with Iran that were supposed to prevent Iran from developing nuclear weapons. That is, until Obama started negotiating, then it became something else entirely.

It began, in 2013, when Obama made a deal in which Iran promised to start, over a period of months, to slow down nuclear weapons development in return for the immediate easing of economic sanctions that were crippling the country.[1076] But the terms of the deal allowed for Iran's nuclear infrastructure to remain intact. This first step agreement merely gave the mullahs of Iran short-term political cover and economic relief, and the world was no more secure.

Maybe Obama didn't realize this, but the Iranian government did. Despite the deal, they declared their intention to continue their nuclear program.[1077] Iranian Foreign Minister Mohammad Javad Zarif claimed that the Obama administration publicly mischaracterized the terms of the deal, telling CNN "we did not agree to dismantle anything."[1078] Iranian president Hassan Rouhani said of the deal that "world powers surrendered to Iranian nation's [sic] will."[1079]

Congress was justifiably skeptical of Iran, and bipartisan sanctions legislation started gaining momentum. This prompted Obama to declare, during his 2014 State of the Union address, that he would veto any Iran sanctions bill passed by Congress.[1080] It's hard to imagine why Obama was so trusting of Iran, especially when the Iranians went out of their way to honor the terrorist responsible for the 1983 Marine barracks bombing in Beirut in January of 2014.[1081] Yet the worst was still to come.

The capstone of Obama's pro-Iranian foreign policy came on July 14, 2015, with a nuclear deal concluded between Iran and six world powers. In return for an unenforceable agreement to curtail their nuclear program, Iran got a bonanza of benefits at the expense of the safety and security of the United States and its allies in the Middle East. As part of the deal, economic sanctions against Iran were lifted, providing Iran with as much as $150 billion, which even Obama's Ambassador to the UN agrees could be funneled to military and terrorist activities.[1082]

What happened? How did such a rotten deal come to be? According to former Secretary of State Henry Kissinger, what began as a multilateral negotiation to prevent Iran from developing nuclear weapons, became "an essentially bilateral negotiation over the scope of that capability."[1083] And the resulting deal had America's allies in the Middle East—including Israel, Saudi Arabia, and Egypt—afraid that Obama abandoned them in favor of a mutual enemy.[1084]

Obama's claim that the deal makes America safer couldn't be further from the truth. He was so desperate to achieve a deal, any deal, with Iran, that he reportedly gave in to eighty percent of Iran's demands.[1085] Ultimately, the deal does not prevent Iran from obtaining a nuclear weapon, and leaves their enrichment infrastructure intact. Obama's nuclear deal allows Iran to block inspections of nuclear sites, and allows Russia and China to supply Iran with weapons.[1086] What could possibly go wrong? Oh, and Iran, by secret side-deal with the U.N., will be allowed to self-inspect some of its most sensitive facilities. Some of those same facilities are currently being expanded by the Iranian government.

To sum up this sad story, Obama cut a nuclear deal with Iran that does nothing at all to deter their nuclear program, writes them an enormous check to be used however they see fit, gives them military aid from some of our most dangerous rivals in the region, and allows them to dictate terms to the international community. All we got to show for this exercise in futility was a boost to Obama's already gargantuan ego and a significant loss of influence in this pivotal region.

200.Kowtowing to Iran

If the particulars of the Iran nuclear deal fail concern you, you would not be alone; the deal received harsh criticism from both the left and the right, after all. What we find even harder to fathom, however, are the incredible lengths to which Obama went in order to secure such a lopsided deal and then defend it when Iran didn't abide by its terms.

As the deal was being ironed out, for example, the Obama administration was fully aware that Iran was no more than three months away from producing enough enriched fissile material to make a nuclear weapon, but kept that information secret, claiming publicly that Iran was more than a year away from being able to make a nuclear bomb.[1087]

As the negotiations took shape, Obama must have been aware of how bad the deal would look to his countrymen, because he took to the airwaves to declare that he could make this deal *without* Senate approval.[1088] The United States Constitution is quite clear when it comes to international treaties. According to Article II, Section 2, Clause 2, the president "shall have power, by and with the advice and consent of the Senate, to make treaties, provided two-thirds of the Senators present concur..." But, as with so many other things, Obama was not one to let the Constitution get in his way. A week after the deal was struck, it was revealed that the White House actually blocked Congress from being able to review certain aspects of the nuclear deal. Why keep such a secret from Congress? The answer to that question can't be good.[1089]

Nor would Obama let the stated intentions of the spiritual leader of Iran give him pause in his quest to cement his legacy, even as he rallied the Iranian people behind the impending deal by chanting "death to America!" Obama, for reasons that simply cannot be explained, downplayed the remarks.[1090]

To top off the corrupt arrogance of Obama's policy towards Iran, it was revealed in the *New York Times* that Obama's foreign policy guru - Ben Rhodes, a man with zero foreign policy experience - was tasked with convincing Obama's media allies that the deal was good.[1091] Rhodes created a media echo-chamber where lies made out of whole cloth by Rhodes were mindlessly repeated in the MSM until the lies became "conventional wisdom" which supposedly only a fool could reject. Rhodes spun the story that Iran was now in the hands of "moderates" whom the United States could trust and only hate-filled, war-mongering Republicans who were on the side of Iran's hard-liners could have a problem with the deal. As an exercise in promoting a con, this is fantastic, but as the end result will be a nuclear-armed Iran governed by the same Muslim radicals who have caused untold bloodshed in Iran and around the world, it wasn't such a good thing.

Yet none of these attempts by Obama to spin the deal as a positive for Americans and cement his legacy as a diplomatic success are quite as damning as Iran's actions after the deal was finalized and Obama's complete failure to respond. In 2015, Obama said that the Iran Deal "is not built on trust, it is built on verification."[1092] When Secretary of State Kerry was asked what might constitute a violation of the deal, he admitted that Iran could purchase conventional weapons, violating a U.N. embargo, without violating the nuclear deal—a loophole Iran immediately took advantage of.[1093] Yet, even though Obama made many concessions to the Iranian regime to get a deal passed, Iran flagrantly violated the terms of the deal on multiple occasions, with no pushback from Obama or his surrogates.

In January 2016, a few months after the deal with Iran was reached, the Iranian Navy seized two American patrol boats in the Persian Gulf.[1094] The official explanation was that the boats made a navigational error. What was never explained was why our boats surrendered without a fight, nor why no other U.S. ships in the area were dispatched to assist. After our sailors were released back to U.S. custody, Iran's state media released video footage of them being captured, including video of one sailor apologizing for entering Iranian waters. Despite this attempt to humiliate America and the U.S. military, Secretary of State Kerry actually *thanked* Iran after our sailors were released.[1095]

Further testing just how far they could go, a couple months later, Iran conducted tests on nuclear-capable ballistic missiles inscribed with the Arabic phrase: "Israel Must be Wiped Out"—at the same time Vice-President Biden was visiting Jerusalem.[1096] What purpose could nuclear capable ballistic missiles (with a hateful message inscribed on the side) serve but to prepare Iran's military for a day when nuclear weapons will someday be deployed? Aren't they supposed to have committed themselves to a purely peaceful nuclear program? In spite of this insulting display with its clear implication that Iran still desires nuclear warheads, the Obama administration's response was muted. While Congress considered the ballistic missile test a violation of the agreement, the Obama administration claimed otherwise. In fact, reports later surfaced that Obama chose *not* to respond to this test for fear of undermining the agreement.[1097]

Eventually, Obama conceded that Iran hadn't been honoring the "spirit" of the deal, but still claimed they had been following the "letter" of it. But, even then, he was covering for Iran's transgressions. According to some analysts, the ballistic missile test was indeed a violation of one element of the deal, and, in addition to the missile test, there had been suspicious activity around a known nuclear site, and Iran's uranium stockpiles had increased despite the fact enrichment was supposed to have been halted under the interim agreement.[1098]

All of the Obama administration's actions are based upon a fear that any vigorous American action to oppose Iran will lead to the collapse of the nuclear deal, which Obama claimed would actually prevent Iran from acquiring nuclear weapons.[1099] Obama has repeatedly given Iran the benefit of the doubt, if not blatantly turning a blind eye to non-compliance with the deal that he has said is supposed to prevent Iran from getting nuclear weapons. Despite this, as part of Obama's deal, the United States has pledged to assist Iran in defending their nuclear program.[1100] That's right; the deal intended to stop Iran from gaining nuclear weapons requires the United States to help Iran defend its nuclear program. It's hard to get more accommodating to an enemy nation than that.

Conclusions

How will the historians of the future assess the presidency of Barack Obama? He would like to be remembered as the president that saved America from another Great Depression, the president that ushered in a new era of government transparency and accountability, the president that cut taxes for the middle class, and lowered the cost of healthcare while providing coverage for all Americans. He'll want history to remember him for making America safer from the threat of terrorism, all while improving the nation's standing in the world. He'll expect the shortcomings of his presidency to be attributed to his predecessor, with his own, unblemished presidency to be an unquestionable success.

It would be a great legacy, if any of it were true.

As patriotic Americans, we felt it was our duty to document the truth about Obama's presidency so that his legacy is defined by the facts, not by his false narrative.

We've seen an economy hobble along thanks to a failed stimulus, new taxes, and regulations. We've seen more people leave the workforce during the so-called "recovery" than the recession that preceded it. More people live in poverty and are on welfare, disability, and food stamps. Obama has broken the engine of economic growth, and Americans are, year by year, becoming poorer and less able to build wealth. Are these the results of successful economic policy?

Our freedoms have also been compromised, and our Constitution ignored. Obama has sought the power to indefinitely detain American citizens, and government spying has exploded on his watch. Freedom of speech, religion, and the press are under attack. When Obama realizes his agenda won't make it through Congress, he merely imposes it via executive fiat. If there are laws he doesn't want to enforce, he ignores them. Obama's assault on the 2nd Amendment at the end of his first term puts an exclamation point on a relentless policy of placing Americans at the mercy of an all-powerful government.

Is it any wonder, then, that we are now more divided than at any time since the Civil War – culturally, economically, politically, the "great uniter" has been brutally divisive instead, urging members of certain ethnic, gender, or religious identities to think tribally, rather than see themselves as Americans.[1104] Americans are losing hope, and believe our best times are behind us and that things will only get worse from here on.[1105] Their dissatisfaction with "politics as usual" has run so hotly that, on Obama's watch, the Democratic Party has suffered the loss of over a thousand elected offices in state and federal government and countless more in local government - the most in American history to be lost from the party of the sitting president. And now, both political parties face populist uprisings and uncertain futures. This sort of division, turmoil, and despair is a far cry from the hopeful words of his 2004 Democratic National Convention speech in which he denounced the notion that there were red states and blue states and promised to make his rising career about uniting us all.

Obama is also a spectacular failure abroad. Obama raved about the death of Al Qaeda during his 2012 reelection campaign, but that organization is rapidly growing, as are ISIS and Boko Haram. He's offended and alienated our allies, kowtowed to our enemies, and made us less safe. All across the Muslim world, radicalism is growing and regimes that stood for decades are toppling in favor of theocratic, terror-sponsoring Jihadis. Christianity is being driven from the Middle East, and the world's only Jewish state is under siege. Waves of refugees are flooding Europe and bringing economic chaos and social upheaval with them, all while our allies, reeling, look to the United States and see nothing but indecision and moral cowardice. In South America, Communism is again on the rise and, in Russia, a form of strongman-led nationalist socialism is taking hold with disastrous results. Putin has attacked and annexed territory, China threatens the entire Pacific Rim, and the United States has no response.

We counted 200 separate reasons to view Obama as the worst President in United States history. And yet, there is only one real reason that Obama is as ineffective as he is - his personality exudes weakness. How far we've fallen from "The buck stops here" and "Ask not what your country can do for you..." As we survey the disaster of Obama's presidency, it is vitally important that the next generation (who will have to pay for our mistake in electing Obama *twice*) fully understands his record and shows better judgment in the voting booth, placing a higher value on strength of character and moral clarity going forward, so that America can once again be the beacon of economic and personal freedom, the shining city on a hill, that it once was.

About The Authors

Matt Margolis is a full time architectural designer and longtime blogger. In November 2003, Matt founded Blogs for Bush, which became one of the most popular political blogs during the 2004 presidential campaign, earning him an invitation to the Republican National Convention. Since then, Matt has launched a number of successful blogs and has been an invited guest on local and national media. Matt lives with his wife and son in Upstate New York.

Follow Matt on Twitter @mattmargolis

Mark Noonan is a longtime blogger and Navy veteran. He has been living in the southern Nevada area for more than a decade and has lived in places as diverse as California, Virginia and, for a time, Italy. Catholic and Distributist, Noonan writes on a wide variety of subjects and has appeared in old and new media over the years.

Sources

1 P.J. Gladnick, "60 Minutes Broadcast Edits Out Laughable Obama Claim as 4th Best President", *Newsbusters*, 12/16/2011; (http://newsbusters.org/blogs/pj-gladnick/2011/12/16/60-minutes-broadcast-edits-out-laughable-obama-claim-4th-greatest-presi)

2 Michael D. Shear and Gardiner Harris, "With High-Profile Help, Obama Plots Life After Presidency", *New York Times*, 8/16/2015; (http://www.nytimes.com/2015/08/17/us/politics/with-high-profile-help-obama-plots-life-after-presidency.html)

3 Frank Newport, "Americans Downbeat on State of U.S., Prospects for Future," *Gallup*, 1/21/2013, (http://www.gallup.com/poll/160046/americans-downbeat-state-prospects-future.aspx)

4 *Ibid.*

5 *Ibid.*

6 Walter Hickey, "Obama Really Wishes He Never Gave This Speech About the Debt Ceiling," *Business Insider*, 01/14/2013 (http://www.businessinsider.com/obama-voted-against-debt-ceiling-increase-2006-2013-1)

7 Talman Bradley, "Obama White House Discloses Two More Lobbyist Waivers Granted," *ABC News*, 03/10/2009, (http://abcnews.go.com/blogs/politics/2009/03/obama-white-hou/)

8 "Support Human Mission to Moon by 2020," *Politifact*, 02/15/2010, (http://www.politifact.com/truth-o-meter/promises/obameter/promise/339/support-human-mission-to-moon-by-2020/)

9 "Reduce earmarks to 1994 levels," *Politifact*, 2/19/2010, (http://www.politifact.com/truth-o-meter/promises/obameter/promise/431/reduce-earmarks-to-1994-levels/)

10 "No Proposal to End Taxes for Seniors Making Less Than $50,000," *Politifact*, 04/15/2009, (http://www.politifact.com/truth-o-meter/promises/obameter/promise/24/end-income-tax-for-seniors-making-less-than/)

11 Josh Gerstein, "President Obama Hails Return to PAYGO," *Politico*, 02/13/2010, (http://www.politico.com/news/stories/0210/32921.html)

12 Mary Bruce, "Obama Argues Rising Gas Costs are Not His Fault," *ABC News*, 02/25/2012, (http://abcnews.go.com/blogs/politics/2012/02/obama-argues-rising-gas-costs-are-not-his-fault/)

13 "Obama Unveils Plan to Wean Americans Off Foreign Oil," *Montreal Gazette*, 8/5/2008, (http://www.canada.com/story.html?id=9ffe2146-39a6-4aa2-bd31-5c868b744214)

14 "Pipeline Politics: Misguided Obama Blocks Keystone Pipeline," *Chicago Tribune*, 01/19/2012, (http://www.chicagotribune.com/news/opinion/editorials/ct-edit-pipeline-20120119,0,3017097.story)

15 Greg McDonald, "Flashback: Obama Argued Against Mandate in 2008," *Newsmax*, 03/29/2012, (http://www.newsmax.com/Newsfront/Obamacare-Clinton-mandate-court/2012/03/29/id/434199)

16 Todd Beamon, "Rules Issued for Obamacare's Individual Mandate," Newsmax, 01/30/2013, (http://www.newsmax.com/Newsfront/individual-manage-regulations-issued/2013/01/30/id/488132)

17   "Obama's Speech on Economic Policy", *New York Times*, 10/13/2008; (http://
      www.nytimes.com/2008/10/13/us/politics/13obama-text.html?
      pagewanted=print&_r=0)

18   Glenn Greenwald, "The Real Story Of How 'Untouchable' Wall Street Execs Avoided
      Prosecution" Business Insider, 1/23/2013; (http://www.businessinsider.com/why-
      wall-street-execs-werent-prosecuted-2013-1)

19   "News Conference by the President" The White House, 10/6/2011; (http://
      www.whitehouse.gov/the-press-office/2011/10/06/news-conference-president)

20   Glenn Greenwald, "The Real Story Of How 'Untouchable' Wall Street Execs Avoided
      Prosecution" Business Insider, 1/23/2013; (http://www.businessinsider.com/why-
      wall-street-execs-werent-prosecuted-2013-1)

21   Matthew Boyle, "Report: Cronyism, Political Donations Likely Behind Obama,
      Holder Failure to Charge any Bankers After 2008 Financial Meltdown," *The Daily
      Caller*, 08/07/2012, (http://dailycaller.com/2012/08/07/report-cronyism-political-
      donations-likely-behind-obama-holder-failure-to-charge-any-bankers-after-2008-
      financial-meltdown)

22   *Ibid*

23   "Justice Inaction: The Department of Justice's Unprecedented Failure to Prosecute
      Big Finance," *Government Accountability Institute*, 08/2012; Retrieved at http://g-a-
      i.org/wp-content/uploads/2012/08/DOJ-Report-8-61.pdf

24   Perry Chiaramonte, "Forgotten by FEMA: Staten Island's Sandy victims vent over
      lack of aid," *Fox News*, 11/8/2012, (http://www.foxnews.com/us/2012/11/08/
      volunteers-step-in-for-fema-in-storm-ravaged-nyc-borough)

25   Kate Zernike, "Gasoline Runs Short, Adding Woes to Storm Recovery", *New York
      Times*, 11/1/2012; (http://www.nytimes.com/2012/11/02/nyregion/gasoline-
      shortages-disrupting-recovery-from-hurricane.html)

26   Billy Hallowell, "Hurricane Sandy Victim Who Hugged Obama in Viral Photo Claims
      He Broke Aid Promise, Sent Her 'Disturbing' Form Letter," *The Blaze*, 1/4/2013
      (http://www.theblaze.com/stories/2013/01/04/hurricane-sandy-victim-in-viral-
      photo-claims-obama-broke-aid-promise-sent-her-disturbing-form-letter-
      response/)

27   Lisa L Colangelo, "Exclusive: City Controller Scott Stringer Launching Audit of Build
      it Back Hurricane Sandy Home Re-Building Program", *New York Daily News*,
      4/17/2014; (http://www.nydailynews.com/new-york/exclusive-city-audit-build-
      back-article-1.1759058)

28   Keith Koffler, "Election Over, Obama Returns to Golf," *White House Dossier*,
      11/10/2012, (http://www.whitehousedossier.com/2012/11/10/election-obama-
      returns-golf/)

29   Roger Runningen and Margaret Talev, "Obama Promising Millions in Aid for
      California's Drought," *Bloomberg*, 2/14/2014 (http://www.bloomberg.com/news/
      2014-02-14/obama-promising-millions-in-aid-for-california-s-drought.html)

30   Pete Kasperowitz, "House passes California drought bill to override Obama on
      environment," *The Hill*, 2/5/2014 (http://thehill.com/blogs/floor-action/votes/
      197585-house-picks-people-over-fish-with-california-drought-bill)

31   Central Valley Project. (n.d.). In *Wikipedia*. Retrieved March 30, 2014, from http://
      en.wikipedia.org/wiki/Central_Valley_Project

32   Kurtis Alexander, "Drought: Feds cut water to Central Valley farmers to zero," *San
      Francisco Gate*, 2/22/2014 (http://www.sfgate.com/news/article/Drought-Feds-cut-
      water-to-Central-Valley-farmers-5256131.php)

33   Pete Kasperowitz, "House passes California drought bill to override Obama on
      environment," *The Hill*, 2/5/2014 (http://thehill.com/blogs/floor-action/votes/
      197585-house-picks-people-over-fish-with-california-drought-bill)

34   Bobby Jindal. *Leadership and Crisis*. Washington D.C.: Regnery Pub, 2010. Print.

35   Karl Rove, "Yes, the Gulf Spill is Obama's Katrina," *Wall Street Journal*, 5/27/2010,
      (http://online.wsj.com/article/
      SB10001424052748704717004575268752362770856.html)

36   John M. Broder, "Report Slams Administration for Underestimating Gulf Spill," *New York Times*, 10/6/2010, (http://www.nytimes.com/2010/10/07/science/earth/07spill.html)

37   Abby Ohlheiser, "Activists release a fourth undercover video as the battle over Planned Parenthood intensifies", *Washington Post*, 7/30/2015; (https://www.washingtonpost.com/news/acts-of-faith/wp/2015/07/30/activists-release-a-fourth-undercover-video-as-the-battle-over-planned-parenthood-intensifies/)

38   Lena H. Sun, "Obama officials warn states about cutting Medicaid funds to Planned Parenthood", *Washington Post*, 4/19/2016; (https://www.washingtonpost.com/news/post-nation/wp/2016/04/19/obama-officials-warn-states-about-cutting-medicaid-funds-to-planned-parenthood/)

39   Steven Ertelt, "Obama Punishes Kansas for De-Funding Planned Parenthood by Cutting Its Title X Funding", LifeNews, 8/26/2015; (http://www.lifenews.com/2015/08/26/obama-punishes-kansas-for-de-funding-planned-parenthood-by-cutting-its-medicaid-funding/)

40   "Tuition Costs of Colleges and Universities," *National Center for Education Statistics*, accessed 12/08/2012

41   Kathleen Kingsbury, "College Costs Stall As Borrowing Falls, Study Says," *Reuters*, 10/24/12, (http://www.reuters.com/article/2012/10/24/us-education-college-costs-idUSBRE89N06R20121024)

42   Mary Beth Marklein, "College Costs Going Up At Slower Rate," *USA Today*, 10/24/12, (http://www.usatoday.com/story/news/nation/2012/10/23/college-tuition-costs/1643921/)

43   Jordan Weissmann, "53% of Recent College Grads Are Jobless or Underemployed—How?", The Atlantic, 4/23/2012; (http://www.theatlantic.com/business/archive/2012/04/53-of-recent-college-grads-are-jobless-or-underemployed-how/256237/)

44   The White House, The Press Office. (2013) Executive Order -- White House Initiative on Educational Excellence for African Americans. Retrieved from http://www.whitehouse.gov/the-press-office/2012/07/26/executive-order-white-house-initiative-educational-excellence-african-am

45   Neil Munro, "Obama backs race-based school discipline policies," Daily Caller, 7/27/2012, (http://dailycaller.com/2012/07/27/obama-backs-race-based-school-discipline-policies/)

46   Michael Meyers, "Obama's Executive Order Puts Blacks In the Corner At the U.S. Department of Education," The Huffington Post, August 7, 2012, (http://www.huffingtonpost.com/michael-meyers/obamas-hbcu-executive-order_b_1726291.html)

47   Charles C. Johnson and Ryan Girdusky, "As college student, Eric Holder participated in 'armed' takeover of former Columbia University ROTC office," *The Daily Caller*, 9/30/2012 (http://dailycaller.com/2012/09/30/as-college-sophomore-eric-holder-participated-in-armed-takeover-of-former-columbia-university-rotc-office/)

48   Patrick Howley, "Al Sharpton Talking to White House About New Attorney General Pick", *The Daily Caller*, 9/25/2014; (http://dailycaller.com/2014/09/25/al-sharpton-talking-to-the-white-house-about-new-attorney-general-pick/)

49   Patrick Howley, "Obama Attorney General Pick: Voter ID Laws Are About Taking Back What Dr. King Won', *The Daily Caller*, 11/9/2014; (http://dailycaller.com/2014/11/09/obama-attorney-general-pick-voter-id-laws-are-about-taking-back-what-dr-king-won/)

50   Judson Phillips, "Loretta Lynch and the GOP surrender caucus", *Washington Times*, 1/30/2015; (http://www.washingtontimes.com/news/2015/jan/30/judson-phillips-loretta-lynch-and-gop-surrender-ca/?page=all)

51   Matthew Boyle, "Loretta Lynch: Illegal Aliens Have Right to Work As Much As American Citizens", *Breitbart*, 1/28/2015; (http://www.breitbart.com/big-government/2015/01/28/loretta-lynch-illegal-aliens-have-right-to-work-as-much-as-american-citizens/)

52   Ginger Gibson, "Attorney General Nominee Omitted HSBC Interview From Senate Questionnaire", *International Business Times*, 1/27/2015; (http://www.ibtimes.com/ attorney-general-nominee-loretta-lynch-omitted-hsbc-interview-senate-questionnaire-1796924)

53   Guatham Nagesh, "U.S. Plans to Give Up Oversight of Web Domain Manager," *Wall Street Journal*, 3/14/2014 (http://online.wsj.com/news/articles/ SB10001424052702303546204579439653103639452)

54 L. Gordon Crovitz, "America's Internet Surrender," *Wall Street Journal*, 3/18/2014 (http://online.wsj.com/news/articles/ SB10001424052702303563304579447362610955656)

55   *Ibid.*

56   *Ibid.*

57 "FCC Official Warns Obama-backed Net Neutrality Plan Would Bring 'Immediate' Internet Tax", *Fox News*, 11/17/2014; (http://www.foxnews.com/politics/ 2014/11/17/fcc-official-warns-obama-backed-net-neutrality-plan-will-bring-backdoor-tax-on/)

58   Phil Kerpen, "Obama's Taxing Plan to Regulate the Internet," *CNSNews*, 11/13/2014; (http://cnsnews.com/commentary/phil-kerpen/obama-s-taxing-plan-regulate-internet)

59   Michael Mandel, "Obama's Plan to Regulate the Internet Would Do More Harm Than Good", *Washington Post*, 11/14/2014; (http://www.washingtonpost.com/ opinions/obamas-internet-rules-would-do-more-harm-than-good/ 2014/11/14/64a795d0-6b82-11e4-a31c-77759fc1eacc_story.html)

60   Brendan Sasso, "Republican FCC Commissioner: Public Is Being Misled About Net-Neutrality Plan", *National Journal*, 2/10/2015; (http://www.nationaljournal.com/ tech/republican-fcc-commissioner-public-is-being-misled-about-net-neutrality-plan-20150210)

61   "61% Oppose Federal Regulation of the Internet" *Rasmussen Reports*, 11/13/2014; (http://www.rasmussenreports.com/public_content/lifestyle/general_lifestyle/ november_2014/61_oppose_federal_regulation_of_the_internet)

62   Alina Selyukh and Roberta Rampton, "Exclusive: White House says net neutrality legislation not needed", *Reuters*, 1/15/2015; (http://www.reuters.com/article/ 2015/01/15/us-usa-internet-neutrality-exclusive-idUSKBN0KO2JO20150115)

63   Devindra Hardawar, "FCC approves net neutrality rules, reclassifies broadband as a utility", *Engadget*, 2/26/2015; (https://www.engadget.com/2015/02/26/fcc-net-neutrality/)

64   Jessica Vaughn, "ICE Document Details 36,000 Criminal Alien Releases in 2013," Center for Immigration Studies, May 12, 2014 (http://www.cis.org/ICE-Document-Details-36000-Criminal-Aliens-Release-in-2013)

65   Stephen Dinan, "Feds released hundreds of immigrant murderers, drunk drivers, sex-crimes convicts," *Washington Times*, 5/12/20142 (http://www.washingtontimes.com/ news/2014/may/12/feds-released-hundreds-immigrant-murderers-drunken/? page=2)

66   Jessica Vaughn, "ICE Document Details 36,000 Criminal Alien Releases in 2013," Center for Immigration Studies, May 12, 2014 (http://www.cis.org/ICE-Document-Details-36000-Criminal-Aliens-Release-in-2013)

67   Tony Lee, "Obama: Amnesty Bill That Rewards Illegals Means 'Everyone Play The Same Rules'," *Breitbart*, 3/26/2014 (http://www.breitbart.com/Big-Government/ 2014/03/26/Obama-Amnesty-Bill-that-Rewards-Illegals-Means-Everyone-Plays-By-the-Same-Rules)

68 Brandon Darby, "Leaked DHS Report Reveals Obama Admin Deception on Border Crisis", *Breitbart*, 7/7/2014; (http://www.breitbart.com/Breitbart-Texas/ 2014/07/07/Leaked-Internal-DHS-Report-Admits-Lack-of-Deportation-Significant-Factor-in-Border-Crisis)

69 "Child Border Surge Includes Mara Salvatrucha Gang Elements", *Investors Business Daily,* Editorial, 7/9/2014; (http://news.investors.com/ibd-editorials/070914-708067-border-surge-includes-significant-criminal-element.htm)

70 Josh Siegal,"What's Driving the Latest Surge of Illegal Immigration From Central America", Daily Signal, 12/29/2015; (http://dailysignal.com/2015/12/29/whats-driving-the-latest-surge-of-illegal-immigration-from-central-america/)

71 Todd Starnes, "Immigration Crisis: Tuberculosis Spreading at Camps", *Fox News,* 7/7/2014; (http://www.foxnews.com/opinion/2014/07/07/immigration-crisis-tuberculosis-spreading-at-camps/)

72 "U.S. General: Border Security an "Existential" Threat to National Security", *CBS DC,* 7/7/2014; (http://washington.cbslocal.com/2014/07/07/us-general-border-security-an-existential-threat-to-national-security/)

73 Jessia Chasmer, "Amid border crisis, Obama to take 15-day vacation in Martha's Vineyard," *Washington Times,* 7/10/2014 (http://www.washingtontimes.com/news/2014/jul/10/amid-border-crisis-obama-take-15-day-vacation-mart/)

74 Jessica Vaughan, "Don't Blame the Border Crisis on a 'Bush-era' Law," *National Review,* 7/10/2014 (http://www.nationalreview.com/article/382463/dont-blame-border-crisis-bush-era-law-jessica-vaughan)

75 Susan Crabtree, "White House stands by claim that border security is stronger than ever," *Washington Examiner,* 7/11/2014 (http://washingtonexaminer.com/white-house-stands-by-claim-that-border-security-is-stronger-than-ever/article/2550730)

76 Brandon Darby, "Leaked DHS Report Reveals Obama Admin Deception on Border Crisis," Breitbart, 7/7/2014 (http://www.breitbart.com/Breitbart-Texas/2014/07/07/Leaked-Internal-DHS-Report-Admits-Lack-of-Deportation-Significant-Factor-in-Border-Crisis)

77 Sarah Carter, "Gov't Confirms Authenticity of Contract Request for 'Escort Services for Unaccompanied Alien Children' at the Border," *The Blaze,* 6/20/2014, (http://www.theblaze.com/stories/2014/06/20/govt-confirms-authenticity-of-contract-request-for-escort-services-for-unaccompanied-alien-children-at-the-border/)

78 "TRANSCRIPT: President Obama's Remarks at Univision Town Hall", *Fox News,* 9/20/2012; (http://insider.foxnews.com/2012/09/20/transcript-president-obamas-remarks-at-univision-town-hall)

79 Aaron Blake, "Obama: I 'probably' can't legalize immigrants myself", *Washington Post,* 7/17/2013; (http://www.washingtonpost.com/blogs/post-politics/wp/2013/07/17/obama-i-probably-cant-legalize-immigrants-myself/)

80 "President Obama Vows To Act Alone, Use Executive Powers To Tackle Immigration Reform", *Fox News Latino,* 6/30/2014; (http://latino.foxnews.com/latino/politics/2014/06/30/same-song-same-verse-president-obama-threatens-to-act-alone-on-immigration/)

81 Dave Boyer, "Obama offers amnesty to 5 million illegal immigrants, defies GOP", *Washington Times,* 11/20/2014; (http://www.washingtontimes.com/news/2014/nov/20/obama-offers-amnesty-to-millions-of-illegal-immigr/)

82 Jonathan Karl, "Obama's Long Lost Campaign Promise", ABC News, 2/17/2014; (http://abcnews.go.com/blogs/politics/2014/02/obamas-long-lost-campaign-promise/)

83 "Transcript of President Barack Obama with Univision", Los Angeles Times, 10/25/2010; (http://latimesblogs.latimes.com/washington/2010/10/transcript-of-president-barack-obama-with-univision.html)

84 Mark Krikorian, "Obama's Unprecedented Amnesty", National Review, 11/18/2014; (http://www.nationalreview.com/article/392887/obamas-unprecedented-amnesty-mark-krikorian)

85 Brandon Darby, "Catch and Release 2.0 - Leaks Highlight Teardown of Immigration Enforcement", *Breitbart,* 1/11/2015; (http://www.breitbart.com/big-government/2015/01/11/exclusive-catch-and-release-2-0-leaks-highlight-teardown-of-immigration-enforcement/)

86   Stephen Dinan, "Obama's Amnesty to Impose Billions in Costs on States, Lawsuit Alleges", *Washington Times*, 1/11/2015; (http://www.washingtontimes.com/news/2015/jan/11/obama-amnesty-for-illegal-immigrants-to-impose-bil/)

87   Stephen Dinan, "IRS to Pay Back-Refunds to Illegal Immigrants Who Didn't Pay Taxes", *Washington Times*, 2/11/2015; (http://www.washingtontimes.com/news/2015/feb/11/irs-pay-back-refunds-illegal-immigrants-who-didnt-/?page=all)

88   Peter Kirsanow, "After Obama's Amnesty, Illegal Aliens Could Decide U.S. Elections", *National Review*, 2/16/2015; (http://www.nationalreview.com/corner/398677/after-obamas-amnesty-illegal-aliens-could-decide-us-elections-peter-kirsanow)

89   Ben Kamisar and Kyle Balluck, "Judge Blocks Obama Order on Immigration", *The Hill*, 2/17/2015; (http://thehill.com/blogs/blog-briefing-room/232918-judge-blocks-obama-order-on-immigration)

90   Daniel Halper, "Obama: 'Consequences' for ICE Officials Who Don't Follow Executive Amnesty", *The Weekly Standard*, 2/25/2015; (http://www.weeklystandard.com/blogs/obama-consequences-ice-officials-who-dont-follow-executive-amnesty_866479.html)

91   Stephen Dinan, "Judge Accuses Obama Lawyers of Misleading Him, Refuses to Restart Amnesty", *Washington Times*, 4/7/2015; (http://www.washingtontimes.com/news/2015/apr/7/obama-motion-immediately-restart-amnesty-rejected-/)

92   Motoko Rich "'No Child' Law Whittled Down by White House,", *New York Times*, 07/06/2012, (http://www.nytimes.com/2012/07/06/education/no-child-left-behind-whittled-down-under-obama.html)

93   Lindsey Burke, Brittany Corona, Jennifer A. Marshall, Rachel Sheffield and Sandra Stotsky "Common Core National Standards and Tests: Empty Promises and Increased Federal Overreach Into Education," *The Heritage Foundation*, 10/7/2013 (http://www.heritage.org/research/reports/2013/10/common-core-national-standards-and-tests-empty-promises-and-increased-federal-overreach-into-education)

94   Brittany Corona, "No Child Left Behind Waivers: Tethers to the Feds," *The Heritage Foundation*, 10/6/2013 (http://www.heritage.org/research/reports/2010/01/a-smarter-path-to-a-race-to-the-top-in-education-reform)

95   Blaine Greteman, "Federal Bureaucrats Declare 'Hunger Games' More Complex Than 'The Grapes of Wrath'", *The New Republic*, 10/29/2013; http://www.newrepublic.com/article/115393/common-core-standards-make-mockery-novels-complexity

96   Fr. John Zuhlsdorf, "Obama Math: 'Common Core' Curriculum to Infect Catholic Schools?", *Fr Z's Blog*, 8/19/2013; http://wdtprs.com/blog/2013/08/obamamath-common-core-curriculum-to-infect-catholic-schools/

97   Al Baker, "Common Core Curriculum Now Has Critics on the Left," *New York Times*, 2/16/2014 (http://www.nytimes.com/2014/02/17/nyregion/new-york-early-champion-of-common-core-standards-joins-critics.html?hp&_r=3)

98   Lynn Adler, "U.S. 2009 Foreclosures Shatter Record Despite Aid," *Reuters*, 01/14/2010, (http://www.reuters.com/article/2010/01/14/us-usa-housing-foreclosures-idUSTRE60D0LZ20100114)

99   "1.8 Million U.S. Properties With Foreclosure Filings in 2012" *RealtyTrac*, 01/14/2013

100 "2012 Foreclosure Activity Up in 57 Percent of Metro Areas...," *RealtyTrac*, 01/28/2013

101 Les Christie, "Foreclosures Hit 6 Year Low in 2013", *CNN Money*, 1/16/2014; http://money.cnn.com/2014/01/16/real_estate/foreclosure-crisis/

102 Brena Swanson, "Realty Trac: Monthly Foreclosure Filings Reverse Course, Rise 8%", *Housing Wire*, 2/13/2014; http://www.housingwire.com/articles/28952-realtytrac-foreclosure-filings-reverse-course-rise-8

103 Binyamin Appelbaum, "Cautious Moves on Foreclosures Haunting Obama," *New York Times*, 08/19/2012, (http://www.nytimes.com/2012/08/20/business/economy/slow-response-to-housing-crisis-now-weighs-on-obama.html)

104   Chris Isidore, "Home Prices Rebound," *CNN Money*, 9/25/2012 (http://
money.cnn.com/2012/09/25/real_estate/home-prices/index.html)

105   Edward J. Pinto, "The Next Housing Bailout? Big Trouble Brewing at the FHA," *The
Atlantic*, 11/16/2012, (http://www.theatlantic.com/business/archive/2012/11/the-
next-housing-bailout-big-trouble-brewing-at-the-fha/265359/)

106   Margaret Chadbourn, "U.S. Federal Housing Administration to tap $1.7 bln in
taxpayer fund," *Reuters*, 9/27/2013 (http://www.reuters.com/article/2013/09/27/
usa-housing-bailout-idUSW1N0G702P20130927)

107   Dana Bash and Emily Sherman, "Sotomayor 'Wise Latina' Quote Used on Multiple
Occasions," *CNN Politics*, 06/05/2009, (http://politicalticker.blogs.cnn.com/
2009/06/05/sotomayor-wise-latina-quote-used-on-multiple-occasions/)

108   Ed Whelan, "Former Puerto Rican Nationalist Nominated to North American
Supreme Court," *National Review Online – Bench Memos*, (http://
www.nationalreview.com/bench-memos/49993/former-puerto-rican-nationalist-
nominated-north-american-supreme-court/ed-whelan)

109   Ed Morrissey, "New DHS Folly: the Domestic Extremism Lexicon." *Hot Air*,
05/01/2009, (http://hotair.com/archives/2009/05/01/new-dhs-folly-the-domestic-
extremism-lexicon/)

110   Ben Conery, "Kagan Kicked out Campus Recruiters at First Chance," *Washington
Times*, 05/12/2010, (http://www.washingtontimes.com/news/2010/may/12/kagan-
kicked-out-campus-recruiters-at-first-chance)

111   John Byrne, "Kagan Helped Shield Saudis from 9/11 Lawsuits," *The Raw Story*,
05/11/2010, (http://www.rawstory.com/rs/2010/05/11/kagan-helped-shield-
saudis-911-lawsuits/)

112   US Energy Information Administration, http://www.eia.gov/coal/ accessed
12/08/2012

113   Steve Mufson, "The Last Minute Obama-McCain Coal Debate," *Washington Post*,
11/3/2008, (http://newsweek.washingtonpost.com/postglobal/energywire/
2008/11/the_last_minute_obama-mccain_c.html)

114   Michael Bastasch, "Report: More Than 200 Coal-Fired Generators Slated for
Shutdown," *Daily Caller*, 09/21/2012 (http://dailycaller.com/2012/09/21/report-
more-than-200-coal-fired-generators-slated-for-shutdown/)

115   "Obama Administration Imposes Five-Year Drilling Ban on Majority of Offshore
Areas," House Natural Resources Committee, Press Release, 11/08/2011 (http://
naturalresources.house.gov/news/documentsingle.aspx?DocumentID=267985)

116   Wendy Koch, "Obama bans offshore oil drilling in Atlantic waters," USA Today,
12/2/2010, (http://usatoday30.usatoday.com/news/washington/environment/
2010-12-02-oildrill02_ST_N.htm)

117 Julie Seymour, "Pump Prices Running Out of Gas - Fall Below $3 for First Time in
More than Three and a Half Years", *CNS News*, 11/1/2014, (http://cnsnews.com/
mrctv-blog/julia-seymour/pump-prices-running-out-gas-fall-below-3-first-time-
more-three-and-half)

118   "Obama threatens to wield veto pen to counter GOP-led Congress" *Fox News*,
12/29/2014; (http://www.foxnews.com/politics/2014/12/29/obama-threatens-to-
wield-veto-pen-to-counter-gop-led-congress/)

119 Juliet Eilperin and Katie Zezima, "Obama vetoes Keystone XL bill", *Washington Post*,
2/24/2015; (http://www.washingtonpost.com/news/post-politics/wp/2015/02/24/
keystone-xl-bill-a-k-a-veto-bait-heads-to-presidents-desk/)

120 Juliet Eilperin and Steven Mufson, "State Department releases Keystone XL final
environmental impact statement", *Washington Post*, 1/31/2014; (https://
www.washingtonpost.com/business/economy/state-to-release-keystones-final-
environmental-impact-statement-friday/2014/01/31/3a9bb25c-8a83-11e3-
a5bd-844629433ba3_story.html)

121   Kelly David Burke, "Obama administration cuts back oil shale development", Fox
News, 6/22/2013; (http://www.foxnews.com/politics/2013/06/22/obama-
administration-cuts-back-oil-shale-development/)

122 Mike Brownfield, "EPA Blocks Oil Drilling in Alaska", Daily Signal, 4/25/2011; (http://dailysignal.com/2011/04/25/epa-blocks-oil-drilling-in-alaska/)

123 "Oil and Gas Production on Federal Lands Still a Disappointment", Institute for Energy Research, 4/24/2014 (http://instituteforenergyresearch.org/analysis/oil-and-gas-production-on-federal-lands-still-a-disappointment/)

124 Darrell Issa, "Obama's Bad Policy, Harmful Regulations Add to Gas Prices," US News and World Report, 05/27/2011, (http://www.usnews.com/opinion/articles/2011/05/27/obamas-bad-policy-harmful-regulations-add-to-gas-prices)

125 "Obama and Reid's Energy Tax Puts Ideology Above Economics," Pete Sepp, *US News and World Report*, 03/07/2012, (http://www.usnews.com/opinion/blogs/on-energy/2012/03/07/obama-and-reids-energy-tax-puts-ideology-above-economics)

126 "American economy stronger than Obama incompetence" *Washington Times*; 1/1/2015; (http://www.washingtontimes.com/news/2015/jan/1/editorial-american-economy-stronger-than-obama-inc/)

127 Jessica Gavora, "How Title IX Became a Political Weapon", *Wall Street Journal* 6/7/2015; http://www.wsj.com/articles/how-title-ix-became-a-political-weapon-1433715320)

128 John Hinderaker, "The Obama Justice Department's Insane Attack on North Carolina", *Power Line;* 5/4/2016; (http://www.powerlineblog.com/archives/2016/05/the-obama-justice-departments-insane-attack-on-north-carolina.php)

129 Ryan T. Anderson, "Obama Unilaterally Rewrites Law, Imposes Transgender Policy on Nation's Schools", *Daily Signal*, 5/13/2016; (http://dailysignal.com/2016/05/13/obama-unilaterally-rewrites-law-imposes-transgender-policy-on-nations-schools/)

130 Julie Hirschfeld Davis, "Obama Defends Transgender Directive for School Bathrooms", *New York Times*, 5/16/2016; (http://www.nytimes.com/2016/05/17/us/politics/obama-defends-transgender-directive-for-school-bathrooms.html)

131 Julie Hirschfeld Davis and Matt Apuzzo, "U.S. Directs Public Schools to Allow Transgender Access to Restrooms", *New York Times*, 5/12/2016; (http://www.nytimes.com/2016/05/13/us/politics/obama-administration-to-issue-decree-on-transgender-access-to-school-restrooms.html)

132 Caleb Howe, "These 12 States Are Fighting Back Against Obama's Leftist Bathroom Bullying" *Redstate*, 5/15/2016; (http://www.redstate.com/absentee/2016/05/14/12-states-fighting-back-obamas-leftist-bathroom-bullying/)

133 Mario Loyola, "Obama's Dictatorial Transgender Proclamation", *National Review*, 5/16/2016; (http://www.nationalreview.com/article/435413/bathroom-wars-obamas-proclamation-dictatorial-unconstitutional)

134 "Barack Obama's Acceptance Speech" *New York Times*, 8/28/2008; (http://www.nytimes.com/2008/08/28/us/politics/28text-obama.html)

135 Jerome Hudson, "22 Times Obama Admin Declare Climate Change a Greater Threat Than Terrorism", Breitbart, 11/14/2015; (http://www.breitbart.com/big-government/2015/11/14/22-times-obama-admin-declared-climate-change-greater-threat-terrorism/)

136 Melanie Hunter, "Obama Links Islamic Terrorism to Climate Change", *CNS News*, 5/20/2015; (http://cnsnews.com/news/article/melanie-hunter/obama-links-islamic-terrorism-climate-change)

137 Stephen Dinan, "Obama clean energy loans leave taxpayers in $2.2 billion hole", *Washington Times*, 4/27/2015; (http://www.washingtontimes.com/news/2015/apr/27/obama-backed-green-energy-failures-leave-taxpayers/)

138 Rowan Scarborough; "Pentagon orders commanders to prioritize climate change in all military actions", *Washington Times*, 2/7/2016; (http://www.washingtontimes.com/news/2016/feb/7/pentagon-orders-commanders-to-prioritize-climate-c/)

139 Andrew Follett, "Obama's NASA Budget Is All About Global Warming, Not Space", *Daily Caller*, 2/10/2016; (http://dailycaller.com/2016/02/10/obamas-nasa-budget-is-all-about-global-warming-not-space/)

140 Marita Noon, "Killing Coal: The Obama Administration's Intentional Assault on an Industry" *Breitbart*, 1/19/2016; (http://www.breitbart.com/big-government/2016/01/19/killing-coal-the-obama-administrations-intentional-assault-on-an-industry/)

141 Hans von Spokovsky, "Attorney General Lynch Looks Into Prosecuting 'Climate Change Deniers'" *Daily Signal*, 3/10/2016; (http://dailysignal.com/2016/03/10/attorney-general-lynch-looking-into-prosecuting-climate-change-deniers/)

142 Rowan Scarborough; "Pentagon wrestles with bogus climate warnings as funds shifted to green agenda", *Washington Times*, 6/1/2014; (http://www.washingtontimes.com/news/2014/jun/1/pentagon-wrestles-with-false-climate-predictions-a/)

143 Keith Johnson, "How Carbon Dioxide Became a 'Pollutant'", *Wall Street Journal*, 4/18/2009; (http://www.wsj.com/articles/SB124001537515830975)

144 Nicholas Loris, "EPA Formally Declares CO2 a Dangerous Pollutant", *The Daily Signal*, 12/7/2009; (http://dailysignal.com/2009/12/07/epa-formally-declares-co2-a-dangerous-pollutant/)

145 Evan Lehmann, "Senate Abandons Climate Effort, Dealing Blow to President", *New York Times*, 7/23/2010; (http://www.nytimes.com/cwire/2010/07/23/23climatewire-senate-abandons-climate-effort-dealing-blow-88864.html)

146 Keith Goldberg, "High Court Stay Could Spell Doom For EPA's Clean Power Plan", *Law360*, 2/16/2016; (http://www.law360.com/articles/757509/high-court-stay-could-spell-doom-for-epa-s-clean-power-plan)

147 Jim DeMint, "How Obama will celebrate 'Earth Day'", *Washington Times* 4/21/2016; (http://www.washingtontimes.com/news/2016/apr/21/jim-demint-obama-bypasses-senate-approval-of-paris/)

148 Sen James Lankford, "Obama Raided $500M for Zika to Finance UN's Green Climate Fund" *Daily Signal*, 5/23/2016; (http://dailysignal.com/2016/05/23/obama-raided-500m-for-zika-to-finance-uns-green-climate-fund)

149 The White House, The Press Office. Memorandum For The Heads of Executive Departments and Agencies. Retrieved from http://www.whitehouse.gov/the-press-office/freedom-information-act

150 The White House, The Press Office (2009). Executive Order 13489 -- Presidential Records. Retrieved from http://www.whitehouse.gov/the_press_office/ExecutiveOrderPresidentialRecords

151 Jim Snyder & Danielle Ivory, "Obama Cabinet Flunks Disclosure Test With 19 in 20 Ignoring Law," *Bloomberg*, 9/27/2012 (http://www.bloomberg.com/news/2012-09-28/obama-cabinet-flunks-disclosure-test-with-19-in-20-ignoring-law.html)

152 Tom Schoenberg, "Obama Visitor Logs Must be Made Public, Lawyer Tells Court," *Bloomberg*, 09/18/2012, (http://www.bloomberg.com/news/2012-09-18/obama-visitor-logs-must-be-public-lawyer-tells-court.html)

153 Hadas Gold, "Media protest White House photo ban," *Politico*, 11/21/13; (http://www.politico.com/blogs/media/2013/11/whca-protests-white-house-photo-ban-178077.html)

154 Paul Bedard, "Vacationer in Chief: Tens of Millions Spent on 38 Obama Holidays", *Washington Examiner*, 3/7/2015; (http://www.washingtonexaminer.com/vacationer-in-chief-tens-of-millions-spent-on-38-obama-holidays/article/2561162)

155 "Michelle Obama's August 2010 Vacation in Spain...," *Judicial Watch*, 04/26/2012, (http://www.judicialwatch.org/press-room/press-releases/michelle-obamas-august-2010-vacation-in-spain-cost-american-taxpayers-467585-according-to-records-obtained-by-judicial-watch/)

156 Paul Bedard, "Michelle Obama's Africa Trip Cost More Than $424,142," *US News and World Report*, 10/04/2011, (http://www.usnews.com/news/blogs/washington-whispers/2011/10/04/michelle-obamas-africa-vacation-cost-more-than-432142)

157 Malia Zimmerman, "Residents Alerted to Obamas' Hawaiian Holiday Plans," *Hawaii Reporter*, 11/27/2012, (http://www.hawaiireporter.com/residents-alerted-to-obamas-hawaiian-holiday-plans/123)

158   Keith Koffler, "Obama Returns to Hawaii at an Added Cost of Over $3 Million," *White House Dossier*, 01/02/2013;, (http://www.whitehousedossier.com/2013/01/02/obama-returns-hawaii-added-cost-3-million/)

159   Tony Lee, "Media Ignores Lavish Obama Vacations, Slammed Bush for Mountain Biking", *Breitbart*, 3/26/2013; (http://www.breitbart.com/big-journalism/2013/03/26/obamas-vacation-more-lavishly-than-bushes/)

160   "Documents Obtained by Judicial Watch Reveal Obama 2013 Vacations, Leno Show Appearance, Cost Taxpayers $7,396,531 for Flight Expenses," *Judicial Watch*, 2/27/2014 (http://www.judicialwatch.org/press-room/press-releases/2013-vacations-cost-taxpayers/)

161 Greg Campbell, "Obamas to Take Third Vacation in Three Months", *TPNN*, 2/16/2015; (http://www.tpnn.com/2015/02/16/obamas-to-take-third-vacation-in-three-months/)

162 Morgan Chalfant, "Obama Books $12M Martha's Vineyard Mansion for Penultimate Presidential Vacataion", *Washington Free Beacon*, 7/7/2015: (http://freebeacon.com/politics/obama-books-12m-marthas-vineyard-mansion-for-penultimate-presidential-summer-vacation/)

163   (n.d.). Retrieved from http://en.wikipedia.org/wiki/Staycation

164   Hugo Gye and Louise Boyle, "Obama Fund-Raises $4.5 Million from Celebs in Just 8 Hours in NY," *Mail Online*, 06/14/2012, (http://www.dailymail.co.uk/news/article-2159554/Barack-Obama-New-York-President-jets-evening-star-studded-fundraisers.html)

165   Toby Harnden, "Is the Taxpayer Funding Obama's Reelection Campaign?," *Mail Online*, 04/26/2012, (http://www.dailymail.co.uk/news/article-2135763/This-does-pass-straight-face-test-Obama-accused-wasting-tax-payers-money-fund-raising-events-election.html)

166   Brett LoGiurato, "Republicans Have Filed A Formal Complaint Into Obama's 'Misuse Of Taxpayer Dollars'" *Business Insider*, 4/25/2012, (http://www.businessinsider.com/rnc-complaint-on-obama-travel-2012-4)

167   Jeffrey Klein, "Obama Leaves Cities on Hook for Expensive Fundraiser Security Costs," *Examiner*, 08/22/2012, (http://www.examiner.com/article/obama-leaves-cities-on-hook-for-expensive-fundraiser-security-costs)

168   Elizabeth Dinan, "Obama refuses to pay Portsmouth $30K for campaign visit costs," *Seacost Online*, 12/20/2012, (http://www.seacoastonline.com/articles/20121220-NEWS-212200416)

169   "City Demands Obama Team Pay Police Tab," *Wall Street Journal*, 8/2/2012, (http://online.wsj.com/article/SB10000872396390443545504577563152319884314.htm)

170   Awr Hawkins, "Obama Admin Gave Classified Info to Bin Laden Filmmakers," *Breitbart*, 11/15/2012, (http://www.breitbart.com/Big-Peace/2012/11/15/Obama-Admin-Discussed-Classifed-Information-With-Osama-bin-Laden-Filmmakers)

171   Daniel Greenfield, "Obama Donors Got $21,000 in Government Money for Every $1 They Gave," *Frontpage Magazine*, 11/25/2012, (http://frontpagemag.com/2012/dgreenfield/obama-donors-got-21000-in-government-money-for-every-1-they-gave/)

172   Ronnie Green and Matthew Mosk, "Green Bundler With the Golden Touch," The Center for Public Integrity, 03/30/2011, (http://www.publicintegrity.org/2011/03/30/3845/green-bundler-golden-touch/)

173   Devin Dwyer, "Watchdogs Question Obama Donor Influence in 'Fiscal Cliff' Meetings," *ABC News*, 11/28/2012, (http://abcnews.go.com/blogs/politics/2012/11/watchdogs-question-donor-influence-in-obama-fiscal-cliff-meetings/)

174   Dave Levinthal, "Obama Inauguration Sponsors Spent Millions Influencing Government," Center for Public Integrity, *TruthOut*, 01/21/2013, (http://truth-out.org/news/item/14037-obama-inauguration-sponsors-spent-millions-influencing-government)

175 Ashley Portero, "Obama's Organizing for Action Could Lead to Government Corruption, Watchdogs Fear," *International Business Times*, 02/20/2013; http://www.ibtimes.com/obamas-organizing-action-could-lead-government-corruption-watchdogs-fear-1095592)

176 T.W. Farnam, "The Influence Industry: Obama gives administration jobs to some big fundraisers," *Washington Post*, 3/7/2012, (http://articles.washingtonpost.com/2012-03-07/politics/35447935_1_bundlers-obama-administration-steve-spinner)

177 Lachlan Markar, "Report: 80% of DOE Green Energy Loans Went to Obama Backers," *The Foundry*, 11/14/2011, (http://blog.heritage.org/2011/11/14/report-80-of-doe-green-energy-loans-went-to-obama-backers/)

178 The White House, Office of the Press Secretary. (2012). Remarks by the President in State of the Union Address [Press release]. Retrieved from http://www.whitehouse.gov/the-press-office/2012/01/24/remarks-president-state-union-address

179 Mike McIntire and Michael Luo, "White House Opens Door to Big Donors, and Lobbyists Slip In," *The New York Times*, 04/14/2012, (http://www.nytimes.com/2012/04/15/us/politics/white-house-doors-open-for-big-donors.html)

180 *Ibid.*

181 Matthew Boyle, "LightSquared CEO Made Curious Max Donation to DNC While Seeking White House Audience," *The Daily Caller*, 02/24/2012, (http://dailycaller.com/2012/02/24/lightsquared-ceo-made-curious-max-donation-to-dnc-while-seeking-white-house-audience/)

182 Matthew Boyle, "LightSquared CEO Resigns Amid Revelations of Company's Proximity to Obama White House," *The Daily Caller*, 02/28/2012, (http://dailycaller.com/2012/02/28/lightsquared-ceo-resigns-amid-revelations-of-companys-proximity-to-obama-white-house/)

183 Matthew Boyle, "Documents: LightSquared Shaping up as FCC's Solyndra," *Daily Caller*, 02/21/2012, (http://dailycaller.com/2012/02/21/documents-lightsquared-shaping-up-as-the-fccs-solyndra/)

184 David Willman, "Cost, Need Questioned in $433 Million Smallpox Drug Deal," *Los Angeles Times*, 11/13/2011, (http://articles.latimes.com/2011/nov/13/nation/la-na-smallpox-20111113)

185 Chuck Neubauer, "Obama Donors Got Deal; Depositors Get 'Stiffed Again'," *Washington Times*, 06/10/2012, (http://www.washingtontimes.com/news/2012/jun/10/obama-donors-get-deal-depositors-get-stiffed-again/)

186

187 Vince Coglianese, "White House Won't Deny $500,000 Purchases Access to President Obama," *The Daily Caller*, 02/25/2013, (http://dailycaller.com/2013/02/25/white-house-wont-deny-500000-purchases-access-to-president-obama-video/)

188 Nicholas Confessore, "Obama's Backers Seek Big Donors to Press Agenda," *The New York Times*, 02/22/2013, (http://www.nytimes.com/2013/02/23/us/politics/obamas-backers-seek-deep-pockets-to-press-agenda.html?_r=3&)

189 Wynton Hall, "Democrats Blast Obama's Bundler-Turned-Treasury Nominee", *Breitbart*, 12/28/2014; (http://www.breitbart.com/big-government/2014/12/28/democrats-blast-obamas-bundler-turned-treasury-nominee/)

190 Nicholas Confessore and Sheryl Gay Stolberg, "Well-Trod Path: Political Donor to Ambassador," *New York Times*, 01/18/2013, (http://www.nytimes.com/2013/01/19/us/politics/well-trod-path-political-donor-to-ambassador.html)

191 "List of Ambassadorial Appointments" *American Foreign Service Association*, Accessed 6/2/2016; (http://www.afsa.org/ambassadorlist.aspx)

192 Fred Lucas, "23: That's How Many Obama Bundlers Have Been Nominated for Ambassadorships — And Now a Democrat Is Speaking Out," *The Blaze*, 2/7/2014 (http://www.theblaze.com/stories/2014/02/07/23-thats-how-many-obama-bundlers-have-been-nominated-for-ambassadorships-and-now-a-democrat-is-speaking-out/)

193 Tim Cavanaugh, "Konnichi-Whaa? Experts debate Caroline Kennedy's Japan cred," *Daily Caller*, 4/3/2013 (http://dailycaller.com/2013/04/03/konnichi-whaa-experts-debate-caroline-kennedys-japan-cred/)

194 "Obama's ambassador pick for Norway bobbles Senate history test, but still likely to nab job," Fox News, 1/23/2014 (http://www.foxnews.com/politics/2014/01/23/obama-ambassador-pick-for-norway-fails-senate-history-test-but-still-likely-to/)

195 Eyder Peralta, "Ambassador To Argentina Nominee Has Never Been To the Country," *The Two-Way*, 2/7/2014 (http://www.npr.org/blogs/thetwo-way/2014/02/07/273106029/ambassador-to-argentina-nominee-has-never-been-to-the-country)

196 Al Kamen, "Obama ambassador nominees — Baucus, Bell and Tsunis — hit bumps in hearings," Washington Post, 1/30/2014 (http://www.washingtonpost.com/politics/obama-ambassador-nominees--baucus-bell-and-tsunis--hit-bumps-in-hearings/2014/01/30/824d6b40-89e8-11e3-a5bd-844629433ba3_story.html)

197 *Ibid.*

198 "Obama far outpaces predecessors in appointing donors to foreign posts," *Fox News*, 2/10/2014 (http://www.foxnews.com/politics/2014/02/10/obama-far-outpaces-predecessors-in-appointing-donors-to-foreign-posts/)

199 Henri J. Barkey, "Obama's ambassador nominees are a disservice to diplomacy," *Washington Post*, 7/6/2014 (http://www.washingtonpost.com/opinions/obamas-ambassador-nominees-are-a-disservice-to-diplomacy/2014/02/06/2273ef9e-8e86-11e3-b227-12a45d109e03_story.html)

200 Michael Isikoff, "Facing Opposition, Obama Intel Pick Pulls Out," *Newsweek*, 3/9/09 (http://www.newsweek.com/facing-opposition-obama-intel-pick-pulls-out-76211)

201 "Intelligence Failures," *National Review*, 3/4/2009 (http://www.nationalreview.com/articles/227003/intelligence-failure/editors)

202 Chris Jacobs, "Donald Berwick's Rationed Transparency", *The Heritage Foundation*, 6/27/2013 (http://www.heritage.org/research/commentary/2013/6/donald-berwicks-rationed-transparency)

203 Paul Mirengoff, "Boring From Within", *Powerline*, 3/29/2010 (http://www.powerlineblog.com/archives/2010/03/025876.php)

204 Mario Trujlio, "Obama nomination of Mumia Abu Jamal lawyer stirs controversy," *The Hill*, 1/9/2014 (http://thehill.com/blogs/blog-briefing-room/news/194950-obama-nomination-of-mumia-abu-jamal-lawyer-stirs-controversy)

205 Burgess Everett, "Democrats help block Obama's DOJ pick," Politico, 3/5/2014 (http://www.politico.com/story/2014/03/senate-blocks-debo-adegbile-justice-department-104297.html)

206 "Obama's DHS pick a major Democratic donor, senators question credentials," *Fox News*, 10/18/2013 (http://www.foxnews.com/politics/2013/10/18/obamas-dhs-pick-major-democratic-donor-senator-questions-credentials/)

207 Stephen Dinan, "DHS nominee Jeh Johnson lacks immigration experience," *Washington Times*, 10/18/2013 (http://www.washingtontimes.com/news/2013/oct/18/dhs-jeh-johnson-nominee-lacks-immigration-experien/)

208 Jess Bravin and Jared A. Favole, "Surprised Pick for Homeland Security," *Wall Street Journal*, 10/17/2013 (http://online.wsj.com/news/articles/SB20001424052702303680404579141881388674454)

209 Jordan Schachtel, "Official Who Claimed al Qaeda 'On The Run' Obama's Pick to Head DHS," *Breitbart*, 10/24/2013 (http://www.breitbart.com/Big-Peace/2013/10/24/President-Obama-s-Left-Hand-Man-Appointed-to-Lead-DHS)

210 Tom Gardner, "Illegal immigrants have 'earned the right to be U.S. citizens', says Homeland Security Secretary," *Daily Mail*, 1/27/2014

211 Andrew Malcolm, "Obama's green jobs czar Van Jones quits under fire," Top of The Ticket, 9/6/2009 (http://latimesblogs.latimes.com/washington/2009/09/obama-adviser-van-jones.html)

212 Chip Johnson, "Timing Of Protest Is Suspect / Mumia supporters disrupt youth event," *San Francisco Gate*, 10/9/1999 (http://www.sfgate.com/bayarea/johnson/article/Timing-Of-Protest-Is-Suspect-Mumia-supporters-2903851.php)

213 Tony Lee, "Radical Obama Regulatory Chief Cass Sunstein Resigns," *Breitbart*, 8/5/2012 (http://www.breitbart.com/Big-Government/2012/08/05/Radical-Obama-Regulatory-Chief-Cass-Sunstein-Resigns)

214 Adam Brickley, "Obama Appoints Pro-Gay Activist Who Promotes Pro-Gay Clubs in Public Schools to be 'Safe Schools' Czar," *CNSNews*, 6/17/2009 (http://www.cnsnews.com/news/article/obama-appoints-pro-gay-activist-who-promotes-pro-gay-clubs-public-schools-be-safe)

215 Kerry Picket, "Kevin Jennings's longtime foe, 'Mass Resistance'," *Washington Times*, 12/8/2009 (http://www.washingtontimes.com/weblogs/watercooler/2009/dec/08/kevin-jennings-longtime-foe-time-mass-resistance/)

216 Kathy Shaidle, "'Science Czar' John P. Holdren's disturbing beliefs about America, capitalism and humanity" *Examiner*, 7/16/2009 (http://www.examiner.com/article/science-czar-john-p-holdren-s-disturbing-beliefs-about-america-capitalism-and-humanity)

217 Benjamin Lesser and Greg B. Smith, "Buildings sprang up as donations rained down on Bronx Borough President Adolfo Carrion," New York Daily News, 3/1/2009 (http://www.nydailynews.com/new-york/bronx/buildings-sprang-donations-rained-bronx-borough-president-adolfo-carrion-article-1.367969)

218 Michelle Malkin, "Czar Wars: The Phantom Menaces," *New York Post*, 7/26/2009 (http://nypost.com/2009/07/26/czar-wars-the-phantom-menaces/)

219 Michelle Malkin, "The Trouble with Obama's Energy Czar," *Human Events*, 12/12/2008 (http://www.humanevents.com/2008/12/12/the-trouble-with-obamas-energy-czar/)

220 "Browner is an environmental radical - and a socialist (seriously)," *Washington Examiner*, 1/7/2009 (http://washingtonexaminer.com/browner-is-an-environmental-radical-and-a-socialist-seriously/article/25170)

221 Seton Motley, "New FCC 'Chief Diversity Officer' Co-Wrote Liberal Group's 'Structural Imbalance of Political Talk Radio'," *Newbusters*, 8/6/2009 (http://newsbusters.org/blogs/seton-motley/2009/08/06/new-fcc-chief-diversity-officer-co-wrote-liberal-groups-structural-imb)

222 Seton Motley, "Audio: FCC's Diversity Czar: 'White People' Need to be Forced to 'Step Down' 'So Someone Else Can Have Power," *Newbusters*, 8/6/2009 (http://newsbusters.org/blogs/seton-motley/2009/09/23/fccs-diversity-czar-white-people-need-be-forced-step-down-so-someone-0)

223 Jesse Byrnes, "McCain: Ebola czar does not 'fit the bill'" The Hill, 10/17/2014; (http://thehill.com/policy/healthcare/221157-mccain-ebola-czar-does-not-fit-the-bill)

224 "ISIS Czar a Terrorist Sympathizer Once Fired by Obama for Hamas Ties", *Judicial Watch*, 12/2/2015 (http://www.judicialwatch.org/blog/2015/12/isis-czar-a-terrorist-sympathizer-once-fired-by-obama-for-hamas-ties/)

225 Eric Owens, "Supremes Smack Down Obama Administration 9-0 For 13th TIME SINCE 2012," Daily Caller, 6/27/2014 (http://dailycaller.com/2014/06/27/supremes-smack-down-obama-administration-9-0-for-13th-time-since-2012/)

226 Ilya Shapiro, "Obama's Abysmal Record Before the Supreme Court," CATO Institute, 2/11/2016 (http://www.cato.org/blog/obamas-abysmal-record-supreme-court)

227 Jonathan Weisman, "Appointments Challenge Senate Role, Experts Say," *New York Times*, 01/07/2012 (http://www.nytimes.com/2012/01/08/us/politics/experts-say-obamas-recess-appointments-could-signify-end-to-a-senate-role.html)

228 Stephen Dinan, "Obama Recess Appointments Unconstitutional," *Washington Times*, 1/25/2013 (http://www.washingtontimes.com/news/2013/jan/25/federal-court-obama-broke-law-recess-appointments/)

229 Julian Hattern, "Obama dealt second court defeat over NLRB recess appointments," *The Hill*, 5/16/2013 (http://thehill.com/blogs/regwatch/labor/300273-court-rules-against-nlrb-recess-appointment)

230 Larry O'Dell. "NLRB Recess Appointments Ruled Unconstitutional By Virginia Appeals Court," *Associated Press*, 7/17/2013 (http://www.huffingtonpost.com/2013/07/17/nlrb-appointments-unconstitutional_n_3613034.html)

231 Robert Barnes, "Supreme Court questions Obama's recess appointment power," *Washington Post*, 1/13/2014 (http://www.washingtonpost.com/politics/2014/01/13/15869f86-7c87-11e3-9556-4a4bf7bcbd84_story.html)

232 "Obama to Order Expansion of Overtime Pay for Millions of Workers", *Fox News*, 3/12/2014; (http://www.foxnews.com/politics/2014/03/12/obama-to-reportedly-order-expansion-overtime-pay-for-millions-workers/)

233 Benjamin Goad, "Biz Stunned by Obama Overtime Move", *The Hill*, 3/12/2014; (http://thehill.com/blogs/regwatch/business/200658-biz-stunned-as-obama-gives-millions-overtime)

234 Kate Scanlon, "Can Obama Raise Your Taxes Without Congressional Approval?" *Daily Signal*, 3/3/2015; (http://dailysignal.com/2015/03/03/can-obama-raise-taxes-without-congressional-approval/?utm_source=facebook&utm_medium=social&utm_campaign=tds03042015RAISE TAXES)

235 Amy Payne, "Obama Wants Power to Raise Debt Limit by Himself, Anytime," *The Foundry*, 12/05/2012, (http://blog.heritage.org/2012/12/05/morning-bell-obama-wants-power-to-raise-debt-limit-by-himself-anytime/)

236 Steve Holland and Mark Felsenthal, "Obama's opening 'fiscal cliff' bid seeks debt limit hike, stimulus," *Reuters*, 11/29/2012, (http://www.reuters.com/article/2012/11/30/us-usa-fiscal-offer-idUSBRE8AT02C20121130)

237 Marc Ambinder, "Obama Won't go to Court Over Defense of Marriage Act," *National Journal*, 02/24/2011, (http://www.nationaljournal.com/obama-won-t-go-to-court-over-defense-of-marriage-act-20110223)

238 Robert Pear, "Fewer Youths to Be Deported in New Policy," *New York Times*, 08/18/2011, (http://www.nytimes.com/2011/08/19/us/19immig.html)

239 *Ibid.*

240 Donna St. George and Brady Dennis, "Growing Share of Hispanic Voters Helped Push Obama to Victory," *The Washington Post*, 11/07/2012, (http://www.washingtonpost.com/politics/decision2012/growing-share-of-hispanic-voters-helped-push-obama-to-victory/2012/11/07/b4087d0a-28ff-11e2-b4e0-346287b7e56c_story.html)

241 Julia Preston, "In Big Shift, Latino Vote Was Heavily for Obama," *New York Times*, 11/06/2008, (http://www.nytimes.com/2008/11/07/us/politics/07latino.html)

242 Dr. Milton R. Wolf, "ObamaCare Waiver Corruption Must Stop," *The Washington Times*, 05/20/2011, (http://www.washingtontimes.com/news/2011/may/20/obamacare-waiver-corruption-must-stop/)

243 "Remarks by President Obama to the People of Africa", The White House, 7/28/2015; https://www.whitehouse.gov/the-press-office/2015/07/28/remarks-president-obama-people-africa

244 Jeffrey H. Anderson, "Obama Continues to Violate His Own 'Stimulus' Law by Not Releasing Quarterly Reports", *The Weekly Standard*, 1/26/2013. (http://www.weeklystandard.com/article/obama-continues-violate-his-own-stimulus-law-not-releasing-quarterly-reports/697896)

245 Grace-Marie Turner, "70 Changes to ObamaCare... -So Far", Galen Institute, 1/28/2016; (http://galen.org/newsletters/changes-to-obamacare-so-far/)

246 Josh Rogin, "Exclusive: Obama Declines to Add Names to Russian Sanction List", *The Daily Beast*, 12/19/2013, (http://www.thedailybeast.com/articles/2013/12/19/exclusive-obama-declines-to-add-names-to-russian-sanction-list.html)

247 "Obama's Magnitsky Walkback", *The Wall Street Journal*, 1/5/2014, (http://online.wsj.com/news/articles/SB10001424052702304591604579290880748745144)

248 Christoph Reuter, "Assad's New Bomb: Syrian Regime Hasn't Abandoned Chemical Weapons", *Der Spiegel*, 5/8/2014; (http://www.spiegel.de/international/world/evidence-mounts-of-chlorine-gas-attacks-in-syria-a-968108.html)

249 Joe Cunningham, "Obama's Iran Deal Violates A Law Obama Signed In 2012", *RedState*, 10/8/2015; (http://www.redstate.com/joesquire/2015/10/08/obamas-iran-deal-violates-law-obama-signed-2012/)

250 James Rosen, "EXCLUSIVE: U.S. officials conclude Iran deal violates federal law", *Fox News*, 10/9/2015; (http://www.foxnews.com/politics/2015/10/08/exclusive-us-officials-conclude-iran-deal-violates-federal-law.html)

251 "Victimizing the Borrowers: Predatory Lending's Role in the Subprime Mortgage Crisis", *Knowledge @ Wharton*, 2/20/2008; (http://knowledge.wharton.upenn.edu/article/victimizing-the-borrowers-predatory-lendings-role-in-the-subprime-mortgage-crisis/)

252 Sean Higgins, "Bank of America gets 2-for-1 deal in Justice Dept. settlement", *Washington Examiner*, 6/1/2016; (http://www.washingtonexaminer.com/bank-of-america-gets-half-off-its-justice-dept.-settlement/article/2592705)

253 Byron York, "Justice Department Steers Money to Favored Groups", *Washington Examiner*, 8/5/2010; (http://www.washingtonexaminer.com/justice-department-steers-money-to-favored-groups/article/11539)

254 Sean Higgins, "Bank of America gets 2-for-1 deal in Justice Dept. settlement", *Washington Examiner*, 6/1/2016; (http://www.washingtonexaminer.com/bank-of-america-gets-half-off-its-justice-dept.-settlement/article/2592705)

255 Sean Higgins, "Bank of America gets 2-for-1 deal in Justice Dept. settlement", *Washington Examiner*, 6/1/2016; (http://www.washingtonexaminer.com/bank-of-america-gets-half-off-its-justice-dept.-settlement/article/2592705)

256 John Nolte, "Obama Pivots to Economy for 21st Time," *Breitbart*, 11/8/2013 (http://www.breitbart.com/Big-Government/2013/11/08/obama-pivots-to-economy-for-20th-time)

257 Alan M. Collinge, "President Obama's horrible, terrible legacy on student loans", *The Hill*, 5/13/2016; (http://thehill.com/blogs/congress-blog/education/279512-president-obamas-horrible-terrible-legacy-on-student-loans)

258 *Ibid.*

259 Jeff Cox, "Average College Debt Rose to $24,000 in 2009", *New York Times*, 10/21/2010; (http://www.nytimes.com/2010/10/22/education/22debt.html)

260 Jeff Cox, "Student debt load growing, so are delinquencies", *CNBC*, 3/8/2016; (http://www.cnbc.com/2016/03/08/student-debt-load-growing-so-are-delinquencies.html)

261 Kim Parker, "The Boomerang Generation", *Pew Research Center*, 3/15/2012; (http://www.pewsocialtrends.org/2012/03/15/the-boomerang-generation/)

262 Julie Pace, "Obama to propose tax hikes for the wealthy, free community college", *Christian Science Monitor*, 1/18/2015; (http://www.csmonitor.com/USA/Latest-News-Wires/2015/0118/Obama-to-propose-tax-hikes-for-the-wealthy-free-community-college-video)

263 " Breakthrough White Paper: Four Year Colleges vs. Community Colleges", Breakthrough Collaborative, (https://www.breakthroughcollaborative.org/sites/default/files/BTResearch-4yr_vs_2yr_colleges.pdf)

264 David Eldrige, "Report Flunks Obama's 'Free' Community College Plan", *Inside Sources*, 1/7/2016; (http://www.insidesources.com/report-flunks-obamas-free-community-college-plan/)

265 "Car Allowance Rebate System", *Wikipedia*, accessed 12/18/2012; http://en.wikipedia.org/wiki/Car_Allowance_Rebate_System

266 Edmunds,. (2015). Cash for Clunkers Results Finally In: Taxpayers Paid $24,000 per Vehicle Sold, Reports Edmunds.com. (http://www.edmunds.com/about/press/cash-for-clunkers-results-finally-in-taxpayers-paid-24000-per-vehicle-sold-reports-edmundscom.html)

267 Jennifer Santis, "The Cash for Clunkers Conundrum", *EMagazine*, 1/2/2013; (http://www.emagazine.com/blog/the-cash-for-clunkers-conundrum)

268 Nick Bunkley, "Government Will End Clunker Program Early." *New York Times*, 8/20/2009; (http://www.nytimes.com/2009/08/21/business/21clunkers.html)

269 Peter Ferrara, "President Obama: The Biggest Government Spender In World History" *Forbes*, 6/14/2012; (http://www.forbes.com/sites/peterferrara/2012/06/14/president-obama-the-biggest-government-spender-in-world-history/)

270 "Examiner Editorial: Big-spending Obama frames himself as scrooge," *Washington Examiner*, 5/24/2012; (http://www.washingtonexaminer.com/examiner-editorial-big-spending-obama-frames-himself-as-scrooge/article/650536)

271 Terrence P. Jeffrey, "Obama Has Presided Over 5 of 6 Largest Deficits in U.S. History," *CNSNews*, 10/30/2013 (http://www.cnsnews.com/news/article/terence-p-jeffrey/obama-has-presided-over-5-6-largest-deficits-us-history)

272 Government data from http://www.usgovernmentspending.com/spending_chart_1929_2017USk_11s1li011mcn_G0f_Deficits_In_Inflation-adjusted_Dollars

273 "The Debt to the Penny and Who Holds It," Treasury Direct, Accessed 1/23/2016 (http://www.treasurydirect.gov/NP/debt/current)

274 "U.S. Debt Reaches 100 Percent of Country's GDP," *Fox News*, 8/4/2011 (http://www.foxnews.com/politics/2011/08/04/us-debt-reaches-100-percent-countrys-gdp/)

275 Tyler Durden, "US Ends 2012 With 103.8% Debt To GDP," *Zero Hedge*, 1/30/2013 (http://www.zerohedge.com/news/its-official-us-debtgdp-passes-100)

276 Calculation by the authors based on government data.

277 Zachary Goldfarb, "S&P downgrades U.S. credit rating for first time," Washington Post, 8/6/2011; (http://www.washingtonpost.com/business/economy/sandp-considering-first-downgrade-of-us-credit-rating/2011/08/05/gIQAqKeIxL_story.html)

278 Richard Sisk, "Hagel Says Cuts to Pay and Benefits are Needed," *Military.com News*, 11/5/2013 (http://www.military.com/daily-news/2013/11/05/hagel-says-cuts-to-pay-and-benefits-are-needed.html?comp=7000024213943&rank=1)

279 "Number of Military Families on Food Stamps Has Nearly Doubled Since Obama Took Office," *Fox New Insider*, 2/18/2014 (http://foxnewsinsider.com/2014/02/18/number-military-families-food-stamps-has-nearly-doubled-obama-took-office)

280 Chris Edwards, "Overpaid Federal Workers," *Downsizing The Federal Government*, 8/2013 (http://www.downsizinggovernment.org/overpaid-federal-workers)

281 Alan Bjerga, "Food-Stamp Usage Climbs to Record, Reviving Campaign Issue," Bloomberg, 9/4/2012, (http://www.bloomberg.com/news/2012-09-04/food-stamp-use-climbed-to-record-46-7-million-in-june-u-s-says.html)

282 Patrick Burke, "First Term: Food Stamp Recipients Increased 11,133 Per Day Under Obama," *CNS News*, 1/21/2013, (http://cnsnews.com/news/article/first-term-food-stamp-recipients-increased-11133-day-under-obama)

283 Brittany Stepniak, "Food Stamp Growth: 75X Greater Than Job Growth," *Wealth Wire*, 11/2/2012, (http://www.wealthwire.com/news/economy/4098)

284 Elizabeth Harrington, "Food Stamp Rolls in America Now Surpass the Population of Spain," *CNS News*, February 13, 2013, (http://cnsnews.com/news/article/food-stamp-rolls-america-now-surpass-population-spain)

285 http://www.fns.usda.gov/sites/default/files/pd/SNAPsummary.pdf Accessed 3/18/2016

286 Caroline May, "Exclusive: Robert Rector Details 370 Percent Increase of Able-Bodied Adults Without Dependents on Food Stamps," *Breitbart*, 1/14/2016, (http://www.breitbart.com/big-government/2016/01/14/exclusive-robert-rector-details-370-increase-of-able-bodied-adults-without-dependents-on-food-stamps/)

287 Joe Schoffstall, "Cost of Food Stamp Fraud More Than Doubles In Three Years," *CNS News*, 4/1/2013, (http://cnsnews.com/blog/joe-schoffstall/cost-food-stamp-fraud-more-doubles-three-years)

288 Ed O'Keefe, "Obama administration targeting food stamp fraud as program reaches record highs," *The Washington Post*, 12/06/2011, (http://www.washingtonpost.com/blogs/federal-eye/post/obama-administration-targeting-food-stamp-fraud-as-program-reaches-record-highs/2011/12/05/gIQAfdM3XO_blog.html)

289 Walter Hamilton, "Disability Claims Rise Even As Work Injuries Decline," *Los Angeles Times*, 8/22/2012) (http://articles.latimes.com/2012/aug/22/business/la-fi-mo-disability-claims-20120822)

290 Source: Social Security Administration extracted on: November 18, 2012

291 Terence P. Jeffrey, "10,988,269: 2013 Closes With Record Number on Disability Getting Highest-Ever Monthly Benefits," *CNS News*, 12/31/2013 (http://www.cnsnews.com/news/article/terence-p-jeffrey/10988269-2013-closes-record-number-disability-getting-highest-ever)

292 Terence P. Jeffrey, "10,988,269: 2013 Closes With Record Number on Disability Getting Highest-Ever Monthly Benefits," *CNS News*, 12/31/2013 (http://www.cnsnews.com/news/article/terence-p-jeffrey/10988269-2013-closes-record-number-disability-getting-highest-ever)

293 Stephen Olmacher, "Social Security Awarding Disability Benefits Without Adequately Reviewing Applications: Report," *Huffington Post*, 9/13/2012 (http://www.huffingtonpost.com/2012/09/13/social-security-disability-benefits_n_1879791.html)

294 Robert Rector, "The Effects of Welfare Reform," *Heritage Foundation*, 03/15/2001, (http://www.heritage.org/research/testimony/the-effects-of-welfare-reform)

295 John Nolte, "Media Fact Checkers Shill for Obama's Gutting of Welfare Reform," *Breitbart*, 8/21/2012, (http://www.breitbart.com/Big-Journalism/2012/08/21/Fact-Checkers-Flak-For-Obamas-Gutting-of-welfare)

296 Eric Pianin, "Why Obama's Welfare Waivers Have Both Sides Seething," *Fiscal Times*, 08/10/2012, (http://www.thefiscaltimes.com/Articles/2012/08/10/Why-Obamas-Welfare-Waivers-Have-Both-Sides-Seething.aspx)

297 Rep. Dave Camp and Rep. John Kline, "Obama's illegal scheme to end welfare work requirements," *Washington Times*, 9/19/2012, (http://www.washingtontimes.com/news/2012/sep/19/obamas-illegal-scheme-to-end-welfare-work-requirem/)

298 David Jackson, "Obama: More work remains in 'war on poverty'," *USA Today*, 1/8/2014 (http://www.usatoday.com/story/theoval/2014/01/08/obama-statement-war-on-poverty-lyndon-johnson/4370259/)

299 David Boyer, "That's rich: Poverty level under Obama breaks 50-year record," *Washington Times*, 1/7/2014 (http://www.washingtontimes.com/news/2014/jan/7/obamas-rhetoric-on-fighting-poverty-doesnt-match-h/)

300 Mark Gongloff, "45 Million Americans Still Stuck Below Poverty Line: Census," *Huffington Post*, 9/16/2014 (http://www.huffingtonpost.com/2014/09/16/poverty-household-income_n_5828974.html)

301 Christopher Ingraham, "Child Poverty in the U.S. is Among the Worst in the Developed World", *Washington Post*, 10/29/2014 (http://www.washingtonpost.com/blogs/wonkblog/wp/2014/10/29/child-poverty-in-the-u-s-is-among-the-worst-in-the-developed-world/)

302 Tanzina Vega, "2 out of 5 Black Children are Living in Poverty". *CNN Money*, 7/14/2015; (http://money.cnn.com/2015/07/14/news/economy/black-children-poverty/)

303 Terrence P. Jeffrey, "65 Percent of Children Live in Households on Federal Aid Programs" *CNS News*, 12/10/2014; (http://cnsnews.com/commentary/terence-p-jeffrey/65-percent-children-live-households-federal-aid-programs)

304 David Jackson, "Obama: Income inequality threatens American Dream," *USA Today*, 12/4/2013 (http://www.usatoday.com/story/news/politics/2013/12/04/obama-income-inequality-speech-center-for-american-progress/3867747/)

305 Peter Ferrara, "Obama's Rising Inequality," *The American Spectator*, 5/8/2013; http://spectator.org/articles/55646/obamas-rising-inequality

306 "Income Inequality Grew Faster Under Obama, According to One Measure," *The Huffington Post*, 9/1/2013; http://www.huffingtonpost.com/2013/09/01/income-inequality-obama_n_3853183.html

307 Bret Baier, "As Obama Hammers 'Income Inequality,' Gap Grows Under His Presidency," *Fox News*, 1/21/2014; http://www.foxnews.com/politics/2014/01/21/as-obama-hammers-income-inequality-gap-grows-under-his-presidency/

308 Nick, Timiraos, "U.S. Incomes End 6-Year Decline, Just Barely," *Wall Street Journal*, 9/16/2014; (http://www.wsj.com/articles/u-s-incomes-edge-higher-as-sluggish-recovery-persists-1410878730)

309 Angelo Young, "Despite Falling US Unemployment, Numbers Of Long-Term Unemployed And Those Who've Given Up On Work Remain High". *International Business Times*, 1/9/2015, (http://www.ibtimes.com/despite-falling-us-unemployment-numbers-long-term-unemployed-those-whove-given-work-1778990)

310 "Average (Mean) Duration of Unemployment" *Federal Reserve Bank of St. Louis*, Accesed 1/23/2015, (http://research.stlouisfed.org/fred2/series/UEMPMEAN/)

311 Brad Plumer, "7 reasons why Congress's failure to extend unemployment insurance matters," *Wonkblog*, 1/14/2014, (http://www.washingtonpost.com/blogs/wonkblog/wp/2014/01/14/an-extension-of-unemployment-insurance-just-failed-in-the-senate/)

312 "Labor Force Statistics from the Current Population Survey", *Bureau of Labor Statistics*, accessed 6/09/2015; (http://data.bls.gov/timeseries/LNS11300000)

313 James Sherk, "Not Looking for Work: Why Labor Force Participation Has Fallen During the Recovery," *The Heritage Foundation*, 9/4/2014; (http://www.heritage.org/research/reports/2014/09/not-looking-for-work-why-labor-force-participation-has-fallen-during-the-recovery)

314 "Alternative Measures of Labor Underutilization", *Bureau of Labor Statistics*, accessed 6/09/2015; (http://www.bls.gov/news.release/empsit.t15.htm)

315 Nick Timiraos and Josh Zumbrun, "The May Jobs Report in 12 Charts," *Real Time Economics*, 6/5/2015; (http://blogs.wsj.com/economics/2015/06/05/the-may-jobs-report-in-12-charts/)

316 Terence P. Jeffrey, "It's Official: Federal Debt Tops $16 Trillion," *CNS News*, 9/4/2012, (http://cnsnews.com/news/article/its-official-federal-debt-tops-16-trillion)

317 Asche Schow, "President Obama's Taxpayer-Backed Green Energy Failures" *Heritage Foundation*, 10/18/2012, (http://blog.heritage.org/2012/10/18/president-obamas-taxpayer-backed-green-energy-failures/)

318 Dave Boyer, "That's rich: Poverty level under Obama breaks 50-year record", *Washington Times*, 1/7/2014; (http://www.washingtontimes.com/news/2014/jan/7/obamas-rhetoric-on-fighting-poverty-doesnt-match-h/)

319 David Rosen, "Looking Beyond Hurricane Sandy" *Counterpunch*, 11/15/2012, (http://www.counterpunch.org/2012/11/15/looking-beyond-hurricane-sandy/)

320 Stephanie Condon, "Obama: "No Such Thing as Shovel-Ready Projects"", CBS News, 10/13/2010; (http://www.cbsnews.com/news/obama-no-such-thing-as-shovel-ready-projects/)

321 James Pethokoukis, "Well, I Think We Have a Final Verdict on the Obama Stimulus," *AEI Ideas*, 12/18/2012, (http://www.aei-ideas.org/2012/11/well-i-think-we-have-a-final-verdict-on-the-obama-stimulus/)

322 James Sherk, "Not Looking for Work: Why Labor Force Participation Has Fallen During the Recovery", *The Heritage Foundation*, 9/4/2014; (http://www.heritage.org/research/reports/2014/09/not-looking-for-work-why-labor-force-participation-has-fallen-during-the-recovery)

323 *Ibid.*

324 "Labor Force Statistics from the Current Population Survey", *U.S. Bureau of Labor Statistics*, Accessed 1/24/2015; (http://data.bls.gov/timeseries/LNS14000000)

325 Wynton Hall, "Richer Democratic States with Lower Unemployment Got Bulk of Obama Stimulus", *Breitbart*, 4/20/2012; (http://www.breitbart.com/big-government/2012/04/20/richer-democratic-states-with-lower-unemployment-got-bulk-of-obama-stimulus/)

326 "Startup America," *The White House*, 1/31/2011; (http://www.whitehouse.gov/economy/business/startup-america)

327 Jim Clifton, "American Entrepreneurship: Dead or Alive?" *Gallup*, 1/13/2015; (http://www.gallup.com/businessjournal/180431/american-entrepreneurship-dead-alive.aspx)

328 *Ibid.*

329 "Liberal Study Finds Entrepreneurs Dying Under Obama," Investors Business Daily, 5/7/2014; (http://news.investors.com/ibd-editorials/050714-700002-liberal-study-finds-obamanomics-killed-the-american-entrepreneur.htm)

330 Max Velthoven, John Kartch, and Ryan Ellis, "Obama has Proposed 442 Tax Hikes Since Taking Office," Americans for Tax Reform, 4/14/2014; (http://www.atr.org/obama-has-proposed-442-tax-hikes-taking-office)

331 Angie Drobnic Holan, "No family making less than $250,000 will see any form of tax increase.'," *The Obamater*, 4/8/2010 (http://www.politifact.com/truth-o-meter/promises/obameter/promise/515/no-family-making-less-250000-will-see-any-form-tax/)

332 Robert Stacy McCain, "Obama Cut Your Taxes, and Other Lies Frank Rich Wants You to Believe In" *The Other McCain*, 10/24/2010; (http://theothermccain.com/2010/10/24/obama-cut-your-taxes-and-other-lies-frank-rich-wants-you-to-believe-in/)

333 Glenn Kessler, "Obama's whopper of a claim on tax cuts," *Washington Post*, 9/7/2011; (http://www.washingtonpost.com/blogs/fact-checker/post/obamas-whopper-of-a-claim-on-tax-cuts/2011/09/06/gIQAmL2h7J_blog.html)

334 Jason, Russell, "All seven of Obama's budgets have proposed tax hikes," Washington Examiner, 2/1/2015; (http://www.washingtonexaminer.com/all-seven-of-obamas-budgets-have-proposed-tax-hikes/article/2559596)

335 Michelle Jamrisko, "U.S. Economy Expands to 0.5% Pace, Weakest in Two Years", *Bloomberg*, 4/28/2016; (http://www.realclearmarkets.com/articles/2016/02/01/barack_obamas_sad_record_on_economic_growth_101987.html)

336 Louis Woodhill, "Barack Obama's Sad Record on Economic Growth", *Real Clear Markets*, 2/1/2016; (http://www.realclearmarkets.com/articles/2016/02/01/barack_obamas_sad_record_on_economic_growth_101987.html)

337 *Ibid.*

338 James Sherk, Not Looking for Work: Why Labor Force Participation Has Fallen During the Recovery", Heritage Foundation, 9/4/2014; (http://www.heritage.org/research/reports/2014/09/not-looking-for-work-why-labor-force-participation-has-fallen-during-the-recover

339 "Labor Force Statistics from the Current Population Survey: Civilian labor force participation rate", Bureau of Labor Statistics, Accessed 1/21/2015; (http://data.bls.gov/timeseries/LNS11300000)

340 "Labor Force Statistics from the Current Population Survey: Employment-population ratio", Bureau of Labor Statistics, Accessed 1/21/2015; (http://data.bls.gov/timeseries/LNS12300000)

341 Jim Hoft, "Gallup CEO: Number of Full-Time Jobs as Percent of Population Is Lowest It's Ever Been (Video)", *Gateway Pundit*, 2/5/2015; (http://www.thegatewaypundit.com/2015/02/gallup-ceo-number-of-full-time-jobs-as-percent-of-population-is-lowest-its-ever-been-video/)

342 Jason Lange, "Obama trumpets rising U.S. wages; data has a more somber tone", *Reuters*, 1/21/2015; (http://www.reuters.com/article/2015/01/21/us-usa-obama-economy-idUSKBN0KU0BC20150121)

343 "Annual growth of the Real Gross Domestic Product (GDP) of the United States from 1990 to 2014", Statista, accessed 2/9/2015; (http://www.statista.com/statistics/188165/annual-gdp-growth-of-the-united-states-since-1990/)

344 P. J. Gladnick, "CNBC Hosts by Guest's Unwelcome Economic Forecast", NewsBusters, 2/11/2015; (http://linkis.com/newsbusters.org/blog/Z9WtE)

345 Howard Schneider, "Middle class decline looms over final years of Obama presidency", Reuters, 1/18/2015; (https://ca.news.yahoo.com/middle-class-decline-looms-over-final-years-obama-130212665--business.html)

346 Neil Irwin, "You Can't Feed a Family With G.D.P.", The Upshot, 9/16/2014; (http://www.nytimes.com/2014/09/17/upshot/you-cant-feed-a-family-with-gdp.html)

347 Annie Lowrey, "Recovery Has Created Far More Low-Wage Jobs Than Better-Paid Ones", New York Times, 4/27/2014; (http://www.nytimes.com/2014/04/28/business/economy/recovery-has-created-far-more-low-wage-jobs-than-better-paid-ones.html)

348 Prashant Gopal, "U.S. home ownership percentage declines to 1995 level", Columbus Dispatch, 10/29/2014; (http://www.dispatch.com/content/stories/business/2014/10/29/ownership-percentage-declines-to-1995-level.html)

349 "Average (Mean) Duration of Unemployment", Federal Reserve Bank of St. Louis, Accessed 1/30/2015; (http://research.stlouisfed.org/fred2/series/UEMPMEAN/)

350 Michael Snyder, "On The Verge Of The Next Economic Crisis, 62 Percent Of Americans Are Living Paycheck To Paycheck", The Economic Collapse, 1/7/2015; (http://theeconomiccollapseblog.com/archives/verge-next-economic-crisis-62-percent-americans-living-paycheck-paycheck)

351 Gayle Trotter, "How Women Have Suffered Under Obama's Policies", The Hill, 5/30/2014; (http://thehill.com/blogs/congress-blog/civil-rights/207468-how-women-have-suffered-under-obamas-policies)

352 "Monthly Labor Review", Bureau of Labor Statistics, 4/2014; (http://www.bls.gov/opub/mlr/2014/article/the-rise-in-women-share-of-nonfarm-employment.htm)

353 Neil Shah, "U.S. Wealth Is Near a Record, Yet Racial Gap Has Widened Since Recession", Real Time Economics, 12/12/2014; (http://blogs.wsj.com/economics/2014/12/12/u-s-wealth-is-near-a-record-yet-racial-gap-has-widened-since-recession/)

354 Young America's Foundation. (2010). Youth Misery Index Grows More Than 50% Under Obama Administration [Press release]. Retrieved from http://www.yaf.org/YouthMiseryIndexGrowsMoreThan50PercentUnderObamaAdministration.aspx

355 Michael Novak, "Obama's Legend", National Review, 8/14/2012; (http://www.nationalreview.com/articles/313899/obama-s-legend-michael-novak)

356 "Ben Shapiro: Fracking Saved the Obama Economy", Front Page Magazine, 1/16/2015; (http://www.frontpagemag.com/2015/truthrevolt-org/ben-shapiro-fracking-saved-the-obama-economy/)

357 Mark J. Perry, "Texas, the 'great American job machine,' is solely responsible for the +1.2M net US job increase since 2007", American Enterprise Intstitute, 1/23/2015; (http://www.aei.org/publication/texas-great-american-job-machine-solely-responsible-1m-net-us-job-increase-since-2007/)

358 "Obama's Economic Growth Gap Now Tops $2 Trillion", Investor's Business Daily, 7/30/2015; (http://www.investors.com/tepid-gdp-growth-leaves-economy-even-further-behind-the-pace/)

359 Huma Khan, "What Does One Get a Queen?" ABC News, 04/01/2009, (http://abcnews.go.com/blogs/politics/2009/04/what-does-one-g/)

360 Toby Harnden, "Barack Obama's gift for the Queen: an iPod, your Majesty," The Telegraph, 04/01/2009, (http://blogs.telegraph.co.uk/news/tobyharnden/9355453/Barack_Obamas_gift_for_the_Queen_an_iPod_your_Majesty/)

361   Emily Yoffe, "Today We Are Gathered … To Hear More About Me," *Slate*, 12/21/2012, (http://www.slate.com/articles/news_and_politics/politics/2012/12/barack_obama_s_eulogy_to_daniel_inouye_told_us_more_about_the_president.html)

362   Mike Flynn, "To Honor Neil Armstrong, Obama Posts Photo of Himself," *Breitbart*, 8/26/2012 (http://www.breitbart.com/Big-Government/2012/08/26/to-honor-neil-armstrong-obama-posts-a-picture-of-himself)

363   "President Obama Honors Rosa Parks Anniversary With Picture of...Himself," *Fox Nation*, 12/02/2012, (http://nation.foxnews.com/obama/2012/12/02/president-obama-honors-rosa-parks-anniversary-picture-himself)

364   The White House (WhiteHouse) "President Obama on President Kennedy and the American spirit —> http://go.wh.gov/j4dUY6 #JFK, pic.twitter.com/1irDH153L1" 22 November 2013 11:34 a.m. Tweet

365   The White House (WhiteHouse) "Rest in peace, Nelson Mandela. pic.twitter.com/4qlqsXLp6e" 5 December 2013 3:07 p.m. Tweet

366   William Bigelow, "Obama Honors Pearl Harbor Dead with Picture of Himself" *Breitbart*, 12/8/2013 (http://www.breitbart.com/Big-Government/2013/12/07/Obama-Inserts-Picture-of-Himself-to-Honor-Pearl-Harbor-Dead)

367   Seth Mandel, "Obama Drops His Name Into the Other Presidential Biographies," *Commentary*, 05/15/2012, (http://www.commentarymagazine.com/2012/05/15/obama-drops-his-name-into-presidential-biographies/)

368   Peggy Noonan, "A New Kind of 'Credibility' Gap" *Wall Street Journal*, 9/2/2013 (http://online.wsj.com/news/articles/SB10001424127887323808204579085560400501346)

369   Ewen MacAskill, "Barack Obama Accused of Giving Partisan Inauguration Speech," *The Guardian*, 01/22/2013, (http://www.guardian.co.uk/world/2013/jan/22/obama-inauguration-speech-republican-compromise)

370   Liz Goodwin, "Conservatives React to Obama Inaugural Speech," *Yahoo News*, 01/22/2013, (http://news.yahoo.com/blogs/ticket/conservatives-react-obama-inaugural-speech-161537952--election.html)

371   Sarah Tanksalvala, "Obama's Inaugural Address Quotes Constitution While Misrepresenting Opposition," *Examiner*, 01/23/2013, (http://www.examiner.com/article/obama-s-inaugural-address-quotes-constitution-while-misrepresenting-opposition)

372   Yuval Levin, "Obama's Second Inaugural," *National Review*, 01/22/2013, (http://www.nationalreview.com/corner/338366/obama-s-second-inaugural-yuval-levin)

373   Ron Fournier, "Post-Partisan No More: Who Is the New Obama?" *National Journal*, 1/22/2013, (http://www.nationaljournal.com/politics/post-partisan-no-more-who-is-the-new-obama-20130122)

374   David Ignatius, "A flat, partisan and pedestrian speech," Washington Post, 1/21/2013, (http://www.washingtonpost.com/blogs/post-partisan/wp/2013/01/21/obama-inaugurala-flat-partisan-and-pedestrian-speech/)

375   *Ibid.*

376   Zachary A. Goldfarb, "Male-female pay gap remains entrenched at White House," *Washington Post*, 7/1/2014; (http://www.washingtonpost.com/politics/male-female-pay-gap-remains-entrenched-at-white-house/2014/07/01/dbc6c088-0155-11e4-8fd0-3a663dfa68ac_story.html)

377   *Ibid.*

378   Foon Rhee, "Obama vows line-by-line budget review," Political Intelligence, 11/25/2008 (http://www.boston.com/news/politics/politicalintelligence/2008/11/obama_vows_line.html)

379   Chris Jacobs, "The Final Obama Budget: Better Never Than Late?" *Conservative Review*, 2/9/2016; (https://www.conservativereview.com/commentary/2016/02/the-final-obama-budget-better-never-than-late)

380 Becket Adams, "How Many Times Has Obama Violated Budget Deadline Laws? (We Have the Answer)", *The Blaze*, 1/28/2014; (http://www.theblaze.com/stories/2014/01/28/how-many-times-has-obama-violated-budget-deadline-laws-we-have-the-answer/)

381 "Obama Promises to Limit No-Bid Contracts," *Boston Globe*, 03/05/2009, (http://www.boston.com/news/nation/washington/articles/2009/03/05/obama_promises_to_limit_no_bid_contracts/)

382 Devin Dwyer, "Senate Democrat Seeks Investigation of Obama's No-Bid Contract for Smallpox Drug," *ABC News*, 11/25/2011, (http://abcnews.go.com/blogs/politics/2011/11/senate-democrat-seeks-investigation-of-obamas-no-bid-contract-for-smallpox-drug/)

383 Reid J. Epstein, "Division over platform at DNC," *Politico*, 9/5/2012, (http://www.politico.com/news/stories/0912/80801.html)

384 Jenny Percival, "Barack Obama compares oil spill to 9/11," *Guardian*, 6/14/2010, (http://www.guardian.co.uk/environment/2010/jun/14/barack-obama-oil-spill-911)

385 Joe Newby, "Tucson event more political rally than memorial service," *Examiner*, 1/13/2011, (http://www.examiner.com/article/tucson-event-more-political-rally-than-memorial-service)

386 Jim Hoft, "Gross. Barack Obama Uses Sandy Hook Massacre to Push Tax Hikes (Video)," *Gateway Pundit*, 12/19/2012, (http://www.thegatewaypundit.com/2012/12/gross-barack-obama-uses-sandy-hook-massacre-to-push-tax-hikes-video/)

387 Josh Blackman, "President Obama and arguments about pending Supreme Court cases," *Constitution Daily*, 6/17/2015; (http://blog.constitutioncenter.org/2015/06/president-obama-and-arguments-about-pending-supreme-court-cases/)

388 Elizabeth Slattery, "Obama's Attempt to Influence Supreme Court on Obamacare Case Breaks Precedent", *Daily Signal*, 6/19/2015; (http://dailysignal.com/2015/06/19/obamas-attempt-to-influence-supreme-court-on-obamacare-case-breaks-precedent/)

389 Matthew Vadum, "National Endowment for the Arts is Trying to Create a Cult of Obama," *The American Spectator*, 09/01/2009, (http://spectator.org/blog/2009/09/01/national-endowment-for-the-art)

390 *Ibid*

391 Ben Shapiro, "At Least 6 Federal Laws and Regulations Violated by the NEA Conference Call," *Breitbart*, 09/22/2009, (http://www.breitbart.com/Big-Hollywood/2009/09/22/At-Least-6-Federal-Laws-and-Regulations-Violated-By-the-NEA-Conference-Call)

392 John F. Kennedy, Address, "The President and the Press" Before the American Newspaper Publishers Association, New York City. 04/27/1961, *The American Presidency Project*, (http://www.presidency.ucsb.edu/ws/index.php?pid=8093)

393 The White House, Office of the Press Secretary (2012) Remarks by the President at the Associated Press Luncheon [Press release] Retrieved from http://www.whitehouse.gov/the-press-office/2012/04/03/remarks-president-associated-press-luncheon

394 Michael Calderone, "Obama Turns to Local Media to Promote Reelection Message," *The Huffington Post*, 08/05/2012, (http://www.huffingtonpost.com/2012/08/05/obama-local-media-reelection_n_1741983.html)

395 Keith Koffler, "White House Sets Ground Rules for Local Interviews," *White House Dossier*, 08/21/2012, (http://www.whitehousedossier.com/2012/08/21/white-house-sets-ground-rules-local-interviews/)

396 "'We did not know': 9 times the Obama administration was blindsided", Fox News, 6/19/2014; (http://www.foxnews.com/politics/2014/06/20/obama-administration-caught-by-surprise/)

397 "Obama says he learned of Clinton using private email through news reports", Fox News, 3/8/2015; (http://www.foxnews.com/politics/2015/03/08/obama-says-learned-clinton-private-emails-news-reports/)

398 Edward-Isaac Dovere, "White House alerted to potential Clinton email problem in August", Politico, 3/6/15; (http://www.politico.com/story/2015/03/hillary-clinton-emails-delays-115824.html)

399 Pablo Martinez Monsivais, "Blindsided by Arab Spring, US sees changes in Mideast influence", NBC News, 12/12/2011; (http://worldnews.nbcnews.com/_news/2011/12/12/9381833-blindsided-by-arab-spring-us-sees-changes-in-mideast-influence)

400 Joshua Berlinger, "BLINDSIDED: Obama's Asia Team Reportedly Partying When North Korea Launched Rocket", Business Insider, 12/14/2012; (http://www.businessinsider.com/report-obamas-asia-team-was-partying-when-north-korea-launched-its-rocket-2012-12)

401 "'We did not know': 9 times the Obama administration was blindsided", Fox News, 6/19/2014; (http://www.foxnews.com/politics/2014/06/20/obama-administration-caught-by-surprise/)

402 "Official: U.S. intelligence surprised by collapse of Yemen government", CBS News, 2/13/2015; (http://www.cbsnews.com/news/obama-administration-surprised-by-collapse-of-yemen-government/)

403 Kate Hicks, "Awkward: Obama Blames Bush for Economy While Standing Next to Him," Townhall, 05/31/2012, (http://townhall.com/tipsheet/katehicks/2012/05/31/awkward_obama_blames_bush_for_economy_while_standing_next_to_him)

404 Matthew Mosk and Brian Ross. "Solyndra Hearing: Blame It On Bush, Say Obama Officials" ABC News. 12/26/2012. (http://abcnews.go.com/Blotter/solyndra-blame-bush-obama-officials/story?id=14513389#.UNsIa2_AcsI)

405 "Second Presidential Debate Full Transcript, Page 9 of 11," ABC News, 10/17/2012, (http://abcnews.go.com/Politics/OTUS/2012-presidential-debate-full-transcript-oct-16/story?id=17493848&page=9#.UNsLmG_AcsI)

406 Mary Bruce, "Obama Blames GOP for Inability to Pass Immigration Reform," ABC News, 09/20/2012, (http://abcnews.go.com/blogs/politics/2012/09/obama-blames-gop-for-inability-to-pass-immigration-reform/)

407 Darlene Superville, "Obama Appeals for an End to Partisan Politics – With a Jab at GOP," Associated Press, 10/30/2010, (http://www.msnbc.msn.com/id/39922794/ns/politics-decision_2010/t/obama-appeals-end-partisan-politics-jab-gop/)

408 Fred Hiatt, "Next Time, Obama May go Over Congress' Head," The Washington Post, 09/04/2012, (http://www.washingtonpost.com/blogs/post-partisan/post/next-time-obama-may-go-over-congresss-head/2012/09/04/9073eb30-f6ba-11e1-8398-0327ab83ab91_blog.html)

409 Ibid.

410 CQ Transcripts, "Sens. Obama and Biden Deliver Remarks in Springfield, IL," The Washington Post, 08/23/2008, (http://www.washingtonpost.com/wp-dyn/content/article/2008/08/28/AR2008082803216.html)

411 "Bring Democrats and Republicans Together to Pass an Agenda," Tampa Bay Time Politifact, 08/31/2012, (http://www.politifact.com/truth-o-meter/promises/obameter/promise/522/bring-democrats-and-republicans-together-pass-agen/)

412 Joel Gehrke, "Obama threatens vetoes of bills requiring him to follow the law," Washington Examiner, 3/12/2014 (http://washingtonexaminer.com/obama-threatens-vetoes-of-bills-requiring-him-to-follow-the-law/article/2545545)

413 Sam Stein, "Top Obama Adviser Tackles 2014, 'The Wire,' Vetoes, Obamacare And Weed" The Huffington Post, 12/29/2014 (http://www.huffingtonpost.com/2014/12/29/drinking-and-talking-dan-pfeiffer-obama_n_6373596.html)

414 Katie Pavilich, "BREAKING: House Passes Final Homeland Security Bill Funding Obama's Executive Amnesty," Townhall, 3/3/2015; (http://townhall.com/tipsheet/katiepavlich/2015/03/03/breaking-house-passes-homeland-security-funding-bill-n1965255)

415   Office of Speaker John Boehner, (Press Release) 12/03/2012. House GOP Leaders Make New Offer to Avert Fiscal Cliff. Retrieved from, http://www.speaker.gov/ press-release/house-gop-leaders-make-new-offer-avert-fiscal-cliff

416   Kathleen Hennessy, "Obama Rejects GOP 'Fiscal Cliff' Offer, Says Tax Rates Must Rise," *Los Angeles Times*, 12/04/2012, (http://www.latimes.com/news/politics/la-pn-obama-rejects-fiscal-cliff-offer-20121204,0,3064040.story)

417   "Carney: "Not Appropriate" For Obama To Comment On Ongoing Secret Service Investigation," *Real Clear Politics*, 4/14/2012, (http://www.realclearpolitics.com/ video/2012/04/14/ carney_not_appropriate_for_obama_to_comment_on_ongoing_secret_service_inv estigation.html)

418   Stephanie Condon, "Obama: 'If I Had a Son, He'd Look Like Trayvon'," *CBS News*, 03/23/2012, (http://www.cbsnews.com/8301-503544_162-57403200-503544/ obama-if-i-had-a-son-hed-look-like-trayvon/)

419   "Obama: Police who arrested professor 'acted stupidly'," *CNN*, 7/23/2009, (http:// www.cnn.com/2009/US/07/22/harvard.gates.interview/)

420   Brian MacQuarrie, "Racial Divide Expected to Persist in U.S.," *The Boston Globe*, 11/20/2012, (http://www.bostonglobe.com/news/nation/2012/11/20/despite-obama-presidency-racial-divide-expected-persist-united-states/ ONPO9LRIasUfGrLYWM3m7H/story.html)

421   John Fund, "Holder's Black Panther Stonewall," *Wall Street Journal*, 8/20/2009; (http:// online.wsj.com/news/articles/ SB10001424052970203550604574361071968458430)

422   Stephanie Condon, "Obama: 'If I had a Son, He'd Look LIke Trayvon'", *CBS News*, 3/23/2012; (http://www.cbsnews.com/news/obama-if-i-had-a-son-hed-look-like-trayvon/)

423   "Editorial: Obama's race-baiting," *Washington Times*, 5/3/2010; (http:// www.washingtontimes.com/news/2010/may/3/obamas-race-baiting/)

424   "Interview with President Obama," *New York Times*, 7/27/2013; (http:// www.nytimes.com/2013/07/28/us/politics/interview-with-president-obama.html)

425   David Remnick, "Going The Distance: On and Off The Road with Barack Obama," *The New Yorker*, 1/27/2014; (http://www.newyorker.com/reporting/ 2014/01/27/140127fa_fact_remnick)

426   Neil Munro, "Hope and Change: Obama Uses Racial Politics to Justify Marijuana Legalization", *Daily Caller*, 1/20/2014; (http://dailycaller.com/2014/01/20/hope-and-change-obama-uses-racial-politics-to-justify-marijuana-legalization/)

427   Susan Jones, "Sebelius: Obamacare Opponents Are Like Those Who Opposed Civil Rights," *CNS News*, 7/17/2013; (http://cnsnews.com/news/article/sebelius-obamacare-opponents-are-those-who-opposed-civil-rights)

428   Tiffany Madison, "MADISON: Holder's Department of Justice is racist, lawless," *Washington Times*, 8/20/2013; (http://communities.washingtontimes.com/ neighborhood/citizen-warrior/2013/aug/20/madison-holders-department-justice-racist-lawless/)

429   Don Lee, "Obama calls for persistence in confronting 'deeply rooted' racism," *Los Angeles Times*, 12/7/2014;, (http://www.latimes.com/nation/la-na-obama-race-police-bet-interview-20141207-story.html)

430   "Advisory: NPR News Interview With President Obama" *NPR*, 12/27/2014; (http:// www.npr.org/about-npr/372903748/advisory-npr-news-interview)

431   Julie Bykowicz, "Most Americans See Race Relations Worsening Since Obama's Election," *Bloomberg*, 12/7/2014; (http://www.bloomberg.com/politics/articles/ 2014-12-07/bloomberg-politics-poll-finds-most-americans-see-race-relations-worsening-since-obamas-election/)

432   Jim Norman, "U.S. Worries About Race Relations Reach a New High," *Gallup*, 4/11/2016; (http://www.gallup.com/poll/190574/worries-race-relations-reach-new-high.aspx)

433 Gallup Daily: Obama Job Approval, (http://www.gallup.com/poll/113980/Gallup-Daily-Obama-Job-Approval.aspx)

434 Jeffrey Jones, "Obama Approval Ratings Still Historically Polarized," *Gallup*, 2/6/2015 (http://www.gallup.com/poll/181490/obama-approval-ratings-historically-polarized.aspx)

435 *Ibid.*

436 *Ibid.*

437 Byron York, "In defeat, Obama tells GOP: My mandate is bigger than yours," *Washington Examiner,* 11/6/14; (http://www.washingtonexaminer.com/in-defeat-obama-tells-gop-my-mandate-is-bigger-than-yours/article/2555866)

438 The White House, Office of the Press Secretary. (2009). News Conference by President Obama [Press release]. Retrieved from http://www.whitehouse.gov/the-press-office/news-conference-president-obama-40209

439 Matt Cover, "Obama Unsure, But State Department Says Egypt Is an Ally," *CNS News*, 9/13/2012, (http://cnsnews.com/news/article/obama-unsure-state-department-says-egypt-ally)

440 David Martosko, "Video Belies Obama 'Apology Tour' Denial," *Daily Caller,* 10/22/2012, (http://times247.com/articles/video-belies-obama-s-apology-tour-denial)

441 The White House, Office of the Press Secretary. (2009). Remarks by President Obama at Strasbourg Town Hall [Press release]. Retrieved from http://www.whitehouse.gov/the-press-office/remarks-president-obama-strasbourg-town-hall

442 The White House, Office of the Press Secretary. (2009). Remarks by President Obama to the Turkish Parliament [Press release]. Retrieved from http://www.whitehouse.gov/the_press_office/Remarks-By-President-Obama-To-The-Turkish-Parliament

443 The White House, Office of the Press Secretary. (2009). Remarks by The President at The Summit of The Americas [Press release]. Retrieved from http://www.whitehouse.gov/the_press_office/Remarks-by-the-President-at-the-Summit-of-the-Americas-Opening-Ceremony

444 "Text of President Obama's Speech in Hiroshima, Japan", *New York Times,* 5/27/2016; (http://www.nytimes.com/2016/05/28/world/asia/text-of-president-obamas-speech-in-hiroshima-japan.html)

445 Christian Datoc, "Obama: 'Hopefully, We Can Learn From' Cuba About Improving Human Rights In America", *Daily Caller,* 3/21/2016; (http://dailycaller.com/2016/03/21/obama-hopefully-we-can-learn-from-cuba-about-improving-human-rights-in-america-video/)

446 Eugene Robinson, "George W. Bush's greatest legacy," *Washington Post,* July 26, 2012 (http://articles.washingtonpost.com/2012-07-26/opinions/35487798_1_african-countries-pepfar-antiretroviral-treatment)

447 Jennifer Loven "Africa Crowds Greet Bush With Hugs, Chants of Thanks," *Boston Globe,* 02/19/2008, (http://www.boston.com/news/world/articles/2008/02/19/africa_crowds_greet_bush_with_hugs_chants_of_thanks/)

448 AIDS Healthcare Foundation. (2012). Obama Budget Decimates Global AIDS Funding [Press release]. http://www.aidshealth.org/archives/news/obama-budget-decimates-global-aids-funding

449 "South Africa: 1,000 Protest Obama AIDS Funding Cuts, Says AHF", Press Release via Reuters, 03/18/2013, (http://www.reuters.com/article/2013/03/18/ca-potus-aids-funding-idUSnBw7gB6XQa+116+BSW20130318)

450 AIDS Healthcare Foundation. (2012). Obama Budget Decimates Global AIDS Funding [Press release]. http://www.aidshealth.org/archives/news/obama-budget-decimates-global-aids-funding

451   Tim Shipman, "Barack Obama Sends Bust of Winston Churchill on its Way Back to Britain," *Telegraph*, 02/14/2009, (http://www.telegraph.co.uk/news/worldnews/barackobama/4623148/Barack-Obama-sends-bust-of-Winston-Churchill-on-its-way-back-to-Britain.html)

452   Ian Drury, "To my special friend Gordon, 25 DVDs: Obama gives Brown a set of classic movies. Let's hope he likes the Wizard of Oz," *Daily Mail*, 3/6/2009, (http://www.dailymail.co.uk/news/article-1159627/To-special-friend-Gordon-25-DVDs-Obama-gives-Brown-set-classic-movies-Lets-hope-likes-Wizard-Oz.html)

453   Andrew Porter, "Barack Obama rebuffs Gordon Brown as 'special relationship' sinks to new low," *Telegraph*, 9/23/2009, (http://www.telegraph.co.uk/news/politics/gordon-brown/6224813/Barack-Obama-rebuffs-Gordon-Brown-as-special-relationship-sinks-to-new-low.html)

454   Z. Byron Wolf, "Awkward Moment During Obama Toast to Queen," *ABC News*, 5/24/2011, (http://abcnews.go.com/blogs/politics/2011/05/awkward-moment-during-obama-toast-to-queen/)

455   Nile Gardiner, "Barack Obama calls France America's strongest ally. The president gives Britain the boot again," *Telegraph*, 1/10/2011, (http://blogs.telegraph.co.uk/news/nilegardiner/100071241/barack-obama-france-is-americas-strongest-ally-the-president-gives-britain-the-boot-again/)

456   "Is the U.S.-U.K. 'special relationship' over?" *The Week*, 3/3/2010, (http://theweek.com/article/index/201339/is-the-us-uk-special-relationship-over)

457   Toby Harnden, "What does the USA think of the 'special relationship'?" *Telegraph*, 3/29/2010, (http://www.telegraph.co.uk/news/worldnews/northamerica/usa/7533241/What-does-the-USA-think-of-the-special-relationship.html)

458   Tim Walker and Nigel Morris, "Barack Obama says David Cameron allowed Libya to become a 's*** show'", The Independent, 3/10/2016; (http://www.independent.co.uk/News/uk/politics/barack-obama-says-david-cameron-allowed-libya-to-become-a-s-show-a6923976.html)

459   Dan Stewart, "Why the U.S.-U.K. Relationship Is Less Special than Ever", *TIME*, 3/11/2016; (http://time.com/4256202/why-the-u-s-u-k-relationship-is-less-special-than-ever/)

460   Alison Little, "Obama's Amazing Threat to Britain: UK Would be at the 'Back of the Queue' After Brexit", *Sunday Express*, 4/23/16; (http://www.express.co.uk/news/politics/663665/Barack-Obama-Britain-back-queue-Brexit)

461   Alastair Jamieson and Jon Schuppe, "Obama Brushes Off London 'Brexit' Backlash With Golf, Shakespeare", *NBC News*, 4/23/2016; (http://www.nbcnews.com/news/world/obama-brushes-london-brexit-backlash-golf-shakespeare-n560966)

462   The White House, Office of the Press Secretary. (2009). Remarks by President Obama [Press release]. Retrieved from http://www.whitehouse.gov/the_press_office/Remarks-By-President-Barack-Obama-In-Prague-As-Delivered/

463   Paul Kengor, "Obama, the Russians, and Missile Defense: Historical Parallels," *Townhall*, 4/1/,2012, (http://townhall.com/columnists/paulkengor/2012/04/01/obama_the_russians_and_missile_defense_historical_parallels/page/full/)

464   *Ibid.*

465   Nile Gardiner, "Barack Obama has insulted 38 million Poles with his crass and ignorant 'Polish death camp' remark," *Telegraph*, 5/30/2012, (http://blogs.telegraph.co.uk/news/nilegardiner/100161347/barack-obama-has-insulted-38-million-poles-with-his-crass-and-ignorant-polish-death-camp-remark/)

466   Scott Wilson, "Where Obama Failed on Forging Peace in the Middle East," *Washington Post*, 07/14/2012; (http://www.washingtonpost.com/politics/obama-searches-for-middle-east-peace/2012/07/14/gJQAQQiKIW_story.html)

467   Tom Cohen, "Obama Calls for Israel's Return to Pre-1967 Borders," *CNN*, 05/19/2011, (http://articles.cnn.com/2011-05-19/politics/obama.israel.palestinians_1_israel-palestinian-conflict-borders-settlements)

468   Robert Tait, "US Condemns 'Provocative' Israel Settlement Building," *The Telegraph*, 12/19/2012, (http://www.telegraph.co.uk/news/worldnews/middleeast/israel/9756199/US-condemns-provocative-Israel-settlement-building.html)

469   Anne Bavefsky, "U.S to Legitimize U.N. Human Rights Council for Three More Years," *National Review*, 11/12/2012; (http://www.nationalreview.com/corner/333240/us-legitimize-un-human-rights-council-three-more-years-anne-bayefsky)

470   Jason Howerton, "Day After DNC 'Jerusalem' Controversy, State Department Still Refuses to Name Israel's Capital," *The Blaze*, 09/06/2012, (http://www.theblaze.com/stories/2012/09/06/day-after-dnc-jerusalem-controversy-state-dept-still-refuses-to-name-israels-capital/)

471   Sharona Schwartz, "Paper Details Obama Admin's Alleged Secret Note Sent to Iran: If Israel Attacks, We Won't Get Involved," *The Blaze*, 09/03/2012, (http://www.theblaze.com/stories/2012/09/03/paper-details-obama-admins-alleged-secret-note-sent-to-iran-if-israel-attacks-we-wont-get-involved/)

472   Keith Koffler, "Obama Insults Netanyahu; Press Fails to Report," *White House Dossier*, 11/08/2011, (http://www.whitehousedossier.com/2011/11/08/reuters-confirms-obama-insults-netanyahu/)

473   Roee Nahmias, "Hamas Says Asked by US to Keep Silent on Talks," *Ynet News*, 06/25/2010, (http://www.ynetnews.com/Ext/Comp/ArticleLayout/CdaArticlePrintPreview/1,2506,L-3910714,00.html)

474   Anne Bayefsky, "Obama's Real Record on Israel," *Fox News*, 10/23/2012; (http://www.foxnews.com/opinion/2012/10/23/obama-real-record-on-israel/)

475   "Israel on the Outs, Again," *New York Post*, 07/14/2012; (http://www.nypost.com/p/news/opinion/editorials/israel_on_the_outs_again_U3SLVPX0LjPG4V8ojjqnpN)

476   Jonathan S. Tobin, "Will Obama Blame Israel for Abbas' 'No'?", *Commentary*, 3/7/14 (http://www.commentarymagazine.com/2014/03/07/will-obama-blame-israel-for-abbas-no-peace-process-jewish-state/)

477   Michael R. Gordon, "Kerry Expresses Regret After Apartheid Remark," *New York Times*, 4/28/2014 (http://www.nytimes.com/2014/04/29/world/middleeast/kerry-apologizes-for-remark-that-israel-risks-apartheid.html)

478   Patrick Goodenoiugh, "State Dept. Slams Netanyahu: 'Overstated', 'Oversimplification', 'Scary'"; *CNS News*, 3/4/2015; (http://cnsnews.com/news/article/patrick-goodenough/state-dept-slams-netanyahu-overstated-oversimplification-scary)

479   Thomas Rose, "Obama Campaign Team Arrives in Israel to Defeat Netanyahu in March Elections", *Breitbart*, 1/26/2015; (http://www.breitbart.com/big-government/2015/01/26/obama-campaign-team-arrives-in-israel-to-defeat-netanyahu-in-march-elections/)

480   Hana Levi Julian, "US Declassifies Report, Exposes Details on Israel's Nuclear Program", *The Jewish Press*, 3/25/2015; (http://www.jewishpress.com/news/breaking-news/us-declassifies-report-exposes-details-on-israels-nuclear-program/2015/03/25/)

481   J.E. Dyer, "Obama Let 40 Year Old Oil Supply Guarantee to Israel Expire in November 2014", *The Jewish Press*, 3/17/2015; (http://www.jewishpress.com/indepth/analysis/j-e-dyer/obama-let-40-year-old-oil-supply-guarantee-to-israel-expire-in-november-2014/2015/03/17/)

482   Jennifer Rubin, "Backlash blows away FAA's Israel flight ban", *Washington Post*, 7/24/2014; (https://www.washingtonpost.com/blogs/right-turn/wp/2014/07/24/backlash-blows-away-faas-israel-flight-ban/)

483   Adam Entous and Danny Yadron, "U.S. Spy Net on Israel Snares Congress,' *Wall Street Journal*, 12/29/2015 (http://www.wsj.com/articles/u-s-spy-net-on-israel-snares-congress-1451425210)

484 David Efune, "Ed Koch on Chuck Hagel Nomination: Obama's Reneging on His Conveyed Support for Israel Has Come Earlier Than I Thought," *Algemeiner*, 01/07/2013, (http://www.algemeiner.com/2013/01/07/ed-koch-on-chuck-hagel-nomination-obamas-reneging-on-his-conveyed-support-for-israel-has-come-earlier-than-i-thought/)

485 Jordan Michael Smith, "How Hagel Angered the GOP," *The National Interest*, 01/11/2013, (http://nationalinterest.org/commentary/how-hagel-angered-the-gop-7957)

486 John Cornyn, "White I Can't Support Hagel," *CNN Opinion*, 01/11/2013, (http://www.cnn.com/2013/01/10/opinion/cornyn-hagel)

487 Republican Jewish Coalition. (2012). RJC: Appointment of Hagel Would Be A "Slap in the Face" for Pro-Israel Americans [Press release]. Retrieved from http://www.rjchq.org/2012/12/rjc-appointment-of-hagel-would-be-a-slap-in-the-face-for-pro-israel-americans/)

488 Paul Mirengoff, "Report: Hagel Said State Department Controlled by Israel," *Powerline*, 02/14/2013, (http://www.powerlineblog.com/archives/2013/02/report-hagel-said-state-department-controlled-by-israel.php)

489 Jennifer Rubin, "Hagel: Israel Heading Towards 'Apartheid'," *The Washington Post*, 02/19/2013, (http://www.washingtonpost.com/blogs/right-turn/wp/2013/02/19/hagel-israel-heading-toward-apartheid/)

490 Mike Flynn, "Hagel Limps into Pentagon," *Breitbart*, 02/26/2013, (http://www.breitbart.com/Big-Government/2013/02/26/Hagel-Limps-into-Pentagon#disqus_thread)

491 "Ash Carter to be Defense Secretary nominee: reports", Washington Times, 12/2/2014; (http://www.washingtontimes.com/news/2014/dec/2/ash-carter-be-defense-secretary-nominee-reports/)

492 Joel E Pollak, "Top Ten Worst John Kerry Foreign Policy Mistakes", *Breitbart*, 12/30/2012; (http://www.breitbart.com/national-security/2012/12/30/top-ten-worst-john-kerry-foreign-policy-mistakes/)

493 Jeff Duntz, "Krauthammer: Hillary Achieved Nothing As Secretary of State," *Truth Revolt*, 2/18/2014 (http://www.truthrevolt.org/news/krauthammer-hillary-achieved-nothing-secretary-state)

494 Jennifer Rubin, "Obama team admits failure on Russian reset", *Washington Post*, 2/4/2014; (http://www.washingtonpost.com/blogs/right-turn/wp/2013/02/04/obama-team-admits-failure-on-russian-reset/)

495 John Sexton, "Senate Report Faults State Department for Lack of Security in Benghazi," *Breitbart*, 1/15/2014 (http://www.breitbart.com/InstaBlog/2014/01/15/Senate-Report-Faults-State-Department-for-Lack-of-Security-in-Benghazi)

496 http://hotair.com/archives/2014/07/25/john-kerry-still-the-only-secretary-of-state-in-20-years-to-fail-at-cease-fire-efforts-in-mideast/

497 Jeremy Bender, "US is Now in an 'Awkward' Position over Syria and Iraq", *Business Insider*, 12/2/2014; (http://www.businessinsider.com/us-sharing-skies-with-syria-and-iran-2014-12)

498 Michael R Gordon and Steven Erlanger, "U.S. EFforts to Broker Russia-Ukraine Diplomacy Fails", *The New York Times*, 3/5/2014; (http://www.nytimes.com/2014/03/06/world/europe/ukraine.html?_r=0)

499 "Kerry Makes Climate Change a 'Top-Tier Diplomatic Priority", *Fox News*, 3/12/2014; (http://www.foxnews.com/politics/2014/03/12/kerry-makes-climate-change-his-first-policy-initiative-top-tier-diplomatic/)

500 Mark Murray, "ISIS Threat: Fear of Terror Attack Soars to 9/11 High, NBC News/WSJ Poll Finds", *NBC News*, 9/9/2014; (http://www.nbcnews.com/politics/first-read/isis-threat-fear-terror-attack-soars-9-11-high-nbc-n199496)

501 Rick Maze, "Obama Plan Calls for New Tricare Fee Hikes," *Army Times*, 09/19/2011, (http://www.armytimes.com/article/20110919/NEWS/109190318/Obama-plan-calls-new-Tricare-fee-hikes)

502 Bill Gertz, "Trashing Tricare," *Washington Free Beacon*, 02/27/2012, (http://freebeacon.com/trashing-tricare/)

503 *Ibid*

504 Louise Radnofsky, "Military Families Balk at Health Fee," *Wall Street Journal*, 10/10/2012, (http://online.wsj.com/article/SB10000872396390443294904578046873641438216.html)

505 Michael Graham, "Michael Graham: Women poor fit for fight," *Boston Herald*, 1/24/2013 (http://bostonherald.com/print/news_opinion/opinion/op_ed/2013/01/michael_graham_women_poor_fit_fight)

506 "Marines delay demale fitness plan after half fail pull-up test," *Associated Press*, 1/2/2014 (http://www.foxnews.com/politics/2014/01/02/marines-delay-female-fitness-plan-after-half-fail-pullup-test/)

507 "Retired Marine says proposed unisex uniform change is 'appalling'," Fox News, 10/25/2013 (http://www.foxnews.com/politics/2013/10/25/retired-marine-proposed-unisex-uniform-change-is-appalling/?intcmp=latestnews)

508 Ken Klukowski, "Pentagon Taps Anti-Christian Extremist For Religious for Religious Tolerance Policy", *Breitbart*, 4/28/2013; http://www.breitbart.com/Big-Peace/2013/04/28/Pentagon-Consults-Extremist-Who-Calls-Christians-Monsters-and-Enemies-of-the-Constitution-to-Develop-Religious-Tolerance-Policyh

509 Ken Klukowski, "Pentagon May Court Martial Soldiers who Share Christian Faith", *Breitbart*, 5/1/2013; http://www.breitbart.com/Big-Peace/2013/05/01/Breaking-Pentagon-Confirms-Will-Court-Martial-Soldiers-Who-Share-Christian-Faith

510 Andrew Tilghman, "Bible verse sends former Marine back to court", *Military Times*, 5/27/2015; (http://www.militarytimes.com/story/military/2015/05/27/marine-monifa-sterling-bible-verse-court-case/28010365/)

511 Todd Starnes, "US Army Defines Christian Ministry as 'Domestic Hate Group'", *Fox News*, 10/14/2013; http://www.foxnews.com/opinion/2013/10/14/us-army-defines-christian-ministry-as-domestic-hate-group/

512 Jim Kouri, "U.S. military is No. 1 Islamic terrorism target," *Examiner*, 12/8/2011 (http://www.examiner.com/article/u-s-military-is-no-1-islamic-terrorism-target)

513 Greg Botelho and Joe Sterling, "FBI: Navy Yard shooter 'delusional,' said 'low frequency attacks' drove him to kill," *CNN*, (http://edition.cnn.com/2013/09/25/us/washington-navy-yard-investigation/)

514 "Fort Hood shooter snapped over denial of request for leave, Army confirms," *Fox News*, 4/7/2014 (http://www.foxnews.com/us/2014/04/07/fort-hood-shooter-snapped-over-denial-request-for-leave-army-confirms/)

515 J.D. Gordon, "GORDON: Purging America's military," *Washington Times*, 11/12/2013 (http://www.washingtontimes.com/news/2013/nov/12/gordon-transforming-the-us-military/)

516 Sara Carter, "Blaze Sources: Obama Purging Military Commanders," *TheBlaze*, 10/23/2013 (http://www.theblaze.com/stories/2013/10/23/military-sources-obama-administration-purging-commanders/)

517 *Ibid.*

518 *Ibid.*

519 Ellie Hall, "Obama Told Military Leaders: Accept Gays in Military or Step Down, Admiral Says". *Buzzfeed*, 3/31/2014 (http://www.buzzfeed.com/elliehvhall/obama-told-military-leaders-accept-gays-in-military-or-step)

520 Kerry Eleveld, "Obama Talks All Things LGBT With The Advocate," *Advocate*, 12/23/2008 (http://www.advocate.com/news/2008/12/23/obama-talks-all-things-lgbt-the%C2%A0advocate?page=0,1)

521 Jeff Zeleny, "No 'Yes' Men, Obama Says," The Caucus, 12/27/2007 (http://thecaucus.blogs.nytimes.com/2007/12/17/no-yes-men-obama-says/)

522 Andrew Refferty, "American Drone Deaths Highlight Controversy," *NBC News*, 03/05/2013; (usnews.nbcnews.com/_news/2013/02/05/16856963-american-drone-deaths-highlight-controversy)

523 Jon Swaine, "Barack Obama 'Has Authority to Use Drone Strikes to Kill Americans on US Soil'," *The Telegraph*, 03/06/2013, (http://www.telegraph.co.uk/news/worldnews/barackobama/9913615/Barack-Obama-has-authority-to-use-drone-strikes-to-kill-Americans-on-US-soil.html)

524 "Brennan: Due Process Not Necessary to Kill Americans for Potential Future Actions," *Breitbart*, 02/07/2013, (http://www.breitbart.com/Breitbart-TV/2013/02/07/Brennan-Killing-Americans-Without-Due-Process-Not-Because-of-What-They-Did-But-What-They%20Might%20Do)

525 Jake Miller, "Paul's Filibuster Provokes Answer From Holder," *CBS News*, 03/07/2013, (http://www.cbsnews.com/8301-250_162-57573102/pauls-filibuster-provokes-answer-from-holder/)

526 Glenn Greenwald, "Chilling Legal Memo From Obama DoJ Justifies Assassination of US Citizens", *The Guardian*, 2/5/2013; http://www.theguardian.com/commentisfree/2013/feb/05/obama-kill-list-doj-memo

527 Marion Blakey, "Out of Balance: Obama Cut Weapons Too Much, Personnel Not Enough," *AOLDefense*, 03/14/2012, (http://defense.aol.com/2012/03/14/out-of-balance-obama-cut-weapons-too-much-personnel-not-enough/)

528 Adam Kredo, "Obama to kill Navy's Tomahawk, Hellfire missile programs in budget decimation," *Washington Times*, 3/25/2014 (http://www.washingtontimes.com/news/2014/mar/25/obama-kill-navys-tomahawk-hellfire-missile-program)

529 *Ibid.*

530 James Rosen, "Proposed Defense Cuts Would Hit Some Bases, Spare Others", *The Washington Post*, 2/24/2014; http://www.mcclatchydc.com/2014/02/24/219237/proposed-defense-cuts-would-hit.html

531 Ben Shapiro, "Obama's Historic Defense Cuts Spell Disaster," Breitbart, 2/25/2014 (http://www.breitbart.com/Big-Government/2014/02/25/defense-budget-cuts-history)

532 Dan De Luce, "Pentagon Plans to Shrink US Army to Pre-WWII Level," *Agence France-Presse*, 2/24/2014; http://news.yahoo.com/pentagon-proposes-shrink-us-army-pre-wwii-level-183915098.html;_ylt=AwrTWf1X8gtTyCsAGVTQtDMD

533 Kristina Wong, "Pentagon Budget Slashes Benefits". *The Hill*, 2/24/2014; http://thehill.com/blogs/defcon-hill/budget-appropriations/199050-hagel-unveils-basics-of-2015-defense-budget-request

534 William Bigelow, "Administration Defends Obama Trips to Tyrannical Regimes," *Breitbart*, 11/16/2012, (http://www.breitbart.com/Big-Government/2012/11/15/Administration-Defends-Obama-Trips-To-Tyrannical-Regimes)

535 Brian Knowlton, "4 Nations With Child Soldiers Keep U.S. Aid," *New York Times*, 10/28/2010, (http://www.nytimes.com/2010/10/29/world/africa/29soldiers.html)

536 David Axe, "Questions Abound as China Unveils Another Stealth Jet," *Wired*, 09/16/2012, (http://www.wired.com/dangerroom/2012/09/questions-abound-as-china-unveils-another-stealth-jet/)

537 Marc S. Reisch, "China Accused of Stealing DuPont Trade Secrets," *Chemical and Engineering News*, 02/09/2011, (http://cen.acs.org/articles/90/web/2012/02/China-Accused-Stealing-DuPont-Trade.html)

538 Jeffrey Mervis, "GAO Says White House Broke the Law by Holding Science Meetings With China," *Science*, 10/12/2011, (http://news.sciencemag.org/scienceinsider/2011/10/gao-says-white-house-broke-the-law.html)

539 Pete Kasperowicz, "'Everything is Confidential':Obama Stiffs Congress on Details of Cuban Spy Swap", *The Blaze*, 12/22/2014, (http://www.theblaze.com/stories/2014/12/22/everything-is-confidential-obama-stiffs-congress-on-details-of-cuban-spy-swap/)

540 United States Senate Committee on Foreign Relations. (2014). Chairman Menendez's Statement on the Release of Alan Gross [Press release]. Retrieved from http://www.foreign.senate.gov/press/chair/release/chairman-menendezs-statement-on-the-release-of-alan-gross

541 Rebecca Kaplan, "Congress deeply divided over Obama's Cuba deal", *CBS News,* 12/17/2014; (http://www.cbsnews.com/news/congress-deeply-divided-over-obamas-cuba-deal/)

542 Carole E Lee and William Maudlin, "Obama Faces Battle with Congress Over Cuba", *Wall Street Journal,* 12/21/2014; (http://www.wsj.com/articles/obama-faces-battle-with-congress-over-cuba-1419211849)

543 Dave Boyer, "Obama to lift Cuba from list of terrorist sponsors", Washington Times, 4/14/2015; (http://www.washingtontimes.com/news/2015/apr/14/obama-removes-cuba-state-sponsor-terror-list/)

544 David Steinberg, "Day After Obama Removes Cuba from Terror Sponsor List, Terror Group Sponsored by Cuba Kills 10", *PJ Media,* 4/15/2015; (http://pjmedia.com/tatler/2015/04/15/day-after-obama-removes-cuba-from-terror-sponsor-list-terror-group-sponsored-by-cuba-kills-10/)

545 Keith Johnson, "The link between Venezuela and Cuba", *Tico Times* 2/27/2014; (http://www.ticotimes.net/2014/02/27/the-link-between-venezuela-and-cuba)

546 Girish Gupta, "Venezuela's role in warming Cuba - US relations", *Christian Science Monitor,* 12/17/2014; (http://www.csmonitor.com/World/Americas/Latin-America-Monitor/2014/1217/Venezuela-s-role-in-warming-Cuba-US-relations-video)

547 Alberto de la Cruz, "Cuba and North Korea send Special Forces to Venezuela to prop up dictatorship", *Babalú Blog,* 5/21/2016; (http://babalublog.com/2016/05/21/cuba-and-north-korea-send-special-forces-to-venezuela-to-prop-up-dictatorship/)

548 Ana Quintana, "Congressional Oversight Needed as Obama Administration Moves to Remove Cuba From State Sponsors of Terrorism List", *The Heritage Foundation,* 1/29/2015; (http://www.heritage.org/research/reports/2015/01/congressional-oversight-needed-as-obama-administration-moves-to-remove-cuba-from-state-sponsors-of-terrorism-list)

549 Tony Lee, "Palin Mocked in 2008 for Warning Putin May Invade Ukraine if Obama Elected", *Breitbart,* 2/28/2014; http://www.breitbart.com/Big-Peace/2014/02/28/Flashback-Palin-Mocked-in-2008-for-Warning-Putin-May-Invade-Ukraine-if-Obama-Elected-President

550 Laura Smith-Spark, Diana Magnay and Ingrid Formanek, "Russian Upper House Approves Use of Military Force in Ukraine", *CNN,* 3/1/2014; http://www.cnn.com/2014/03/01/world/europe/ukraine-politics/

551 "Krauthammer on Ukraine: 'Everybody is shocked by the weakness of Obama's statement," Fox News, 2/28/2014 (http://www.foxnews.com/politics/2014/02/28/krauthammer-on-ukraine-everybody-is-shocked-by-weakness-obama-statement/)

552 Daniel Harper, "Obama Skips National Security Team Meeting on Russia, Ukraine," Weekly Standard, 3/1/2014 (http://www.weeklystandard.com/blogs/obama-skips-national-security-team-meeting-russia-ukraine_783659.html)

553 Kirit Radia, "Russian Deputy PM Laughs at Obama's Sanctions," ABC News, 3/17/2014 (http://abcnews.go.com/blogs/headlines/2014/03/russian-deputy-pm-laughs-at-obamas-sanctions/)

554 Emily Friedman, "Mitt Romney Says Russia is No. 1 Geopolitical Foe", *ABC News,* 3/26/2012; http://news.yahoo.com/mitt-romney-says-russia-no-1-geopolitical-foe-214249733--abc-news.html

555 Nile Gardiner, "Barack Obama is proving an embarrassing amateur on the world stage compared to George W. Bush," *The Telegraph,* 8/30/2013 (http://blogs.telegraph.co.uk/news/nilegardiner/100233454/barack-obama-is-proving-an-embarrassing-amateur-on-the-world-stage-compared-to-george-w-bush/)

556 Shadee Ashtari, "Americans View U.S. Power, Respect Slipping On Global Stage, Poll Shows," *Huffington Post,* 12/4/2013 (http://www.huffingtonpost.com/2013/12/04/us-power-global_n_4385160.html)

557 Nico Hines, "Senior UK Defense Advisor: Obama Is Clueless About 'What He Wants To Do In The World'," *The Daily Beast*, 1/14/2013, (http://www.thedailybeast.com/articles/2014/01/15/senior-uk-defense-advisor-obama-is-clueless-about-what-he-wants-to-do-in-the-world.html)

558 Maayana Miskin, "Report: Israel, Saudi Arabia Plan Iran Strike", *Arutz Sheva 7*, 11/17/2013, (http://www.israelnationalnews.com/News/News.aspx/174092#.UrNDJuInip0)

559 Barbara Starr, "U.S., Chinese warships come dangerously close," *CNN*, 12/13/2013 (http://www.cnn.com/2013/12/13/politics/us-china-confrontation/)

560 "Iran Sending Warships Close To US Borders," Associated Press, 2/8/2014 (http://abcnews.go.com/International/wireStory/iran-sending-warships-close-us-borders-22424767)

561 Oren Dorell, "Iranian warships heading to USA to show reach," *USA Today*, 2/11/2014 (http://www.usatoday.com/story/news/world/2014/02/10/iran-warships-threat-to-usa-coast/5365335/)

562 Will Englund and Kathy Lally, "Ukraine, Under Pressure from Russia, Puts Brakes on E.U. Deal," *The Washington Post*, November 21, 2013; http://www.washingtonpost.com/world/europe/ukraine-under-pressure-from-russia-puts-brakes-on-eu-deal/2013/11/21/46c50796-52c9-11e3-9ee6-2580086d8254_story.html

563 Will Englund, "U.S. relations with Russia face critical tests in 2014 as Putin, Obama fail to fulfill expectations," Washington Post, 1/2/2014 (http://www.washingtonpost.com/world/europe/us-relations-with-russia-face-critical-tests-in-2014-as-putin-obama-fail-to-fulfill-expectations/2014/01/02/a46c880c-4562-11e3-95a9-3f15b5618ba8_story.html)

564 "North Korea's Shadowy Arms Trade", *The Associated Press*, July 17, 2013; http://www.theguardian.com/world/2013/jul/18/history-north-korea-arms-dealing

565 "Philippines Accuse China of Military Buildup at South China Sea", *Agence France-Presse*, June 30, 2013; http://www.ndtv.com/article/world/philippines-accuses-china-of-military-buildup-at-south-china-sea-386029

566 Fred Dews, "Lessons From World War I: is Today's China the German of 1914? Where is the Next Global Flashpoint?", *Brookings Institute*, November 13, 2013; http://www.brookings.edu/blogs/brookings-now/posts/2013/11/lessons-world-war-one-china-germany-global-flashpoint

567 "Starving North Koreans Forced to Survive on Diet of Grass and Tree Bark," *Amnesty International*, 7/15/2010, (http://www.amnesty.org/en/news-and-updates/starving-north-koreans-forced-survive-diet-grass-and-tree-bark-2010-07-14)

568 Gerard Hunt, "From Bread Basket to Basket Case: Land Seizures from White Farmers Have Cost Zimbabwe 7 Billion Pounds," The Daily Mail, 08/03/2011, (http://www.dailymail.co.uk/news/article-2022014/Mugabes-land-seizures-white-farmers-cost-Zimbabwe-7bn.html)

569 Charlies Devereaux and Raymond Colitt, "Venezuelans Faring Better but Economy is Crumbling." *Bloomberg*, 03/08/2013, (http://www.dispatch.com/content/stories/national_world/2013/03/08/venezuelans-faring-better-but-economy-is-crumbling.html)

570 "The Economic Freedom of the World" The Fraser Institute, (http://www.freetheworld.com/countrydata.php?country=C135)

571 Terry Miller, "U.S. Economic Freedom Continues to Fade", *Wall Street Journal*, 1/31/2016; (http://www.wsj.com/articles/u-s-economic-freedom-continues-to-fade-1454281752)

572 Nicole V. Crain and W. Mark Crain, "The Impact of Regulatory Costs on Small Firms," SBA Office of Advocacy, September, 2010

573 "The Cost of Federal Regulation to the U.S. Economy, Manufacturing and Small Business", National Association of Manufacturers; (http://www.nam.org/Data-and-Reports/Cost-of-Federal-Regulations/Federal-Regulation-Executive-Summary.pdf)

574 Elizabeth Harrington, "Report: Cost of Federal Regulation Reached $1.88 Trillion in 2014", Free Beacon, 5/12/2015; (http://freebeacon.com/issues/report-cost-of-federal-regulation-reached-1-88-trillion-in-2014/)

575 Stephen Dinan, "Feds Sting Amish Farmer Selling Raw Milk," *Washington Times*, 04/29/2011, (http://www.washingtontimes.com/news/2011/apr/28/feds-sting-amish-farmer-selling-raw-milk-locally/)

576 "Regulator Without a Peer," *Wall Street Journal*, 4/16/2014 (http://online.wsj.com/news/articles/SB10001424052702304311204579505953682216682)

577 Alex Newman, "Obama Imposed 75,000 Pages of New Regulations in 2014," *The New American*, 12/30/2014, (http://www.thenewamerican.com/usnews/constitution/item/19803-obama-imposed-75-000-pages-of-new-regulations-in-2014)

578 James Gattuso, "20,642 New Regulations Added in the Obama Presidency," *The Daily Signal*, 5/23/2016 (http://dailysignal.com/2016/05/23/20642-new-regulations-added-in-the-obama-presidency/)

579 Stacy Swimp, "Did President Obama Malign Right to Work Laws?" *Washington Times*, 5/2/2012, (http://communities.washingtontimes.com/neighborhood/frederick-douglass-model-ages/2012/may/2/did-president-obama-malign-right-work-laws/)

580 Mark J. Perry, "Since 2009, Right to Work States Created 4x as Many Jobs as Forced Union States...," *American Enterprise Institute*, 11/24/2012, (http://www.aei-ideas.org/2012/11/since-2009-right-to-work-states-have-created-4x-as-many-jobs-as-forced-union-states-and-may-have-help-obamas-re-election/)

581 *Ibid.*

582 Macon Phillips, "Facts Are Stubborn Things," *The White House Blog*, 8/4/2009, (http://www.whitehouse.gov/blog/Facts-Are-Stubborn-Things)

583 "Big Brother Obama is Watching," *Washington Times*, 9/14/2011, (http://www.washingtontimes.com/news/2011/sep/14/big-brother-obama-is-watching/)

584 Joel Pollack, "Obama Now Scapegoating Jewish Donor Adelson," *Breitbart*, 08/08/2012, (http://www.breitbart.com/Big-Government/2012/08/08/Obama-Now-Scapegoating-Jewish-Donor-Adelson)

585 Christopher Bedford, "Obama Steps Up Anti-Koch Campaign With Online Petition," *The Daily Caller*, 02/29/2012, (http://dailycaller.com/2012/02/29/obama-steps-up-anti-koch-campaign-with-online-petition/)

586 Doug Schoen, "The Obama Campaign's Nixonian 'White House Enemies List'," *Forbes*, 05/14/2012, (http://www.forbes.com/sites/dougschoen/2012/05/14/the-obama-white-house-enemies-list/)

587 Jeff Zeleny, "Opponents Call Obama Remarks 'Out of Touch'", *The New York Times*, 4/12/2008, http://www.nytimes.com/2008/04/12/us/politics/12campaign.html?_r=0

588 Lachlan Markay, "An Extreme Position on Extremism", *The Washington Free Beacon*, 4/5/2013; http://freebeacon.com/an-extreme-position-on-extremism/

589 "Equal Opportunity and Treatment Incidents," http://www.judicialwatch.org/wp-content/uploads/2013/08/2161-docs.pdf

590 Charles Rollet, "Defense Department guide calls Founding Fathers 'extremist'," *Daily Caller*, 8/23/2013 (http://dailycaller.com/2013/08/23/defense-department-guide-calls-founding-fathers-extremist/)

591 "Gallup Sued by DOJ After Unfavorable Obama Polls, Employment Numbers," *Breitbart*, 09/06/2012, (http://www.breitbart.com/Big-Government/2012/09/06/gallup-doj-axelrod)

592 Aruna Viswanatha and Lauren Tara Lacapra, "U.S. government slams S&P with $5 billion fraud lawsuit," *Reuters*, 2/5/2013, (http://www.reuters.com/article/2013/02/05/us-mcgrawhill-sandp-civilcharges-idUSBRE9130U120130205)

593 "Treasury chief Geithner sought revenge on S&P: McGraw," New York Post, 1/21/2014 (http://nypost.com/2014/01/21/treasury-chief-geithner-sought-revenge-on-sp-mcgraw/)

594   "US DOT Proposes Broader Use of Even Data Recorders to Help Improve Vehicle Safety," NHTSA 46-10, 12/07/2012, (http://www.nhtsa.gov/About+NHTSA/Press +Releases/U.S.+DOT+Proposes+Broader+Use+of+Event+Data+Recorders+to +Help+Improve+Vehicle+Safety)

595   *Ibid.*

596   The National Center for Public Policy Research. (2012). Obama Administration Rushes "Creepy Black Box" Mandate on All New Car Buyers [Press release]. Retrieved from http://www.nationalcenter.org/PR-Black_Boxes_Cars_121312.html

597   C. J. Ciaramella, "Justice Dept. Proposes Lying, Hiding Existence of Records Under New FOIA Rule," *The Daily Caller*, 10/24/2011, (http://dailycaller.com/2011/10/24/ justice-dept-proposes-lying-hiding-existence-of-records-under-new-foia-rule)

598   Mark Tapscott, "'Most transparent' White House ever rewrote the FOIA to suppress politically sensitive docs", Washington Examiner, 3/18/2014; (http:// www.washingtonexaminer.com/most-transparent-white-house-ever-rewrote-the- foia-to-suppress-politically-sensitive-docs/article/2545824)

599   Ted Bridis and Jack Gillum, "US Cites security more to censor, deny records," *Associated Press*, 4/17/2014; (http://news.yahoo.com/us-cites-security-more-censor- deny-records-180650460.html)

600   Megan R. Wilson, "White House formally exempts office from FOIA regs," The Hill, 3/16/2015; (http://thehill.com/homenews/administration/235900-white-house- exempts-office-from-foia-regs)

601   Lisa Desjardins, "The War Over Coal Is Personal," *CNN*, 7/17/12, (http:// www.cnn.com/2012/07/17/us/embed-america-energy-war)

602   "Potential Impacts Of EPA Air, Coal Combustion Residuals, And Cooling Water Regulations," *NERA Economic Consulting*, September 2011 (http:// www.americaspower.org/sites/default/files/ NERA_Four_Rule_Report_Sept_21.pdf)

603   The White House, Office of the Press Secretary. (2013). Remarks by the President in the State of the Union Address [Press release]. Retrieved from http:// www.whitehouse.gov/the-press-office/2013/02/12/remarks-president-state-union- address

604   Coral Davenport, "Obama to Take Action to Slash Coal Pollution", New York Times, 6/1/2014; (http://www.nytimes.com/2014/06/02/us/politics/epa-to-seek-30- percent-cut-in-carbon-emissions.html)

605   Amy Harder, "EPA Set to Unveil Climate Proposal," *Wall Street Journal*, 5/26/2014 (http://online.wsj.com/news/articles/ SB10001424052702304811904579585843675203708)

606   Michael Bastasch, "Obama Unilaterally Pushes Cap-And-Trade On Unwilling States," *Daily Caller*, 6/2/2014, (http://dailycaller.com/2014/06/02/obama- unilaterally-pushes-cap-and-trade-on-unwilling-states//)

607   Stephen Dinan, "Email Tells Feds to Make Squester as Painful as Promised," *Washington Times*, 03/05/2013, (http://www.washingtontimes.com/news/2013/ mar/5/email-tells-feds-make-sequester-painful-promised/)

608   Judson Berger, "Park Ranger: Supervisors Pushed Sequester Cuts That Visitors Would See," *Fox News*, 03/09/2013, (http://www.foxnews.com/politics/ 2013/03/08/park-ranger-claims-supervisors-pushed-sequester-cuts-that-visitors- would-notice/)

609   Kathleen Hennessey, "Detained immigrants released; officials cite sequester cuts," *Los Angeles Times*, 2/26/13, (http://articles.latimes.com/2013/feb/26/news/la-pn- detained-immigrants-sequester-20130226)

610   Dylan Matthews, "Here is every previous government shutdown, why they happened and how they ended," *Washington Post*, 9/25/13, (http://www.washingtonpost.com/ blogs/wonkblog/wp/2013/09/25/here-is-every-previous-government-shutdown- why-they-happened-and-how-they-ended/)

611 "Closure of War Memorials Continues to Cause Conflict," *4NBC Washington*, 10/4/2013 (http://www.nbcwashington.com/news/local/Closure-of-War-Memorials-Continues-to-Cause-Conflict-226481851.html)

612 Jillian Kay Melchior, "Park Service Knew World War II Veterans Would be Locked Out", National Review Online, 3/10/2014 (http://www.nationalreview.com/article/373015/park-service-knew-world-war-ii-veterans-would-be-locked-out-jillian-kay-melchior)

613 Elizabeth Shield, "Armed Guards Kick Senior Citizens Out of Yellowstone Park," *Breitbart*, 10/8/2013, (http://www.breitbart.com/InstaBlog/2013/10/08/Senior-Citizens-Kicked-Out-Treated-Harshly-at-Yellowstone-Park)

614 Warner Todd Huston, "Obama Forcing Shut Down of Parks the Feds Don't Even Fund," *Brietbart*, 10/4/2013, (http://www.breitbart.com/Big-Government/2013/10/03/Obama-Forcing-Shut-Down-of-Parks-the-Feds-Don-t-Even-Fund)

615 Jacqui Heinrich, "Lake Mead Property Owners Forced Out Until Shutdown Ends," *13 Action News*, 10/4/2013, (http://ktnv.com/news/local/Lake-Mead-Property-Owners-Forced-Out-Until-Gov-Shutdown-Ends-226557661.htm)

616 Ed O'Keefe, "Eleanor Holmes Norton Confronts Obama on D.C. Budget Bill," *Washington Post*, 10/9/13 (http://www.washingtonpost.com/blogs/post-politics/wp/2013/10/09/eleanor-holmes-norton-confronts-obama-on-d-c-budget-bill/)

617 Ronn Torossian, "Millions Paid to Liberal Public Relations Firms," *Frontpage Magazine*, 10/30/2012, (http://frontpagemag.com/2012/ronn-torossian/millions-paid-to-liberal-public-relations-firms/)

618 Tyler Durden, "Foodstamps Surge by Most in One Year to New All Time High, in Delayed Release," *Zero Hedge*, 11/10/2012, (http://www.zerohedge.com/news/2012-11-10/foodstamps-surge-most-one-year-new-all-time-record-delayed-release)

619 Juliet Eilperin, "White House Delayed Enacting Rules Ahead of 2012 Election to Avoid Controversy", *Washington Post*, 12/13/2013 (http://www.washingtonpost.com/politics/white-house-delayed-enacting-rules-ahead-of-2012-election-to-avoid-controversy/2013/12/14/7885a494-561a-11e3-ba82-16ed03681809_story.html)

620 Juliet Eilperin, "White House Delayed Enacting Rules Ahead of 2012 Election to Avoid Controversy", *Washington Post*, 12/13/2013; http://www.washingtonpost.com/politics/white-house-delayed-enacting-rules-ahead-of-2012-election-to-avoid-controversy/2013/12/14/7885a494-561a-11e3-ba82-16ed03681809_story.html

621 Mary Bruce and Jake Tapper, "At White House Request, Lockheed Martin Drops Plan to Issue Layoff Notices," *ABC News*, 10/01/2012, (http://abcnews.go.com/blogs/politics/2012/10/at-white-house-request-lockheed-martin-drops-plan-to-issue-layoff-notices/)

622 Mike Flynn, "Obama Urges Companies to Break Law for His Reelection," *Breitbart*, 10/02/2012, (http://www.breitbart.com/Big-Government/2012/10/02/obama-urges-companies-to-break-federal-law-for-his-reelection)

623 "2012 Presidential Election, Virginia," *Politico*, 11/29/2012, (http://www.politico.com/2012-election/map/#/President/2012/VA)

624 Michael Medved, "The Great Political Migration," *The Daily Beast*, 08/27/2011, (http://www.thedailybeast.com/articles/2011/08/27/census-data-shows-people-are-moving-from-blue-to-red-states.html)

625 Bill Sammon, Shannon Beam and Fox News Staff, "GOP Sounds Alarm Over Obama Decision to Move Census to White House," *Fox News*, 02/09/2009, (http://www.foxnews.com/politics/2009/02/09/gop-sounds-alarm-obama-decision-census-white-house/)

626 *Ibid*

627 David Crary, "Census Counts Gay Marriages Even in States That Don't Allow Them," *The Huffington Post*, 04/05/2010, (http://www.huffingtonpost.com/2010/04/05/census-counts-gay-marriag_n_526396.html)

628 Meredith Simons, "Census Launches Campaign to Hear More From Latinos," *Houston Chronicle*, 10/01/2009, (http://www.chron.com/news/nation-world/article/Census-launches-campaign-to-hear-more-from-Latinos-1732032.php)

629 Michelle Malkin, "Obama's Politicized, Profligate US Census," *Michelle Malkin*, 04/07/2009, (http://michellemalkin.com/2010/04/07/obamas-politicized-profligate-u-s-census/)

630 Kenneth R. Bazinet and Michasel McAuliff, "Bill Clinton Made Joe Sestak Job Offer on Behalf of Administration to Leave Race, White House Says," *New York Daily News*, 05/28/2010, (http://www.nydailynews.com/news/politics/bill-clinton-made-joe-sestak-job-offer-behalf-administration-leave-race-white-house-article-1.178586)

631 Hans von Spakovsky, "Sestak Job Offer Violated Federal Law?" *The Foundry*, 06/01/2010, (http://blog.heritage.org/2010/06/01/sestak-job-offer-violated-federal-law/)

632 18 U.S.C. 211: U.S. Code – Section 211: Acceptance or Solicitation to Obtain Appointive Public Office, *FindLaw*, accessed at, http://codes.lp.findlaw.com/uscode/18/I/11/211

633 John Bresnahan and Jake Sherman, "DoJ Nixes Sestak Special Counsel," *Politico*, 05/24/2010, (http://www.politico.com/news/stories/0510/37713.html)

634 Frank Ahrens, "Treasury Pick Misfiled Using Off-the-Shelf Tax Software," *The Washington Post*, 01/22/2009, (http://www.washingtonpost.com/wp-dyn/content/article/2009/01/21/AR2009012103552.html)

635 Carrie Budoff Brown, "Sebelius Paid Over $7,000 in Back Taxes." *Politico*, 03/31/2009, (http://www.politico.com/news/stories/0309/20728.html)

636 Matt Kelley, "Tax Snafus Add up for Obama Team," *USA Today*, 02/05/2009, (http://usatoday30.usatoday.com/news/washington/2009-02-05-solis-husband-taxes_N.htm)

637 Huma Khan, "Another Tax Problem for Obama Nominee," *ABC News*, 02/03/2009, (http://abcnews.go.com/blogs/politics/2009/02/another-tax-pro/)

638 Andrew Malcolm, "36 Obama Aids Owe $833,000 in Back Taxes," *Investors Business Daily*, 01/26/2012, (http://news.investors.com/politics-andrew-malcolm/012612-599002-obama-white-house-staff-back-taxes.htm)

639 Stephen Dinan, "Tax Cheats got $1.4 Billion in Stimulus Loans," *Washington Times*, 06/27/2012, (http://www.washingtontimes.com/news/2012/jun/27/gao-1-billion-in-tax-credits-went-to-cheats/)

640 John Fund, "Holder's Black Panther Stonewall," *Wall Street Journal*, 8/20/2013 (http://online.wsj.com/news/articles/SB10001424052970203550604574361071968458430)

641 Jan Crawford, "New Black Panther Case Spurs Civil Rights Commission to Challenge DOJ," *CBS News*, 07/14/2010 (http://www.cbsnews.com/8301-504564_162-20010581-504564.html)

642 Josh Gerstein, "Eric Holder: Black Panther Case Focus Demeans 'My People'", Politico, 3/1/2011; (http://www.politico.com/blogs/under-the-radar/2011/03/eric-holder-black-panther-case-focus-demeans-my-people-033839)

643 John Solomon, "Exclusive: FBI Blocked in Corruption Probe Involving Senators Reid, Lee," *Washington Times*, 3/13/2014 (http://www.washingtontimes.com/news/2014/mar/13/fbi-blocked-in-corruption-probe-involving-sens-rei/)

644 Pete Williams and Frank Thorp, "Obama invokes executive privilege over DOJ documents," *NBC News*, 6/20/2012; (http://firstread.nbcnews.com/_news/2012/06/20/12317893-obama-invokes-executive-privilege-over-doj-documents)

645 "AP Exclusive: US Ordered Delay in Intern's Arrest," *Associated Press*, 01/15/2013, (http://news.yahoo.com/ap-exclusive-us-ordered-delay-interns-arrest-172424335.html)

646 Sally Goldenberg, "Sanitation Department's Slow Cleanup Was a Budget Protest," *New York Post*, December 30, 2010; http://nypost.com/2010/12/30/sanitation-departments-slow-snow-cleanup-was-a-budget-protest/

THE LEGACY OF BARACK OBAMA

647 Jennifer Gould Keil and Frank Rosario, "De Blasio 'getting back at us' by not plowing: UES residents," *New York Post*, 1/21/2014 (http://nypost.com/2014/01/21/upper-east-side-residents-feel-spurned-after-plow-delay/)

648 Michael S. Schmidt, "Hillary Clinton Used Personal Email Account at State Dept., Possibly Breaking Rules", *New York Times*, 3/3/2015; (http://www.nytimes.com/2015/03/03/us/politics/hillary-clintons-use-of-private-email-at-state-department-raises-flags.html)

649 Sharyl Attkisson, "Hillary Clinton's Email: the Definitive Timeline", SharylAttkison.com, 5/27/2016; (https://sharylattkisson.com/hillary-clintons-email-the-definitive-timeline/)

650 "State Won't Release 18 Emails Between Clinton and Obama That Were on Her Private Server—But Says They Are Not Classified", *CNS News*, 1/30/2016; (http://www.cnsnews.com/news/article/cnsnewscom-staff/spokesman-says-state-wont-release-18-emails-between-clinton-and-obama)

651 Andrew McCarthy, "Why the Justice Department Won't Work with the FBI on Clinton's E-mail Case", *National Review*, 1/23/2016; (http://www.nationalreview.com/article/430211/hillary-clinton-email-fbi-department-justice-obama)

652 Stephen Dinan, "State Dept: Review of Hillary Clinton's emails may wait until after election", *Washington Times*, 3/1/2016; (http://www.washingtontimes.com/news/2016/mar/1/review-clinton-emails-may-come-after-election/)

653 "State Department Hid Key Clinton Benghazi Email from Judicial Watch" *Judicial Watch*, 4/26/2016; (http://www.judicialwatch.org/press-room/press-releases/state-department-hid-key-clinton-benghazi-email-from-judicial-watch/)

654 Matthew Boyle, "Priebus: Menendez's Allegedly Criminal Link to Democratic Megadonor 'Stinks to High Heaven'", *Breitbart*, 3/9/2015; (http://www.breitbart.com/big-government/2015/03/09/priebus-menendezs-allegedly-criminal-link-to-democratic-megadonor-stinks-to-high-heaven/)

655 Keith Laning, "Report: US Attorney Investigating Christie Bridge Scandal", *The Hill*, 1/9/2014 (http://thehill.com/blogs/transportation-report/highways-bridges-and-roads/194931-new-jersey-us-attorney-investigating)

656 Paul Bond, "'2016: Obama's America' Filmmaker Indicted for Violating Campaign Finance Laws," *The Hollywood Reporter*, 1/23/2014 (http://www.hollywoodreporter.com/news/2016-obamas-america-filmmaker-indicted-673670)

657 Jennifer G. Hickey and John Gizzi, Dershowitz, "Law Enforcement Experts Slam D'Souza Targeting," *Newsmax*, 1/29/2014 (http://www.newsmax.com/Newsfront/DSouza-Dershowitz-targeting-selective/2014/01/29/id/549845)

658 Andrew C. McCarthy, "Amnesty, but Not for D'Souza" *National Review*, 2/1/2014 (http://www.nationalreview.com/article/370097/amnesty-not-dsouza-andrew-c-mccarthy/)

659 Huma Khan, "President Obama Fires Controversial Inspector General," ABC News, June 12, 2009, (http://abcnews.go.com/blogs/politics/2009/06/president-obama-fires-controversial-inspector-general/)

660 The Cajun Boy, "Will Obama's Firing of an Inspector General Evolve Into a Major Scandal?," *Gawker*, June 16, 2009, (http://gawker.com/5292275/will-obamas-firing-of-an-inspector-general-evolve-into-a-major-scandal)

661 Robert Stacy McCain, "IG-Gate: 'Hush Money' Charge in Sacramento Mayor's Sex Scandal Was Part of Probe," *American Spectator*, November, 23 2009, (http://spectator.org/blog/2009/11/23/ig-gate-hush-money-charge-in-s)

662 John Kinsellagh, "Obama fires Inspector General Gerald Walpin without cause," *Examiner*, 6/18/2009, (http://www.examiner.com/article/obama-fires-inspector-general-gerald-walpin-without-cause)

663 Matthew Boyle, "Sebelius Violated Hatch Act and May be Fired, Obama Administration Lawyers Find," *The Daily Caller*, 09/12/2012, (http://dailycaller.com/2012/09/12/sebelius-violated-hatch-act-and-may-be-fired-obama-administration-lawyers-find/)

664 The White House, Office of the Special Counsel. Report of Prohibited Political Activity Under the Hatch Act OSC File No. HA-12-1989 (Kathleen A. Sebelius). 08/23/2012. Accesssed at http://www.osc.gov/documents/hatchact/Hatch%20Act %20Report%20on%20HHS%20Secretary%20Kathleen%20Sebelius.pdf Accessed November 18, 2012

665 The White House, Office of the Special Counsel. Information on Hatch Act. Accessed at http://www.osc.gov/haFederalPenalties.htm

666 Lee Stranahan, "Pigford: NYT Pegs Obama for Vote-Buying Scheme", *Breitbart*, April 25, 2013; http://www.breitbart.com/Big-Government/2013/04/26/New-York-Times-Reveals-Obama-s-Maneuvers-And-Motives-On-Pigford

667 Lee Stranahan, "New Obama 'Pigford' Farmers Settlement Designed for Fraud", *Breitbart*, September 25, 2012; http://www.breitbart.com/Big-Government/2012/09/25/New-Obama-Farmers-Settlements-Designed-For-Fraud

668 Sharon LaFraniere, "U.S. Opens Spigot After Farmers Claim Discrimination", *New York Times*, April 25, 2013; http://www.nytimes.com/2013/04/26/us/farm-loan-bias-claims-often-unsupported-cost-us-millions.html

669 *Ibid.*

670 *Ibid.*

671 Joel Gehrke, "Emails Show Obama Admin Used DOE Loan Money to Help Harry Reid's 2010 Campaign," *Washington Examiner*, 10/31/2012, (http://washingtonexaminer.com/emails-show-obama-admin-used-doe-loan-money-to-help-harry-reids-2010-campaign/article/2512249)

672 Tom Schoenberg,"Car Companies XP Vehicles, Limnia Sue U.S. Over Loans," *Bloomberg*, 01/10/2013, (http://www.bloomberg.com/news/2013-01-10/car-companies-xp-vehicles-limnia-sue-u-s-over-loans.html)

673 Ronnie Green, "Obama administration Agreed to Solyndra's Loan Days After Insiders Foresaw Firm's Failure," *The Center for Public Integrity*, 09/14/2011, (http://www.publicintegrity.org/2011/09/14/6465/obama-administration-agreed-solyndra-loan-days-after-insiders-foresaw-firms-failure)

674 Michael Beckel, "Before Collapse and Government Investigations, Solar Company Solyndra Was a Rising Star," *OpenSecrets*, 09/14/2011, (http://www.opensecrets.org/news/2011/09/solar-company-solyndra-rising-star.html)

675 Matthew Mosk and Brian Ross, "Solyndra: Blame it on Bush, Say Obama Officials," *ABC News*, 09/14/2011, (http://abcnews.go.com/Blotter/solyndra-blame-bush-obama-officials/story?id=14513389)

676 Jonathan Karl, "Exclusive: Jobs 'Saved or Created' in Congressional Districts That Don't Exist," *ABC News*, 11/6/2009, (http://abcnews.go.com/Politics/jobs-saved-created-congressional-districts-exist/story?id=9097853)

677 Bill McMorris, "$6.4 Billion Stimulus Goes to Phantom Districts," *Watchdog.org*, 11/17/2009, (http://watchdog.org/1530/6-4-billion-stimulus-goes-to-phantom-districts/)

678 Conn Carroll, "Morning Bell: The Fake Jobs of Obama's Failed Stimulus," *The Foundry*, 11/17/2009, (http://blog.heritage.org/2009/11/17/morning-bell-the-fake-jobs-of-obamas-failed-stimulus/)

679 Devlin Barrett, Danny Yadron and Damian Paletta, "U.S. Suspects Hackers in China Breached About 4 Million People's Records, Officials Say", *Wall Street Journal*, 6/5/2015; (http://www.wsj.com/articles/u-s-suspects-hackers-in-china-behind-government-data-breach-sources-say-1433451888)

680 Priya Anand, "OM Hack May Have Affected 32 Million Government Employees", *Market Watch*, 7/7/2015; (http://www.marketwatch.com/story/opm-hack-may-have-affected-32-million-government-employees-2015-07-08)

681 Sean Gallagher, "Encryption 'Would Not Have Helped' at OPM, says DHS Official", *arstechnica*, 6/16/2015; (http://arstechnica.com/security/2015/06/encryption-would-not-have-helped-at-opm-says-dhs-official/)

682 Sean Gallagher, "Hack of Government Employee Records Discovered by Product Demo", *arstechnica*, 6/11/2015; (http://arstechnica.com/security/2015/06/report-hack-of-government-employee-records-discovered-by-product-demo/)

683 Shane Harris, "Spies Warned Feds about OPM Mega-Hack Danger", *The Daily Beast*, 6/30/2015; (http://www.thedailybeast.com/articles/2015/06/30/spies-warned-feds-about-opm-mega-hack-danger.html)

684 Cory Bennett, "Feds Warn: Hackers Sending Fake E-Mails to OPM Hack Victims", *The Hill*, 7/1/2015; (http://thehill.com/policy/cybersecurity/246661-feds-warn-hackers-sending-fake-emails-to-opm-hack-victims)

685 Paul Conway, "How Obama's Poor Judgment Led to the Chinese Hack of OPM", *The Daily Signal*, 7/27/2015; (http://dailysignal.com/2015/07/27/how-obamas-poor-judgment-led-to-the-chinese-hack-of-opm/)

686 David Boyer, "Obama still backs OPM chief despite massive data breach," *Washington Times*, 6/17/2015; ("http://www.washingtontimes.com/news/2015/jun/17/obama-still-backs-opm-chief-despite-data-breach/)

687 http://pjmedia.com/blog/bombshell-justice-department-only-selectively-complies-with-freedom-of-information-act-pjm-exclusive/

688 http://pjmedia.com/blog/epa-accused-of-waiving-foia-fees-for-left-wing-groups-over-conservative-ones/

689 http://blog.ap.org/2014/09/19/8-ways-the-obama-administration-is-blocking-information/

690 http://oversight.house.gov/report/a-new-era-of-openness-how-and-why-political-staff-at-dhs-interfered-with-the-foia-process/

691 Cathy Milbourne, "EPA Finds Greenhouse Gases Pose Threat to Public Health, Welfare; Proposed Finding Comes in Response to 2007 Supreme Court Ruling", *United States Environmental Protection Agency*, press release, 4/17/2009, (http://yosemite.epa.gov/opa/admpress.nsf/0/0ef7df675805295d8525759b00566924)

692 Terence P. Jeffrey, "Obama Doesn't Rule Out Bypassing Congress and Using EPA Regulations to Cap Carbon Emissions," CNS News, 11/4/2010 (http://cnsnews.com/news/article/obama-doesn-t-rule-out-bypassing-congress-and-using-epa-regulations-cap-carbon)

693 Lachlan Markay, "Video: EPA Official Compares Agency Enforcement to Roman Crucifixions", *The Foundry*, 4/25/2012, (http://blog.heritage.org/2012/04/25/video-epa-official-compares-agency-enforcement-to-roman-crucifictions/)

694 Steve Everly, "EPA's watchdog covered up the agency's missteps," *The Hill*, 1/4/2014 (http://thehill.com/blogs/congress-blog/energy-environment/194314-epas-watchdog-covered-up-the-agencys-missteps)

695 http://dailycaller.com/2012/11/12/epa-chiefs-secret-alias-email-account-revealed/

696 Stephen Dinan, "Newly Released Emails Show EPA Director's Extensive Use of Fictional Alter Ego", *Washington Times*, 6/2/2013, (http://www.washingtontimes.com/news/2013/jun/2/newly-released-emails-show-epa-directors-extensive/)

697 Kevin Freking, "Lisa Jackson Resigns: EPA Administrator Stepping Down" Huffington Post, 12/27/2013, (http://www.huffingtonpost.com/2012/12/27/lisa-jackson-resigns-epa-administrator_n_2370019.html)

698 Michael Bastasch, "Vitter: EPA FOIA scandal 'no different than the IRS disaster'," *Daily Caller*, 5/17/2013, (http://dailycaller.com/2013/05/17/vitter-epa-foia-scandal-no-different-than-the-irs-disaster/)

699 C J Ciaramella, "Senators Question Leak of Private Farmer Info", *The Washington Free Beacon*, June 6, 2013; http://freebeacon.com/senators-question-epa-leak-of-private-farmer-info/

700 Tuskegee syphilis experiment. (n.d.). In Wikipedia. Retrieved April 6, 2014, from http://en.wikipedia.org/wiki/Tuskegee_syphilis_experiment

701 Michael Bastach, "Report: EPA Tested Deadly Pollutants on Humans to Push Obama Admin's Agenda", *The Daily Caller*, 4/2/2014 (http://dailycaller.com/2014/04/02/report-epa-tested-deadly-pollutants-on-humans-to-push-obama-admins-agenda/)

702 Kerry Picket, "This is How the EPA Finds People for Pollution Exposure Experiments", *Breitbart*, 4/3/2014 (http://www.breitbart.com/Big-Government/2014/04/03/This-Is-How-The-EPA-Finds-People-For-Pollution-Exposure-Experiments)

703 Michael Bastach, "Report: EPA Tested Deadly Pollutants on Humans to Push Obama Admin's Agenda", *The Daily Caller*, 4/2/2014 (http://dailycaller.com/2014/04/02/report-epa-tested-deadly-pollutants-on-humans-to-push-obama-admins-agenda/)

704 *Ibid.*

705 "Press Release: Obama Campaign Announces National Veterans Advisory Committee; 11/12/2007"; *The American Presidency Project*, accessed 5/19/2014; (http://www.presidency.ucsb.edu/ws/?pid=91891)

706 Bob Brewin, "VA Comes Under Fire as Claims Backlog Tops 900,000, Again," *NextGov*, 3/27/13 (http://www.nextgov.com/defense/2013/03/va-comes-under-fire-claims-backlog-tops-900000-again/62124/)

707 Jamie Reno, "Veterans Die Waiting For Benefits As VA Claims Backlog Builds," *Daily Beast*, 2/9/2013 (http://www.thedailybeast.com/articles/2013/02/09/veterans-die-waiting-for-benefits-as-va-claims-backlog-builds.html)

708 Aaron Glantz, "Number of Veterans Who Die Waiting for Benefits Claims Skyrockets," *Daily Beast*, 12/20/2012 (http://www.thedailybeast.com/articles/2012/12/20/number-of-veterans-who-die-waiting-for-benefits-claims-skyrockets.html)

709 "Senators Call for Probe into VA Hospital Deaths Allegedly Tied to Delayed Care", *Fox News*, 4/24/2014,(http://www.foxnews.com/politics/2014/04/24/senators-call-for-probe-into-va-hospital-deaths-allegedly-tied-to-delayed-care/)

710 Geoff Dyer, "Veterans scandal risks engulfing Obama," *Financial Times*, 5/16/2014 (http://www.ft.com/intl/cms/s/0/328546c0-dd10-11e3-8546-00144feabdc0.html)

711 Becket Adams, "Eric Holder: No Immediate Plans to Investigate VA Scandal," *The Blaze*, 5/14/2014 (http://www.theblaze.com/stories/2014/05/14/eric-holder-no-immediate-plans-to-investigate-va-scandal/)

712 "Whistleblowers describe VA culture of retaliation to lawmakers at hearing," *Fox News*, 7/9/2014 (http://www.foxnews.com/politics/2014/07/09/whistleblowers-tell-lawmakers-there-is-culture-retaliation-at-va/)

713 Jonathan Karl, "Obama's Pick for VA Health Supervised Scandal-Tainted Hospital," *ABC News*, 5/16/2014 (http://abcnews.go.com/blogs/politics/2014/05/obamas-pick-for-va-health-supervised-scandal-tainted-hospital/)

714 Guy Benson, "Surprise: WH Says Obama Found Out About VA Scandal On the News," *Townhall*, 5/19/2014, (http://townhall.com/tipsheet/guybenson/2014/05/19/number-nine-albuquerque-va-hospital-accused-of-manipulating-wait-times-n1840291)

715 Jim McElhatton, "He Knew! Obama Told of Veterans Affairs Health Care Debacle as far Back as 2008", *Washington Times*, 5/18/2014; (http://www.washingtontimes.com/news/2014/may/18/obama-warned-about-va-wait-time-problems-during-20/)

716 Martin Matishak, "Report: One-third of vets on pending medical care list already dead", *The Hill*, 7/13/2015; (http://thehill.com/policy/defense/247752-report-one-third-of-vets-waiting-medical-care-already-dead)

717 Richard A. Serrano, "Gun Store Owner Had Misgivings About ATF Sting," *Los Angeles Times*, 09/11/2011, (http://www.latimes.com/news/nationworld/nation/la-na-atf-guns-20110912,0,7686272,full.story)

718 Ken Ellingwood, Richard A. Serrano and Tracy Wilkinson, "Mexico Still Waiting for Answers on Fast and Furious Gun Program," *The Los Angeles Times*, 09/19/2011, (http://articles.latimes.com/2011/sep/19/world/la-fg-mexico-fast-furious-20110920)

719 David Keene, "Fast and Furious Cover-Up at Holder's Justice," *Washington Times*, 07/06/2012, (http://www.washingtontimes.com/news/2012/jul/6/fast-and-furious-cover-up-at-holders-justice/)

720 Alan Silverleib, "House Holds Holder in Contempt," *CNN*, 06/29/2012, (http://www.cnn.com/2012/06/28/politics/holder-contempt/index.html)

721 William LaJeunesse, Laura Prabucki and Fox News Staff, "Congressional Report Blames Five ATF Employees for Fast and Furious Debacle," *Fox News*, 07/31/2012, (http://www.foxnews.com/politics/2012/07/30/republicans-to-issue-report-blaming-five-atf-employees-for-fast-and-furious/)

722 "Issa-Grassley Report Links Fast and Furious to 'Widespread' Justice Department Failures," *Fox News*, 10/29/2012, (http://www.foxnews.com/politics/2012/10/29/issa-grassley-report-links-fast-furious-to-widespread-justice-dept-failures/)

723 Caitlin Dickson, "IRS Scandal's Central Figure, Lois Lerner, Described as 'Apolitical'," *Daily Beast*, 5/14/2013,(http://www.thedailybeast.com/articles/2013/05/14/irs-scandal-s-central-figure-lois-lerner-described-as-apolitical.html)

724 Patrick Howley, "Twelve different IRS units nationwide targeted conservatives," *Daily Caller*, 6/25/2013, (http://dailycaller.com/2013/06/25/twelve-different-irs-units-nationwide-targeted-conservatives/)

725 Kerry Picket, "IRS Employee: D.C. Told Us to Target Tea Party," *Breitbart*, 6/2/2013 (http://www.breitbart.com/Big-Government/2013/06/02/IRS-Employee-Washington-D-C-Told-Us-To-Target-Tea-Party-Oragnizations)

726 "Judicial Watch: New Documents Show IRS HQ Control of Tea Party Targeting", *Judicial Watch*, 5/14/2014, (http://www.judicialwatch.org/press-room/press-releases/judicial-watch-new-documents-show-irs-hq-control-tea-party-targeting/)

727 Stephen Dinan, "IRS officials thought Obama wanted crackdown on tea party groups, worried about negative press," Washington Times, 9/17/2013, (http://www.washingtontimes.com/news/2013/sep/17/report-irs-staff-acutely-aware-tea-party-antipathy)

728 Vince Coglianese, "IRS's Shulman Had More Public White House Visits Than Any Cabinet Member", *The Daily Caller*, 5/29/2013, (http://dailycaller.com/2013/05/29/irss-shulman-had-more-public-white-house-visits-than-any-cabinet-member)

729 Patrick Howley, "White House, IRS exchanged confidential taxpayer info," *Daily Caller*, 10/9/2013, (http://dailycaller.com/2013/10/09/white-house-irs-exchanged-confidential-taxpayer-info/)

730 Paul Bedard, "Treasury: IRS targeted 292 Tea Party groups, just 6 progressive groups," *Washington Examiner*, 6/27/2013, (http://washingtonexaminer.com/article/2532456)

731 Patrick Howley, "IRS Agents' Testimony: No Progressive Groups Were Targeted by IRS", *Daily Caller*, 4/7/2014, (http://dailycaller.com/2014/04/07/committee-staff-report-no-progressive-groups-were-targeted-by-irs/)

732 Stephan Dinan, "House Republicans find 10% of tea party donors audited by IRS," Washington Times, 5/7/2014 (http://www.washingtontimes.com/news/2014/may/7/house-republicans-find-10-of-tea-party-donors-audi/)

733 Joel Gehrke, "Report: IRS denied tax-exempt status to pro-lifers on behalf of Planned Parenthood," *Washington Examiner*, 5/16/2013, (http://washingtonexaminer.com/article/2529750)

734 Matthew Boyle, "Romney Donor Vandersloot: I was audited twice by IRS, once by DOL & investigated by by former Senate staffer," *Breitbart*, 5/19/2013 (http://www.breitbart.com/Big-Government/2013/05/19/Businessman-Frank-VanderSloot-I-was-audited-twice-by-IRS-once-by-DOL-investigated-by-Senate-staffer-after-giving-1-million-to-Romney-Super-PAC)

735 "Eric Bolling: I Was Audited After Criticizing Obama," *Fox News*, 5/16/2013 (http://nation.foxnews.com/irs-targeting-tea-party/2013/05/16/eric-bolling-i-was-audited-after-criticizing-obama)

736 Caroline May, "The 'strange' IRS audit of a Romney fundraiser and her extended family," *Daily Caller*, 6/6/2013, (http://dailycaller.com/2013/06/06/the-strange-irs-audit-of-a-romney-fundraiser-and-her-extended-family/)

737 Ben Wolfgang and Dave Boyer, "Former GOP Senate candidate Christine O'Donnell told her tax records were breached," *Washington Times*, 7/17/2013 (http://www.washingtontimes.com/news/2013/jul/17/former-gop-senate-candidate-christine-odonnell-tol/)

738 John Solomon and Ben Wolfgang, "The long line of conservatives targeted by the IRS," *Washington Times*, 10/3/2013, (http://www.washingtontimes.com/news/2013/oct/3/irs-targeted-dr-ben-carson-after-prayer-breakfast-/)

739 Alex Pappas, "Ben Carson: White House Wanted Apology for 'Offending' Obama", *Daily Caller*, 4/14/2014; (http://dailycaller.com/2014/04/14/ben-carson-white-house-wanted-apology-for-offending-obama/)

740 John Nolte, "Report: IRS Covered Up Scandal Until After Election," *Breitbart*, 5/17/2013, (http://www.breitbart.com/Big-Journalism/2013/05/17/Report-Irs-Covered-up-Scandal-before-Election)

741 James Pethokoukis, "Did the IRS's Tea Party suppression get Obama reelected?," American Enterprise Institute, 6/20/2013, (http://www.aei-ideas.org/2013/06/the-asterisk-president-did-the-irss-tea-party-suppression-get-obama-reelected/)

742 Neil Munro, "Covert cronies? Obama's attorney general appoints Obama donor to investigate Obama's IRS," Daily Caller, 1/8/2014, (http://dailycaller.com/2014/01/08/covert-cronies-obamas-attorney-general-appoints-obama-donor-to-investigate-obamas-irs/)

743 Lauren French, "Two Democrats Call for Ethics Probe into J. Russell George's Work as IRS Inspector General", *Politico*, 2/7/14, (http://www.politico.com/morningtax/0214/morningtax12951.html)

744 Josh Hicks, "Obama donor leading Justice Department's IRS investigation," *Washington Post*, 1/9/2014 (http://www.washingtonpost.com/politics/980c010a-796a-11e3-8963-b4b654bcc9b2_story.html)

745 Devlin Barrett, "Criminal Charges Not Expected in IRS Probe," *Wall Street Journal*, 1/13/14 (http://online.wsj.com/news/articles/SB10001424052702303819704579318983271821584)

746 Jeff Dunetz, "Obamacare Victim Appears On Fox News; Gets IRS Audit," *Truth Revolt*, 11/29/2013, (http://www.truthrevolt.org/news/obamacare-victim-appears-fox-news-gets-irs-audit)

747 Kimberly A. Strassel, "IRS Targeting and 2014," *Wall Street Journal*, 1/16/2014 (http://online.wsj.com/news/articles/SB10001424052702304603704579324783339931114)

748 Michael Cieply and Nicholas Confessore, "Leaning Right in Hollywood, Under a Lens," *New York Times*, 1/22/2014

749 "'Not even a smidgen of corruption': Obama downplays IRS, other scandals," *Fox News*, 2/3/2014 (http://www.foxnews.com/politics/2014/02/03/not-even-smidgen-corruption-obama-downplays-irs-other-scandals/)

750 Staff Report, "Lois Lerner's Involvement in the IRS Targeting of Tax-Exempt Organizations," *Committee on Oversight and Government Reform*, 3/11/14 (http://oversight.house.gov/wp-content/uploads/2014/03/Lerner-Report1.pdf)

751 Katie Pavlich, "BREAKING: New Emails Show Lois Lerner Was in Contact With DOJ About Prosecuting Tax Exempt Groups," *Townhall*, 4/16/2014 (http://townhall.com/tipsheet/katiepavlich/2014/04/16/breaking-new-emails-show-lois-lerner-contacted-doj-about-prosecuting-tax-exempt-groups-n1825292)

752 Gregory Korte, "House holds former IRS official Lerner in contempt," *USA Today*, 5/7/2014 (http://www.usatoday.com/story/news/politics/2014/05/07/lois-lerner-contempt-of-congress/8815051/)

753 "The IRS Loses Lerner's Emails", *The Wall Street Journal, Review and Outlook*, 6/13/2014; (http://online.wsj.com/articles/the-irs-loses-lerners-emails-1402700540)

754 Allahpundit, "IRS Regulations Require E-Mails That are 'Federal Records' to be Stored in Separate, Permanent System", *Hot Air*, 6/17/2014; (http://hotair.com/archives/2014/06/17/irs-regulations-require-e-mails-that-are-federal-records-to-be-stored-in-separate-permanent-system/)

755 Patric Howley, "IRS CANCELLED Contract with Email-Storage Firm Weeks After Lerner's Computer Crash," *Breitbart*, 6/22/2014 (http://dailycaller.com/2014/06/22/irs-cancelled-contract-with-email-storage-firm-weeks-after-lerners-computer-crash/)

756 Dave Boyer, "Obama's 'phony' scandals line draws GOP retort," 7/25/2013 (http://www.washingtontimes.com/news/2013/jul/25/obamas-phony-scandals-line-draws-gop-retort/)

757 Mark Steyn, "Re: If Only Mitt Would Stop Preventing Us From Doing Our Jobs Sequel," *National Review Online – The Corner*, (http://www.nationalreview.com/corner/321063/re-if-only-mitt-would-stop-preventing-us-doing-our-jobs-sequel-mark-steyn#)

758 Colleen Curry, "Lawyers Rally in Defense of Anti-Muslim Filmaker," *ABC News*, 10/05/2012, (http://abcnews.go.com/US/jailed-anti-muslim-filmmaker-support-free-speech-lawyers/story?id=17397897)

759 "California Man Behind anti-Muslim Video Sentenced to Prison," *The Associated Press*, 11/07/2012, (http://www.foxnews.com/entertainment/2012/11/07/california-man-behind-anti-muslim-film-sentenced-to-prison/)

760 "Gov't Says Wood is Illegal if U.S. Workers Produce It," *Gibson Guitar: Press release*, 08/25/2011, (http://www.gibson.com/absolutenm/templates/FeatureTemplatePressRelease.aspx?articleid=1340&zoneid=6)

761 *Ibid.*

762 Victor Keith, "What Gibson Guitars Did with the Wood the Government Returned," *American Thinker*, 2/2/2014 (http://www.americanthinker.com/blog/2014/02/what_gibson_guitars_did_with_the_wood_the_government_returned.html)

763 Anthony Martin, "Federal Raid on Gibson Guitars – Retaliatory Harassment?," *Examiner*, 08/29/2011, (http://www.examiner.com/article/federal-raid-on-gibson-guitars-retaliatory-harassment)

764 Becket Adams, "Feds Drop Case After Gibson Guitar Agrees to Pay $300k Penalty," *The Blaze*, 08/06/2012, (http://www.theblaze.com/stories/2012/08/06/feds-drop-case-after-gibson-guitars-agrees-to-pay-300k-penalty/)

765 Victor Keith, "What Gibson Guitars Did with the Wood the Government Returned," *American Thinker*, 2/2/2014 (http://www.americanthinker.com/blog/2014/02/what_gibson_guitars_did_with_the_wood_the_government_returned.html)

766 Elizabeth White, "Obama Says Gitmo Facility Should Close," *Washington Post*, 6/24/2007, (http://www.washingtonpost.com/wp-dyn/content/article/2007/06/24/AR2007062401046_pf.html)

767 Michael McAuliff, "Indefinite Detention Ruling Backed by Civil Liberties Groups," *Huffington Post*, 9/13/2012, (http://www.huffingtonpost.com/2012/09/13/indefinite-detention-national-defense-authorization-act-ndaa_n_1880315.html)

768 Michael McAuliff, "Indefinite Detention Ban Stayed by Appeals Judge in NDAA Case," *Huffington Post*, 09/18/2012, (http://www.huffingtonpost.com/2012/09/18/indefinite-detention-ban-_n_1893652.html)

769 Charlie Savage, "U.S. Tries to Make It Easier to Wiretap the Internet," *New York Times*, 09/27/2012, (http://www.nytimes.com/2010/09/27/us/27wiretap.html)

770 Peter Yost, "Federal Surveillance Rises Sharply Under Obama," *Associated Press*, 10/01/2012, (http://www.washingtonguardian.com/big-brother-listening)

771 David Kravets, "Feds Say Mobile-Phone Location Data Not 'Constitutionally Protected'," *Wired*, 9/5/2012, (http://www.wired.com/threatlevel/2012/09/feds-say-mobile-phone-location-data-not-constitutionally-protected/)

772 Julia Angwin, "U.S. Terrorism Agency to Tap a Vast Database of Citizens," *Wall Street Journal*, 12/13/2012, (http://online.wsj.com/article/SB10001424127887324478304578171623040640006.html)

773 "JW Obtains Records Detailing Obama administration's Warrantless Collection of Citizens' Personal Financial Data," *Judicial Watch*, 6/27/2013 (http://www.judicialwatch.org/press-room/press-releases/jw-obtains-records-detailing-obama-administrations-warrantless-collection-of-citizens-personal-financial-data/)

774 Richard Pollock, "CFPB's data-mining on consumer credit cards challenged in heated House hearing," *Washington Examiner*, 9/13/2013 (http://washingtonexaminer.com/cfpbs-data-mining-on-consumer-credit-cards-challenged-in-heated-house-hearing/article/2535726)

775 Richard Pollock, "Federal Consumer Bureau Data-Mining Hundreds of Millions of Consumer Credit Card Accounts, Mortgages", *Washington Examiner*, 1/28/2014, (http://washingtonexaminer.com/federal-consumer-bureau-data-mining-hundreds-of-millions-of-consumer-credit-card-accounts-mortgages/article/2543039)

776 Dave Levinthal, "Obama's 2012 campaign is watching you," *Politico*, 3/16/2012, (http://www.politico.com/news/stories/0312/74095.html)

777 Ethan Roeder, "I Am Not Big Brother," *New York Times*, 12/5/2012, (http://www.nytimes.com/2012/12/06/opinion/i-am-not-big-brother.html)

778 Ed Lasky, "Big Brother Obama is Watching," *American Thinker*, 03/17/2012, (http://www.americanthinker.com/blog/2012/03/big_brother_obama_is_watching.html)

779 Kara Brandeisky, "The Surveillance Reforms Obama Supported Before He Was President", *Pro Publica*, August 7, 2013; http://www.propublica.org/article/the-surveillance-reforms-obama-supported-before-he-was-president

780 James Risen, "Obama's Wiretapping Stand Enrages Many Supporters", *The New York Times*, July 2, 2008, http://www.nytimes.com/2008/07/02/world/americas/02iht-obama.1.14161755.html?_r=0

781 Glenn Greenwald, "NSA Collecting Phone Records of Millions of Verizon Customers Daily", *The Guardian*, June 5th, 2013; http://www.thedailybeast.com/articles/2013/06/07/nsa-surveillance-program-explained-here-s-why-we-re-freaking-out.html

782 Siobhan Gorman, Evan Perez and Janet Hook, "U.S. Collects Vast Data Trove", *The Wall Street Journal*, June 7, 2013; http://online.wsj.com/news/articles/SB10001424127887324299104578529112289298922

783 Barton Gellman and Laura Poitras, "U.S., British Intelligence Mining Data from Nine U.S. Internet Companies in Broad Secret Program", *The Washington Post*, June 6th, 2013; http://www.washingtonpost.com/investigations/us-intelligence-mining-data-from-nine-us-internet-companies-in-broad-secret-program/2013/06/06/3a0c0da8-cebf-11e2-8845-d970ccb04497_story_2.html

784 *Ibid.*

785 The Editorial Board, "President Obama's Dragnet," *New York Times*, 6/6/2013 (http://www.nytimes.com/2013/06/07/opinion/president-obamas-dragnet.html)

786 "Judge deals blow to NSA phone data program," *Fox News*, 12/17/2013 (http://www.foxnews.com/politics/2013/12/17/judge-deals-nsa-defeat-on-bulk-phone-collection/)

787 Greta Van Susteren, "OBAMA ADMINISTRATION has some EXPLAINING TO DO," *Gretawire*, 1/16/2014 (http://gretawire.foxnewsinsider.com/2014/01/16/obama-administration-and-new-york-times-have-some-explaining-to-do/?dtoc)

788 Ajit Pai, "The FCC Wades Into the Newsroom", *The Wall Street Journal*, 2/10/2014; http://online.wsj.com/news/articles/SB10001424052702304680904579366903828260732

789 Michael Hausam, "First Amendment Victory! FCC Pulls Plug on News Monitoring Program", *Independent Journal Review*, 2/21/2014, http://www.ijreview.com/2014/02/116865-breaking-fcc-pulls-proposed-monitoring-program/

790 Bob Woodward, "Obama's Sequester Deal-Changer," *The Washington Post*, 02/22/2013, (http://articles.washingtonpost.com/2013-02-22/opinions/37238840_1_jack-lew-treasury-secretary-rob-nabors)

791 Brett LoGiurato, "Bob Woodward: A 'Very Senior' White House Person Warned Me I'd 'Regret' What I'm Doing," *Business Insider*, 02/27/2013, (http://www.businessinsider.com/bob-woodward-obama-sequester-white-house-reporting-price-politics-2013-2)

792 Maureen Callahan, "Beat the Pres," *New York Post*, 03/03/2013, (http://www.nypost.com/p/news/opinion/opedcolumnists/beat_the_press_96IFrUNync5zuBZTiZ6aUL)

793 Ron Fournier, "Why Bob Woodward's Fight With the White House Matters to You," *National Journal*, 02/28/2013, (http://www.nationaljournal.com/politics/why-bob-woodward-s-fight-with-the-white-house-matters-to-you-20130228)

794 "WMAL Exclusive: Woodward's Not Alone – Fmr. Clinton Aide Davis Says He Received White House Threat," *WMAL AM 630*, 02/28/2013, (http://www.wmal.com/common/page.php?pt=WMAL+EXCLUSIVE%3A+Woodward%27s+Not+Alone+-+Fmr.+Clinton+Aide+Davis+Says+He+Received+White+House+Threat&id=8924&is_corp=0)

795 "Transparency and Open Government," The White House, (http://www.whitehouse.gov/the_press_office/TransparencyandOpenGovernment)

796 Margaret Sullivan, "Leak Investigations Are an Assault on the Press, and on Democracy, Too," *New York Times*, 5/14/2013 (http://publiceditor.blogs.nytimes.com/2013/05/14/leak-investigations-are-an-assault-on-the-press-and-on-democracy-too/)

797 Mark Sherman, "Gov't Obtains Wide AP Phone Records in Probe", *Associated Press*, 5/13/2013 (http://www.ap.org/Content/AP-In-The-News/2013/Govt-obtains-wide-AP-phone-records-in-probe)

798 *Ibid.*

799 Mackenzie Weinger, "AP boss: Sources won't talk anymore," *Politico*, 6/19/2013 (http://www.politico.com/story/2013/06/ap-sources-93054.html)

800 Ann E. Marimow, "A rare peek into a Justice Department leak probe," *Washington Post*, 5/19/2013 (http://www.washingtonpost.com/local/a-rare-peek-into-a-justice-department-leak-probe/2013/05/19/0bc473de-be5e-11e2-97d4-a479289a31f9_story.html)

801 Michael Isikoff, "DOJ confirms Holder OK'd search warrant for Fox News reporter's emails," *NBC News*, 5/27/2013 (http://investigations.nbcnews.com/_news/2013/05/23/18451142-doj-confirms-holder-okd-search-warrant-for-fox-news-reporters-emails)

802 Michael Barone, "Michael Barone: More than all past presidents, Obama uses 1917 Espionage Act to go after reporters," *Washington Examiner*, 5/22/2013 (http://washingtonexaminer.com/michael-barone-more-than-all-past-presidents-obama-uses-1917-espionage-act-to-go-after-reporters/article/2530340)

803 "The Obama administration and the Press," *Committee to Protect Journalists*, 10/10/2013, (http://cpj.org/reports/2013/10/obama-and-the-press-us-leaks-surveillance-post-911.php)

804 *Ibid.*

805 Andre Tartar, "David Axelrod Talks with John Heilmann: A Constitutional Amendment to Overturn Citizens United?," *New York Magazine*, 06/12/2012, (http://nymag.com/daily/intel/2012/06/david-axelrod-on-how-to-overturn-citizens-united.html)

806 "U.S. Supreme Court: Citizens United v Federal Election Commission"; 12/21/2010, PDF Document retrieved from http://www.supremecourt.gov/opinions/09pdf/08-205.pdf

807 Eugene Volokh, "The 'People's Rights Amendment' and the Media," *The Volokh Conspiracy*, 4/26/2012, (http://www.volokh.com/2012/04/26/the-peoples-rights-amendment-and-the-media/)

808 Julian Pecquet, "Health Plans Ordered to Cover Birth Control Without Co-Pays," *The Hill*, 01/20/2012, (http://thehill.com/blogs/healthwatch/health-reform-implementation/205413-obama-administration-orders-health-plans-to-cover-birth-control-without-co-pays)

809 "HHS Mandate Information Central," *The Becket Fund*, (http://www.becketfund.org/hhsinformationcentral/)

810 "Attorney: Hobby Lobby to Defy Morning-After Pill Insurance Requirement While Lawsuit is Pending," *Associated Press*, 12/27/2012, (http://www.newser.com/article/da3ee7s01/attorney-hobby-lobby-to-defy-morning-after-pill-insurance-requirement-while-lawsuits-pending.html)

811 Rick Ungar, "Here Are The 23 Executive Orders On Gun Safety Signed Today By The President," *Forbes*, 1/16/2013; (http://www.forbes.com/sites/rickungar/2013/01/16/here-are-the-23-executive-orders-on-gun-safety-signed-today-by-the-president/)

812 Dean Chambers, "State leaders resist President Obama's new gun control regulations," *Examiner*, 01/17/2013 (http://www.examiner.com/article/state-leaders-resist-president-obama-s-new-gun-control-regulations)

813 AWR Hawkins, "Obama Uses Executive Actions To Bypass Congress on Gun Control Again," *Breitbart*, 8/29/2013; (http://www.breitbart.com/big-government/2013/08/29/obama-uses-executive-actions-to-bypass-congress-enact-more-gun-control/)

814 Fred Lucas, "Obama administration's Two Quiet New Executive Actions on Who Can Buy a Gun," *The Blaze*, 1/3/2014; (http://www.theblaze.com/stories/2014/01/03/obama-administrations-two-quiet-new-executive-actions-on-who-can-buy-a-gun/)

815 Paul Bedard, "Obama to Ban Bullets by Executive Action, Threatens Top-Selling AR-15 Rifle", *The Washington Examiner*, 2/27/2015, (http://www.washingtonexaminer.com/article/2560750)

816 Mary Katherine Ham, "ATF on Proposed AR15 Ammo Ban: Nevermind, for Now", *Hot Air*, 3/10/2015; (http://hotair.com/archives/2015/03/10/atf-on-proposed-ar15-ammo-ban-nevermind-for-now/)

817 "Obama Issues Executive Actions on Guns" NRA-ILA, 1/8/2016; (https://www.nraila.org/articles/20160108/obama-issues-executive-actions-on-guns)

818 Charlotte Davis, "Reconciliation and Obamacare A 'Bad Mix,'" *The Foundry*, 2/8/2010, (http://dailysignal.com/2010/02/18/reconciliation-and-obamacare-a-"bad-mix")

819 Ray Locker, "Republican's Health Vote a 'Decision of Conscience'," *USA Today*, 11/09/2009, (http://usatoday30.usatoday.com/news/washington/2009-11-08-cao-votes-yes-for-health-bill_N.htm)

820 Richard Pollack, "Groups led by inside trader, child abuser got Obamacare co-op loans," *Washington Examiner*, 4/3/2013, (http://washingtonexaminer.com/groups-led-by-inside-trader-child-abuser-got-obamacare-co-op-loans/article/2526140)

821 *Ibid.*

822 Richard Pollack, "Failed Iowa entrepreneur awarded $112 million for Obamacare co-ops," *Washington Examiner*, 3/26/2013, (http://washingtonexaminer.com/failed-iowa-entrepreneur-awarded-112-million-for-obamacare-co-ops/article/2525456)

823 Richard Pollack, "U.S. gave troubled Florida firm $129 million for new Ohio Obamacare health insurance cooperative," *Washington Examiner*, 3/5/2013, (http://washingtonexaminer.com/u.s.-gave-troubled-florida-firm-129-million-for-new-ohio-obamacare-health-insurance-cooperative/article/2523337)

824 Richard Pollack, "Insurer with NY's 'worst' record of complaints gets $340M Obamacare loan," *Examiner*, 2/21/2013, (http://washingtonexaminer.com/obama-ally-got-340-million-to-set-up-health-care-co-ops/article/2522229)

825 Rep. Phil Roe, M.D., "CO-OP failures put spotlight on ACA's many shortcomings," *The Hill*, 1/14/2016, (http://thehill.com/special-reports/healthcare-january-14-2016/265827-co-op-failures-put-spotlight-on-acas-many)

826 Eric Pianin., "More Bad News for the Remaining Obamacare Co-ops," *Fiscal Times*, 3/18/2016, (http://www.thefiscaltimes.com/2016/03/18/More-Bad-News-Remaining-Obamacare-Co-ops)

827 Dan Mangan, "President: 7.1 million enrolled in Obamacare," CNBC, 4/1/2014 (http://www.cnbc.com/id/101543801)

828 Guy Benson, "Confirmed: Many of Obamacare's 'Eight Million Enrollments' are Duplicates," *Townhall*, 5/7/2014 (http://townhall.com/tipsheet/guybenson/2014/05/07/confirmed-many-of-obamacares-8-million-enrollees-are-duplicates-n1834786)

829 Avik Roy, "RAND Comes Clean: Obamacare's Exchanges Enrolled Only 1.4 Million Previously Uninsured Individuals," *Forbes*, 4/9/2014 (http://www.forbes.com/sites/theapothecary/2014/04/09/rand-comes-clean-obamacares-exchanges-enrolled-only-1-4-million-previously-uninsured-individuals/)

830 Avik Roy, "New McKinsey Survey: 74% of Obamacare Sign-Ups Were Previously Insured", *Forbes*, 5/10/2014, (http://www.forbes.com/sites/theapothecary/2014/05/10/new-mckinsey-survey-74-of-obamacare-sign-ups-were-previously-insured/)

831 "Report: Obamacare contractors paid to do nothing," *CBS News*, 5/14/2014 (http://www.cbsnews.com/news/report-obamacare-contractors-paid-to-do-nothing/)

832 Sarah Hurtubise, "Yet Another Obamacare Contractor Office Paid to do Nothing," *Daily Caller*, 5/20/2014 (http://dailycaller.com/2014/05/20/yet-another-obamacare-contractor-office-paid-to-do-nothing/)

833 Bill Allison, "Good enough for government work? The contractors building Obamacare," *Sunlight Foundation*, 10/9/2013 (http://sunlightfoundation.com/blog/2013/10/09/aca-contractors/)

834 Akash Chougule, "White House Hired Sham Foreign Company for Obamacare, Employees 'Do Nothing'," *The Blaze*, 5/22/2014, (http://www.theblaze.com/contributions/white-house-hired-sham-foreign-company-for-obamacare-employees-do-nothing/)

835 David Morgan "U.S. administration defends Obamacare contractor after UK probe," Reuters, 7/16/2013 (http://www.reuters.com/article/2013/07/16/us-usa-healthcare-serco-idUSBRE96F18J20130716)

836 Brett Norman and David Nather, "Obamacare delay sparks new mandate fight," *Politico*, 2/10/2014 (http://www.politico.com/story/2014/02/obamacare-employer-mandate-delay-103338.html)

837 James Taranto, "OmertàCare," *Wall Street Journal*, 2/12/2014 (http://online.wsj.com/news/articles/SB10001424052702304888404579378833508471324)

838 Chris Stirewalt, "Thought Police: Firms must swear ObamaCare not a factor in firings," *Fox News*, 2/11/2014 (http://www.foxnews.com/politics/2014/02/11/thought-police-firms-must-swear-obamacare-not-factor-in-firings/)

839 Sam Baker, "HHS finalizes over 1,200 waivers under healthcare reform law," *The Hill*, 01/06/12, (http://thehill.com/blogs/healthwatch/health-reform-implementation/202791-hhs-finalizes-more-than-1200-healthcare-waivers)

840 Paul Conner, "Labor unions primary recipients of Obamacare waivers," *Daily Caller*, 1/6/2012, (http://dailycaller.com/2012/01/06/labor-unions-primary-recipients-of-obamacare-waivers/)

841 Charlie Spierling, "Interior Secretary nominee Sally Jewell received Obamacare waiver for REI," *Washington Examiner*, 2/7/2013, (http://washingtonexaminer.com/interior-secretary-nominee-sally-jewell-received-obamacare-waiver-for-rei/article/2520821)

842 Rebecca Riffkin, "Cost Still a Barrier Between Americans and Medical Care", *Gallup*, 11/28/2014; (http://www.gallup.com/poll/179774/cost-barrier-americans-medical-care.aspx)

843 *Ibid.*

844 Lori Montgomery and Shailagh Murray, " In Deal With Stupak, White House Announces Executive Order on Abortion" *Washington Post*, 3/21/10 (http://voices.washingtonpost.com/44/2010/03/white-house-announces-executiv.html)

845 Rep. Bart Stupak Announces His Retirement After Health Care Controversy, *Fox News*, 4/09/10 (http://www.foxnews.com/politics/2010/04/09/rep-bart-stupak-retire/)

846 Caroline May, "$1 abortion surcharge in Obamacare," *Daily Caller*, 3/13/2012 (http://dailycaller.com/2012/03/13/1-abortion-premium-in-obamacare/)

847 Sean Higgins, "Bart Stupak: 'Perplexed and disappointed' that White House undid Obamacare abortion compromise," *Washington Examiner*, 9/5/2012 (http://washingtonexaminer.com/bart-stupak-perplexed-and-disappointed-that-white-house-undid-obamacare-abortion-compromise/article/2507073)

848 Rep. Steve Stockman (StockmanSenate). "Remember, when Republicans suggested delaying ObamaCare because the site doesn't work Democrats called that 'terrorism' and shut down govt." 10/21/2013, 9:45 PM. Tweet.

849 Ian Schwartz, "Howard Dean: I Wonder If Obama Has 'The Legal Authority' To Fix Obamacare," *Real Clear Politics*, 11/14/2013 (http://www.realclearpolitics.com/video/2013/11/14/howard_dean_i_wonder_if_obama_has_the_legal_authority_to_fix_obamacare.html)

850 Eugene Kontorovich, "The Obamacare 'Fix' Is Illegal," *Politico*, 11/23/2013 (http://www.politico.com/magazine/story/2013/11/the-obamacare-fix-is-illegal-100254.html)

851 John Yoo, "ObamaCare debacle much worse for constitution, presidency than Katrina was for Bush," *FoxNews*, 11/21/2013 (http://www.foxnews.com/opinion/2013/11/21/obamacare-is-no-katrina-it-much-worse/)

852 John Hayward, "Obama threatens to veto the measure he just called for," *Breitbart*, 11/14/2013 (http://www.breitbart.com/InstaBlog/2013/11/14/Obama-threatens-to-veto-the-measure-he-just-called-for)

853 John Fund, "Who Says Obama Hasn't United the Country?" *The Corner*, 12/20/2013 (http://www.nationalreview.com/corner/366828/who-says-obama-hasnt-united-country-john-fund)

854 Juliet Eilperin and Amy Goldstein, "White House delays health insurance mandate for medium-sized employers until 2016," *Washington Post*, 2/10/2014 (http://www.washingtonpost.com/national/health-science/white-house-delays-health-insurance-mandate-for-medium-sized-employers-until-2016/2014/02/10/ade6b344-9279-11e3-84e1-27626c5ef5fb_story.html)

855 Elise Viebeck, "New O-Care Delay to Help Midterm Dems", *The Hill*, 3/3/2014; http://thehill.com/blogs/healthwatch/health-reform-implementation/199784-new-obamacare-delay-to-help-midterm-dems

856 Ian Schwartz, "Turley: Obama's 'Become The Very Danger The Constitution Was Designed To Avoid'," *Real Clear Politics*, 12/4/2013 (http://www.realclearpolitics.com/video/2013/12/04/turley_obamas_become_the_very_danger_the_constitution_was_designed_to_avoid.html)

857 Paige Winfield Cunningham, "Threats, Deals Got Drug Companies on Board With Obama," *Washington Times*, 05/31/2012, (http://www.washingtontimes.com/news/2012/may/31/threats-deals-got-drug-companies-on-board-with-oba)

858 The White House. Transparency and Open Government. Retrieved from http://www.whitehouse.gov/the_press_office/TransparencyandOpenGovernment

859 Kim Palmer, "Cleveland Clinic announces job cuts to prepare for Obamacare," *Reuters*, 9/18/2013 (http://www.reuters.com/article/2013/09/18/us-usa-health-clevelandclinic-idUSBRE98H14V20130918)

860 Paul Davidson and Barbara Hansen, "A job engine sputters as hospitals cut staff," *USA Today*, 10/13/2013 (http://www.usatoday.com/story/money/business/2013/10/13/hospital-job-cuts/2947929/)

861 Sarah Hurtubise, "Fourth Georgia hospital closes due to Obamacare payment cuts," *Daily Caller*, 2/18/2014 (http://dailycaller.com/2014/02/18/fourth-georgia-hospital-closes-due-to-obamacare-payment-cuts/)

862 Cheryl K Chumley, "New York Doctors Flee ObamaCare: 'I Plan to Retire'", *The Washington Times*, 10/29/2013; http://www.washingtontimes.com/news/2013/oct/29/new-york-doctors-flee-obamacare-i-plan-retire/

863 Chip Reid, "Obama Reneges on Health Care Transparency," *CBS News*, 01/07/2010, (http://www.cbsnews.com/8301-18563_162-6064298.html)

864 Patrick Howly, "Obamacare Architect: Lack of Transparency Was Key Because 'Stupidity Of The American Voter' Would Have Killed Obamacare," *Daily Caller*, 11/9/2014; (http://dailycaller.com/2014/11/09/obamacare-architect-lack-of-transparency-was-key-because-stupidity-of-the-american-voter-would-have-killed-obamacare/)

865 Jeffrey Young, "Health Care Costs To Exceed A Record $20,000 Per Year For Families With Insurance, Study Says," *Huffington Post*, 5/15/12, (http://www.huffingtonpost.com/2012/05/15/health-care-costs-record_n_1516380.html)

866 Kathryn Smith, "Businesses Brace For Health Care Cost Increase, Report Says," *Politico*, 8/8/12, (http://www.politico.com/news/stories/0812/79494.html)

867 Byron Tau, "Papa John's: 'Obamacare' will raise pizza prices," *Politico*, 8/7/2012, (http://www.politico.com/politico44/2012/08/papa-johns-obamacare-will-raise-pizza-prices-131331.html)

868 Janean Chun, "John Metz, Denny's Franchisee And Hurricane Grill & Wings Owner, Imposes Surcharge For Obamacare," *Huffington Post*, 11/14/2012, (http://www.huffingtonpost.com/2012/11/13/john-metz-hurricane-grill-wings-dennys_n_2122412.html)

869 2012 Annual Report Of The Boards Of Trustees Of The Federal Hospital Insurance And Federal Supplementary Medical Insurance Trust Funds," *Social Security & Medicare Trustees Report*

870 Ricardo Alonso-Zaldivar, "Medicare Official Doubts Health Care Law Savings," *Associated Press*, 1/26/11, (http://www.nbcnews.com/id/41277495/ns/health-health_care/t/medicare-official-doubts-health-care-law-savings)

871 Stephen Ohlemacher, "Finances look worse for Medicare, Social Security," *Associated Press*, 5/14/11, (http://usatoday30.usatoday.com/news/topstories/2011-05-13-2916218767_x.htm)

872 "The GOP's New York Spanking," *Wall Street Journal*, 5/26/11, (http://online.wsj.com/article/SB10001424052702304520804576345442590223566.html)

873 Editorial, "Return Control To The Patient," *The Tampa Tribune*, 10/15/11, (http://www2.tbo.com/news/opinion/2011/oct/15/meopino1-return-control-to-the-patient-ar-272052/)

874 Julie Reiskin, "The wrong way to fix Medicare spending," *Denver Post*, 5/5/2011, (http://www.denverpost.com/opinion/ci_17993137)

875 Steve Gelsi, "Boeing Cutting 30% of Executives at Defense Unit," *Marketwatch*, 11/2/2012; (http://www.marketwatch.com/story/boeing-cutting-30-of-executives-at-defense-unit-2012-11-07)

876 Kavita Kumar, "Energizer to Slash Workforce by 10 Percent, Close Three Factories," *St Louis Post-Dispatch*, 11/08/2012; (http://www.stltoday.com/business/local/energizer-to-slash-workforce-by-percent-close-three-factories/article_2a72c60e-29e8-5a71-94c9-2d4a3b34a0fe.html)

877 Steven Mufson, "After Obama Reelection, Murray Energy CEO Reads Prayer, Announces Layoffs," *Washington Post*, November 9, 2012, (http://articles.washingtonpost.com/2012-11-09/business/35505834_1_coal-slurry-prayer-web-site)

878 Henry Blodget, "Exclusive: Layoffs at Groupon," *Business Insider*, 11/08/2012, (http://www.businessinsider.com/groupon-layoffs-2012-11)

879 Scott Sloan, "Stanford Brake to Layoff 75," *Lexington Herald-Leader*, 11/07/2012, (http://www.kentucky.com/2012/11/07/2398967/brake-company-in-stanford-laying.html)

880 Gregory J. Wilcox, "Updated: Rocketdyne Lays Off 100 – Mostly in San Fernando Valley," *LA Daily News*, 11/08/2012, (http://www.dailynews.com/business/ci_21952197/rocketdyne-lays-off-100-mostly-san-fernando-valley)

881   Paul Bedard, "Jobs shock: Mass layoffs at 3-year high," *Washington Examiner*, 1/2/2013 (http://washingtonexaminer.com/jobs-shock-mass-layoffs-at-3-year-high/article/2517456#.UOY377njk44)

882   Neil Shirley, "Shirley: Medical Device Tax Will Impact Jobs and Costs," *Ventura County Star*, 10/27/2012, (http://www.vcstar.com/news/2012/oct/27/shirley-medical-device-tax-will-impact-jobs-and/)

883 Stephen Dinan, "Obamacare will push 2 million workers out of labor market: CBO," *Washington Times*, 2/4/2014 (http://www.washingtontimes.com/news/2014/feb/4/cbo-obamacare-push-2m-workers-out-labor-market/)

884   Dan Mangan, "99% of Obamacare applications hit a wall," *CNBC*, 10/4/2013 (http://www.cnbc.com/id/101087965)

885   Devin Dwyer, "Memo Reveals Only 6 People Signed Up for Obamacare on First Day," *ABC News*, October 31, 2013, (http://abcnews.go.com/blogs/politics/2013/10/memo-reveals-only-6-people-signed-up-for-obamacare-on-first-day/)

886 "Less Than Half of One Percent of HealthCare.gov Visitors Complete Obamacare Enrollment," *Breitbart*, October 16, 2013, (http://www.breitbart.com/Big-Government/2013/10/16/one-half-one-percent-obamacare-enrollment)

887   Joe Johns and Z. Byron Wolf, "First on CNN: Obama administration warned about health care website," *CNN*, October 30, 2013 (http://www.cnn.com/2013/10/29/politics/obamacare-warning/)

888   Elizabeth Harrington, "Obama administration Knew of Healthcare.gov Security Risks Before Launch," *Free Beacon*, 12/19/2013 (http://freebeacon.com/obama-admin-knew-of-healthcare-gov-security-risks-before-launch/)

889   Staryl Attkisson, "High security risk found after HealthCare.gov launch," *CBS News*, 12/20/2013 (http://www.cbsnews.com/news/high-security-risks-found-after-healthcaregov-launch/)

890 Associated Press, "Obamacare site can't handle it when you have a baby," *New York Post*, 1/3/2014 (http://nypost.com/2014/01/03/adding-a-baby-to-obamacare-plan-not-easy/)

891 Patrick Howley, "Michelle Obama's Princeton classmate is executive at company that built Obamacare website," *Daily Caller*, 10/25/2013 (http://dailycaller.com/2013/10/25/michelle-obamas-princeton-classmate-is-executive-at-company-that-built-obamacare-website/)

892 Avik Roy, "Obama Officials In 2010: 93 Million Americans Will Be Unable To Keep Their Health Plans Under Obamacare," *Forbes*, 10/31/2013 (http://www.forbes.com/sites/theapothecary/2013/10/31/obama-officials-in-2010-93-million-americans-will-be-unable-to-keep-their-health-plans-under-obamacare/)

893 "Reid hammered by GOP after claiming all ObamaCare 'horror stories' untrue," *Fox News*, 2/27/2014 (http://www.foxnews.com/politics/2014/02/27/reid-hammered-by-gop-after-claiming-all-obamacare-horror-stories-untrue/)

894 Sarah Kliff, "If You Like Your Health Plan, You Might Lose It. Again.", *Vox*, 4/24/2014; (http://www.vox.com/2014/4/24/5641356/if-you-like-your-health-plan-you-might-lose-it-again)

895   Alexis Levinson, "Poll: If voters had known they'd lose insurance, Romney would have won" *Daily Caller*, 11/22/2013 (http://dailycaller.com/2013/11/22/poll-if-voters-had-known-theyd-lose-insurance-romney-would-have-won/)

896   Neil Munro, "Obama denies 'you can keep it' videotaped promises," *Daily Caller*, 11/5/2013 (http://dailycaller.com/2013/11/05/obama-denies-you-can-keep-it-videotaped-promises/)

897   Noel Sheppard, "CNN: White House Pressuring Insurance Companies to Not Criticize ObamaCare," *Newsbusters*, 10/29/2013 (http://newsbusters.org/blogs/noel-sheppard/2013/10/30/cnn-white-house-pressuring-insurance-companies-not-criticize-obamacar)

898   Larry O'Connor, "White House Bullied Beckel For Backing Obamacare Delay," *Breitbart*, 10/24/2013 (http://www.breitbart.com/Big-Journalism/2013/10/24/White-House-Bullied-Beckel-For-Backing-Obamacare-Delay)

899 "Students suffer ObamaCare sticker shock as premiums soar, plans get cut," *FoxNews*, 11/18/2013 (http://www.foxnews.com/politics/2013/11/18/students-suffer-sticker-shock-from-obamacare/)

900 Andrew Adams, "New health care law makes finding cancer coverage difficult, family says," *KSL.com*, 11/29/2013 (http://www.ksl.com/?sid=27834668)

901 Lucy McCalmont, "A health care 'success story' that isn't," *Politico*, 11/19/13 (http://www.politico.com/story/2013/11/jessica-sanford-obamacare-100046.html)

902 Angie Drobnic Holan, "Lie of the Year: If you like your health care plan you can keep it' 12/12/2013 (http://www.politifact.com/truth-o-meter/article/2013/dec/12/lie-year-if-you-like-your-health-care-plan-keep-it/)

903 "An Analysis of Health Insurance Premiums Under the Patient Protection and Affordable Care Act," *Congressional Budget Office*, 11/30/2009, (http://www.cbo.gov/publication/41792)

904 Aimee Picchi, "For some, Obamacare deductibles deliver sticker shock," *CBS News*, 12/9/2013 (http://www.cbsnews.com/news/obamacare-deductibles-deliver-hefty-sticker-shock/)

905 Patrick Howly, "Obama Adviser Jonathan Gruber In 2009: Obamacare Will NOT Be Affordable," *Daily Caller*, 12/30/2014; (http://dailycaller.com/2014/12/30/obama-adviser-jonathan-gruber-in-2009-obamacare-will-not-be-affordable/)

906 "Review and Outlook: Its Up to the Voters, Now," *Wall Street Journal*, 07/02/2012, (http://online.wsj.com/article/SB10001424052702304782404577490842520348690.html)

907 Kate Pavlich, "Obama: I Have Not Raised Taxes," Townhall, 09/24/2012, (http://townhall.com/tipsheet/katiepavlich/2012/09/24/obama_i_have_not_raised_taxes)

908 Alyene Senger and John Fleming, "ObamaCare's 18 New Tax Hikes," *Heritage Foundation*, 08/20/2012, (http://blog.heritage.org/2012/08/20/obamacares-18-new-tax-hikes/)

909 Qassim Adbul-Zahra, "Al-Qaeda Making Comeback in Iraq, Officials Say," *The Associated Press*, 10/09/2012; (http://www.usatoday.com/story/news/world/2012/10/09/al-qaeda-iraq/1623297/)

910 Jill Dougherty, "European Official: Al-Qaeda Threat in Northern Africa 'Spreading'," *CNN*, 10/03/2012; (http://security.blogs.cnn.com/2012/10/03/al-qaeda-threat-in-northern-africa-spreading/)

911 Bridget Johnson, "General Tells Senators al-Qaeda Has 'Grown Fourfold in Last Five Years'" *PJ Media*, 1/27/2015; (http://pjmedia.com/tatler/2015/01/27/general-tells-senators-al-qaeda-has-grown-fourfold-in-last-five-years/)

912 Bridget Johnson, "General Tells Senators al-Qaeda Has 'Grown Fourfold in Last Five Years'" *PJ Media*, 1/27/2015; (http://pjmedia.com/tatler/2015/01/27/general-tells-senators-al-qaeda-has-grown-fourfold-in-last-five-years/)

913 Rowan Scarborough, "Bush Policies he Reviled are Crux of Obama's Arsenal," *Washington Times*, 05/15/2012, (http://www.washingtontimes.com/news/2012/may/15/bush-policies-he-reviled-part-of-obamas-arsenal/)

914 "Administration Reportedly Works Against Resolution to Recognize Deaths," *Politifact*, 03/05/2010, (http://www.politifact.com/truth-o-meter/promises/obameter/promise/511/recognize-armenian-genocide/)

915 Nile Gardiner, "The U-Turn President: Barack Obama's Top Ten Flip Flops," *Telegraph*, 04/11/2011, (http://blogs.telegraph.co.uk/news/nilegardiner/100083104/the-u-turn-president-barack-obama-top-ten-flip-flops/)

916 "Flashback: Obama Calls Mubarak's Egypt 'Stallwart ally,' 'Force for Good," *Breitbart*, 09/13/2012, (http://www.breitbart.com/Breitbart-TV/2012/09/13/Flashback-Obama-Calls-Mubaraks-Egypt-Stallwart-Ally-Force-For-Good)

917 CNN Wire Staff, "Obama Says Egypt's Transition 'Must Begin Now'," *CNN*, 02/02/2011, (http://www.cnn.com/2011/POLITICS/02/01/us.egypt.obama/index.html)

918 Stephen Brown, "Obama's Disappearance on Darfur," *Frontpage*, 08/03/2012, (http://frontpagemag.com/2012/stephenbrown/obama%E2%80%99s-disappearance-on-darfur/)

919 Jennifer Rubin, "Obama to Israel: Never Mind," *Washington Post*, 03/06/2012, (http://www.washingtonpost.com/blogs/right-turn/post/obama-to-israel-never-mind/2012/03/06/gIQA1T3BvR_blog.html)

920 Amy Davidson, "John Brennan's Kill List," *The New Yorker*, 01/07/2013, (http://www.newyorker.com/online/blogs/closeread/2013/01/john-brennans-kill-list.html)

921 "Brennan: Due Process Not Necessary to Kill Americans for Potential Future Actions," *Breitbart*, 02/07/2013, (http://www.breitbart.com/Breitbart-TV/2013/02/07/Brennan-Killing-Americans-Without-Due-Process-Not-Because-of-What-They-Did-But-What-They%20Might%20Do)

922 Steve Emerson, "John Brennan Wrong for CIA," *Newsmax*, 02/05/2013, (http://www.newsmax.com/Emerson/John-Brennan-Wrong-for-CIA/2013/02/05/id/489057)

923 *Ibid.*

924 "National Security Hawks Call for Brennan's Resignation," *Fox News*, 09/29/2010, (http://www.foxnews.com/politics/2010/09/29/national-security-hawks-brennans-resignation/)

925 Joel B. Pollak, "Brennan Breaks Record: Most 'No' Votes Ever for a CIA Director," *Breitbart*, 03/08/2013, (http://www.breitbart.com/Big-Peace/2013/03/08/Brennan-Breaks-Record-Most-No-Votes-Ever-for-CIA-Director)

926 Larry O'Conner, "Flashback: Obama Sent Three Representatives to Michael Brown Funeral", *Truth Revolt*, 1/12/2015; (http://www.truthrevolt.org/news/flashback-obama-sent-three-representatives-michael-brown-funeral)

927 Ashley Collman and David Martosko, "America Snubs Historic Paris Rally", *Daily Mail*, 1/11/2015; (http://www.dailymail.co.uk/news/article-2905678/America-snubs-historic-Paris-rally-Holder-skipped-early-Kerry-India-Obama-Biden-just-stayed-home-leave-no-U-S-presence-anti-terror-march-joined-global-leaders.html)

928 *Ibid.*

929 Patrick Howley, "'A PETULANT CHILD': Former Secret Service Agent Blasts Obama For Blaming Service For Skipping Paris March", *Daily Caller*, 1/13/2015; (http://dailycaller.com/2015/01/13/a-petulant-child-former-secret-service-agent-blasts-obama-for-blaming-service-for-skipping-paris-march/)

930 Neil Munro, "White House Slams French Cartoons, Amid Election-Time Threats From Islamists", *Daily Caller*, 9/19/2012; (http://dailycaller.com/2012/09/19/white-house-slams-french-cartoon-amid-election-time-threats-from-islamists/)

931 Katrina Trinko, "Obama: 'The Future Must Not Belong To Those Who Slander the Prophet of Islam'", *National Review*, 9/25/2015; (http://www.nationalreview.com/corner/328483/obama-future-must-not-belong-those-who-slander-prophet-islam-katrina-trinko)

932 Andrew McCarthy, "Why It's So Hard for Obama to Call Terrorism *Terrorism*", PJ Media, 1/7/2015; (http://pjmedia.com/andrewmccarthy/2015/01/07/why-its-so-hard-for-obama-to-call-terrorism-terrorism/)

933 The White House, Office of the Press Secretary. (2010). Remarks by President Obama and Prime Minister Cameron of the United Kingdom in Joint Press Availability [Press release]. Retrieved from http://www.whitehouse.gov/the-press-office/remarks-president-obama-and-prime-minister-cameron-united-kingdom-joint-press-avail

934 Jason Allardyce and Tony Allen-Mills, "Revealed: Document exposes US double-talk on Lockerbie," *Sunday Times*, 7/25/2010, (http://www.thesundaytimes.co.uk/sto/news/uk_news/National/article353568.ece)

935 Thom Shanker and Rick Gladstone, "Iran Fired on Military Drone in First Such Attack, U.S. Says," *New York Times*, 11/08/2012, (http://www.nytimes.com/2012/11/09/world/middleeast/pentagon-says-iran-fired-at-surveillance-drone-last-week.html)

936 "Iran Fired on U.S Drone Before Vote," *Wall Street Journal*, 11/09/2012, (http://online.wsj.com/article/SB10001424127887324439804578107191429662874.html)

937 "The Muslim Brotherhood," *Jewish Virtual Library*, accessed 12/30/2012, (http://www.jewishvirtuallibrary.org/jsource/Terrorism/muslimbrotherhood.html

938 "Muslim Brotherhood Envoys Met With White House Officials in DC," *Fox News*, 04/05/2012, (http://www.foxnews.com/politics/2012/04/05/muslim-brotherhood-envoys-met-with-white-house-officials-in-dc/)

939 Steve Emerson and John Rossomando, "A Red Carpet for Radicals at the White House," *IPT News*, 10/21/2012; (http://www.investigativeproject.org/3777/a-red-carpet-for-radicals-at-the-white-house)

940 Caroline May, "Obama Admin Unilaterally Changes Law to Immigrants with 'Limited' Terror Contacts into US", *The Daily Caller*, 2/5/14; http://dailycaller.com/2014/02/05/obama-admin-changes-immigration-law-allows-immigrants-who-supported-terrorists-into-us/

941 Patricia Zengerle, "U.S. Eases Rules to Admit More Syrian Refugees, After 31 Last Year", *Reuters*, 2/5/2014; http://www.reuters.com/article/2014/02/05/us-syria-crisis-usa-refugees-idUSBREA141ZQ20140205

942 Laura Koran, "Obama pledge to welcome 10,000 Syrian refugees far behind schedule" *CNN*, 4/1/2016; (http://www.cnn.com/2016/04/01/politics/obama-pledge-10000-syrian-refugees-falling-short/)

943 "Obama Administration Assures Governors Refugee Vetting Is Rigorous" *CBS New York*, 11/21/2015; (http://newyork.cbslocal.com/2015/11/21/united-states-syrian-refugee-vetting)

944 Daniel Greenfield, "1 In 4 Swedish Women will be Raped As Sexual Assaults Increase 500%", *Frontpage*, 1/29/2013; (http://www.frontpagemag.com/point/175434/1-4-swedish-women-will-be-raped-sexual-assaults-daniel-greenfield)

945 "Guide to nationalist parties challenging Europe", *BBC*, 5/23/2016; (http://www.bbc.com/news/world-europe-36130006)

946 Chuck Ross, "FBI Director Admits US Can't Vet All Syrian Refugees For Terror Ties ", *The Daily Caller*, 10/21/2015; (http://dailycaller.com/2015/10/21/fbi-director-admits-us-cant-vet-all-syrian-refugees-for-terror-ties-video/)

947 Matt Vespa, "31 States: North Dakota Joins Majority Of Governors Refusing To Relocate Syrian Refugees, Cites Security Concerns", *Townhall*, 11/18/2015; (http://townhall.com/tipsheet/mattvespa/2015/11/18/31-states-north-dakota-joins-majority-of-governors-refusing-to-relocate-syrian-refugees-cites-security-concerns-n2082522)

948 Jess Bravin and Gary Fields, "Terror Trial Likely to Leave New York City," *Wall Street Journal*, 01/30/2010, (http://online.wsj.com/article/SB10001424052748703389004575033000474040096.html)

949 Jason Ryan and Huma Khan, "In Reversal, Obama Orders Guantanamo Military Trial for 9/11 Mastermind Khalid Sheikh Mohammed'" *ABC*, 04/04/2011, (http://abcnews.go.com/Politics/911-mastermind-khalid-sheikh-mohammed-military-commission/story?id=13291750)

950 William Bigelow, "Report Faules Obama for Ignoring Persecution of Christians", *Breitbart*, 5/7/2014; (http://www.breitbart.com/national-security/2014/05/07/report-faults-obama-administration-for-ignoring-persecution-of-christians/)

951 Barbara Boland, "Pew Study: Christians are the World's Most Oppressed Religious Group", *CNS News*; 2/6/2014; (http://cnsnews.com/news/article/barbara-boland/pew-study-christians-are-world-s-most-oppressed-religious-group)

952 Jeremy Reynalds, "Sudan Bombings Kill More Nuba Christians Around Christmas," *Assist News Service*, 12/31/2012)(http://www.assistnews.net/STOS/2012/s12120143.htmRIE

953 Mark Salmon and Sean Duffy, "Religious Persecution in Pakistan", *National Review Online*, 6/17/14; (http://www.nationalreview.com/article/380554/religious-persecution-pakistan-matt-salmon-sean-duffy)

954 Daniel Greenfield, "Christian Refugee From Mosul Describes Being Forced Out by Muslim Neighbors, *FrontPage*, 8/12/2014; (http://www.frontpagemag.com/2014/dgreenfield/christian-refugee-from-mosul-describes-being-forced-out-by-muslim-neighbors-video/)

955 Todd Starnes, "Team Obama Wins Fight to Have Christian Home-School Family Deported", *Fox News*, 3/3/14; http://www.foxnews.com/opinion/2014/03/03/team-obama-wins-fight-to-have-christian-home-school-family-deported/

956 "Obama's New Asylum Decree Favors Muslims Over Christians", *Investors Business Daily*, 2/21/14; http://news.investors.com/ibd-editorials/022114-690860-obama-immigration-reforms-seem-to-come-with-religious-test.htm

957 Ed Morrissey, "Friday night news dump: Obama bypasses Congress, funds Palestinian Authority," *Hot Air*, 04/28/2012 (http://hotair.com/archives/2012/04/28/friday-night-news-dump-obama-bypasses-congress-funds-palestinian-authority/)

958 Steven Lee Meyers, "U.S. Move to Give Egypt $450 Million in Aid Meets Resistance," *New York Times*, 09/28/2012, (http://www.nytimes.com/2012/09/29/world/middleeast/white-house-move-to-give-egypt-450-million-in-aid-meets-resistance.html)

959 Erick Stackelbeck, "Muslim Brotherhood: A Global Terrorist Influence," *CBN News*, February 1, 2011, (http://www.cbn.com/cbnnews/world/2011/february/muslim-brotherhood-a-global-terrorist-influence/)

960 "A short course 14: The Muslim Brotherhood's Strategic Plan", Shariah: The Threat To America; (http://shariahthethreat.org/a-short-course-1-what-is-shariah/a-short-course-14-the-muslim-brotherhood%E2%80%99s-strategic-plan/)

961 Robert Satloff and Patrick Clawson, "U.S. Military Aid to Egypt: Assessment and Recommendations", *The Washington Institute*, 7/8/98; http://www.washingtoninstitute.org/policy-analysis/view/u.s.-military-aid-to-egypt-assessment-and-recommendations

962 "Congress Spending Package Restricts Aid to Egypt, Pakistan", *Associated Press*, 12/16/2011; http://www.foxnews.com/politics/2011/12/16/congress-spending-package-restricts-aid-to-egypt-pakistan/

963 Matthew Lee, "US Oks Egypt Aid Despite Congressional Concerns", *The Guardian*, 3/22/2012; http://www.theguardian.com/world/feedarticle/10158648

964 Awr Hawkins, "Obama Bypasses Congress, Gives $1.5 Billion to the Muslim Brotherhood," *Breitbart*, 3/21/2012 (http://www.breitbart.com/Big-Peace/2012/03/21/obama-bypasses-congress-gives-1-5-billion-to-muslim-brotherhood)

965 "Millions of Egyptians Demand Morsi's Downfall", *Al Monitor*, 6/30/2013; http://www.al-monitor.com/pulse/originals/2013/06/egyptians-demonstrate-in-large-numbers-against-morsi.html

966 Jim Sciutto and Elise Labott, "U.S. to Cut Some Military Aid to Egypt After Coup, Turmoil", *CNN*, 10/9/2013; http://www.cnn.com/2013/10/08/us/egypt-aid/

967 The White House, "Executive Order: Review and Disposition of Individual's Detained at the Guantanamo Bay Naval Base and Closure of Detention Facilities," 01/22/2009, (http://www.whitehouse.gov/the_press_office/ClosureOfGuantanamoDetentionFacilities)

968 Matt Sledge and Ryan J. Reilly, "NDAA Signed Into Law By Obama Despite Guantanamo Veto Threat, Indefinite Detention Provisions," Huffington Post, 1/3/2013 (http://www.huffingtonpost.com/2013/01/03/ndaa-obama-indefinite-detention_n_2402601.html)

969 Helene Cooper, "Obama Nears Goal for Guantánamo With Faster Pace of Releases", *New York Times*, 1/5/2015; (http://www.nytimes.com/2015/01/06/us/obama-nears-goal-for-guantanamo-with-faster-pace-of-releases.html?_r=0)

970 "Former CIA Officer: Admin's Release of Gitmo Prisoners Is 'Insane'" *Fox New Insider*, 1/17/2015; (http://insider.foxnews.com/2015/01/17/former-cia-officer-obama-administrations-release-guantanamo-bay-terror-prisoners-insane)

971 "'Extraordinary Admission' by Chuck Hagel as He Exits: He Was Pressured by WH to Release Terrorists", *BizPac Review*, 1/31/2015; (http://www.bizpacreview.com/2015/01/31/extraordinary-admission-by-chuck-hagel-as-he-exits-he-was-pressured-by-wh-to-release-terrorists-176765)

972 "5 Yemeni Detainees Released from Guantanamo", *The Week*, 1/14/2015; (http://www.theweek.com/speedreads/533663/5-yemeni-detainees-released-from-guantanamo)

973 Rebecca Kheel, "US official: Gitmo transfers have resulted in American deaths", *The Hill*, 3/23/2016; (http://thehill.com/policy/defense/274083-pentagon-official-americans-killed-by-former-gitmo-detainees)

974 Alissa J. Rubin, "Former Taliban Officials Say U.S. Talks Started," *New York Times*, 01/28/2012, (http://www.nytimes.com/2012/01/29/world/asia/taliban-have-begun-talks-with-us-former-taliban-aides-say.html)

975 Judicial Watch Blog, "Obama Negotiates With Taliban Over Gitmo Prisoners," *Judicial Watch*, 02/02/2012, (http://www.judicialwatch.org/blog/2012/02/obama-negotiates-with-taliban-over-gitmo-prisoners/)

976 Robert Tilford, "Clinton Evasive About Listing Taliban as Terrorist Organization," *Examiner*, 09/12/2012, (http://www.examiner.com/article/clinton-evasive-about-listing-taliban-as-terrorist-organization)

977 Jake Tapper, "Fellow Soldiers Call Bergdahl a Deserter, Not a Hero", *CNN*, 6/4/2014; (http://www.cnn.com/2014/06/01/us/bergdahl-deserter-or-hero/)

978 Charles Spiering, "Former Officer: Soldiers were 'Threatened' if they Question Bergdahl Story," *Breitbart*, 6/2/2014 (http://www.breitbart.com/Big-Government/2014/06/02/Former-Officer-Soldiers-Were-Threatened-if-They-Questioned-Bergdahl-Story)

979 James Rosen, "EXCLUSIVE: Bergdahl declared jihad in captivity, secret documents show," *Fox News*, 6/6/2014 (http://www.foxnews.com/politics/2014/06/06/exclusive-bergdahl-declared-jihad-secret-documents-show/)

980 Justin Sink, "Bergdahl blame shifting to Hagel?" *The Hill*, 6/10/2014 (http://thehill.com/blogs/blog-briefing-room/208803-obama-shifting-blame-for-bergdahl-trade-to-hagel)

981 Barbara Starr, "Officials: Detainee swapped for Bergdahl suspected of militant activities", *CNN* 1/29/2015; (http://edition.cnn.com/2015/01/29/politics/bergdahl-swap-prisoner-militant-activity/index.html)

982 "Bowe Bergdahl Will be Charged With Desertion, Sources Say", *NBC News*, 3/25/2015; (http://www.nbcnews.com/storyline/bowe-bergdahl-released/do-not-publish-bowe-bergdahl-charged-desertion-xyz-says-n330036)

983 Dan Martosko, "Obama administration has SLASHED budget for domestic bombing prevention by 45 per cent, says former Homeland Security Assistant Secretary," *Daily Mail*, 4/16/2013, (http://www.dailymail.co.uk/news/article-2310110/Obama-administration-SLASHED-budget-domestic-bombing-prevention-45-cent-says-Homeland-Security-Assistant-Secretary.html)

984 "Boston Bomber Could Have Been Deported After 2009 Arrest," *Judicial Watch Blog*, 04/29/2013, (http://www.judicialwatch.org/blog/2013/04/boston-bomber-could-have-been-deported-after-2009-conviction/)

985 "FBI Interviewed Dead Boston Bombing Suspect Years Ago", *CBS News*, 04/19/2013, (http://www.cbsnews.com/8301-201_162-57580534/fbi-interviewed-dead-boston-bombing-suspect-years-ago/)

986 "Boston Marathon Bombings: Barack Obama Statement on Suspect's Capture," *The Telegraph*, 04/20/2013, (http://www.telegraph.co.uk/news/worldnews/barackobama/10007338/Boston-Marathon-bombings-Barack-Obama-statement-on-suspects-capture.html)

987 Robert Spencer, "Boston Jihad Bombers YouTube Page Features Videos by Sheikh Feiz Mohammed," *Jihad Watch*, 4/19/2013, (http://www.jihadwatch.org/2013/04/boston-jihad-bombers-youtube-page-features-videos-by-sheikh-feiz-mohammed-who-called-on-muslims-to-k.html)

988 Hillary Chabot and David Wedge, "FBI's concern was Qaeda, not Chechens, says Sen." *Boston Herald*, 4/24/2013, (http://bostonherald.com/news_opinion/local_coverage/2013/04/fbi_s_concern_was_qaeda_not_chechens_says_sen)

989 Richard Miniter, "President Obama's Greatest Foreign Policy Failure: Killing bin Laden," *Forbes*, 9/13/2012; (http://www.forbes.com/sites/richardminiter/2012/09/13/president-obamas-greatest-foreign-policy-failure-killing-bin-laden/)

990 *Ibid.*

991 Stephen F. Hayes and Thomas Joscelyn, "How America Was Misled on al Qaeda's Demise", *Wall Street Journal*, 3/5/2015; (http://www.wsj.com/articles/stephen-hayes-and-tomas-joscelyn-how-america-was-misled-on-al-qaedas-demise-1425600796)

992 *Ibid.*

993 Richard Esposito and Brian Ross, "Investigators: Northwest Bomb Plot Planned by Al-Qaeda in Yemen," *ABC*, 12/26/2009, (http://abcnews.go.com/Blotter/al-qaeda-yemen-planned-northwest-flight-253-bomb-plot/story?id=9426085)

994 Charlie Savage, "Holder Backs a Miranda Limit for Terror Suspects," *The New York Times*, 05/09/2010, (http://www.nytimes.com/2010/05/10/us/politics/10holder.html)

995 Catherine Herridge and Fox News Staff, "Lawmakers Blast Administration for Calling Fort Hood Massacre 'Workplace Violence'," *Fox News*, 12/07/2011, (http://www.foxnews.com/politics/2011/12/06/military-growing-terrorist-target-lawmakers-warn/)

996 The White House, Office of the Press Secretary (2009). Remarks by the President at Memorial Service at Fort Hood [Press Release]. Retrieved from http://www.whitehouse.gov/the-press-office/remarks-president-memorial-service-fort-hood

997 "Authorities: Man Charged in Blast at Ariz. Social Security Office Researched Terrorist Bombs," *The Associated Press*, 12/03/2012, (http://www.foxnews.com/us/2012/12/03/authorities-man-charged-in-blast-at-ariz-social-security-office-researched/)

998 Dave Gibson, "No Terrorism Charges for Iraqi Man Accused of Arizona Bomb Attack," *Examiner*, 12/04/2012, (http://www.examiner.com/article/no-terrorism-charges-for-iraqi-man-accused-of-arizona-bomb-attack)

999 Sean Gorman, "Cruz is right: Obama doesn't link Islam to terrorism", *Politifact*, 11/30/2015; (http://www.politifact.com/virginia/statements/2015/nov/30/ted-cruz/cruz-right-obama-doesnt-link-islam-terrorismerrori/)

1000 Craig Bannister, "VIDEO: WH Censors French President Saying 'ISLAMIST Terrorism'" MRCTV, 4/1/2016; (http://www.mrctv.org/blog/video-wh-censors-reference-islamist-terrorism-french-president)

1001 Kevin Johnson and Mary Bowerman, "FBI, DOJ issue new transcript of Orlando 911 call amid outrage", USA Today, 6/20/2016; (http://www.usatoday.com/story/news/nation-now/2016/06/20/many-outraged-reference-isil-omitted-orlando-911-transcript/86139678/)

1002 Jim Treacher, "Loretta Lynch: We May Never Know Why That Islamic Terrorist Killed All Those People," Daily Caller, 6/21/2016; (http://dailycaller.com/2016/06/21/loretta-lynch-we-may-never-know-why-that-islamic-terrorist-killed-all-those-people/)

1003 Meghan Keneally, "San Bernardino Shooting Investigated as 'Act of Terrorism'" ABC News, 12/4/2015; (http://abcnews.go.com/US/san-bernardino-shooting-investigated-act-terrorism/story?id=35573368)

1004 Ralph Ellis, Ashley Fantz, Faith Karimi and Eliott C. McLaughlin, "Orlando shooting: 49 killed, shooter pledged ISIS allegiance", CNN, 6/12/2016; (http://www.cnn.com/2016/06/12/us/orlando-nightclub-shooting/)

1005 John R. Schindler, "The Intelligence Lessons of San Bernardino", *Observer*, 12/14/15; (http://observer.com/2015/12/the-intelligence-lessons-of-san-bernardino/)

1006 Katie Pavlich, "Neighbor Didn't Report Suspicious Activity of San Bernardino Killers For Fear of Being Called Racist", *Townhall*, 12/3/2015; (http://townhall.com/tipsheet/katiepavlich/2015/12/03/neighbor-didnt-report-suspicious-activity-of-san-bernardino-killers-for-fear-of-being-called-racist-n2088543)

1007 Cecilia Kang and Eric Lichtblau, "F.B.I. Error Locked San Bernardino Attacker's iPhone", *New York Times*, 3/2/2016; (http://www.nytimes.com/2016/03/02/technology/apple-and-fbi-face-off-before-house-judiciary-committee.html)

1008 Michael Daly, "Omar Mateen, Terrorist Who Attacked Orlando Gay Club, Had Been Investigated by FBI" *Daily Beast*, 6/12/2016; (http://www.thedailybeast.com/articles/2016/06/12/omar-mateen-id-d-as-orlando-killer.html)

1009 Christian Datoc, "FBI Called Off Investigation Of Orlando Shooter Because They Thought His Coworkers Were Racist", *The Daily Caller* 6/13/2016; (http://dailycaller.com/2016/06/13/fbi-called-off-investigation-of-orlando-shooter-because-they-thought-his-coworkers-were-racist/)

1010 "Ex-CIA Chief Petraeus Testifies Benghazi Attack was al Qaeda-linked Terrorism," *CNN*, 11/16/2012, (http://www.cnn.com/2012/11/16/politics/benghazi-hearings/index.html)

1011 Jake Tapper, "Documents Back up Claims of Requests Requests for Greater Security in Benghazi," *ABC*, 10/19/2012, (http://abcnews.go.com/blogs/politics/2012/10/documents-back-up-claims-of-requests-for-greater-security-in-benghazi/)

1012 Awr Hawkins, "Panetta's Testimony Calls Obama's Benghazi Explanations in to Question," *Breitbart*, 02/09/2013; (http://www.breitbart.com/Big-Peace/2013/02/08/Panetta-s-Testimony-Calls-Obama-s-Benghazi-Explanations-Into-Question)

1013 Arshad Mohammed and Tabassum Zakaria, "Clinton Forcefully Defends Handling of Benghazi Attack," *Reuters*, 01/23/2013, (http://www.reuters.com/article/2013/01/23/us-usa-libya-clinton-idUSBRE90M0SM20130123)

1014 Kerry Picket, "Benghazi Survivors Remain Gagged by Federal Law," *Breitbart*, 02/20/2013, (http://www.breitbart.com/Big-Peace/2013/02/20/Benghazi-Survivors-Remained-Gagged-By-Federal-Law)

1015 Marina Koren, "We Now Know Who's to Blame for Benghazi," *National Journal*, 1/15/2014 (http://www.nationaljournal.com/congress/we-now-know-who-s-to-blame-for-benghazi-20140115)

1016 John Parkinson, "White House Failed to Protect Benghazi Mission, House Report Concludes," *ABC News*, 2/11/2014 (http://abcnews.go.com/Politics/white-house-failed-protect-benghazi-mission-house-report/story?id=22460489)

1017 "Libyan President to NBC: Anti-Islam Film Had 'Nothing to do with' US Consulate Attack," *NBC News*, 09/26/2012, (http://worldnews.nbcnews.com/_news/2012/09/26/14105135-libyan-president-to-nbc-anti-islam-film-had-nothing-to-do-with-us-consulate-attack)

1018 Brendan Bordelon, "Krauthammer: New Benghazi Email A 'Classic Cover-Up Of A Cover-Up'" *The Daily Caller*, 4/29/2014 (http://dailycaller.com/2014/04/29/krauthammer-new-benghazi-email-classic-cover-up-of-a-cover-up-and-that-is-a-serious-offense/)

1019 "Judicial Watch: Newly Released Documents Confirm White House Officials Set Hillary Clinton's Benghazi Response", *Judicial Watch*, 6/29/2015; (http://www.judicialwatch.org/press-room/press-releases/judicial-watch-newly-released-documents-confirm-white-house-officials-set-hillary-clintons-benghazi-response/)

1020 Sara A Carter, "Secret Memo Suggests White House Ignored SOS from Iranian Opposition", *Washington Examiner*, 2/27/2012; (http://www.washingtonexaminer.com/article/318891)

1021 David French, "The Utter Chaos of the 's Egypt Policy", *National Review*, 7/2/2013; (http://www.nationalreview.com/corner/352604/utter-chaos-obama-administrations-egypt-policy-david-french)

1022 Zeke J. Miller, "Obama Condemns Egyptian Violence, But Doesn't Halt Aid", *Time*, 8/15/2013; (http://swampland.time.com/2013/08/15/obama-condemns-egyptian-violence-but-doesnt-halt-aid/)

1023 S.A. Miller, "The knives are out: Panetta eviscerates Obama's 'red line' blunder on Syria", *Washington Times*, 10/7/2014; (http://www.washingtontimes.com/news/2014/oct/7/panetta-decries-obama-red-line-blunder-syria/)

1024 Noah Rothman, "Panetta: Obama's bad decisions on Syria and Iraq led to rise of ISIS," *Hot Air*, 9/22/2014; (http://hotair.com/archives/2014/09/22/obama-syria-iraq-panetta/)

1025 Spencer Ackerman, "What Surge? Afghanistan's Most Violent Places Stay Bad, Despite Extra Troops," *Wired*, 8/23/2012; (http://www.wired.com/2012/08/afghanistan-violence-helmand/)

1026 Julie Pace and Ken Dilanian, "US Counterterrorism Strategy in Yemen Collapses Amid Chaos," *Associated Press*, (http://www.military.com/daily-news/2015/03/24/us-counterterrorism-strategy-in-yemen-collapses-amid-chaos.html)

1027 Council on Foreign Relations, "Sectarian Conflict in Lebanon", Accessed 6/14/2016; (http://www.cfr.org/global/global-conflict-tracker/p32137#!/conflict/sectarian-conflict-in-lebanon)

1028 David Schenker, "Lebanon Unstable and Insecure", The Washington Institute, 6/12/2014; (http://www.washingtoninstitute.org/policy-analysis/view/lebanon-unstable-and-insecure)

1029 Ian Hanchett, "Fmr. Obama Ambassador: Middle East Destabilizing More Rapidly Than Under Bush," Breitbart, 3/28/2015; (http://www.breitbart.com/video/2015/03/28/fmr-obama-amb-middle-east-destabilizing-more-rapidly-than-under-bush/)

1030 Nick Gass, "Bob Gates: U.S. has no Middle East strategy 'at all'," *Politico*, 5/19/2015; (http://www.politico.com/story/2015/05/robert-gates-us-no-middle-east-strategy-118083.html)

1031 Mark Mazzetti and Matt Apuzzo, "Inquiry Weighs Whether ISIS Analysis Was Distorted", *New York Times*, 8/25/2015; (http://www.nytimes.com/2015/08/26/world/middleeast/pentagon-investigates-allegations-of-skewed-intelligence-reports-on-isis.html)

1032 Shane Harris and Nancy A. Yousef, "Exclusive: 50 Spies Say ISIS Intelligence Was Cooked", *Daily Beast*, 9/9/2015; (http://www.thedailybeast.com/articles/2015/09/09/exclusive-50-spies-say-isis-intelligence-was-cooked.html)

1033 Pamela Engel, "'Something's wrong': The ISIS intelligence scandal just hit Obama's inner circle", *Business Insider*, 9/11/2015; (http://www.businessinsider.com/obama-administration-and-isis-intelligence-2015-9)

1034 Stephen F. Hayes, "Obama's Intel Scandal", *The Weekly Standard*, 12/7/2015; (http://www.weeklystandard.com/obamas-intel-scandal/article/1070543)

1035 Tom LoBianco, "Former intel chief says WH worried over re-elect 'narrative'", CNN, 12/2/2015; (http://www.cnn.com/2015/12/01/politics/michael-flynn-obama-isis/)

1036 Michael Hastings, "How Obama Decided to Intervene in Libya", *Rolling Stone*, 10/13/2011; (http://www.rollingstone.com/politics/news/inside-obamas-war-room-20111013)

1037 http://www.theatlantic.com/international/archive/2016/04/obamas-worst-mistake-libya/478461/

1038   Bill Gertz, "Islamic State Rises in Libya," *Washington Free Beacon*, 3/20/2015; (http://freebeacon.com/national-security/islamic-state-rises-in-libya/)

1039 Dominic Tierney, "The Legacy of Obama's 'Worst Mistake'" *The Atlantic*, 4/15/2016; (http://www.theatlantic.com/international/archive/2016/04/obamas-worst-mistake-libya/478461/)

1040 Garikai Chengu, "Libya: From Africa's Wealthiest Democracy Under Gaddafi to Terrorist Haven After US Intervention", *Counterpunch*, 10/20/2015; (http://www.counterpunch.org/2015/10/20/libya-from-africas-wealthiest-democracy-under-gaddafi-to-terrorist-haven-after-us-intervention/)

1041 "Obama Defends Military Mission in Libya, Says U.S. Acted to 'Prevent a Massacre'" Fox News, 3/28/2011; (http://www.foxnews.com/politics/2011/03/28/obama-delivers-address-nation-libya-intervention.html)

1042 "Obama warns Syria not to cross 'red line'," *CNN*, 8/21/2012 (http://www.cnn.com/2012/08/20/world/meast/syria-unrest/)

1043 Alistair Dawber, "John Kerry says Assad's Syria regime HAS used sarin chemical weapons against rebels - despite Barack Obama insisting that was a 'red line' for US," *The Independent*, 4/25/2013 (http://www.independent.co.uk/news/world/middle-east/john-kerry-says-assads-syria-regime-has-used-sarin-chemical-weapons-against-rebels--despite-barack-obama-insisting-that-was-a-red-line-for-us-8588774.html)

1044 Dianne Feinstein. (2013). Feinstein statement on syria. [press release] 4/25/2013 (http://www.feinstein.senate.gov/public/index.cfm/press-releases?ID=4423d4a4-a602-4e7d-823f-77aade545e91)

1045 Joby Warrick, "More than 1,400 killed in Syrian chemical weapons attack, U.S. says," *Washington Post*, 8/30/2013 (http://www.washingtonpost.com/world/national-security/nearly-1500-killed-in-syrian-chemical-weapons-attack-us-says/2013/08/30/b2864662-1196-11e3-85b6-d27422650fd5_story.html)

1046 Molly Hunter and Shushannah Walshe, "Britain Won't Join in a Syrian Attack," *ABC News*, 8/29/2013 (http://abcnews.go.com/International/britain-join-syrian-attack/story?id=20104801)

1047 Paul Singer, "Opposition to Syria Attack Emerges in Congress", *USA Today*, 9/2/2013 (http://www.usatoday.com/story/news/politics/2013/09/01/congress-syria-rand-paul-kerry/2752965/

1048 Jonathan Karl, "Obama on Syria: 'My Credibility Is Not on the Line'," *ABC News*, 9/4/2013 (http://abcnews.go.com/blogs/politics/2013/09/obama-on-syria-my-credibility-is-not-on-the-line/)

1049 Paul Steinhauser and John Helton, "CNN Poll: Public Against Syria Strike Resolution", *CNN*, 9/9/2013 (http://www.cnn.com/2013/09/09/politics/syria-poll-main)

1050 Olivier Knox, "Kerry Vows 'Unbelievably Small' Strike on Syria", *Yahoo News*, 9/9/2013 (http://news.yahoo.com/-kerry-vows-%E2%80%98unbelievably-small%E2%80%99-strike-on-syria--150302777.html)

1051 Joel Gehrke, "Obama waives ban on arming terrorists to allow aid to Syrian opposition," *Washington Examiner*, 9/17/2013 (http://washingtonexaminer.com/obama-waives-ban-on-arming-terrorists-to-allow-aid-to-syrian-opposition/article/2535885)

1052 Julian Pecquet, "Obama Administration Reaches Syria Weapons Deal With Russia", *The Hill*, 9/26/2013 (http://thehill.com/blogs/global-affairs/un-treaties/324999-obama-administration-reaches-syria-deal-with-russia)

1053 Joby Warrick, "Syria blamed for missed deadline on chemical arsenal," *Washington Post*, 12/30/2013 (http://www.washingtonpost.com/world/national-security/syria-blamed-for-missed-deadline-on-chemical-arsenal/2013/12/30/8356c350-719d-11e3-8b3f-b1666705ca3b_story.html)

1054 Josh Rogin, "Senators: Kerry Admits Obama's Syria Policy Is Failing," *The Daily Beast*, 2/4/2014 (http://www.thedailybeast.com/articles/2014/02/03/senators-kerry-admits-obama-s-syria-policy-is-failing.html)

1055 Global Terrorism Index 2015; Institute for Economics and Peace (PDF); (http://economicsandpeace.org/wp-content/uploads/2015/11/Global-Terrorism-Index-2015.pdf)

1056 Aminu Abubakar, "As Many as 200 Girls Abducted by Boko Haram, Nigerian Officials Say", *CNN*, 4/16/2014; (http://www.cnn.com/2014/04/15/world/africa/nigeria-girls-abducted/)

1057 Morgan Lorraine Roach, "Boko Haram: Addressing the Threat Before it Strikes", *Heritage Foundation Issue Brief 3549*, 3/22/2012; (http://www.heritage.org/research/reports/2012/03/boko-haram-threat-of-the-nigerian-islamist-insurgency)

1058 Josh Rogin, "Hillary's State Department Refused to Brand Boko Haram as Terrorists", The Daily Beast, 5/7/2014; (http://www.thedailybeast.com/articles/2014/05/07/hillary-s-state-department-refused-to-brand-boko-haram-as-terrorists.html)

1059 James Simpson, "Obama Accused of Obstructing Battle against Boko Haram to Promote Axelrod's Nigerian Muslim Client", Accuracy in Media, 3/24/2015; (http://www.aim.org/aim-column/obama-accused-of-obstructing-battle-against-boko-haram-to-promote-axelrods-nigerian-muslim-client/)

1060 Robert Marquand, "Obama Singles Out Boko Haram and Nigeria Declares 'Total War' on Shadowy Group", *Christian Science Monitor*, 5/29/2014; (http://www.csmonitor.com/World/Africa/2014/0529/Obama-singles-out-Boko-Haram-and-Nigeria-declares-total-war-on-shadowy-group-video)

1061 Global Terrorism Index 2015; Institute for Economics and Peace (PDF); (http://economicsandpeace.org/wp-content/uploads/2015/11/Global-Terrorism-Index-2015.pdf)

1062 Charlotte Florence, "Boko Haram Benefitted from State Department Inaction", *Daily Signal*, 5/12/2014; (http://dailysignal.com/2014/05/12/boko-haram-benefitted-state-department-inaction/)

1063 Elise Jordan, "How Obama Lost Afghanistan", *The Daily Beast*, 4/5/2014; http://www.thedailybeast.com/articles/2014/04/05/how-obama-lost-afghanistan.html

1064 James Warren, "President Obama Lost Faith in Afghanistan Mission, Can't Stand President Karzai: Gates' Memoir", *New York Daily News*, 1/7/2014; http://www.nydailynews.com/news/politics/president-obama-lost-faith-afghanistan-mission-article-1.1569274

1065 Ali Meyer, "74% of U.S. Afghan Casualties After Obama Ordered Troops Increased", *CNS News*, 1/9/2014; http://cnsnews.com/news/article/ali-meyer/74-us-afghan-casualties-came-after-obama-ordered-troops-increased

1066 David Zucchino, "Opium cultivation soars in Afghanistan, U.N. reports," *Los Angeles Times*, 11/13/2013 (http://articles.latimes.com/2013/nov/13/world/la-fg-wn-opium-cultivation-soars-afghanistan-20131113)

1067 Associated Press, "Obama threatens Karzai with full US withdrawal," *New York Post*, 2/26/2014 (http://nypost.com/2014/02/26/obama-threatens-karzai-with-full-us-withdrawal/)

1068 Matthew Rosenberg and Michael D. Shear, "In Reversal, Obama Says U.S. Soldiers Will Stay in Afghanistan to 2017", *New York Times*, 10/15/2015; (http://www.nytimes.com/2015/10/16/world/asia/obama-troop-withdrawal-afghanistan.html)

1069 Yaroslav Trofimov and Margherita Stancati, "Afghan Elections Point to Runoff, Waning Karzai Influence," *Wall Street Journal*, 4/7/2014; (http://online.wsj.com/news/articles/SB10001424052702304819004579485482622918584)

1070 Elise Jordan, "How Obama Lost Afghanistan", *The Daily Beast*, 4/5/2014; http://www.thedailybeast.com/articles/2014/04/05/how-obama-lost-afghanistan.html

1071 James Gordon Meek, "Barack Obama Purges Web Site Critique of Surge in Iraq", *New York Daily News*, 7/14/2008 (http://www.nydailynews.com/news/politics/barack-obama-purges-web-site-critique-surge-iraq-article-1.349828)

1072 Josh Rogin, "How the Obama Administration Bungled the Iraq Withdrawal Negotiations", *Foreign Policy*, 10/21/2011 (http://thecable.foreignpolicy.com/posts/2011/10/21/how_the_obama_administration_bungled_the_iraq_withdrawal_negotiations)

1073 "Obama Announces Complete Withdrawal of U.S. Forces From Iraq by End of 2011," *Fox News*, 10/21/2011 (http://www.foxnews.com/politics/2011/10/21/obama-to-speak-about-iraq-troop-levels/)

1074 "Violence in Iraq Increases Following US Withdrawal", *Catholic Online*, 3/11/2012 (http://catholic.org/international/international_story.php?id=45135)

1075 Liz Sly, "Al-Qaeda-Linked Force Captures Fallujah Amid Rise in Violence in Iraq", *The Washington Post*, January 3, 2014; http://www.washingtonpost.com/world/al-qaeda-force-captures-fallujah-amid-rise-in-violence-in-iraq/2014/01/03/8abaeb2a-74aa-11e3-8def-a33011492df2_story.html

1076 Francesca Chambers, "Revealed: How Obama SET FREE the merciless terrorist warlord now leading the ISIS horde blazing a trail of destruction through Iraq," *Daily Mail (UK)*, 6/13/2014 (http://www.dailymail.co.uk/news/article-2657231/Revealed-Obama-RELEASED-warlord-head-ISIS-extremist-army-five-years-ago.html)

1077 Nick Hallett, "Dirty Bomb Fears After ISIS Seize Uranium," *Breitbart*, July 11, 2014 (http://www.breitbart.com/Breitbart-London/2014/07/11/Dirty-Bomb-Fears-after-ISIS-Seize-Uranium)

1078 Wikipedia contributors, "Capital punishment in Iran," *Wikipedia*, The Free Encyclopedia, http://en.wikipedia.org/wiki/Capital_punishment_in_Iran (accessed February 14, 2014).

1079 "Statement By The President On First Step Agreement On Iran's Nuclear Program", The White House, 11/23/2013; (https://www.whitehouse.gov/the-press-office/2013/11/23/statement-president-first-step-agreement-irans-nuclear-program)

1080 "Iran Say to Continue Building at Arak Nuclear Site Despite Deal", *Reuters*, November 27, 2013; http://www.reuters.com/article/2013/11/27/us-iran-nuclear-arak-idUSBRE9AQ0U120131127

1081 Tom Cohen, "Iran on Nuke Deal: 'We Did Not Agree to Dismantle Anything'", *CNN*, January 23, 2014; http://www.cnn.com/2014/01/22/politics/iran-us-nuclear/index.html

1082 Daniel Halper, "Iran's Rouhani: 'World Powers Surrendered to Iranian Nation's Will'", *The Weekly Standard*, January 14, 2014; http://www.weeklystandard.com/blogs/irans-rouhani-world-powers-surrendered-iranian-nations-will_774616.html

1083 Julian Pecquot, "Obama: 'I will veto' new Iran sanctions," *The Hill*, 1/28/2014 (http://thehill.com/blogs/global-affairs/middle-east-north-africa/196750-obama-to-congress-i-will-veto-your-iran)

1084 "Iran FM Zarif Honors American-Murdering Hezbollah Terrorist, 'Signals Insincerity' Behind Tehran's Latest Moves", *The Tower*, January 14, 2014; http://www.thetower.org/experts-iran-fm-signals-insincerity-honoring-american-murdering-hezbollah-terrorist/

1085 Daniel Bassali, "Wolf Blitzer Makes a Fool Out of Susan Rice on Iran Funding of Terrorists", *The Washington Free Beacon*, 7/15/2015; (http://freebeacon.com/national-security/wolf-blitzer-makes-a-fool-of-susan-rice-on-iran-funding-terrorists/)

1086 Henry A. Kissinger, "Speeches and Public Statements; Opening Statement by Dr. Henry A Kissinger Before the United States Senate Committee on Armed Services", 1/29/2015; (http://www.henryakissinger.com/speeches/012915.html)

1087 Yaroslav Trofimov, "Like Israel, U.S. Arab Allies Fear Obama's Iran Nuclear Deal", *Wall Street Journal*, 3/4/2015; (http://www.wsj.com/articles/like-israel-u-s-arab-allies-fear-obamas-iran-nuclear-deal-1425504773)

1088 Jordan Schachtel, "Report: Obama has Agreed to 80 percent of Iran's Demands in Nuclear Talks", *Breitbart*, 1/30/2015; (http://www.breitbart.com/national-security/2015/01/30/report-obama-agrees-to-80-percent-of-irans-demands-in-nuke-talks/)

1089 Winston Hall, "7 Devestasting Facts about Obama's Iran Nuclear Deal," *Breitbart*, 7/17/2015; (http://www.breitbart.com/national-security/2015/07/17/7-devastating-facts-about-obamas-iran-nuclear-deal/)

1090 Eli Lake, "Obama Kept Iran's Short Breakout Time Secret", *Bloomberg View*, 4/21/2015; (http://www.bloombergview.com/articles/2015-04-21/obama-kept-iran-s-short-breakout-time-a-secret)

1091 David E. Sanger, "Obama Sees an Iran Deal That Could Avoid Congress," *New York Times*, 10/20/2014; (http://www.nytimes.com/2014/10/20/us/politics/obama-sees-an-iran-deal-that-could-avoid-congress-.html)

1092 Christian Datoc, "White House, Obama Blocked Congress From Reviewing Secret Aspects Of Iran Deal", *The Daily Caller*, 7/22/2015; (http://dailycaller.com/2015/07/22/white-house-obama-blocked-congress-from-reviewing-secret-aspects-of-iran-deal/)

1093 Guy Taylor and Ben Wolfgang, "Obama downplays Iran 'death to America' remarks, toes hard line on Benjamin Netanyahu," Washington Times, 3/23/2015; (http://www.washingtontimes.com/news/2015/mar/23/obama-downplays-iran-death-to-america-remarks-toes/)

1094 Lee Smith, "Obama's Foreign Policy Guru Boasts of How the Administration Lied to Sell the Iran Deal", *Weekly Standard*, 5/5/2016; (http://www.weeklystandard.com/article/2002252)

1095 "Obama: Iranian nuclear deal 'is not built on trust, it is built on verification.'", *Associated Press*, 7/14/2015; (http://bigstory.ap.org/article/6ee7bbfc43144f3b8afa3c8381251523/obama-iranian-nuclear-deal-not-built-trust-it-built)

1096 Blake Seitz, "Kerry Admits Iran Can Flout Weapons Embargo Without Violating Nuclear Deal", *Washington Free Beacon*, 8/11/2015; (http://freebeacon.com/national-security/kerry-admits-iran-can-flout-weapons-embargo-without-violating-nuclear-deal/)

1097 Helene Cooper and David E. Sanger, "Iran Seizes U.S. Sailors Amid Claims of Spying", *New York Times*, 1/12/2016; (http://www.nytimes.com/2016/01/13/world/middleeast/iran-holds-us-navy-boats-crew.html?_r=0)

1098 Julian Hattem, "Kerry Thanks Iran for Care of U.S. Sailors", *Associated Press*, 1/13/2016: (http://thehill.com/policy/national-security/265730-kerry-thanks-iran-for-care-of-us-sailors)

1099 Jon Gambrell, "Iran fires 2 missiles marked with 'Israel must be wiped out'", *Associated Press*, 3/9/2016: (http://bigstory.ap.org/article/c9e2945ea3ef4dd9972f23cf663ac99e/iran-fires-2-missiles-marked-israel-must-be-wiped-out)

1100 Josh Siegel, "Fear of Undermining Iran Deal Complicates Obama Administration's Response to MIssile Tests", *The Daily Signal*, 3/10/2016; (http://dailysignal.com/2016/03/10/weighing-punishing-iran-over-missile-tests-obama-administration-fears-undermining-nuclear-deal/)

1101 Guy Benson, "Kerry: Iran Can Violate Parts of the Nuclear Deal Without Really Violating the Nuclear Deal", *Townhall*, 8/12/2015; (http://townhall.com/tipsheet/guybenson/2015/08/12/kerry-iran-can-violate-parts-of-the-nuclear-deal-without-really-violating-the-nuclear-deal-n2037589)

1102 Josh Siegel, "Fear of Undermining Iran Deal Complicates Obama Administration's Response to MIssile Tests", *The Daily Signal*, 3/10/2016; (http://dailysignal.com/2016/03/10/weighing-punishing-iran-over-missile-tests-obama-administration-fears-undermining-nuclear-deal/)

1103 Asam Kredo, "U.S. Will Teach Iran to Thwart Nuke Threats", *The Washington Free Beacon*, 7/14/2015; (http://freebeacon.com/national-security/u-s-will-teach-iran-to-thwart-nuke-threats/)

1104 Patrick Henningsen, "Obama Wins Second Term, But America Remains More Divided Than Ever," *Centre for Research on Globalization*, 11/07/2012, (http://www.globalresearch.ca/obama-wins-second-term-but-america-remains-more-divided-than-ever/5310937)

1105 Terence P. Jeffrey, "Poll: Majority Sees America as Declining Power, Facing Economic Difficulty and Rising Crime Rates," *CNS News*, 01/02/2013, (http://cnsnews.com/news/article/poll-majority-sees-america-declining-power-facing-economic-difficulty-and-rising-crime)